Principles of Equity Valuation

I0885483

The book provides a rigorous introduction to corporate finance and the valuation of equity. The first half of the book covers much of the received theory in these areas, such as the relationship between the risk of an equity security and the return that one can expect from it, the effects of leverage (i.e. the borrowing policies of the firm) on the return that one can expect from the firm's shares, and the role that dividends, operating cash flows, and accounting earnings play in the valuation of equity. The second half of the book is more advanced and deals with the important role that 'real options' (i.e. as-yet unexploited investment opportunities) play in the valuation of equity.

Particular focus is on a firm's ability to change or modify its investment opportunity set so that it can use its resources in alternative and more profitable ways. There are a variety of ways in which a firm can exercise this option to change its investment opportunity set, including liquidating its unprofitable investments, spin-offs of its unprofitable investments, divestitures, changing its Chief Executive Officer, mergers and/or takeovers with other firms, filing for bankruptcy, restructuring its operations, and making new capital investments. A firm's ability to make changes like these can add considerable value to its equity, and this book develops and then illustrates the procedures to be applied in valuing the real option values associated with them.

The detailed coverage given to the contribution that real options make to the value of a firm's equity contrasts with the texts generally available in the area, which seldom cover this important topic in any detail. Yet, the analysis summarized in this book shows that real options can make a significant contribution to equity value, particularly for firms with low earnings-to-book ratios or where the book value of a firm's equity is comparatively small.

Ian Davidson is The Head of The School of Business, Management and Economics, and Professor in the Science Policy Research Unit (SPRU) at the University of Sussex, UK.

Mark Tippett is Honorary Professor in the Discipline of Accounting in the Business School at the University of Sydney, Australia.

Principles of Equity Valuation

Ian Davidson and Mark Tippett

Routledge
Taylor & Francis Group
LONDON AND NEW YORK

First published 2012
by Routledge
4 Park Square, Milton Park, Abingdon, Oxon OX14 4RN
605 Third Avenue, New York, NY 10017

Routledge is an imprint of the Taylor & Francis Group, an informa business

British Library Cataloguing in Publication Data
A catalogue record for this book is available from the British Library

Library of Congress Cataloging in Publication Data
A catalog record has been requested for this book

ISBN: 978-0-415-69602-9 (hbk)
ISBN: 978-0-415-69603-6 (pbk)
ISBN: 978-0-203-11261-8 (ebk)

Typeset in Times New Roman
by Cenveo Publisher Services

To Judy and Julie

Iona, Danielle, Kari, Brin and Rhys

Contents

List of figures ix
List of tables xi
Preface xii
Acknowledgements xvi

Introduction 1

1 The measurement of returns on bonds, equities and other financial instruments 9

2 The relationship between return and risk 28

3 Alternative approaches to the relationship between return and risk 53

4 Returns and the capital structure of the firm 80

5 The relationship between equity value, dividends and other cash flow streams 106

6 The relationship between book (accounting) rates of return and the cost of capital for firms and capital projects 137

7 Statistical foundations: first-order stochastic differential equations 155

8 Statistical foundations: systems of and higher-order stochastic differential equations 179

9 Equity valuation: a canonical model 208

10 Equity valuation: non-linearities and scaling 234

11 Equity valuation: multivariate investment opportunity sets 254

12 Equity valuation: higher-order investment opportunity sets, momentum and acceleration 286

Index 306

Figures

2.1 Normal distributions of centred asset returns 29
2.2 Markowitz locus with parameter values $a = 22$, $b = -4.8$ and $c = 0.33$ 33
2.3 Markowitz locus with efficient and inefficient portfolios 34
2.4 Forming portfolios when there is a risk-free asset 36
2.5 Summary graph of Markowitz locus and capital market line 40
2.6 Minimum-variance zero-beta portfolio 46
3.1 Orthogonal portfolio and the capital market line 54
3.2 Roots of the characteristic polynomial

$$\lambda^4 - 4\lambda^3 + 4.6744\lambda^2 - 1.68979\lambda + 0.189089 \\ = (\lambda - 2.22)(\lambda - 1.26)(\lambda - 0.26)^2 = 0$$ 71

4.1 Optimal debt-to-equity ratio 81
4.2 Return on equity against debt-to-equity ratio for US electric utility companies 86
4.3 Return on equity against debt-to-equity ratio for US oil companies 87
4.4 Relationship between the weighted average cost of capital and the debt-to-equity ratio 95
4.5 Relationship between the market value of a levered firm and its debt-to-equity ratio 99
5.1 The cash flow function $C(t) = 1 + \frac{1}{t!}$ 115
5.2 Present value of future cash flows for the cash flow function: $C(t) = 1 + \frac{1}{t!}$ 116
5.3 The cash flow function $C(s) = (s - t)e^{-(s-t)}$, where $s \geq t$ 121
5.4 Present value of future cash flows for the cash flow function $C(s) = (s - t)e^{-(s-t)}$, where $s \geq t$ 122
6.1 Relationship between the net present value V_0 and the discount rate r 143
6.2 Relationship between the net present value V_0 and the discount rate r 150
9.1 Relationship between recursion value η and market value of equity $P(\eta)$ for a risk parameter $\theta = 2$ and where $P(0) = 1$ 227
9.2 Relationship between recursion value η and market value of equity $P(\eta)$ for a risk parameter $\theta = \frac{1}{2}$ and where $P(0) = 1$ 228
9.3 Relationship between recursion value η and market value of equity $P(\eta)$ for a risk parameter $\theta = 4$ and where $P(0) = 1$ 229
10.1 Relationship between recursion value η and the equity valuation function $P(\eta)$, for a risk parameter $\theta = 2$ and where $P(0) = 1$ 236

10.2 Relationship between the recursion value η, the equity valuation function $P(\eta)$ and the best linear approximation to the equity valuation function for a risk parameter $\theta = 2$ and where $P(0) = 1$ 240
10.3 Relationship between the equity valuation function $P(\eta)$ and its fifth-order ($m = 5$) Laguerre power series approximation for a risk parameter $\theta = 2$ and where $P(0) = 1$ 241
10.4 Relationship between the equity valuation function $P(\eta)$ and its 10th-order ($m = 10$) Laguerre power series approximation for a risk parameter $\theta = 2$ and where $P(0) = 1$ 241
10.5 Relationship between the equity valuation function $P(\eta)$ and its 15th-order ($m = 15$) Laguerre power series approximation for a risk parameter $\theta = 2$ and where $P(0) = 1$ 242
10.6 Relationship between the equity valuation function $P(\eta)$ and its 30th-order ($m = 30$) Laguerre power series approximation for a risk parameter $\theta = 2$ and where $P(0) = 1$ 242
11.1 Graph of $P(\eta)$ against η when $P(0) = 1$ and the risk parameter $r/\zeta^2 = \frac{1}{2}$ 276
11.2 Graph of $P(\eta)$ against η when $P(0) = 1$ and the risk parameter $r/\zeta^2 = 1$ 276
11.3 Graph of $P(\eta)$ against η when $P(0) = 1$ and the risk parameter $r/\zeta^2 = \frac{3}{2}$ 277

Tables

1.1 Mortgage repayment schedule 12
1.2 Mortgage repayment schedule for flat rate of interest 14
1.3 Mortgage repayment schedule using Newton–Raphson technique 16
1.4 Share and rights price data for Loca Lola Bottlers 21
1.5 Share and rights price data for Caledonian Highland Bank 26
4.1 Summary of financial transactions for Esther and Hannah 83
4.2 Summary financial information for firm H and firm Z 97
5.1 Relationship between the actual present value of the future cash flows and the present value of the future cash flows as given by the fourth-order approximation formula when $a = 1$ and $\lambda = 0.005$ 119
5.2 Relationship between the actual present value of the future cash flows and the present value of the future cash flows as given by the fourth-order approximation formula when $a = 1$ and $\lambda = 0.10$ 120
5.3 Present value as the Laplace transform of the given cash flow function 123
5.4 Roots z_i of the Laguerre polynomial of order 4 and their associated weights w_i 127
6.1 Accounting (book) data for British Petroleum (BP) PLC 145
6.2 Calculations at first iteration ($n = 0$) for determining the rate of return on British Petroleum (BP) PLC ordinary shares 146
6.3 Determining the rate of return on British Petroleum (BP) PLC ordinary shares 147
9.1 Values of the integral $\frac{1}{2}\int_{-1}^{1} \exp\left(-\frac{2y}{1+z}\right)dz$, where $y = \theta\eta$ 224

Preface

This book is the product of nearly 40 years' teaching and research on the part of each of its authors in British, North American and Australasian universities. One cannot be associated with a discipline in a teaching and research capacity for this period of time without coming to a view about the intellectual foundations on which the discipline is built. Thus, in many ways, this book is a statement of what we believe to be the underlying principles upon which the valuation of equity is based. We would begin by emphasizing that the approach we take to our subject matter has been shaped by some of the intellectual giants of our discipline. At the risk of oversight, we acknowledge the many hours spent in discussion and debate with Ray Chambers, Philip Bell, Angus Deaton, Sir David Tweedie and Geoffrey Whittington. Our intellectual debt to all of them is immense, although we fear that if they were to read the text that follows, they would all feel the time they have so generously given to us might have been better spent doing other things.

A distinguishing feature of our time in higher education is the decline in academic standards expected of students. In our view, it is no coincidence that this has occurred as the research of the discipline has deteriorated into a form that involves little more than a data set and an econometric package. Albert Einstein once remarked that 'what can be observed is really determined by theory'. He said, 'you cannot first know what can be observed, but you must first know a theory, or produce a theory, and then you can define what can be observed.' But theory is hard – often very hard. In our discipline, a competent theorist will have spent many hours absorbing a complicated brew of mathematics, economics and theoretical statistics, if not more. In contrast, 'off-the-shelf' linear software packages can be applied to 'off-the-shelf' data sets with only a limited (and in many instances, no) understanding of the statistical and mathematical principles upon which the empirical analysis is based. This has led to an entirely unsatisfactory situation where many of our prestigious academic journals are clogged up with a kind of 'mindless' empiricism that is capable of resolving few, if any, of the fundamental questions and problems that confront our discipline. Again, one can do little more than quote what Einstein had to say when the research of a discipline descends to this level of mediocrity: 'I have little patience with scientists who take a board of wood, look for its thinnest part, and drill a great number of holes where the drilling is easy.' The pages that follow lay down a challenge to those who would teach and encourage their students to 'drill a great number of holes where the drilling is easy'; that is to say, those who would champion the cause of empirical work based on artificially constructed linear models of the relationship between equity values and their determining variables. A founding father of quantum mechanics has astutely described the probability of obtaining anything useful from procedures like this in the following terms: 'If everything were linear, nothing would influence nothing.'

Some difficult decisions have had to be made about what to include and what to exclude from this book. The first half provides a rigorous introduction to corporate finance and the valuation of equity. The later chapters, comprising the second half of the book, encompass more advanced material on the valuation of equity. In these later chapters especially, the choice of topics may sometimes appear to be curious. For example, little space is devoted to discrete-time equity valuation models despite their overwhelming popularity in the literature. Rather, the analysis in the second half of the book is almost exclusively conducted in continuous time. Although there are many reasons for this, two are worthy of particular mention. First, large organizations will typically conduct millions of transactions in any given day, and so continuous-time models provide a much more realistic description of the way firms evolve in practice. More important, however, is that whilst discrete-time models are usually easier for numerical analysis, simple analytical solutions are more likely to emerge when equity valuation models are formulated in continuous time. The distributional properties of the process realizations can then be determined in a relatively straightforward manner. This contrasts with the corresponding discrete-time equity valuation models, which seldom admit explicit representations and whose distributional properties are therefore much more difficult, if not impossible, to determine.

All the chapters in this book have been developed from lecture notes and other materials distributed to students over our many years of teaching. Our hope is that this will have helped in making the text more 'reader-friendly' than would otherwise have been the case. Before taking a course based on the first six chapters of the book, students would be well advised to have completed a basic service course in accounting that covers the double-entry bookkeeping system, including the preparation of the profit and loss account and the balance sheet. They will also need to have completed a basic service course in probability and statistics and have a rudimentary understanding of matrices, differentiation and integration. The last six chapters of the book emphasize the important role played by 'real options' in the valuation of equity and, in particular, the value that arises out of a firm's ability to change or modify its investment opportunity set in order to use its resources in alternative and more profitable ways. For this part of the book, students will need a more advanced understanding of matrix theory and differential and integral calculus and an elementary understanding of differential equations. They will also need a deeper understanding of probability and statistics than that which is necessary for the first six chapters.

A guiding philosophy in our presentation of this book is that 'knowing is achieved by doing'. It is because of this that each chapter includes five carefully chosen exercises for readers to work through. Detailed solutions for all exercises may be accessed on our website; namely,

http://www.sussex.ac.uk/profiles/236905

We would encourage readers to attempt all the exercises, even if they do so with an eye on the answers provided.

As we read through the manuscript and note its numerous failings, all of them (we might add) of our own making, it occurs to us that it might be wiser to omit any mention of those who have so selflessly given of their time and effort in both commenting on and suggesting improvements in what we have written. At whatever risk, we thank our PhD students Diandian Ma and Xiaojing Song, who between them have read the entire manuscript and have made many penetrating but useful criticisms that resulted in revisions being made to presentation and explanations in several parts of the manuscript. We also thank our former student Gaurav

Chavda, who also made some sharp criticisms of presentation. We owe much to Professor Albert William (Bill) Richardson of McMaster University, who provided written comments on several of the more difficult chapters and whose incisive analysis caused us to rethink the motivation and accuracy of statements made at several points of the manuscript. The co-author of many of our published papers, Mr Huw Rhys formerly of the University of Exeter, has patiently led us through the intricacies of several jointly published proofs. Last but not least, we thank the PhD students in our classes on Equity Valuation at the School of Commerce and Administration in the Victoria University of Wellington, New Zealand, who endured the discomfort of having to work through various parts of the manuscript whilst these were still in early draft form. Their cheerful patience and perseverance in the face of numerous and confusing typographical and other errors is much appreciated.

We would warmly welcome criticisms, corrections and suggestions, both major and minor, from those who have the inclination to provide them.

Ian Davidson,
University of Sussex

Mark Tippett,
University of Sydney
April 2012

'No one can comprehend what goes on under the sun. Despite all his efforts to search it out, man cannot discover its meaning. Even if a wise man claims he knows, he cannot really comprehend it.'

Ecclesiastes, Chapter 8, verse 17

Acknowledgements

The authors gratefully acknowledge the granting of copyright permission from the American Economic Association to reproduce Figure 3 and Figure 4 from Modigliani, F. and Miller, M. (1958) 'The cost of capital, corporation finance and the theory of investment', *American Economic Review*, 48: 261–97.

The authors gratefully acknowledge the granting of copyright permission from Taylor & Francis to reproduce Figure 1, Figure 2 and Figure 3 from Ali Ataullah, Huw Rhys and Mark Tippett, 'Non-linear equity valuation', *Accounting and Business Research,* 39: 57–72. Details of this article can be found on the journal's website: http://www.tandfonline.com.

Introduction

§0-1. In 1937, John Burr Williams argued that an asset's value should be calculated by determining the present value of the future cash flows one expects to receive from it. 'A cow', wrote Williams, 'for her milk. A hen for her eggs, and a stock, by heck, for her dividends. An orchard for fruit, bees for their honey, and stocks, besides, for their dividends.' Thus, said Williams, since future dividends are the cash flows one expects to receive from an equity security, it necessarily follows that one should determine the intrinsic, long-term worth of the given equity security by calculating the present value of the dividends that one expects to receive from it. Nowadays, this approach for determining the intrinsic or fundamental value of an equity security is widely used in the financial markets, although less rigorous methods such as price–earnings multiples are still in evidence. In applying the dividend valuation approach, security analysts and investors determine the intrinsic value of an equity security by first estimating the future stream of dividends they expect the equity security to pay. They will then apply an appropriate discount rate to the estimated stream of dividends in order to determine the fundamental or intrinsic value of the given equity security. If the intrinsic value of the equity security exceeds its market price, they will regard the equity security as a 'good' investment. In contrast, should its market price exceed its intrinsic value, they will label the equity security as a 'bad' investment. It thus follows that the discount rate applied to the dividends a company is expected to pay will be an instrumental determinant of the intrinsic or fundamental value that analysts and investors will calculate for the equity security. Given this, the first chapter of this book is devoted to issues surrounding the calculation of an appropriate discount rate with which to determine the present value of a given cash flow stream. In particular, we identify some of the pitfalls that can arise from the incorrect calculation and averaging of the returns that accrue on equity securities and other financial instruments. This chapter also illustrates and provides a brief introduction to the numerical procedures that can be used to determine the return on fixed-interest securities, such as mortgages and bonds.

It is conventional practice to base the discount rate used in the calculation of the intrinsic value of an equity security on an asset pricing model such as the Capital Asset Pricing Model (CAPM). Under the CAPM, there is a simple linear relationship between the expected return on an asset and the asset's inherent risk as captured by what is known as its 'beta' statistic. In Chapter 2, we develop the CAPM from first principles by using a series of simple numerical examples. We show, in particular, how an asset's beta relates to the returns earned on the myriad of other assets comprising the economy and how beta is influenced by the macroeconomic variables that characterize the economy as a whole. We would emphasize, however, that whilst the CAPM is probably the most commonly encountered asset pricing model in the literature, there are alternative ways of modelling the relationship between asset returns and the risks associated with them. Thus, in Chapter 3, we demonstrate how one can build asset pricing models in which factors other than beta might be interpreted as important determinants of asset returns. This places the largely *ad hoc* nature of the asset pricing formulae that characterize the empirical research of this area of the literature onto a similar footing to the CAPM in the sense that there will be a perfect linear relationship between the average return on an asset and the variables selected as important determining variables in the asset pricing process. The focus of Chapter 3 then moves on to a second and more theoretically plausible approach to asset pricing issues, namely, the Arbitrage Pricing Theory (APT). The basic assumption behind the APT is that it will never be possible to earn a riskless profit from a self-financing (i.e. a zero-cost) investment portfolio. We note how a variety of arbitrage pricing models have arisen out of this basic assumption. Probably the most commonly employed of these uses what is known as the 'characteristic polynomial' associated with the matrix whose elements are the variances and covariances of the assets comprising the economy. The characteristic polynomial identifies what is known as the 'latent roots' or 'eigenvalues' of the variance–covariance matrix, and these are used to isolate the important 'factors' or determinants of returns on the assets comprising a given portfolio. This interpretation of the APT shows that an asset's return has two components. First, there is the component of the return that arises from the set of underlying factors; then, there is a second purely idiosyncratic component of the return. Our analysis in this third chapter is limited to a consideration of the most commonly encountered alternatives to the CAPM to be found in the literature. There are, however, many other approaches to asset pricing theory that, owing to limitations of space, we are unable treat in this chapter.

§0-2. The first three chapters of the book examine how returns ought to be calculated and averaged and articulates the relationships that one might expect to find between the average returns on assets and the various risk measures encountered in the literature. In Chapter 4, our attention focuses on a risk measure that empirical researchers have found to have an instrumental association with equity returns, namely, the ratio of the debt and equity with which firms finance their operating activities. We demonstrate how under certain idealized market conditions the return on the equity of a levered firm will be equal to the return on the equity of an 'equivalent' unlevered firm plus a risk premium that hinges on the ratio of the debt and equity with which the levered firm finances its productive activities. Moreover, in the idealized market conditions on which our analysis is based, firms will finance their operating activities with as much debt as possible. This is because the weighted average cost of the firm's capital will continuously decline as its debt-to-equity ratio grows in magnitude. Unfortunately, when market imperfections are taken into account, it is not hard to show that a firm's weighted average cost of capital will at first decline as debt is substituted for equity in the firm's capital structure. However, a point will eventually be reached where so much debt has been issued that the firm will have difficulty in meeting the interest payments on its debt should it find itself getting into financial difficulties. At this point, both debt and equity holders will demand higher rates of return as compensation for the increased risks they are required to bear and the firm's weighted average cost of capital will begin to rise. Correspondingly, the firm's market value will reach a maximum at this minimum cost of capital and will then fall away as the cost of capital increases in response to the risks posed by the increasing levels of debt comprising the firm's capital structure.

The opening sections of Chapter 5 demonstrate how in a perfect capital market the present value of the dividends paid over the life of a firm must be equal to the present value of its operating cash flows. Hence, whilst one can always determine the value of an equity security by discounting the future dividends it will pay, it is the firm's operating cash flows (and not its dividends) that are the instrumental determinants of its equity value. This has the important consequence that the specific time pattern of dividend payments invoked by a firm will be irrelevant to the valuation of the firm's equity, since every time pattern of dividend payments will have a present value that is equal to the present value of the firm's future operating cash flows. In other words, investors will care little about whether the firm pays niggardly dividends in the immediate future and generous dividends over the longer term or vice versa, since the present value of the dividends it will pay will always be equal to the present value of its future operating cash flows. Moreover, it will often be the case that a firm's operating cash flows can be approximated by a functional form that leads to a simple analytical expression for the present value of the cash flows associated with a firm's equity. In the intermediate sections of Chapter 5, we demonstrate some specific examples of where this will be the case. Importantly, when there is a closed-form solution for the present value of the future cash flows associated with a given discrete-time cash flow function, one can normally differentiate through it to derive closed-form expressions for the present value of alternative discrete-time cash flow functions. However, even when a particular cash flow function does not lead to a closed-form present value expression, it will still normally be possible to obtain a convergent series expansion for the present value of the future cash flows. Examples are given of discrete-time cash flow functions where this is the case. Moreover, the operating cash flows of large firms will typically be composed of thousands of transactions on any given day and so their cash flows will normally evolve in a way that can be closely approximated by a continuous function of time. When this is the case, one can apply the numerical integration procedure of Gauss–Laguerre quadrature to estimate the present value of its future cash flows. Chapter 5 concludes by providing several examples of how the Gauss–Laguerre quadrature procedure is implemented.

Chapter 6 begins with the observation that one will normally take an average of the returns that an equity security has earned in the past in order to estimate the return that one can expect from the given equity security in the future. There are occasions, however, where the market price of an equity security either does not exist or can only be observed infrequently, and this can create difficulties with measuring the past returns on the given equity security. This in turn will make it difficult to estimate the return that one might expect from the equity security in future periods. Hence, in this chapter, we demonstrate how one can estimate the return on a given equity security by using only past profits as determined by the firm's accountants and the book values at which the owners' equity has been recorded in the firm's accounting records. This means that we do not have to use information about the equity security's market prices at any point in our calculations. Several numerical examples illustrate how the estimation procedure is implemented, including some that are based on the profitability figures and book values of firms listed on the London Stock Exchange.

§0-3. Previous chapters summarize how returns are computed and averaged and how assets will be priced so as to provide an expected return compatible with their inherent risks. However, these models of risk and return have little to say about fundamental supply-side issues; in particular, of how the variables comprising a firm's investment opportunity set influence the market value of the firm's equity. In Chapter 7, we lay the foundations for the much fuller treatment that is given in the second half of this book of the impact that supply-side issues can have on equity value. The chapter begins by showing how the Brownian motion on which virtually all of modern asset pricing theory is built is based on a limiting form of the simplest interpretation of the Laplace model of accumulated errors developed towards the end of the eighteenth century by Pierre-Simon, Marquis de Laplace. The chapter then goes on to demonstrate how the Laplace model of accumulated errors can be generalized to more complicated and potentially more useful stochastic processes by merely changing the probabilities that Laplace attributed to the stochastic errors arising in his model. In particular, we formulate the probabilities associated with the Uhlenbeck–Ornstein process, which leads to one of the most widely employed stochastic differential equations in asset pricing theory. The Uhlenbeck–Ornstein process is then used to illustrate the application of the Fokker–Planck equation. The Fokker–Planck equation allows one to determine the distributional properties of a variable directly from the stochastic differential equation through which it evolves, even when there is no closed-form solution for the underlying stochastic differential equation. The final sections of the chapter deal with the problem of determining the properties of functions of stochastic variables. For example, the market value of a firm's equity hinges on the firm's profitability as well as the general outlook for the economy. The firm's profitability and the general economic outlook are both stochastic variables, and so the market value of the firm's equity will be a function of these and many other underlying stochastic variables. Hence, in these final sections of the chapter, we introduce a procedure, named for Kiyoshi Itô, which enables one to determine the distributional properties of a stochastic variable that is itself a function of a more primitive set of underlying stochastic variables.

Chapter 8 continues with our consideration of the impact that supply-side issues can have on the valuation of a firm's equity. The opening sections of this chapter model the factors comprising a firm's investment opportunity set in terms of a first-order vector system of stochastic differential equations. This allows one to capture many of the important interdependences that exist between the factors that most directly influence the value of a firm's equity. Moreover, we demonstrate how one can obtain the solution of a first-order vector system of stochastic differential equations and thereby determine the distributional properties of the individual factors comprising the firm's investment opportunity set. However, stating the evolution of the factors comprising a firm's investment opportunity set in terms of a first-order vector system of differential equations has some significant limitations. In particular, if the momentum and acceleration of factors comprising the firm's investment opportunity set are important determinants of equity value then it will be necessary to consider investment opportunity sets that are characterized by higher-order systems of stochastic differential equations. Recall that a factor's acceleration is defined in terms of its second derivative. However, if a firm's investment opportunity set is stated in terms of a first-order system of stochastic differential equations then, by definition, it will not include the second and higher derivatives of the factors comprising the firm's investment opportunity set. Given this, in this chapter, we develop the theory behind the formulation and solution of the simplest (or canonical) forms of second- (and higher-) order vector systems of stochastic differential equations. In subsequent chapters, we show that that this is an area of considerable importance in equity valuation.

§0-4. Chapter 9 develops the analysis of the previous two chapters into a canonical model of equity valuation. The model assumes 'clean surplus' accounting, by which we mean that changes in the book value of equity are composed exclusively of the profits and losses recorded on the firm's profit and loss account. The analysis of this chapter also invokes what has become the conventional practice of characterizing the firm's investment opportunity set in terms of its abnormal earnings and a second variable that captures all the information relevant to the value of a firm's equity that has not, as yet, been incorporated into the firm's accounting records. One can use these definitions and assumptions to show that there are two complementary aspects to the valuation of the firm's equity. The first of these is determined by discounting the stream of expected future operating cash flows under the assumption that the firm will apply its existing investment opportunity set indefinitely into the future. This is usually referred to as the 'recursion value' of equity. The second element of equity value arises from the fact that the firm will normally have the option of changing or modifying its investment opportunity set so that it can use its resources in alternative and potentially more profitable ways. The potential to change the firm's investment opportunity set gives rise to what is known as the 'adaptation value' of equity. Our analysis in this chapter shows how the adaptation value of equity will have a highly convex and non-linear relationship with the variables comprising the firm's investment opportunity set. This is of particular significance given the penchant amongst empirical researchers for applying purely linear methodologies to estimate the valuation relationships that exist in this area.

Chapter 10 begins with the observation that empirical work dealing with the relationship between the market value of a firm's equity and the variables comprising its investment opportunity set is normally based on some form of linear model that neglects the adaptation options associated with the firm's ability to change or modify its existing operating activities. Given this, the opening sections of this chapter determine the likely form and magnitude of the biases that arise when researchers assume that the market value of a firm's equity is composed exclusively of its recursion value and therefore is linear in its determining variables. We analyse the biases that arise from this assumption using an orthogonal polynomial fitting technique that identifies the relative contribution which the linear and non-linear components of the relationship between equity value and its determining variables make towards overall equity value. The evidence from this procedure is that the non-linearities in equity valuation can be large and significant, particularly for firms where the recursion value of equity is relatively small. Moreover, empirical work conducted in the area is invariably based on market and/or accounting (book) variables that are scaled or deflated in order to facilitate comparisons between firms of different size. Given this, it is important that one appreciates how these deflation procedures might alter or even distort the underlying levels relationships that exist between the market value of equity and its determining variables. In particular, our analysis of this issue shows that deflating data before regression procedures are applied can lead to a form of spurious correlation between the regression variables. This in turn can lead a researcher to the conclusion that a non-trivial relationship exists between the regression variables when in fact the data on which the regression analysis is based are completely unrelated. Examples of spurious correlations arising out of the deflation procedures demonstrated here are not difficult to find in the literature and several illustrations are provided in the later sections of this chapter.

§0-5. The opening sections of Chapter 11 generalize the canonical equity pricing model developed in Chapter 9 so as to remove its dependence on the clean surplus identity and also to allow for the payment of dividends. Our analysis is based on two dirty surplus propositions. The first of these shows how the recursion value of equity is determined when the clean surplus identity does not hold; that is, when there is a form of dirty surplus accounting. The second proposition outlines how the system of stochastic differential equations that characterize the firm's investment opportunity set must be modified so as to encompass dirty surplus accounting. Our analysis of this second proposition is based on a multiplicity of determining variables. We do this because it is highly likely that in practice the market value of a firm's equity will hinge on a large number of determining variables and not just the two (abnormal earnings and the information variable) on which the canonical pricing formula developed in Chapter 9 is based. We then move on to assess the impact that the explicit incorporation of dividend payments into our modelling procedures can have on equity values. In common with results reported in the real options literature, our analysis shows that whilst the recursion value of equity does not hinge on the firm's dividend policy, the adaptation value of equity will be affected by the dividend policy invoked by the firm. Against this, our analysis also shows that, for parsimonious dividend payout assumptions (e.g. dividend payments that are proportional to the recursion value of equity), the 'structure' of the equity valuation formula is similar to the canonical equity valuation formula developed in Chapter 9.

Earlier chapters also assumed that a firm's operating cash flows evolve through an investment opportunity set defined in terms of a first-order system of stochastic differential equations. However, there is mounting empirical evidence showing that the momentum and acceleration (i.e. the first and second derivatives) of the variables comprising the firm's investment opportunity set can also have a significant impact on the market value of a firm's equity. As noted in §0-3 above, however, when an investment opportunity set is defined in terms of a first-order system of stochastic differential equations, it cannot take account of these momentum and acceleration phenomena. In Chapter 12, we address this problem by demonstrating that if a firm's investment opportunity set evolves in terms of a second- (or higher-) order system of stochastic differential equations then the present value of the operating cash flows that it expects to earn will be stated in terms of both the levels and momentum (i.e. first derivative) of the variables comprising its investment opportunity set. This provides an analytical justification for the emerging empirical evidence that finds a significant association between earnings momentum and the market value of equity. Moreover, the results presented here generalize to higher-order systems of stochastic differential equations. It then follows that the acceleration (second derivative), jerk (third derivative), snap (fourth derivative), crackle (fifth derivative) and pop (sixth derivative) of the variables comprising its investment opportunity set can also have a significant impact on the present value of the operating cash flows that a firm expects to earn.

Earlier chapters also assumed that if the recursion value of equity falls away to nothing then the firm will be able to exchange its current investment opportunity set for a suite of assets and/or capital projects that have an inter-temporally known and constant adaptation value. However, it is highly likely that the adaptation value of equity will mirror recursion value in evolving stochastically through time. Unfortunately, the equity pricing formulae developed in previous chapters do not take account of the valuation implications arising from stochastic variations in the adaptation value of equity. Thus, in Chapter 12, we also demonstrate the significant impact that stochastic variations in adaptation value can have on the equity pricing formulae developed in previous chapters. Our analysis shows that the adaptation value of equity is a highly convex function of its determining variables and this in turn implies that there will be a non-linear relationship between the market value of a firm's equity and the variables comprising its investment opportunity set. This again (as in §0-4) points to the limitations of empirical work based on the assumption that there is a purely linear relationship between the market value of a firm's equity and its determining variables.

Selected references

Howell, S., Stark, A., Newton, D., Paxson, D., Cavus, M., Azevedo-Pereira, J. and Patel, K. (2001) *Real Options – Evaluating Corporate Investment Opportunities in a Dynamic World*, London: Financial Times/Prentice Hall, 2001.

Rubinstein, M. (2006) *A History of the Theory of Investments*. Hoboken: Wiley.

Williams, J. (1997) *The Theory of Investment Value*, Burlington, VT: Fraser Publishing.

1 The measurement of returns on bonds, equities and other financial instruments

§1-1. The calculation and indeed, the manipulation of returns pervades our everyday lives. When one opens a bank account or line of credit with a financial institution, the rate of interest on surplus funds and/or the rate of interest on the overdraft facilities we expect to use figure highly in the decisions we make about which bank/and or financial institution we will lend our custom to. When it comes to risky assets such as the shares and bonds of publicly listed companies, we make investment decisions by weighing the returns we expect to get from our proposed investments against the risks that are likely to arise from them. Our retirement plans also hinge crucially on the returns earned by the superannuation funds with which we deposit our retirement funds and on the prospective benefits these returns will enable us to enjoy after we retire. All of this presupposes of course that we have a clear understanding of how the returns on a given portfolio or financial instrument ought to be calculated. Hence, the principal brief of this chapter is to identify the pitfalls that may arise from the incorrect calculation and averaging of the returns that accrue on shares, bonds, portfolios and other financial instruments. We begin our analysis with a consideration of the procedures that can be used to compute the returns on bonds.

§1-2. A bond is a written contract by a debtor to pay a creditor a redemption payment V on an indicated date and to pay a pre-specified amount K (normally termed interest) on a periodic basis. The typical bond mentions a borrowed principal H, called the face value or par value of the bond. Bonds typically make interest payments on a semi-annual basis and are redeemable at par – in which case $V = H$. Consider, then, the purchaser of a bond who demands that his money be invested at a pre-specified rate r. We call this the investment rate. The price the investor will pay for the bond is given by

> the present value of the final redemption payment (V) plus the present value of the remaining interest payments (K)

One can demonstrate how this valuation formula is implemented using the following simple example.

An $H = £100$ par 6 per cent bond pays interest on a semi-annual basis. This means that interest of $K = (0.06/2) \times H = 0.03 \times £100 = £3$ is paid at the mid-point of the year and also at the end of year until such time as the bond is redeemed. The bond is to be redeemed on 30 June 2012. Determine the price to be paid for the bond if (a) the bond is purchased on 1 July 2009, (b) the investment rate is 2 per cent (per half year); that is, $r = 4$ per cent (per annum) compounded *semi-annually* and (c) the bond is redeemable at par; that is $V = £100 = H$.

Now the present value of £100 receivable in three years' time, compounded at 4 per cent (per annum) compounded semi-annually, is

$$\frac{100}{\left(1+\frac{0.04}{2}\right)^{3\times 2}} = \frac{100}{(1.02)^6} = 100 \times 0.8880 = £88.80$$

Likewise, the present value of the interest payments compounded at 4 per cent (per annum) compounded semi-annually is

$$\sum_{t=1}^{6} \frac{100 \times 0.03}{(1.02)^t} = 3 \times 5.6014 = £16.80$$

Hence, the investor would be prepared to pay no more than (£88.80 + £16.80) = £105.60 for the bond.

§1-3. The rate of interest quoted on a bond is normally what is known as the nominal rate of interest. With a given nominal rate r, compounded m times per year, we define the corresponding effective rate of interest to be the rate that would apply if compounding occurred on an annual basis only. One can demonstrate this point by supposing for the example given in §1-2 above that the investment rate is 4.04 per cent *compounded annually*. We would then have that the present value of £100 receivable in three years' time, compounded at an annual rate of 4.04 per cent, would be

$$\frac{100}{(1+0.0404)^3} = \frac{100}{1.1262} = £88.80$$

Likewise, the present value of the interest payments compounded at an annual rate of 4.04 per cent will be

$$\sum_{t=1}^{6} \frac{3}{(1+0.0404)^{t/2}} = \sum_{t=1}^{6} \frac{3}{(\sqrt{1+0.0404})^t} = \sum_{t=1}^{6} \frac{3}{(1.02)^t} = 3 \times 5.6014 = £16.80$$

Hence, the value of the bond is again (£88.80 + £16.80) = £105.60, i.e. the same value as calculated in §1-2 above. This implies that an interest rate of 4 per cent (per annum) compounded semi-annually is equivalent to an interest rate of 4.04 per cent compounded annually. In other words, an effective rate of interest of 4.04 per cent corresponds to a nominal rate of interest of 4 per cent (per annum) compounded semi-annually. The effective rate of interest is often called the Annual Percentage Rate or APR for short. We develop the relationship between the nominal rate of interest and the effective rate of interest (or APR) in further detail in §1-7 below.

§1-4. Suppose I have to repay a loan and I want to confirm the integrity or otherwise of the figures that have been given to me by the lending institution. The principles just enunciated for bond valuation may also be applied here. The present value of the repayments on the loan must be equal to the amount borrowed, or

$$P = \sum_{t=1}^{N} \frac{R}{(1+r)^t}$$

where P is the principal (or the amount) borrowed, N is the number of repayments that will be made on the loan, R is the periodic repayment and r is the investment rate on the loan. One can demonstrate the application of this formula by considering a person who takes out a loan of £2,000 that is to be repaid in 12 equal monthly instalments. The borrowing (investment) rate is 18 per cent (per annum). It thus follows that $P = £2,000$, $r = 0.18/12 = 0.015$ or $1\frac{1}{2}$ per cent (per month), and $N = 12$. Substitution then shows that the monthly repayment R may be obtained by solving the following equation:

$$2,000 = \sum_{t=1}^{12} \frac{R}{(1+0.015)^t}$$

Now, in the exercises at the end of this chapter, the reader will be asked to prove the following result:

$$\sum_{t=1}^{N} \frac{1}{(1+r)^t} = \frac{1}{r}[1-(1+r)^{-N}]$$

Setting $r = 0.015$ in this result, we have

$$\sum_{t=1}^{12} \frac{1}{(1.015)^t} = \frac{1}{0.015}[1-(1.015)^{-12}] = 10.907505$$

It follows from this that the monthly repayment R can be computed from the equation

$$2,000 = \sum_{t=1}^{12} \frac{R}{(1+0.015)^t} = R\sum_{t=1}^{12} \frac{1}{(1+0.015)^t} = 10.907505 \times R$$

or that the monthly repayment is $R = £2{,}000/10.907505 = £183.36$.

One can prove that these calculations are correct by preparing the mortgage repayment schedule exhibited in Table 1.1. The interest payment at the end of the first month is the principal outstanding at the beginning of the month multiplied by the monthly interest rate, or $£2{,}000 \times 0.015 = £30$. This in turn means that the principal repaid at the end of the first month will be the repayment made at the end of the first month less the interest that has accrued over the month, or $£183.36 - £30 = £153.36$. Subtracting this from the opening principal shows that the principal outstanding at the end of the first month will be $£2{,}000 - £153.36 = £1{,}846.64$. The interest payment at the end of the second month will then be the principal outstanding at the beginning of the second month multiplied by the monthly interest rate, or $£1{,}846.64 \times 0.015 = £27.70$. This in turn means that the principal repaid at the end of the second month will be the repayment made at the end of the second month less the interest which has accrued over the second month, or $£183.36 - £27.70 = £155.66$. Subtracting this from the principal outstanding at the end of the first month shows that the principal outstanding

Table 1.1 Mortgage repayment schedule

Date	*Opening principal* £	*Interest* £	*Principal repaid* £	*Closing principal* £
1	2,000.00	30.00	153.36	1,846.64
2	1,846.64	27.70	155.66	1,690.98
3	1,690.98	25.36	158.00	1,532.98
4	1,532.98	22.99	160.37	1,372.62
5	1,372.62	20.59	162.77	1,209.85
6	1,209.85	18.15	165.21	1,044.64
7	1,044.64	15.67	167.69	876.95
8	876.95	13.15	170.21	706.74
9	706.74	10.60	172.76	533.98
10	533.98	8.01	175.35	358.63
11	358.63	5.38	177.98	180.65
12	180.65	2.71	180.65	0.00

at the end of the second month will be £1,846.64 – £155.66 = £1,690.98. Continuing with these calculations shows that the loan will be completely discharged (that is, paid off) by the end of the twelfth month.

Note also that one can calculate the principal outstanding on the loan at any given time by simply calculating the present value of the remaining payments. Thus, suppose the borrower wishes to discharge (i.e. pay off) the loan immediately after making the eighth of the twelve monthly payments that would normally have been made on the loan. This means that there are four monthly payments of $R = £183.36$ that remain to be made on the loan, the first of which is due in one month's time. The present value of these repayments is

$$\sum_{t=1}^{4} \frac{183.36}{(1.015)^t} = \frac{183.36}{0.015}[1-(1.015)^{-4}] = 183.36 \times 3.8544 = £706.74$$

Alternatively, the borrower will have to meet the four monthly repayments that remain to be made on the loan, less the interest that is now avoided by paying the loan off early. Table 1.1 shows that the interest avoided in month 9 amounts to £10.60. Similarly, the interest avoided in months 10, 11 and 12 is £8.01, £5.38 and £2.71, respectively. Hence, the amount necessary to pay out the loan at the end of month eight is $4 \times £183.36 - (£10.60 + £8.01 + £5.38 + £2.71) =$ £706.74, the same figure as that obtained above by determining the present value of the remaining four repayments on the loan. Note how our calculation of the amount necessary to pay out the loan immediately after the eighth monthly payment has been made, £706.74, is exactly the same as the figure for the closing principal in the eighth row of the mortgage repayment schedule summarized in Table 1.1. This result encapsulates a principle that we will stress repeatedly throughout this book, namely, that the market value of any asset will be given by the expected present value of its future cash flows.

§1-5. It is occasionally the case that loan contracts are written in terms of 'flat' rates of interest. Consider then the following example in which a creditor borrows £2,000 repayable in 12 monthly instalments at an interest rate of 18 per cent (per annum) flat. It then follows that the total interest payable is the amount borrowed multiplied by the rate of interest multiplied by the number of years the loan is outstanding, or £2,000 × 0.18 × 1 = £360. Moreover, the total amount to be repaid will be the amount borrowed plus the interest or £2,000 + £360 = £2,360. The repayments at the end of each month will thus be £2,360/12 = £196.67. Now, the interest rate implicit in the above contract is computed by applying the principles summarized in §1-2 above. Hence, one can determine the interest rate by letting the amount borrowed be equal to the present value of the repayments, or

$$2,000=\sum_{t=1}^{12}\frac{196.67}{(1+r)^t}$$

That is,

$$\sum_{t=1}^{12}\frac{1}{(1+r)^t}=\frac{2,000}{196.67}=10.169492$$

Now if one substitutes $r = 0.025$ into the left-hand side of the above equation then it follows that

$$\sum_{t=1}^{12}\frac{1}{(1+r)^t}=\sum_{t=1}^{12}\frac{1}{(1+0.025)^t}=\frac{1}{0.025}\left[1-\frac{1}{(1.025)^{12}}\right]=10.257765$$

This is larger than the actual figure on the right-hand side of the above equation, 10.169492, thereby indicating that the interest rate we have used is too low. Given this, we substitute $r = 0.03$ into the left-hand side of the above equation, to give

$$\sum_{t=1}^{12}\frac{1}{(1+r)^t}=\sum_{t=1}^{12}\frac{1}{(1+0.03)^t}=\frac{1}{0.03}\left[1-\frac{1}{(1.03)^{12}}\right]=9.954004$$

This is now smaller than the actual figure on the right-hand side of the above equation, 10.169492, thereby indicating that the interest rate we have used is too high. One can then approximate the interest rate by using the method of linear interpolation

$$\frac{r-0.025}{0.03-0.025}=\frac{10.169492-10.257765}{9.954004-10.257765}$$

Recall here that 10.257765 is the present value factor corresponding to an interest rate of 2½ per cent. Likewise, 9.954004 is the present value factor corresponding to an interest rate of 3 per cent. Finally, 10.169492 is the present value factor corresponding to the interest rate to be determined, namely, r. Solving this equation for r shows that $r = 0.026453$ or 2.6453 per cent (per month). One can then use this result to prepare the mortgage repayment schedule depicted in Table 1.2. The interest payment at the end of the first month is the principal outstanding at the beginning of the month multiplied by the monthly interest rate, or £2,000 × 0.026453 = £52.91. This in turn means that the principal repaid at the end of the first month will be the repayment made at the end of the first month less the interest that has accrued over the month, or £196.67 − £52.91 = £143.76. Subtracting this from the opening principal shows that the principal outstanding at the end of the first month will be £2,000 − £143.76 = £1,856.24. The interest payment at the end of the second month will

Table 1.2 Mortgage repayment schedule for flat rate of interest

Date	*Opening principal* £	*Interest* £	*Principal repaid* £	*Closing principal* £
1	2,000.00	52.91	143.76	1,856.24
2	1,856.24	49.10	147.57	1,708.67
3	1,708.67	45.20	151.47	1,557.20
4	1,557.20	41.19	155.48	1,401.72
5	1,401.72	37.08	159.59	1,242.13
6	1,242.13	32.86	163.81	1,078.32
7	1,078.32	28.52	168.15	910.17
8	910.17	24.08	172.59	737.58
9	737.58	19.51	177.16	560.42
10	560.42	14.82	181.85	378.58
11	378.58	10.01	186.66	191.92
12	191.92	5.08	191.59	0.33

then be £1,856.24 × 0.026453 = £49.10. This in turn means that the principal repaid at the end of the second month must be £196.67 – £49.10 = £147.57. Subtracting this from the principal outstanding at the end of the first month shows that the principal outstanding at the end of the second month will be £1,856.24 – £147.57 = £1,708.67. Note, however, that the linear interpolation technique employed here has led to a slight error in the estimate of the implicit rate of interest – as is evidenced by the fact that there is 33p that remains to be paid on the loan after the final repayment at the end of the twelfth month.

§1-6. The Newton–Raphson technique is a much more reliable and accurate procedure for estimating the implicit interest rate on loans than the method of linear interpolation demonstrated in §1-5 above. The Newton–Raphson technique uses an iterative 'updating' procedure to estimate the implicit rate of interest and is based on the following formula:

$$r_{n+1} = r_n - \frac{F(r_n)}{F'(r_n)}$$

where r_n is the estimate of the implicit rate of interest at the nth iteration,

$$F'(r_n) = \frac{dF(r_n)}{dr_n}$$

is the derivative of $F(r_n)$ with respect to r_n and

$$F(r_n) = \sum_{t=1}^{N} \frac{1}{(1+r_n)^t} - \frac{B}{R}$$

Here N represents the number of repayments to be made on the loan, B is the principal (i.e. the amount borrowed) and R is the periodic repayment. Thus, for the example given in §1-5 above we have $N = 12$, $B = £2,000$ and $R = £196.67$ per month in which case $B/R = 2,000/196.67 = 10.169492$. Moreover, one can differentiate through the above expression for $F(r_n)$ and thereby show that

$$\frac{dF(r_n)}{dr_n} = F'(r_n) = \sum_{t=1}^{N} \frac{-t}{(1+r_n)^{t+1}}$$

One can then substitute into the above expression for r_{n+1} to give the following iteration formula for estimating the rate of interest on the loan:

$$r_{n+1} = r_n - \frac{F(r_n)}{F'(r_n)} = r_n + \frac{\sum_{t=1}^{12} \frac{1}{(1+r_n)^t} - 10.169492}{\sum_{t=1}^{12} \frac{t}{(1+r_n)^{t+1}}}$$

As an illustration of how this formula may be applied, suppose one uses a 'seed' value for the implicit rate of interest of $r_0 = 0.025 = 2\frac{1}{2}$ per cent. It then follows that

$$\sum_{t=1}^{12} \frac{1}{(1+r_0)^t} - 10.169492 = \sum_{t=1}^{12} \frac{1}{(1.025)^t} - 10.169492 = 0.088273$$

and

$$\sum_{t=1}^{12} \frac{t}{(1+r_0)^{t+1}} = \sum_{t=1}^{12} \frac{t}{(1.025)^{t+1}} = 62.108804$$

The revised estimate r_1, of the implicit rate of interest will then be

$$r_1 = r_0 + \frac{\sum_{t=1}^{12} \frac{1}{(1+r_0)^t} - 10.169492}{\sum_{t=1}^{12} \frac{t}{(1+r_0)^{t+1}}} = 0.025 + \frac{\sum_{t=1}^{12} \frac{1}{(1.025)^t} - 10.169492}{\sum_{t=1}^{12} \frac{t}{(1.025)^{t+1}}}$$

or

$$r_1 = 0.025 + \frac{0.088273}{62.108804} = 0.0264213$$

Continuing with this process for a second iteration, we have

$$r_2 = r_1 + \frac{\sum_{t=1}^{12} \frac{1}{(1+r_1)^t} - 10.169492}{\sum_{t=1}^{12} \frac{t}{(1+r_1)^{t+1}}}$$

or

$$r_2 = 0.0264213 + \frac{\sum_{t=1}^{12} \frac{1}{(1.0264213)^t} - 10.169492}{\sum_{t=1}^{12} \frac{t}{(1.0264213)^{t+1}}} = 0.0264213 + \frac{0.000555}{62.132958}$$

from which we have

$$r_2 = 0.0264213 + \frac{0.000555}{62.132958} = 0.0264303$$

If we continue with this 'updating' procedure then we obtain the following estimates of the implicit rate of interest in subsequent iterations: $r_3 = 0.0264303, r_4 = 0.0264303, r_5 = 0.0264303$, and so on. Hence, the Newton–Raphson algorithm gives a 'correct' estimate of the implicit rate of interest out to seven decimal places by the end of the third iteration. One can confirm that this is the correct implicit interest rate by preparing the mortgage repayment schedule depicted in Table 1.3 using $r = 0.0264303$ as the implicit rate of interest. The interest payment at the end of the first month is the principal outstanding at the beginning of the month multiplied by the monthly interest rate, or £2,000 × 0.0264303 = £52.86. This in turn means that the principal repaid at the end of the first month will be the repayment made at the end of the first month less the interest that has accrued over the month, or £196.67 – £52.86 = £143.81. Subtracting this from the opening principal shows that the principal outstanding at the end of the first month will be £2,000 – £143.81 = £1,856.19. The interest payment at the end of the second month will then be £1,856.19 × 0.0264303 = £49.06. This in turn means that the principal repaid at the end of the second month must be £196.67 – £49.06 = £147.61. Subtracting this from the principal outstanding at the end of the first month shows that the principal outstanding at the end of the second month will be £1,856.19 – £147.61 = £1,708.59. Continuing with these calculations shows that the loan will be completely discharged (i.e. paid off) by the end of the twelfth month. Note that the Newton–Raphson technique employed here leads to a much more accurate estimate of the implicit rate of interest when compared with the linear interpolation procedure employed in §1-5 – as evidenced by the fact that the loan is completely discharged (that is, paid off) after the final repayment at the end of the twelfth month. Note also that the effective rate of interest on the above loan turns out to be $(1 + r)^{12} - 1 = (1.0264303)^{12} - 1 = 0.367583$ or about 36.76 per cent (per annum) – a calculation that we now examine in greater detail.

Table 1.3 Mortgage repayment schedule using Newton–Raphson technique

Date	*Opening principal* £	*Interest* £	*Principal repaid* £	*Closing principal* £
1	2,000.00	52.86	143.81	1,856.19
2	1,856.19	49.06	147.61	1,708.59
3	1,708.59	45.16	151.51	1,557.08
4	1,557.08	41.15	155.51	1,401.57
5	1,401.57	37.04	159.62	1,241.94
6	1,241.94	32.82	163.84	1,078.10
7	1,078.10	28.49	168.17	909.93
8	909.93	24.05	172.62	737.31
9	737.31	19.49	177.18	560.13
10	560.13	14.80	181.86	378.27
11	378.27	10.00	186.67	191.60
12	191.60	5.06	191.60	0.00

§1-7. Suppose one defines r to be the nominal rate of interest (per annum) and m to be the number of times in any given year that the compounding of interest occurs. Hence, after the first compounding, a loan of £1 that accumulates interest at the nominal rate r will have grown to

$$1+\frac{r}{m}$$

At the second compounding, the loan will have grown to

$$\left(1+\frac{r}{m}\right)\times\left(1+\frac{r}{m}\right)=\left(1+\frac{r}{m}\right)^{2}$$

At the third compounding, the loan will have grown to

$$\left(1+\frac{r}{m}\right)^{2}\times\left(1+\frac{r}{m}\right)=\left(1+\frac{r}{m}\right)^{3}$$

Continuing with this process shows that after a full year, the loan will have grown to

$$\left(1+\frac{r}{m}\right)^{m}$$

Given this, one can define the effective rate of interest i as the rate of interest that would apply if compounding occurred on an annual basis (i.e. once a year) only, or

$$1+i=\left(1+\frac{r}{m}\right)^{m}$$

One can demonstrate the effect that compounding more frequently than annually can have on the interest charged on a loan by considering the way interest is calculated on many credit cards. Typical interest rates on credit cards are around 16 per cent (per annum) but the rate is compounded on a monthly (and not an annual) basis. Hence, whilst the nominal rate of interest on the typical credit card is $r = 16$ per cent (per annum), this rate is compounded $m = 12$ times per year, and so the effective rate of interest will be

$$i=\left(1+\frac{r}{m}\right)^{m}-1=\left(1+\frac{0.16}{12}\right)^{12}-1=0.172271$$

or about $i = 17.23$ per cent (per annum). This means that if one started the year with a £1 debt on a credit card and left it there for the whole year without making any repayments then by the end of the year one would owe about £1.1723.

This raises an interesting question: what happens if one lets the number of compoundings, m, become very large and in the limit go off to infinity? It is not hard to show that with an infinite number of compoundings over the year, the effective rate of interest can be calculated from the formula

$$1+i=\lim_{m\to\infty}\left(1+\frac{r}{m}\right)^{m}=e^{r}$$

where $e = 2.718281828$ correct to nine decimal places and $\exp(r) = e^{r}$ is known as the exponential function. Hence, in the case of the credit card example given here where

$r = 0.16$ or 16 per cent (per annum), it follows that if the credit card firm applied continuous compounding (i.e. if it compounded interest an infinite number of times in any given year) then the effective rate of interest on the credit card would be

$$i = e^r - 1 = e^{0.16} - 1 = 0.173511$$

or $i = 17.3511$ per cent. In other words, if one started the year with a £1 debt on a credit card and did nothing about it during the year (i.e. made no repayments during the year) then by the end of the year one would owe about £1.1735. And this will be the 'worst' the credit card company would be able to do, since one cannot compound more frequently than continuously over the year. That is, the effective rate of interest (or APR as in §1-3 above) on the credit card amounts to 17.35 per cent (per annum).

§1-8. Now suppose we have continuous compounding (as in §1-7 above) and that the effective rate of interest, i, is known. To determine the nominal rate of interest, one must solve the following equation for r:

$$1 + i = e^r$$

One can do this by taking (natural) logarithms of both sides of the above equation, giving

$$r = \log(1 + i)$$

Thus, if the effective rate of interest is $i = 10.517092$ per cent (per annum), the reader will be able to confirm that the nominal rate of interest is

$$r = \log(1 + i) = \log(1.10517092) = 0.10$$

or 10 per cent (per annum). The nominal rate r given here is normally called the continuously compounded rate of return when it is calculated in this way. It is the method normally used to compute returns on stocks and shares, as we now demonstrate.

Suppose that one defines P_t to be the price of a share at time t. Then the discretely compounded rate of return on the share, r_t, over the period from time $t - \Delta t$ until time t is computed as follows:

$$r_t = \frac{P_t + D_t - P_{t-\Delta t}}{P_{t-\Delta t}}$$

where D_t is the dividend paid on the share over the period from time $t - \Delta t$ until time t. In contrast, the logarithmic or continuously compounded rate of return, i_t, is computed as

$$i_t = \log\left(\frac{P_t + D_t}{P_{t-\Delta t}}\right) = \log\left(1 + \frac{P_t + D_t - P_{t-\Delta t}}{P_{t-\Delta t}}\right) = \log(1 + r_t)$$

Now here one can use a Taylor series expansion and thereby show

$$\log(1 + r_t) = r_t - \tfrac{1}{2}r_t^2 + \tfrac{1}{3}r_t^3 - \tfrac{1}{4}r_t^4 + \ldots$$

This result has some important implications for the way returns will evolve for firms with different characteristics. If one ignores terms involving r_t^3, r_t^4, r_t^5, etc., all of which are likely to be very small, then one can state the relationship between the continuous and discretely compounded returns as follows:

$$i_t = \log\left(\frac{P_t + D_t}{P_{t-\Delta t}}\right) = \log\left(1 + \frac{P_t + D_t - P_{t-\Delta t}}{P_{t-\Delta t}}\right) = \log(1 + r_t) \approx r_t - \tfrac{1}{2}r_t^2$$

or

$$r_t \approx i_t + \tfrac{1}{2}r_t^2$$

Now one can take expectations across this expression and thereby show

$$E(r_t) \approx E(i_t) + \tfrac{1}{2}E(r_t^2)$$

where $E(r_t)$ is the expected discretely compounded return on the share and $E(i_t)$ is the expected continuously compounded return on the share; furthermore, the variance of the discretely compounded return on the share is

$$\sigma_t^2 = E[r_t - E(r_t)]^2 = E(r_t^2) - [E(r_t)]^2$$

It thus follows that

$$E(r_t) \approx E(i_t) + \tfrac{1}{2}\{\sigma_t^2 + [E(r_t)]^2\}$$

Note here, however, that $[E(r_t)]^2$ will usually be fairly small and can be safely ignored. We thus have

$$E(r_t) \approx E(i_t) + \tfrac{1}{2}\sigma_t^2$$

Now, the empirical evidence shows that σ_t^2 tends to have higher numerical values for 'small' firms when compared with its values for equivalent 'large' firms. Thus, consider two firms – one 'small', the other 'large' – with the same expected continuously compounded return $E(i_t)$. Then one would expect the smaller of the two firms to have the higher discretely compounded return $E(r_t)$; that is, one would expect discretely compounded returns to evidence a 'small-firm' effect. And this is exactly what the empirical evidence shows. See, for example, the article by Fama and French (1992) for a good illustration of the empirical evidence on this matter. This means that one must be extremely careful about the way average returns on shares are calculated – as the following example demonstrates.

§1-9. On 31 July 2009, Rockbottom Oil's ordinary shares were quoted on the stock exchange at $P_0 = £1$ per share. On 31 August 2009, the price of the ordinary shares had fallen to $P_1 = 80$ pence per share. However, by 30 September 2009, the ordinary shares had again risen back to $P_2 = £1$ per share. It thus follows that the discretely compounded rate of return on Rockbottom Oil's ordinary shares for the month of August 2009 turns out to be

$$r_1 = \frac{P_1 - P_0}{P_0} = \frac{0.8 - 1}{1} = -0.2$$

or −20 per cent. Likewise, the discretely compounded rate of return for the month of September 2009 turns out to be

$$r_2 = \frac{P_2 - P_1}{P_1} = \frac{1 - 0.8}{0.8} = 0.25$$

or 25 per cent. Now, the average of these two rates of return is

$$\frac{r_1 + r_2}{2} = \frac{1}{2} \times (-0.2 + 0.25) = 0.025$$

or $2\frac{1}{2}$ per cent. But there is clearly something wrong here, because Rockbottom Oil's share price at the end of July and at the end of September was £1. That is, the price of Rockbottom Oil's ordinary shares started the period at £1 and finished the period at £1 and yet our calculations show that the average monthly return over the period from the end of July until the end of September was $2\frac{1}{2}$ per cent. Surely, the average return ought to be zero because the investor started at the end of July with an investment worth £1 and finished at the end of September with an investment still worth £1! In other words, the investor's wealth has neither increased nor decreased over this period. Fortunately, one can resolve this apparent paradox by computing the average return using the geometric mean. It then follows that the average discretely compounded return on Rockbottom Oil's ordinary shares for the months of August and September 2009 turns out to be

$$\left[\prod_{t=1}^{2}(1 + r_t)\right]^{1/2} - 1 = \sqrt{(1 + r_1)(1 + r_2)} - 1 = \sqrt{(1 - 0.2)(1 + 0.25)} - 1$$

or:

$$\left[\prod_{t=1}^{2}(1 + r_t)\right]^{1/2} - 1 = \sqrt{0.8 \times 1.25} - 1 = 0$$

This average of zero meets with our intuition, since Rockbottom Oil's share price at the end of July and at the end of September was £1. Given this, one would expect the average return over this period to be zero. More generally, the geometric mean of n discretely compounded returns is simply the nth root of one plus the returns multiplied together, less one. Thus, the geometric average of the six monthly returns, r_1, r_2, r_3, r_4, r_5 and r_6 will be

$$\left[\prod_{t=1}^{6}(1 + r_t)\right]^{1/6} - 1 = \sqrt{(1 + r_1)(1 + r_2)(1 + r_3)(1 + r_4)(1 + r_5)(1 + r_6)} - 1$$

In other words, the geometric average return provides the most accurate measure of central tendency for a set of discretely compounded returns.

Note also that the continuously compounded return on Rockbottom Oil's shares for the month of August turns out to be

$$i_1 = \log\left(\frac{P_1}{P_0}\right) = \log\left(\frac{0.8}{1}\right) = \log\left(\frac{4}{5}\right) = \log(4) - \log(5)$$

Likewise, the continuously compounded return on Rockbottom Oil's shares for the month of September is

$$i_2 = \log\left(\frac{P_2}{P_1}\right) = \log\left(\frac{1}{0.8}\right) = \log\left(\frac{5}{4}\right) = \log(5) - \log(4)$$

Hence, the simple average of the continuously compounded rates of return for the months of August and September turns out to be

$$\frac{i_1 + i_2}{2} = \frac{1}{2}\left[\log\left(\frac{0.8}{1}\right) + \log\left(\frac{1}{0.8}\right)\right] = \frac{1}{2}\{[\log(4) - \log(5)] + [\log(5) - \log(4)]\} = 0$$

Recall that since Rockbottom Oil's ordinary shares started the period at $P_0 = £1$ and finished the period at $P_1 = £1$, we would expect the average return to be zero. And this is precisely what we get when we average the continuously compounded returns for Rockbottom Oil's shares. Hence, the simple average return provides the most accurate measure of central tendency for a set of continuously compounded returns. Of course, our analysis here ignores dividends and, most importantly, any new share issues firms might make. We now demonstrate how to calculate returns when dividends are paid and new share issues occur.

§1-10. Consider then the price data for the ordinary shares of Loca Lola Bottlers as summarized in Table 1.4. At the beginning of October, Loca Lola Bottlers announced a one for five rights issue of new shares exercisable on or before 22 November. The issue was at an exercise price of 80 pence per new share, with the 'ex rights' date being at the close of business on 12 October. This means the right to take up the new shares would apply only to shareholders appearing on the register of shareholders on this date – that is, 12 October. Moreover, during November, a dividend of $7\frac{1}{2}$ pence (per share) was declared payable to shareholders appearing on the register of shareholders on 29 November (the 'ex dividend' date). Equipped with this information, one can compute the returns for each month as follows:

Returns for the month ended 31 July:

$$\text{Discretely compounded return} = \frac{1.08 - 1.05}{1.05} = 0.028571$$

$$\text{Continuously compounded return} = \log\left(\frac{1.08}{1.05}\right) = \log(1 + 0.028571) = 0.028171$$

Table 1.4 Share and rights price data for Loca Lola Bottlers

Type of security	*Date*	*Price £*
Ordinary Share	30 Jun	1.05
Ordinary Share	31 Jul	1.08
Ordinary Share	31 Aug	1.15
Ordinary Share	30 Sep	1.11
Ordinary Share	31 Oct	1.00
Share Right	31 Oct	0.16
Ordinary Share	30 Nov	0.93
Ordinary Share	31 Dec	1.15

Returns for the month ended 31 August:

$$\text{Discretely compounded return} = \frac{1.15 - 1.08}{1.08} = 0.064815$$

$$\text{Continuously compounded return} = \log\left(\frac{1.15}{1.08}\right) = \log(1 + 0.064815) = 0.062801$$

Returns for the month ended 30 September:

$$\text{Discretely compounded return} = \frac{1.11 - 1.15}{1.15} = -0.034783$$

$$\text{Continuously compounded return} = \log\left(\frac{1.11}{1.15}\right) = \log(1 - 0.034783) = -0.035402$$

Returns for the month ended 31 October:

$$\text{Discretely compounded return} = \frac{1.00 + 0.2 \times 0.16 - 1.11}{1.11} = -0.070270$$

$$\text{Continuously compounded return} = \log\left(\frac{1.00 + 0.2 \times 0.16}{1.11}\right)$$

$$= \log(1 - 0.070270) = -0.072861$$

Recall that the right to take up new shares is allocated to all shareholders appearing on the register of shareholders on 12 October. This means a shareholder who owned a single share at the beginning of October would own the same share plus the right to subscribe to one-fifth of a new share at the end of October. Hence, the total value of their holding at the end of October would be the share price, £1.00, plus one-fifth of the value of a right to take up a new share, $\frac{1}{5} \times 0.16 = 0.2 \times 0.16$, or $1.00 + 0.2 \times 0.16 = £1.032$.

Returns for the month ended 30 November:

$$\text{Discretely compounded return} = \frac{0.93 + 0.075 - 1.00}{1.00} = 0.005$$

$$\text{Continuously compounded return} = \log\left(\frac{0.93 + 0.075}{1.00}\right) = \log(1 + 0.005) = 0.004988$$

During November, a dividend of $7\frac{1}{2}$ pence (per share) was declared payable to shareholders appearing on the register of shareholders on 29 November (the ‘ex dividend’ date). This means a shareholder who owned a single share at the beginning of November would own the same share at the end of November, plus they will have received a dividend of $7\frac{1}{2}$ pence (per share) during November. Hence, the total value of his holding at the end of November would be the share price, £0.93, plus the dividend, $7\frac{1}{2}$ pence, or $0.93 + 0.075 = £1.005$.

Returns for the month ended 31 December:

$$\text{Discretely compounded return} = \frac{1.15 - 0.93}{0.93} = 0.236559$$

$$\text{Continuously compounded return} = \log\left(\frac{1.15}{0.93}\right) = \log(1 + 0.236559) = 0.212333$$

§1-11. One can then determine the geometric average of the discretely compounded returns computed in §1-10 as follows:

$$\left[\prod_{t=1}^{6}(1+r_t)\right]^{1/6} - 1 =$$

$$[(1.028571)(1.064815)(0.965217)(0.929730)(1.005000)(1.236559)]^{1/6} - 1$$

$$= 0.033900$$

Hence, the geometric average return is approximately 3.39 per cent (per month). Likewise, the simple average of the continuously compounded returns computed in §1-10 turns out to be

$$\frac{0.028171 + 0.062801 - 0.035402 - 0.072861 + 0.004988 + 0.212333}{6} = 0.0333383$$

Hence, the simple average continuously compounded return is approximately 3.33 per cent (per month).

§1-12. Our analysis to date assumes that assets trade (and their market prices are determined) with reasonable frequency, in which case one will be able to determine the return on a given asset over any given interval of time without much difficulty. There are occasions, however, when the market prices of assets are observed infrequently and this can create difficulties with measuring returns on the given assets. Consider, for example, a superannuation fund that reports the cash flows it receives from its contributors (net of pensions paid) on a monthly basis but only reports the market value of its assets on a quarterly basis. Now let $C(t)$ be the accumulated cash flows from contributors (net of pensions paid) from the beginning of a particular quarter up until time t within the given quarter. Moreover, let $M(0)$ be the market value of the superannuation fund's assets at the beginning of the quarter and $M(1)$ be the market value of its assets at the end of the quarter. It then follows that the return i earned by the fund over the quarter that begins at time $t = 0$ and finishes at time $t = 1$ will be implicitly defined by the equation

$$M(0)e^i + \int_0^1 e^{i(1-t)} dC(t) = M(1)$$

where $dC(t) = C(t + dt) - C(t)$ represents the cash flow received from contributors over the instantaneous period from time t until time $t + dt$. Note here that a superannuation fund will normally be composed of thousands of contributors and so its cash flows will typically be the outcome of a large number of transactions on any given day. This will mean that $C(t)$ will evolve in a way that can be closely approximated by the continuous-time assumptions we now invoke. Note also that if the superannuation fund invests its assets at the beginning of the quarter at the rate i, then by the end of the quarter the market value of these assets will have accumulated to $M(0)e^i$. Likewise, the contributions received over the period from time t until time $t + dt$ will accumulate to $e^{i(1-t)}dC(t)$ by the end of the quarter. Hence, if the fund earns a return i then the opening market value of its assets plus its contributions must accumulate to the ending market value of its assets as summarized in the above formula. Now, if we divide through the above equation by e^i, we have

$$M(0)+\int_0^1 e^{-it}dC(t)=M(1)e^{-i}$$

Suppose we approximate the exponential terms in the above expression by the first-order Taylor series expansion $e^{it}\approx 1-it$. Furthermore, assume that the contributions $C(t)$ made by the superannuation fund's beneficiaries from time zero up until time t are a piecewise-linear function of time, namely

$$C(t)=\begin{cases} C(0)+3\left[C\left(\tfrac{1}{3}\right)-C(0)\right]t & \text{for } 0\le t\le \tfrac{1}{3} \\ \left[2C\left(\tfrac{1}{3}\right)-C\left(\tfrac{2}{3}\right)\right]+3\left[C\left(\tfrac{2}{3}\right)-C\left(\tfrac{1}{3}\right)\right]t & \text{for } \tfrac{1}{3}\le t\le \tfrac{2}{3} \\ \left[3C\left(\tfrac{2}{3}\right)-2C(1)\right]+3\left[C(1)-C\left(\tfrac{2}{3}\right)\right]t & \text{for } \tfrac{2}{3}\le t\le 1 \end{cases}$$

It then follows that the instantaneous cash flow at time t will be

$$dC(t)=\begin{cases} 3\left[C\left(\tfrac{1}{3}\right)-C(0)\right]dt & \text{for } 0\le t\le \tfrac{1}{3} \\ 3\left[C\left(\tfrac{2}{3}\right)-C\left(\tfrac{1}{3}\right)\right]dt & \text{for } \tfrac{1}{3}\le t\le \tfrac{2}{3} \\ 3\left[C(1)-C\left(\tfrac{2}{3}\right)\right]dt & \text{for } \tfrac{2}{3}\le t\le 1 \end{cases}$$

Substituting into the above equation then shows

$$\begin{aligned} &3\int_0^{1/3}(1-it)\left[C\left(\tfrac{1}{3}\right)-C(0)\right]dt+3\int_{1/3}^{2/3}(1-it)\left[C\left(\tfrac{2}{3}\right)-C\left(\tfrac{1}{3}\right)\right]dt \\ &\quad+3\int_{2/3}^{1}(1-it)\left[C(1)-C\left(\tfrac{2}{3}\right)\right]dt \\ &\quad\approx M(1)(1-i)-M(0) \end{aligned}$$

Evaluating the integrals in the above expression and collecting terms then shows that

$$i\approx\frac{M(1)-[M(0)-C(1)]}{M(1)-\tfrac{1}{6}\left[C\left(\tfrac{1}{3}\right)-C(0)\right]-\tfrac{1}{2}\left[C\left(\tfrac{2}{3}\right)-C\left(\tfrac{1}{3}\right)\right]-\tfrac{5}{6}\left[C(1)-C\left(\tfrac{2}{3}\right)\right]}$$

will be a first-order approximation for the quarterly return earned by the superannuation fund. Now formulae like this are often used to estimate superannuation fund returns and as a basis for assessing superannuation fund performance, although the first-order approximations employed in deriving them suggest that there is good reason to doubt the accuracy of the returns they yield. More accurate estimates of the return can be obtained by using higher-order approximation procedures and we shall examine some of these in Chapter 5 of this book in particular.

§1-13. The principal objective of this chapter has been to outline how the returns on a given asset or financial instrument are correctly calculated. The return expected from a share, bond or other security is an instrumental determinant of the price that investors will be prepared to pay for the given security. The proper calculation of returns is also important if one wishes to estimate the risks associated with a security or portfolio of assets. The most commonly used returns in the finance literature are the so-called logarithmic (or continuously compounded) return and the discretely compounded return. Our analysis in §1-9 shows that the simple average of the discrete returns earned by a given security over a given period of time will provide a biased and inefficient estimate of the population mean return on the affected security. The appropriate way to average discrete returns is to determine the geometric mean of the given return series. However, the expected value of the geometric mean and the variance of a discrete return series hinge crucially on the precise form of the probability distribution from which the returns are drawn. Moreover, for many (if not most) probability distributions, the evaluation of the expressions for the expected value of the geometric mean is computationally difficult and these cannot be expressed in closed form. Given this, it is fortunate that the simple average of the continuously compounded returns does provide an unbiased and efficient estimate of the population mean return. Moreover, the sample variance of the continuously compounded returns will also provide a consistent estimate of the population variance. Hence, the continuously compounded return is arguably the most reliable method for calculating returns on equity securities. This chapter has also illustrated and provided a brief summary of the numerical procedures that can be used to estimate the returns on fixed-interest securities, such as mortgages and bonds. The method of linear interpolation is probably the best known and most frequently used numerical procedure for estimating the return on fixed-interest securities – probably because it is easily understood and applied. We show, however, that the Newton–Raphson technique has several important advantages over the method of linear interpolation. One of the more important of these is that the Newton–Raphson technique is more accurate than the method of linear interpolation, although the increased accuracy often comes at the cost of significantly greater computational requirements. Finally, we have demonstrated procedures for estimating returns on asset portfolios when market values are published infrequently.

Selected references

Dimson, E., Marsh, P. and Staunton, M. (2002) *Triumph of the Optimists: 101 Years of Global Investment Returns*, Princeton, NJ: Princeton University Press.

Fama, E. and French, K. (1992) 'The cross-section of expected stock returns', *Journal of Finance*, 47: 427–65.

Ibbotson and Associates (2011) *Cost of Capital 2011 Yearbook*. Chicago: Ibbotson and Associates.

Zima, P. and Brown, R. (1996) *Schaum's Outline of Theory and Problems of Mathematics of Finance*, New York: McGraw-Hill.

Exercises

1. Show that

$$\sum_{t=1}^{N} \frac{1}{(1+r)^t} = \frac{1}{r}\left[1 - \frac{1}{(1+r)^N}\right]$$

and hence that a perpetuity of £1 received at the end of each year is worth $\frac{1}{r}$.

2. Show that

$$\sum_{t=1}^{N} \frac{t}{(1+r)^t} = \frac{N-(N+1)(1+r)+(1+r)^{N+1}}{r^2(1+r)^N}$$

Explain how this result and the result reported in Exercise 1 may be used to implement the Newton–Raphson algorithm for determining the implicit rate of interest on the mortgage instrument described in §1-6.

3. Suppose one borrows £2,000 to be repaid in 24 equal monthly instalments. The interest rate is 20 per cent (per annum) flat. Prepare a mortgage repayment schedule showing for each month the opening and ending principal outstanding, the interest for the month, and the amount paid off the principal in each month.
4. In March 2009, the Caledonian Highland Bank PLC announced a one for three rights issue with an exercise price of 225 pence per new share. Shareholders appearing on the Register of Shareholders on 6 April 2009 would be entitled to take up the new shares. The rights to the new shares had to be exercised by the middle of May 2009 at the latest. Relevant prices for Caledonian Highland Bank ordinary shares and the share right are as summarized in Table 1.5. Compute the discretely compounded and the continuously compounded monthly returns for the Caledonian Highland Bank. Also compute the geometric average of the discretely compounded returns and the simple average return of the continuously compounded returns.
5. In §1-12, it was shown that the quarterly return i earned by a superannuation fund on its assets is implicitly defined by the equation

$$M(0)e^i + \int_0^1 e^{i(1-t)} dC(t) = M(1)$$

where $C(t)$ is the function whose value is the accumulated cash flow (net of pensions paid) from the beginning of a particular quarter up until time t within the affected quarter, $M(0)$ is the market value of the superannuation fund's assets at the beginning of the quarter and

Table 1.5 Share and rights price data for Caledonian Highland Bank

Type of security	*Date*	*Price* £
Ordinary Share	31 Dec 2008	2.70
Ordinary Share	31 Jan 2009	2.70
Ordinary Share	28 Feb 2009	2.70
Ordinary Share	31 Mar 2009	3.10
Ordinary Share	30 Apr 2009	2.90
Share Right	30 Apr 2009	0.45
Ordinary Share	31 May 2009	3.00
Ordinary Share	30 Jun 2009	3.15

$M(1)$ is the market value of its assets at the end of the quarter. Assume that accumulated contributions are described by the following piecewise-linear function of time:

$$C(t) = \begin{cases} C(0) + 3\left[C\left(\tfrac{1}{3}\right) - C(0)\right]t & \text{for } 0 \leq t \leq \tfrac{1}{3} \\ \left[2C\left(\tfrac{1}{3}\right) - C\left(\tfrac{2}{3}\right)\right] + 3\left[C\left(\tfrac{2}{3}\right) - C\left(\tfrac{1}{3}\right)\right]t & \text{for } \tfrac{1}{3} \leq t \leq \tfrac{2}{3} \\ \left[3C\left(\tfrac{2}{3}\right) - 2C(1)\right] + 3\left[C(1) - C\left(\tfrac{2}{3}\right)\right]t & \text{for } \tfrac{2}{3} \leq t \leq 1 \end{cases}$$

Use the first-order Taylor series expansion $e^{i(1-t)} \approx 1 + i(1-t)$ and thereby show that

$$i \approx \frac{M(1) - [M(0) - C(1)]}{M(0) + \frac{5}{6}\left[C\left(\frac{1}{3}\right) - C(0)\right] + \frac{1}{2}\left[C\left(\frac{2}{3}\right) - C\left(\frac{1}{3}\right)\right] + \frac{1}{6}\left[C(1) - C\left(\frac{2}{3}\right)\right]}$$

provides an alternative estimate of the quarterly return earned by the superannuation fund. Determine when this formula will lead to higher estimates of superannuation returns than the formula derived in §1-12.

2 The relationship between return and risk

§2-1. In Chapter 1, we identified some of the pitfalls that can arise from the incorrect calculation and averaging of the returns that accrue on shares, bonds, portfolios and other financial instruments. Historical returns are often used to provide guidance about the likely magnitude of future returns on a given security or financial instrument and of the current prices that ought to be paid for them. Moreover, historical returns are also used to assess the risks that are likely to arise from particular investments. Our purpose in this chapter is to summarize the relationships that exist between the returns that arise on particular investments and the risks that must be taken to achieve them. We also determine what implications these relationships will have for the pricing of risky assets. We begin our analysis in the next section with a consideration of how the risks associated with investments shape the returns that we can expect from them. We then go on to demonstrate how assets are priced so as to be compatible with the risks and returns that arise from them.

§2-2. Consider a portfolio comprising $j = 1, 2, 3, 4, \ldots, N$ risky assets. The expected return on the portfolio, $E(R_p)$, will be

$$E(R_p) = \sum_{j=1}^{N} w_j E(R_j)$$

where $E(R_j)$ is the expected return on the jth asset and w_j is the proportion of the investor's wealth that is invested in the jth asset. Sometimes, we will use the symbol $\mu = E(R_p)$ to represent the expected return on the portfolio; the two symbols will be used interchangeably. Thus, the expected return on an $N = 2$ or two-asset portfolio will be computed from the following formula:

$$\mu = E(R_p) = \sum_{j=1}^{2} w_j E(R_j) = w_1 E(R_1) + w_2 E(R_2)$$

We can illustrate the application of this formula by supposing that the expected return on the first asset is $E(R_1) = 0.2$ or 20 per cent (per annum) and the expected return on the second asset is $E(R_2) = 0.1$ or 10 per cent (per annum). With these expected returns, we can rewrite the expected returns formula given above as follows:

$$E(R_p) = 0.2w_1 + 0.1w_2$$

Thus, if the investor puts an equal proportion of their wealth into each asset so that $w_1 = \frac{1}{2} = w_2$ then the expected return on the investor's portfolio will be

$$E(R_p) = 0.2 \times \frac{1}{2} + 0.1 \times \frac{1}{2} = 0.15$$

or 15 per cent (per annum). Of course, the investor can always get a higher expected return by investing a greater proportion of their wealth in the first asset, since this first asset has a higher expected return (20 per cent) than the expected return on the second asset (10 per cent). Thus, if the investor puts $w_1 = \frac{3}{4}$ or 75 per cent of their wealth in the first asset and only $w_2 = \frac{1}{4}$ or 25 per cent of their wealth in the second asset, then the expected return on the investor's portfolio will be

$$E(R_p) = 0.2 \times \frac{3}{4} + 0.1 \times \frac{1}{4} = 0.175$$

or $17\frac{1}{2}$ per cent (per annum). There are, however, no 'free lunches' in this world, and if the investor wants a higher expected return from their portfolio, they will have to take more 'risk' to get it. In other words, the market induces investors to take more risk by rewarding them with higher expected returns when they do so. The only problem here is that we need to decide on what we mean by the term 'risk' as it is applied in portfolio analysis.

§2-3. The conventional assumption here is that asset returns evolve in terms of a normal distribution. We would emphasize that this assumption represents an approximation of reality (especially in relation to extreme returns, i.e. very high and very low returns) and that its principal virtue is in facilitating the tractability of our analysis. Now when returns on the assets comprising a portfolio evolve in terms of a normal distribution, risk is measured by the standard deviation (or variance) of the return on the given portfolio. The standard deviation (or variance) of a distribution measures how 'spread out' or compressed the distribution is. We can illustrate this through Figure 2.1, which summarizes the normal probability distributions associated with the centred returns of four separate portfolios of risky assets. Each of the

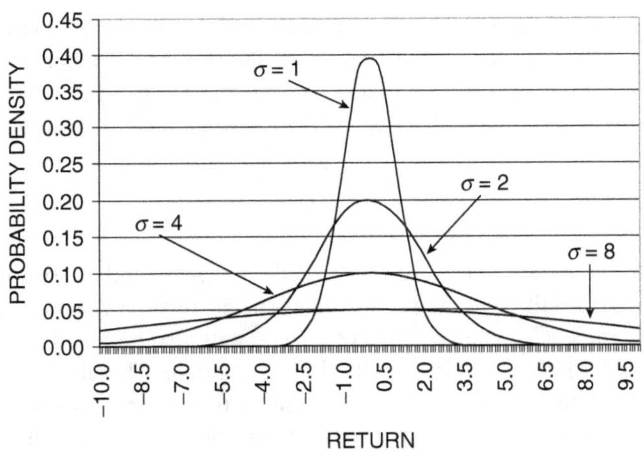

Figure 2.1 Normal distributions of centred asset returns

curves in Figure 2.1 represents a normal distribution with a mean of zero (the returns on all four portfolios have been centred by subtracting the mean or expected return on the portfolio from all possible returns on the portfolio). The most 'compact' and peaked of these normal distributions has a standard deviation $\sigma = 1$. The next most peaked distribution has a standard deviation $\sigma = 2$. The third normal distribution sets $\sigma = 4$ and is quite dispersed compared with the normal distributions with $\sigma = 1$ and $\sigma = 2$. Finally, the most dispersed distribution has a standard deviation of $\sigma = 8$. Note that the larger the standard deviation, the bigger the spread or dispersion in the returns that will be earned on the portfolio. Thus, when $\sigma = 1$, there is virtually no probability of earning a centred return on the portfolio that is below $-3\frac{1}{2}$ per cent or above $3\frac{1}{2}$ per cent (per annum). However, when the portfolio's standard deviation is $\sigma = 8$, there is a relatively large probability of earning a centred return on the portfolio that falls below $-3\frac{1}{2}$ per cent or above $3\frac{1}{2}$ per cent (per annum). This is because the distribution of the centred returns on a portfolio with a standard deviation $\sigma = 8$ is much more dispersed and therefore more risky than is the case with a portfolio of assets with a standard deviation $\sigma = 1$. This explains why risk is usually measured by the standard deviation σ of the distribution of the returns on an asset or portfolio, or, equivalently, the square of the standard deviation, σ^2, which is called the variance of the return on the portfolio.

However, if we are to implement this risk measure then we must determine an expression for the standard deviation or variance of the distribution of returns for a portfolio consisting of many assets. For a portfolio comprising $j = 1, 2, 3, 4, \ldots, N$ assets, it can be shown that the variance of the return on the portfolio, σ_p^2, will be

$$\sigma_p^2 = \sum_{j=1}^{N}\sum_{k=1}^{N} w_j w_k \sigma_{jk}$$

where w_j and w_k are the proportionate investments in the jth and kth assets comprising the portfolio and σ_{jk} is the covariance between the return on the jth asset and the return on the kth asset. Here it will be recalled that the correlation coefficient between the return on the jth asset and the return on the kth asset, ρ_{jk}, is given by

$$\rho_{jk} = \frac{\sigma_{jk}}{\sigma_j \sigma_k}$$

where σ_j is the standard deviation of the return on the jth asset, σ_k is the standard deviation of the return on the kth asset and $-1 \leq \rho_{jk} \leq 1$. Note that the correlation coefficient between the returns on any two assets always lies between -1 and $+1$. It thus follows that the expression for the covariance between the return on the jth asset and the return on the kth asset, σ_{jk}, can be expressed as

$$\sigma_{jk} = \rho_{jk} \sigma_j \sigma_k$$

This in turn will mean that the covariance is easily determined once ρ_{jk}, σ_j and σ_k are known. Note also that the covariance σ_{jk} will have the same sign as the correlation coefficient ρ_{jk}. Hence, if the correlation coefficient is positive, the covariance will also be positive; if the correlation coefficient is negative, the covariance will also be negative. This means that if the covariance between the returns on any two assets is positive then their prices will tend to go up and down together; however, if it is negative then their prices will tend to move in opposite directions. That is, when one asset's price goes up in value, the other asset's price will tend to go down in value, and vice versa.

§2-4. It follows from the above formula that the variance of the return for a two-asset ($N=2$) portfolio will be

$$\sigma_p^2 = \sum_{j=1}^{2}\sum_{k=1}^{2} w_j w_k \sigma_{jk}$$

Now, we can break down the double summation in the above equation into its two components:

$$\sigma_p^2 = \sum_{j=1}^{2}\left(\sum_{k=1}^{2} w_j w_k \sigma_{jk}\right)$$

Expanding the summation associated with the k subscript in the parentheses leads to

$$\sigma_p^2 = \sum_{j=1}^{2}\left(w_j w_1 \sigma_{j1} + w_j w_2 \sigma_{j2}\right)$$

We can then evaluate the summation associated with the j subscript, giving

$$\sigma_p^2 = w_1 w_1 \sigma_{11} + w_1 w_2 \sigma_{12} + w_2 w_1 \sigma_{21} + w_2 w_2 \sigma_{22}$$

Now, the first term on the right-hand side of this equation is the squared proportionate investment in the first asset, $w_1 \times w_1 = w_1^2$, multiplied by the covariance of the first asset's return with its own return, σ_{11}. However, σ_{11} is the same thing as the variance of the first asset's return; that is, $\sigma_{11} = \sigma_1^2$. Likewise, the variance of the second asset's return is $\sigma_{22} = \sigma_2^2$. Finally, $\sigma_{12} = \sigma_{21}$ is the covariance of the return on the first asset with the return on the second asset. Whether we compute the covariance between the return on the first asset and the return on the second asset (σ_{12}) or the covariance between the return on the second asset and the return on the first asset (σ_{21}), we will obtain exactly the same result. Substitution into the above equation then shows that

$$\sigma_p^2 = w_1^2\sigma_1^2 + w_2^2\sigma_2^2 + 2w_1 w_2 \sigma_{12}$$

will be the variance of the return on a two-asset ($N=2$) portfolio.

We can illustrate the application of this result by supposing that $\sigma_1^2 = 0.25$ is the variance of the first asset's return, $\sigma_2^2 = 0.07$ is the variance of the second asset's return and $\sigma_{12} = 0.05$ is the covariance between the return on the first asset and the return on the second asset. Substituting these values into the above equation shows that the variance of the return on the portfolio will be

$$\sigma_p^2 = 0.25w_1^2 + 0.07w_2^2 + 0.10w_1 w_2$$

Moreover, since $w_2 = 1 - w_1$ will be the proportionate investment in the second asset, we have

$$\begin{aligned}\sigma_p^2 &= 0.25w_1^2 + 0.07(1-w_1)^2 + 0.10w_1(1-w_1)\\ &= 0.25w_1^2 + 0.07(1 - 2w_1 + w_1^2) + 0.10(w_1 - w_1^2)\\ &= 0.22w_1^2 - 0.04w_1 + 0.07\end{aligned}$$

is an expression for the variance of the portfolio's return in terms of the proportionate investment made in the first of the two assets.

Now, in §2-2, we have shown that the expected return on the portfolio will be

$$\mu = E(R_p) = w_1E(R_1) + w_2E(R_2) = 0.2w_1 + 0.1w_2$$

or

$$\begin{aligned}\mu &= 0.2w_1 + 0.1(1 - w_1)\\ &= 0.1w_1 + 0.1\end{aligned}$$

Multiplying through this equation by 10 gives $10\mu = w_1 + 1$ or, equivalently,

$$w_1 = 10\mu - 1$$

Now, we can substitute this expression into the formula for the variance given earlier:

$$\begin{aligned}\sigma_p^2 &= 0.22w_1^2 - 0.04w_1 + 0.07\\ &= 0.22(10\mu - 1)^2 - 0.04(10\mu - 1) + 0.07\\ &= 0.22(100\mu^2 - 20\mu + 1) - 0.04(10\mu - 1) + 0.07\\ &= 22\mu^2 - 4.8\mu + 0.33\end{aligned}$$

which gives an expression for the variance of the return on the portfolio, σ_p^2, in terms of the expected return on the portfolio, $\mu = E(R_p)$. This means that the standard deviation of the return on the portfolio will be

$$\sigma_p = \sqrt{22\mu^2 - 4.8\mu + 0.33}$$

This formula encapsulates what is known as the Markowitz locus of the relationship between the expected return on the portfolio and the standard deviation of the return on the portfolio.

§2-5. It is not hard to show that, irrespective of how many assets a portfolio is composed of, the Markowitz locus will always take the following form:

$$\sigma_p = \sqrt{a\mu^2 + b\mu + c}$$

where $a > 0$, $c > 0$ and $b < 0$. We say that a, b and c are the parameters of the Markowitz locus. Thus, for the example developed in §2-4, the parameters of the Markowitz locus are $a = 22$, $b = -4.8$ and $c = 0.33$. A graph of the Markowitz locus with these parameter values appears in Figure 2.2. Thus, if the investor wanted to form a portfolio with an expected return of $\mu = E(R_p) = 0.125$ or 12.5 per cent (per annum) then the portfolio's risk as measured by its standard deviation, would be

$$\sigma_p = \sqrt{22\mu^2 - 4.8\mu + 0.33} = \sqrt{22 \times (0.125)^2 - 4.8 \times 0.125 + 0.33} = \sqrt{\frac{59}{800}} \approx 0.271570$$

This will be the smallest possible level of risk on a portfolio with an expected return of $E(R_p) = 0.125$; that is, the investor will be able to form a portfolio with an expected return

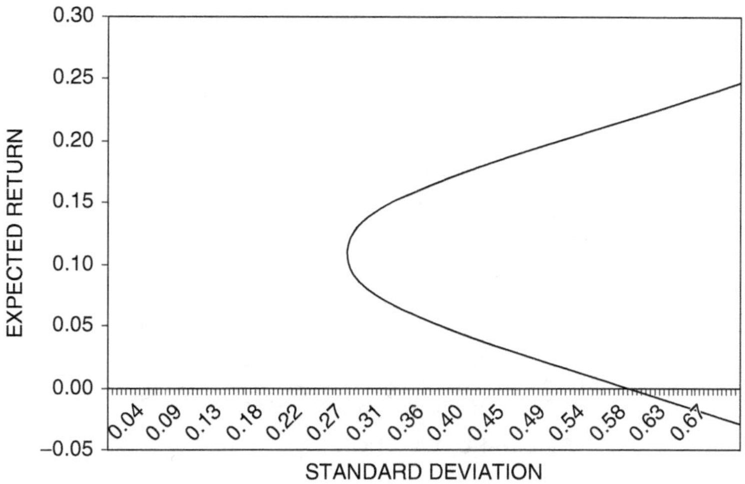

Figure 2.2 Markowitz locus with parameter values $a = 22$, $b = -4.8$ and $c = 0.33$

of $E(R_p) = 0.125$ but with a higher standard deviation than $\sigma_p = 0.271570$. However, the investor will not be able to form a portfolio with an expected return of $E(R_p) = 0.125$ that has a smaller standard deviation than $\sigma_p = 0.271570$.

Note also that we can determine the composition of this minimum-variance portfolio with an expected return of $\mu = E(R_p) = 0.125$ by recalling from §2-4 above that the proportionate investment in the first asset will be

$$w_1 = 10\mu - 1 = 10 \times 0.125 - 1 = \frac{1}{4}$$

This in turn implies that the proportionate investment in the second asset will be $w_2 = 1 - w_1 = 1 - 0.25 = \frac{3}{4}$. Thus, the minimum-variance portfolio with an expected return of $E(R_p) = 0.125$ per annum will be composed of a proportionate investment of $w_1 = \frac{1}{4}$ in the first asset and a proportionate investment of $w_2 = \frac{3}{4}$ in the second asset.

§2-6. We now determine a further crucial property of the Markowitz locus. To do this, consider the portfolios X and Y as marked on the Markowitz locus depicted in Figure 2.3. These two portfolios have the same standard deviation (i.e. the same risk) but the expected return on portfolio X is much higher than the expected return on portfolio Y. Given the choice, which of portfolios X and Y would an investor choose to hold? The investor would obviously choose to hold portfolio X because, for the same level of risk, it offers a much higher expected return than portfolio Y. This means that an investor would never be prepared to hold a portfolio with an expected return that falls below the expected return associated with portfolio D in Figure 2.3. Portfolio D is called the global minimum-variance portfolio because there is no portfolio on the Markowitz locus that has a lower standard deviation (or, equivalently, a lower level of risk). The expected return $E(R_0)$ on the global minimum-variance portfolio in terms of the parameters of the Markowitz locus is $E(R_0) = -b/2a$. Now, for the particular example we have been looking at, the parameters of the Markowitz locus are $a = 22$, $b = -4.8$ and $c = 0.33$, and so the expected return on the global minimum

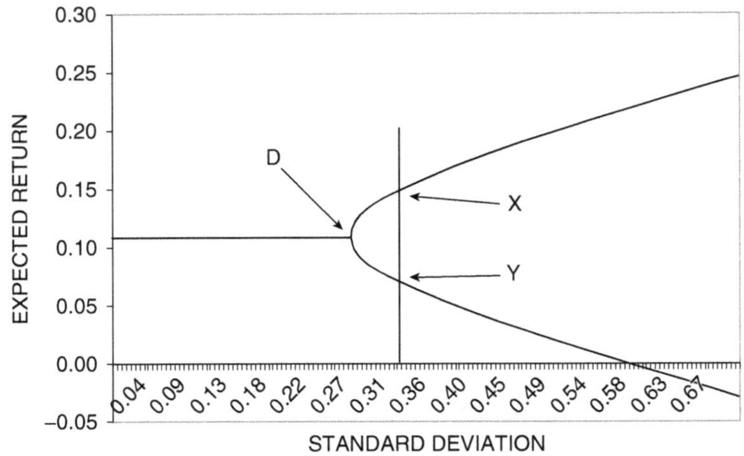

Figure 2.3 Markowitz locus with efficient and inefficient portfolios

variance portfolio is

$$E(R_0) = \frac{-b}{2a} = \frac{4.8}{2 \times 22} = \frac{6}{55} \approx 0.109091 \text{ or } 10.9091 \text{ per cent (per annum)}$$

Now, one can substitute the expected return $\mu = E(R_0) = -b/2a$ on the global minimum-variance portfolio into the Markowitz locus to determine the risk associated with the global minimum-variance portfolio. Doing so shows

$$\sigma_p = \sqrt{a\mu^2 + b\mu + c} = \sqrt{a\left(\frac{-b}{2a}\right)^2 + b\left(\frac{-b}{2a}\right) + c} = \sqrt{\frac{4ac - b^2}{4a}} = \sigma_0$$

Thus, substituting $a = 22$, $b = -4.8$ and $c = 0.33$ into the above expression shows that the standard deviation of the return on the global minimum-variance portfolio for the particular example we have been looking at will be

$$\sigma_0 = \sqrt{\frac{4ac - b^2}{4a}} = \sqrt{\frac{4 \times 0.33 \times 22 - 4.8^2}{4 \times 22}} = \sqrt{\frac{3}{44}} \approx 0.261116$$

Alternatively, we may calculate the same figure by direct substitution into the Markowitz locus:

$$\sigma_p = \sqrt{22\mu^2 - 4.8\mu + 0.33} = \sqrt{22 \times \left(\frac{6}{55}\right)^2 - 4.8 \times \frac{6}{55} + 0.33} = \sqrt{\frac{3}{44}} \approx 0.261116 = \sigma_0$$

Thus, for the particular example considered here it will be impossible to find a portfolio with a standard deviation of less than $\sigma_0 = \sqrt{\frac{3}{44}}$; that is, all portfolios for this example must have $\sigma_p \geq \sqrt{\frac{3}{44}}$. Moreover, since we have previously shown that 'rational' investors will only hold portfolios that have an expected return in excess of the expected return on the global minimum-variance portfolio, we can now define

$$\sigma_p = \sqrt{a\mu^2 + b\mu + c} \text{ for } \mu \geq \frac{-b}{2a}$$

as the Markowitz Efficient Frontier.

§2-7. Now, suppose that in addition to the ($N = 2$) risky assets on which the above example is based there is a risk-free asset in the economy. This will be an asset with a sure (i.e. certain) return and will therefore have no risk. This in turn means that the standard deviation of the return on the riskless asset will be zero. Consider then a risk-free asset with a sure return $R_f = \frac{1}{30} = 3\frac{1}{3}$ per cent (per annum) as depicted on the vertical axis of the graph in Figure 2.4. Now, if we form a portfolio by investing some of our funds in the risk-free asset and the balance of our funds in the risky asset B, then the expected returns on the portfolio are defined by the chord R_fB. However, we can do much better than this. If we invest some of our funds in the risk-free asset and the balance of our funds in the risky asset M then the expected returns on the portfolio are defined by the chord R_fM. Note how the chord R_fM strictly dominates the chord R_fB since, for the same risk, any portfolio on R_fM has a higher expected return in comparison to the equivalent portfolio on the chord R_fB. The chord R_fM is called the Capital Market Line. When a risk-free asset is available, the Capital Market Line gives the maximum possible expected return that can be earned for any given level of risk and takes the following form:

$$E(R_p) = R_f + \gamma\sigma_p$$

where R_f is the return on the risk-free asset, σ_p is the portfolio's risk (as measured by the standard deviation of the return on the portfolio), γ is the slope of the Capital Market Line and $E(R_p)$ is the expected return on the portfolio. The parameter γ is often referred to as 'the market price of risk' since it summarizes the additional risk that an investor will have to take in order to obtain a particular expected return on their portfolio.

The portfolio M depicted in Figure 2.4 is called the market portfolio. The market portfolio is comprised of all assets in the economy in proportion to their overall market values. We can illustrate this point by considering an economy comprised of just three assets. The first asset has a market value of £1. The second asset has a market value of £2. The third asset has a market value of £3. The market portfolio will then be comprised of a

$$w_1 = \frac{1}{1+2+3} = \frac{1}{6}$$

proportionate investment in the first asset, a

$$w_2 = \frac{2}{1+2+3} = \frac{1}{3}$$

proportionate investment in the second asset and a

$$w_3 = \frac{3}{1+2+3} = \frac{1}{2}$$

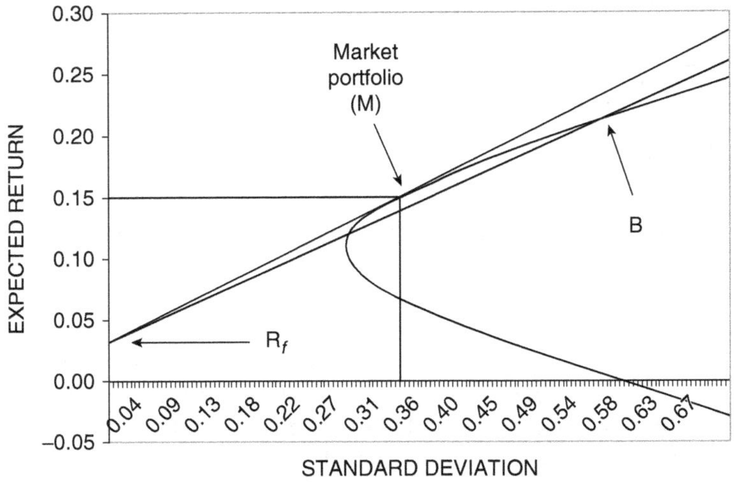

Figure 2.4 Forming portfolios when there is a risk-free asset

proportionate investment in the third asset. Unfortunately, not all assets in the economy are traded on active markets, and this will mean that it is seldom, if ever, that one will be able to identify the exact composition of the market portfolio M. The best that one can hope for is to find a good approximation or 'surrogate' for the market portfolio, such as the Financial Times–London Stock Exchange (FTSE) All Share Index. The FTSE All Share Index is comprised of the equity securities of approximately 600 companies and covers some 98 per cent of the total capitalized value of shares traded on the London Stock Exchange.

§2-8. We can determine an explicit formula for the slope γ of the Capital Market Line in terms of the risk-free rate of interest and the parameters that characterize the Markowitz locus by solving the formula describing the Capital Market Line for

$$\sigma_p = \frac{\mu - R_f}{\gamma}$$

We can then equate the resultant with the formula for the Markowitz locus, namely,

$$\frac{\mu - R_f}{\gamma} = \sigma_p = \sqrt{a\mu^2 + b\mu + c}$$

where, it will be recalled, $\mu = E(R_p)$ is the expected return on the portfolio. Squaring both sides of this equation then shows

$$\frac{\mu^2 - 2\mu R_f + R_f^2}{\gamma^2} = a\mu^2 + b\mu + c$$

Now, multiplying through by γ^2 and collecting terms, we have

$$(a\gamma^2 - 1)\mu^2 + (b\gamma^2 + 2R_f)\mu + (c\gamma^2 - R_f^2) = 0$$

Note, however, that this is a quadratic equation in $\mu = E(R_p)$. We can therefore determine its two roots:

$$\mu = \frac{-(b\gamma^2 + 2R_f) \pm \sqrt{(b\gamma^2 + 2R_f)^2 - 4(a\gamma^2 - 1)(c\gamma^2 - R_f^2)}}{2(a\gamma^2 - 1)}$$

We have shown through Figure 2.4 in §2-7 above, however, that the Capital Market Line is tangential to the Markowitz locus at one point only, namely, at the market portfolio M. This in turn will mean that the discriminant in the above expression for the roots of μ will have to be zero:

$$(b\gamma^2 + 2R_f)^2 - 4(a\gamma^2 - 1)(c\gamma^2 - R_f^2) = 0$$

Expanding this expression gives

$$b^2\gamma^4 + 4b\gamma^2 R_f + 4R_f^2 - 4ac\gamma^4 + 4a\gamma^2 R_f^2 + 4c\gamma^2 - 4R_f^2 = 0$$

Cancelling and collecting terms then gives

$$(b^2 - 4ac)\gamma^4 + 4(R_f b + R_f^2 a + c)\gamma^2 = 0$$

It thus follows that the slope parameter, or equivalently the market price of risk, for the Capital Market Line will be

$$\gamma = \sqrt{\frac{-4(R_f b + R_f^2 a + c)}{b^2 - 4ac}}$$

where a, b and c are the parameters of the Markowitz locus and R_f is the risk-free rate of interest.

We can illustrate the application of this formula by using the $N = 2$ risky asset example employed to date. For this example, we assumed that the risk-free rate of interest is $R_f = \frac{1}{30}$ or $3\frac{1}{3}$ per cent (per annum). Now, we know from §2-4 above that the Markowitz locus for our two-asset portfolio is given by:

$$\sigma_p = \sqrt{22\mu^2 - 4.8\mu + 0.33}$$

It then follows that the parameters for the Markowitz locus are $a = 22$, $b = -4.8$ and $c = 0.33$. Substituting these parameter values into the expression for γ gives

$$\gamma = \sqrt{\frac{-4(R_f b + R_f^2 a + c)}{b^2 - 4ac}} = \sqrt{\frac{-4[\frac{1}{30} \times (-4.8) + (\frac{1}{30})^2 \times 22 + 0.33]}{(-4.8)^2 - 4 \times 22 \times 0.33}} = \frac{1}{3}\sqrt{\frac{7}{6}}$$

or $\gamma \approx 0.360041$ will be the market price of risk. This will mean that for every unit increase in the expected return, the risk (or standard deviation) associated with the return on the portfolio will have to increase by approximately 0.36. This result also means that the Capital Market Line for the $N = 2$ risky asset example employed to date will take the following form:

$$E(R_p) = R_f + \gamma\sigma(R_p) = \tfrac{1}{30} + \tfrac{1}{3}\sqrt{\tfrac{7}{6}}\sigma_p$$

Recall that when a risk-free asset is available, the Capital Market Line gives the maximum possible expected return that can be obtained by combining a proportionate investment in the risk-free asset with a complementary proportionate investment in the market portfolio.

§2-9. One can also use the analysis in §2-7 and §2-8 above to determine the expected return $E(R_m)$ and variance σ_m^2 on the market portfolio. It will be recalled from Figure 2.4 in §2-7 that a positively sloped chord drawn from the risk-free rate of return on the expected return axis will cut the Markowitz locus twice at the following expected returns:

$$\mu = \frac{-(b\gamma^2 + 2R_f) \pm \sqrt{(b\gamma^2 + 2R_f)^2 - 4(a\gamma^2 - 1)(c\gamma^2 - R_f^2)}}{2(a\gamma^2 - 1)}$$

We also noted, however, that the Capital Market Line is just tangential to the Markowitz locus at the expected return on the market portfolio. This in turn will mean that the chord representing the Capital Market Line will have only one point of tangency with the Markowitz locus or, equivalently, that the discriminant in the above expression must be zero. Hence, if we set this discriminant to zero, it follows that the expected return on the market portfolio will have to be

$$E(R_m) = \frac{-(b\gamma^2 + 2R_f)}{2(a\gamma^2 - 1)}$$

Substituting the slope of the Capital Market Line, $\gamma = \frac{1}{3}\sqrt{\frac{7}{6}}$, the parameters associated with the Markowitz locus, $a = 22$, $b = -4.8$ and $c = 0.33$, as well as the risk-free rate $R_f = \frac{1}{30}$, will then imply

$$E(R_m) = \frac{-(2R_f + b\gamma^2)}{2(a\gamma^2 - 1)} = \frac{-(2 \times \frac{1}{30} - 4.8 \times \frac{7}{54})}{2(22 \times \frac{7}{54} - 1)} = \frac{\frac{5}{9}}{\frac{200}{54}} = 0.15$$

that is, that the expected return on the market portfolio for the two-asset example we have been looking at will be $E(R_m) = 15$ per cent (per annum). Moreover, we can determine the proportionate investments in the two risky assets for the market portfolio by using the analysis in §2-4 above, where we have shown that the proportionate investment in the first asset, w_1, corresponding to an expected return of $E(R_p) = \mu$ will be

$$w_1 = 10\mu - 1$$

Now consider the market portfolio, which has an expected return of $E(R_m) = 15$ per cent (per annum). Substituting into the above expression shows

$$w_1 = 10E(R_m) - 1 = 10 \times 0.15 - 1 = \frac{1}{2}$$

This in turn implies $w_2 = 1 - w_1 = 1 - \frac{1}{2} = \frac{1}{2}$. This means that the market portfolio is comprised of an equal proportionate investment in each of the two risky assets on which our example is based.

§2-10. We can also use these weights to determine the variance σ_m^2 on the market portfolio. From §2-4 above, it will be recalled that the variance of the return on a two-asset portfolio can be written as

$$\sigma_p^2 = w_1^2\sigma_1^2 + w_2^2\sigma_2^2 + 2w_1w_2\sigma_{12}$$

where for the example employed to date we have that $\sigma_1^2 = 0.25$ is the variance of the return on the first asset, $\sigma_2^2 = 0.07$ is the variance of the return on the second asset and $\sigma_{12} = 0.05$ is the covariance between the return on the first asset and the return on the second asset. Hence, substituting these expressions and the fact that $w_1 = \frac{1}{2} = w_2$ are the proportionate investments in the two assets shows that the variance of the return on the market portfolio will be

$$\sigma_m^2 = \left(\frac{1}{2}\right)^2 \times 0.25 + \left(\frac{1}{2}\right)^2 \times 0.07 + 2\left(\frac{1}{2} \times \frac{1}{2}\right) \times 0.05 = 0.105$$

There are, however, two other ways in which we can calculate the above variance. The first of these arises from the fact that we can use the Markowitz locus (as in §2-8) with an expected return on the market portfolio of $\mu = E(R_m) = 0.15$, in which case we have

$$\sigma_m^2 = 22[E(R_m)]^2 - 4.8E(R_m) + 0.33$$

or:

$$\sigma_m^2 = 22 \times (0.15)^2 - 4.8 \times 0.15 + 0.33 = 0.105$$

Note how this gives the same value for the variance of the return on the market portfolio, $\sigma_m^2 = 0.105$, as with our previous calculations. Moreover, we can also use the Capital Market Line (as in §2-8) to determine the variance of the return on the market portfolio:

$$E(R_m) = \frac{1}{30} + \frac{1}{3}\sqrt{\frac{7}{6}}\sigma_m$$

Thus, substituting $E(R_m) = 0.15$ into the above equation shows

$$\frac{3}{20} = \frac{1}{30} + \frac{1}{3}\sqrt{\frac{7}{6}}\sigma_m$$

and solving for σ_m we have

$$\sigma_m = \left(\frac{3}{20} - \frac{1}{30}\right) \times 3 \times \sqrt{\frac{6}{7}} = \frac{7}{20} \times \sqrt{\frac{6}{7}} \approx 0.324037$$

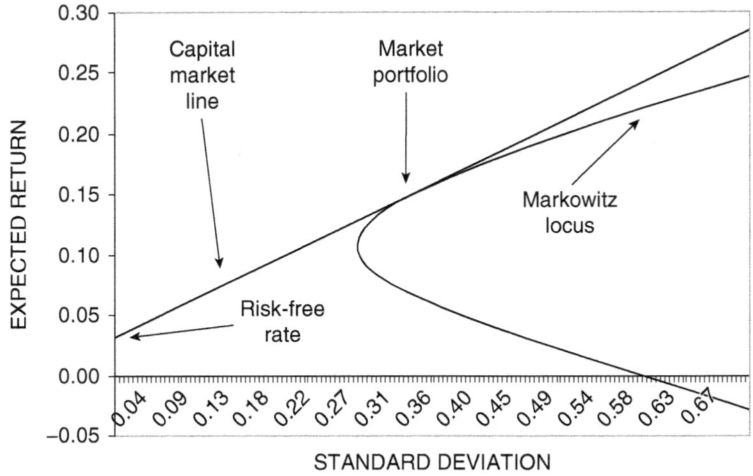

Figure 2.5 Summary graph of Markowitz locus and capital market line

It follows from this that

$$\sigma_m^2 = \left(\frac{7}{20} \times \sqrt{\frac{6}{7}}\right)^2 = \frac{49}{400} \times \frac{6}{7} = \frac{21}{200} = 0.105$$

Again this agrees with previous calculations for the variance of the return on the market portfolio. One can summarize the results relating to the two risky asset portfolio example employed to date in terms of the graph depicted in Figure 2.5. Recall (as in §2-8) that the Markowitz locus for our two asset portfolio takes the form:

$$\sigma_p = \sqrt{22\mu^2 - 4.8\mu + 0.33}$$

whilst the Capital Market Line is

$$E(R_p) = \frac{1}{30} + \frac{1}{3}\sqrt{\frac{7}{6}}\sigma_p$$

The risk-free rate of interest is $R_f = \frac{1}{30}$ or $3\frac{1}{3}$ per cent (per annum). Moreover, the market portfolio has an expected return of $E(R_m) = 0.15$ or 15 per cent (per annum), with a variance of $\sigma_m^2 = 0.105$.

§2-11. Now, we can use the simple example on which Figure 2.5 is based to show that risky assets must satisfy a result known as the Capital Asset Pricing Model (CAPM). The most important input for the CAPM is what is known as the asset's beta. The beta of the *j*th asset comprising the market portfolio is defined as follows:

$$\beta_j = \frac{\text{Cov}(R_j, R_m)}{\sigma_m^2} = \frac{\sigma_{jm}}{\sigma_m^2}$$

where R_j is the return on the jth asset, R_m is the return on the market portfolio, σ_m^2 is the variance of the return on the market portfolio and $\text{Cov}(R_j, R_m) = \sigma_{jm}$ is the covariance between the return on the jth asset and the return on the market portfolio. Thus, for the simple two-asset ($N = 2$) portfolio considered to date, we have shown in §2-9 above that the market portfolio is comprised of an equal proportionate investment in each risky asset; that is, $w_1 = \frac{1}{2}$ and $w_2 = \frac{1}{2}$. This in turn will mean that the return on the market portfolio will be

$$R_m = w_1 R_1 + w_2 R_2 = \tfrac{1}{2} R_1 + \tfrac{1}{2} R_2$$

where R_1 is the return on the first of the two risky assets and R_2 is the return on the second risky asset. We can substitute the expression for the return on the market portfolio given here into the expression for the covariance between the return on the first asset and the return on the market portfolio and thereby show

$$\text{Cov}(R_1, R_m) = \text{Cov}(R_1, \tfrac{1}{2} R_1 + \tfrac{1}{2} R_2) = \tfrac{1}{2}\sigma_1^2 + \tfrac{1}{2}\text{Cov}(R_1, R_2) = \tfrac{1}{2}\sigma_1^2 + \tfrac{1}{2}\sigma_{12}$$

Now, from §2-4 above, we have $\sigma_1^2 = 0.25$ and $\text{Cov}(R_1, R_2) = \sigma_{12} = 0.05$ for the two-asset example we have been working with to date. Substitution then shows

$$\text{Cov}(R_1, R_m) = \sigma_{1m} = \frac{1}{2} \times 0.25 + \frac{1}{2} \times 0.05 = 0.15$$

It then follows that the first asset's beta will be

$$\beta_1 = \frac{\text{Cov}(R_1, R_m)}{\sigma_m^2} = \frac{0.15}{0.105} = \frac{10}{7}$$

where, from §2-10 above, $\sigma_m^2 = 0.105$ is the variance of the return on the market portfolio. Now the CAPM says that the relationship between the expected return on an asset and its beta will be

$$E(R_j) = R_f + [E(R_m) - R_f]\beta_j$$

Moreover, we have previously assumed (as in §2-7) that the risk-free rate of interest is $R_f = \frac{1}{30}$ or $3\frac{1}{3}$ per cent (per annum), whilst in §2-9 we have shown that the expected return on the market will be $E(R_m) = \frac{3}{20}$ or 15 per cent (per annum). Hence, substituting the risk-free rate, the expected return on the market portfolio and the first asset's beta, $\beta_1 = \frac{10}{7}$, into the expression for the CAPM shows that

$$E(R_1) = R_f + [E(R_m) - R_f]\beta_1 = \frac{1}{30} + \left(\frac{3}{20} - \frac{1}{30}\right)\frac{10}{7} = \frac{1}{5} = 0.2$$

that is, the expected return on the first asset will be $E(R_1) = 20$ per cent (per annum). Note how this is the expected return assumed for the first asset when we began our analysis of this two-asset portfolio in §2-2 above. Observe also how an asset's beta captures the sensitivity of its return to the return on the market portfolio. Thus, the first asset's beta of $\beta_1 = \frac{10}{7}$ signifies that if in a given year the market has a return of one per cent in excess of the risk-free rate of return, then one would expect the first asset to have a return of $\frac{10}{7} \approx 1.4286$ per cent in excess of the risk-free rate of return. In other words, assets with betas that exceed unity will tend to outperform the market during 'bull' markets but correspondingly, do worse than the market as a whole during 'bear' markets.

Similar procedures show that the second asset's return will have the following covariance with the return on the market portfolio:

$$\text{Cov}(R_2, R_m) = \text{Cov}(R_2, \tfrac{1}{2}R_1 + \tfrac{1}{2}R_2) = \tfrac{1}{2}\text{Cov}(R_1, R_2) + \tfrac{1}{2}\sigma_2^2 = \tfrac{1}{2}\sigma_{12} + \tfrac{1}{2}\sigma_2^2$$

It will be recalled from §2-4, however, that $\text{Cov}(R_1, R_2) = \sigma_{12} = 0.05$ and $\sigma_2^2 = 0.07$. Hence, substitution shows that the covariance of the return on the second asset with the return on the market portfolio will be

$$\text{Cov}(R_2, R_m) = \sigma_{2m} = \frac{1}{2} \times 0.05 + \frac{1}{2} \times 0.07 = 0.06$$

We can then use the fact that $\sigma_m^2 = 0.105$ is the variance of the return on the market portfolio (as in §2-10) to show that the second asset's beta will be

$$\beta_2 = \frac{\text{Cov}(R_2, R_m)}{\sigma_m^2} = \frac{0.06}{0.105} = \frac{4}{7}$$

Substituting this result into the CAPM shows

$$E(R_2) = R_f + [E(R_m) - R_f]\beta_2 = \frac{1}{30} + \left(\frac{3}{20} - \frac{1}{30}\right) \times \frac{4}{7} = 0.10$$

or that the expected return on the second asset will be $E(R_1) = 10$ per cent (per annum). Note again how this is the expected return assumed for the second asset when we began our analysis of this two-asset portfolio in §2-2 above.

It is not hard to show that the weighted average beta for the economy as a whole will be unity – where the weights are given by the proportionate investments for the assets comprising the market portfolio. Thus, for our two-asset example, we have (as in §2-9 above) that $w_1 = \frac{1}{2}$ and $w_2 = \frac{1}{2}$ for the market portfolio whilst $\beta_1 = \frac{10}{7}$ for the first risky asset and $\beta_2 = \frac{4}{7}$ for the second risky asset. This in turn will mean that the weighted average beta for the economy as a whole will be

$$w_1\beta_1 + w_2\beta_2 = \frac{1}{2} \times \frac{10}{7} + \frac{1}{2} \times \frac{4}{7} = 1$$

or unity, as required.

§2-12. There are several points about the CAPM that we need to emphasize. The first stems from the fact that $E(R_m) - R_f$ (which is the expected return on the market portfolio less the return on the risk-free asset) is often referred to as 'the equity risk premium'. Now, we have previously noted (in §2-7 above) that it is seldom, if ever, that one will be able to identify the exact composition of the market portfolio. This in turn will mean that it is very difficult to determine the exact magnitude of the equity risk premium. Indeed, there is a great deal of speculation and often acrimonious debate in the literature about the magnitude of the equity risk premium, with estimates for the UK economy varying from as little as 3 per cent to as high as 7 per cent (per annum). However, it is unlikely that this issue can ever be resolved, owing to our inability to identify the exact composition of the market portfolio.

A second point of importance stems from the fact that the CAPM details the relationship between the return an investor can expect on an asset, $E(R_j)$, and what is known as its 'systematic (or market) risk' as captured by the asset's beta β_j. Unfortunately, expectations are seldom realized in practice, and this will mean that the actual return R_j on the asset over any given period will be comprised of an expected component as defined by the CAPM and a residual or unexpected component. This in turn will mean that one can represent the *ex poste* return on the asset in the following terms:

$$R_j = R_f + (R_m - R_f)\beta_j + \varepsilon_j$$

where R_m is the *ex poste* return on the market portfolio, R_f is the risk-free rate of return and ε_j is the unexpected component of the return over the given period. Now, we can use the above expression to determine the variance of the return, σ_j^2, on the asset:

$$\sigma_j^2 = \sigma_m^2\beta_j^2 + \sigma^2(\varepsilon_j)$$

where σ_m^2 is the variance of the rate of return on the market portfolio and $\sigma^2(\varepsilon_j)$ is referred to as the unsystematic risk or, equivalently, the idiosyncratic risk associated with the given asset's return. Now, the first component on the right-hand side of the above expression for the variance – namely, $\sigma_m^2\beta_j^2$ – is called the systematic (or 'market') component of the asset's risk and refers to the component of total risk that is common to all securities. In §3-11 of Chapter 3 we show that an asset's systematic (i.e. its market) risk can never be diversified away. In contrast, the unsystematic risk $\sigma^2(\varepsilon_j)$ associated with an asset's return can be diversified away as the investor adds more and more securities to his investment portfolio.

§2-13. The analysis that leads to the CAPM is based on the assumption that a risk-free asset is always available in the economy. When, however, there is no risk-free asset in the economy, an equilibrium relationship between risky asset returns can still be developed in terms of what is known as the minimum-variance zero-beta portfolio. One can demonstrate this model in terms of an example based on a portfolio that is composed of three risky assets whose expected returns are summarized in the vector

$$\underset{\sim}{e} = \begin{pmatrix} 0.10 \\ 0.15 \\ 0.20 \end{pmatrix}$$

where the first element indicates that $E(R_1) = 0.1 = 10$ per cent (per annum) is the expected return on the first asset, the second element indicates that $E(R_2) = 0.15 = 15$ per cent (per annum) is the expected return on the second asset and the third element indicates that $E(R_3) = 0.2 = 20$ per cent (per annum) is the expected return on the third asset. Moreover, the variances of the returns on the three assets and the covariances between their returns are as defined in the following variance–covariance matrix:

$$\Omega = \begin{pmatrix} 0.2 & 0.1 & 0.2 \\ 0.1 & 0.4 & 0.1 \\ 0.2 & 0.1 & 1.0 \end{pmatrix}$$

Hence, the variance of the return for the first asset as given in the first row and first column of this matrix is $\sigma_{11} = \sigma_1^2 = 0.2$; the variance of the return on the second asset as given in the second row and second column is $\sigma_{22} = \sigma_2^2 = 0.4$; and the variance of the return for the third asset as given in the third row and third column is $\sigma_{33} = \sigma_3^2 = 1.0$. Furthermore, the covariance of the first asset's return with the second asset's return as given in the first row and second column is $\sigma_{12} = 0.1$. Note that this is the same as the covariance of the second asset's return with the first asset's return as given in the second row and first column: $\sigma_{21} = 0.1 = \sigma_{12}$. Likewise, the covariance of the first asset's return with the third asset's return as given in the first row and third column is $\sigma_{13} = 0.2 = \sigma_{31}$. Finally, the covariance of the second asset's return with the third asset's return as given in the second row and third column is $\sigma_{23} = 0.1 = \sigma_{32}$. These considerations mean that the matrix Ω is symmetric; that is, the entries above the diagonal (or variance terms) are a mirror image of the entries appearing below the diagonal terms.

In Exercise 3 at the end of this chapter, the reader will be asked to show that the Markowitz locus corresponding to the expected returns vector $\underset{\sim}{e}$ and the variance–covariance matrix Ω given above is

$$\sigma_p = \sqrt{\frac{160}{3}\mu^2 - 12\mu + \frac{17}{20}}$$

where $\mu = E(R_p)$ is the expected return on the portfolio and σ_p is the standard deviation of the return on the portfolio. Now suppose the market portfolio has an expected return of $\mu = E(R_m) = \frac{3}{20} = 15$ per cent (per annum). Then substitution into the Markowitz locus shows that the standard deviation of the return on the market portfolio, σ_m, will be

$$\sigma_m = \sqrt{\frac{160}{3}\left(\frac{3}{20}\right)^2 - 12\left(\frac{3}{20}\right) + \frac{17}{20}} = \frac{1}{2}$$

Moreover, in Exercise 3, the reader will be asked to show that the market portfolio is composed of a $w_1 = \frac{1}{4}$ proportionate investment in the first asset, a $w_2 = \frac{1}{2}$ proportionate investment in the second asset and a $w_3 = \frac{1}{4}$ proportionate investment in the third asset. This will mean that the return on the market portfolio, R_m, can be expressed as

$$R_m = \tfrac{1}{4}R_1 + \tfrac{1}{2}R_2 + \tfrac{1}{4}R_3$$

where R_1 is the return on the first risky asset, R_2 is the return on the second risky asset and R_3 is the return on the third risky asset. Given this, we may compute the covariance between the return on the first asset and the return on the market portfolio:

$$\text{Cov}(R_1, R_m) = \text{Cov}(R_1, \tfrac{1}{4}R_1 + \tfrac{1}{2}R_2 + \tfrac{1}{4}R_3) = \tfrac{1}{4}\sigma_1^2 + \tfrac{1}{2}\text{Cov}(R_1, R_2) + \tfrac{1}{4}\text{Cov}(R_1, R_3)$$

This will mean that the first asset's beta turns out to be

$$\beta_1 = \frac{\text{Cov}(R_1, R_m)}{\sigma_m^2} = \frac{\frac{1}{4} \times \frac{1}{5} + \frac{1}{2} \times \frac{1}{10} + \frac{1}{4} \times \frac{1}{5}}{(\frac{1}{2})^2} = \frac{\frac{3}{20}}{\frac{1}{4}} = \frac{3}{5}$$

Likewise, the covariance between the return on the second asset and the return on the market portfolio will be:

$$\mathrm{Cov}(R_2, R_m) = \mathrm{Cov}(R_2, \tfrac{1}{4}R_1 + \tfrac{1}{2}R_2 + \tfrac{1}{4}R_3) = \tfrac{1}{4}\mathrm{Cov}(R_2, R_1) + \tfrac{1}{2}\sigma_2^2 + \tfrac{1}{4}\mathrm{Cov}(R_2, R_3)$$

This means that one can use the data from the variance–covariance matrix Ω to show that the second asset's beta will be

$$\beta_2 = \frac{\mathrm{Cov}(R_2, R_m)}{\sigma_m^2} = \frac{\frac{1}{4} \times \frac{1}{10} + \frac{1}{2} \times \frac{2}{5} + \frac{1}{4} \times \frac{1}{10}}{(\frac{1}{2})^2} = \frac{\frac{1}{4}}{\frac{1}{4}} = 1$$

Finally, the covariance between the return on the third asset and the return on the market portfolio will be

$$\mathrm{Cov}(R_3, R_m) = \mathrm{Cov}(R_3, \tfrac{1}{4}R_1 + \tfrac{1}{2}R_2 + \tfrac{1}{4}R_3) = \tfrac{1}{4}\mathrm{Cov}(R_3, R_1) + \tfrac{1}{2}\mathrm{Cov}(R_3, R_2) + \tfrac{1}{4}\sigma_3^2$$

This means the beta for the third asset will be

$$\beta_3 = \frac{\mathrm{Cov}(R_3, R_m)}{\sigma_m^2} = \frac{\frac{1}{4} \times \frac{1}{5} + \frac{1}{2} \times \frac{1}{10} + \frac{1}{4} \times 1}{(\frac{1}{2})^2} = \frac{\frac{7}{20}}{\frac{1}{4}} = \frac{7}{5}$$

Unfortunately, one cannot use the betas determined here in conjunction with the CAPM to determine the expected returns on the three assets, since a risk-free asset does not exist in this economy.

§2-14. It can be shown, however, that the expected return on every risky asset can be stated in terms of a linear combination of the expected return on the market portfolio, $E(R_m) =$ 15 per cent, as given above and a minimum-variance zero-beta portfolio whose expected return $E(R_z)$ and standard deviation of return $\sigma(R_z)$ always fall on the Markowitz locus. The minimum-variance zero-beta portfolio is determined by passing a chord from the market portfolio down to the vertical or expected return axis and then passing a horizontal line across from the expected return axis to the Markowitz locus as illustrated in Figure 2.6. The chord from the market portfolio down to the vertical or expected return axis will take the following form:

$$E(R_m) = E(R_z) + \gamma\sigma_m$$

where $E(R_z)$ is the expected return on the zero-beta portfolio, γ is the slope of the chord, $E(R_m)$ is the expected return on the market portfolio and σ_m is the standard deviation of the return on the market portfolio. Here it is important to note that the slope γ of the chord and the slope of the Markowitz locus are identical at the market portfolio since at this point the chord is tangential to the Markowitz locus. Hence, determining the slope of the Markowitz locus at this point, we have

$$\frac{d\sigma_p}{d\mu} = \frac{d}{d\mu}\left(\sqrt{\tfrac{160}{3}\mu^2 - 12\mu + \tfrac{17}{20}}\right) = \frac{\frac{320}{3}\mu - 12}{2\sqrt{\frac{160}{3}\mu^2 - 12\mu + \frac{17}{20}}} = \frac{\frac{320}{3}\mu - 12}{2\sigma_p}$$

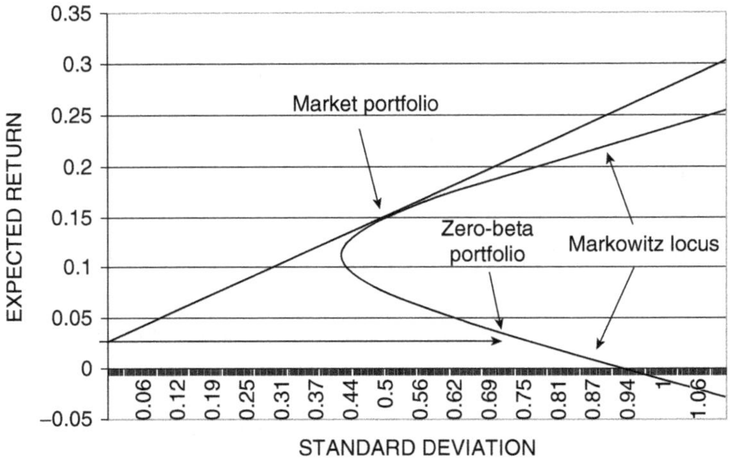

Figure 2.6 Minimum-variance zero-beta portfolio

Evaluating this expression at the mean, $\mu = E(R_m) = \frac{3}{20} = 15$ per cent, and standard deviation, $\sigma_p = \sigma_m = \frac{1}{2}$, of the market portfolio shows

$$\frac{d\sigma_p}{d\mu} = \frac{\frac{320}{3}\mu - 12}{2\sigma_p} = \frac{\frac{320}{3} \times \frac{3}{20} - 12}{2 \times \frac{1}{2}} = 4$$

However, the slope measured here is the rate of change in the standard deviation σ_p with respect to the change in the mean μ. From Figure 2.6, however, it is clear that what we require is the rate of change in the mean μ with respect to the change in the standard deviation σ_p, that is, $d\mu/d\sigma_p$. Now, under certain regularity conditions that are satisfied here, it may be shown that

$$\frac{d\mu}{d\sigma_p} = \left(\frac{d\sigma_p}{d\mu}\right)^{-1} = \frac{1}{4}$$

in which case it follows that the slope of the chord will be $\gamma = \frac{1}{4}$. Moreover, we also know that the expected return on the market portfolio is $\mu = E(R_m) = \frac{3}{20}$ and that the market portfolio has a standard deviation of $\sigma_m = \frac{1}{2}$. Substituting these three parameters into the mathematical expression for the chord given above shows

$$E(R_m) = \frac{3}{20} = E(R_z) + \gamma\sigma_m = E(R_z) + \frac{1}{4} \times \frac{1}{2}$$

Hence, solving the above equation for the expected return on the zero-beta portfolio, we have $E(R_z) = \frac{1}{40} = 2\frac{1}{2}$ per cent (per annum). The zero-beta portfolio with this return is marked on the lower (inefficient) segment of the Markowitz locus in Figure 2.6. This highlights an important property of the minimum-variance zero-beta portfolio, namely, that the zero-beta portfolio is always an inefficient portfolio. In light of our discussion in §2-6 above, the zero-beta portfolio is a portfolio that no rational investor will ever wish to hold, since there will always be an alternative portfolio with the same standard deviation as the zero-beta portfolio but which has a higher expected return.

§2-15. We can identify further properties of the zero-beta portfolio for the example considered here by looking at portfolios that involve the following proportionate investments across the three risky assets:

$$\underset{\sim}{w} = \begin{pmatrix} \frac{5}{2} \\ -\frac{3}{2} \\ 0 \end{pmatrix} + \psi \begin{pmatrix} 1 \\ -2 \\ 1 \end{pmatrix}$$

where ψ is a parameter that can take on any numerical value. Thus, the portfolios defined here will have a proportionate investment of $w_1 = \frac{5}{2} + \psi$ in the first asset, a proportionate investment of $w_2 = -\frac{3}{2} - 2\psi$ in the second asset and a proportionate investment of $w_3 = \psi$ in the third asset. Note that

$$w_1 + w_2 + w_3 = \left(\frac{5}{2} + \psi\right) + \left(-\frac{3}{2} - 2\psi\right) + \psi = 1$$

that is, the total of the proportionate investments is unity, as required (and this will be so irrespective of the value assumed by the parameter ψ). Moreover, we can use the expected returns vector given in §2-13 above to determine the expected return on portfolios comprised of these proportionate investments:

$$E(R_z) = w_1 E(R_1) + w_2 E(R_2) + w_3 E(R_3) = \left(\frac{5}{2} + \psi\right)\frac{1}{10} + \left(-\frac{3}{2} - 2\psi\right)\frac{3}{20} + \psi\frac{1}{5}$$

Collecting terms in the above expression shows

$$E(R_z) = \left(\frac{5}{20} - \frac{9}{40}\right) + \left(\frac{1}{10} - \frac{6}{20} + \frac{1}{5}\right)\psi = \frac{1}{40} = 0.025$$

or that the expected return on portfolios comprised of these proportionate investments will be $E(R_z) = 2\frac{1}{2}$ per cent (per annum), and this will be so irrespective of the value assumed by the parameter ψ. Moreover, using the betas calculated in §2-13 for the three risky assets, we can also show that the beta, β_z, for these zero-beta portfolios will have to be

$$\beta_z = w_1\beta_1 + w_2\beta_2 + w_3\beta_3 = \left(\frac{5}{2} + \psi\right)\frac{3}{5} + \left(-\frac{3}{2} - 2\psi\right)1 + \psi\frac{7}{5}$$
$$= \left(\frac{3}{2} - \frac{3}{2}\right) + \left(\frac{3}{5} - 2 + \frac{7}{5}\right)\psi = 0$$

That is, these portfolios will all have a beta of zero, and again this will be so irrespective of the specific value assumed by the parameter ψ. This will mean that the returns on these portfolios will have no systematic relationship with the return on the market portfolio. Finally, the variance of the return for these portfolios can be computed from the formula

$$\sigma_z^2 = w_1^2\sigma_1^2 + w_2^2\sigma_2^2 + w_3^2\sigma_3^2 + 2w_1w_2\sigma_{12} + 2w_1w_3\sigma_{13} + 2w_2w_3\sigma_{23}$$

where w_j is the proportionate investment in the $j = 1, 2, 3$ risky assets, σ_j^2 is the variance of the return on the jth asset and σ_{jk} is the covariance of the return on the jth asset with the return on the kth asset. Substituting the relevant proportionate investments and the variances and covariances from the variance–covariance matrix Ω, defined in §2-13 above, into the above expression, we have

$$\sigma_z^2 = \left(\frac{5}{2}+\psi\right)^2 \frac{1}{5} + \left(-\frac{3}{2}-2\psi\right)^2 \frac{2}{5} + \psi^2 1$$
$$+2\left(\frac{5}{2}+\psi\right)\left(-\frac{3}{2}-2\psi\right)\frac{1}{10} + 2\psi\left(\frac{5}{2}+\psi\right)\frac{1}{5} + 2\psi\left(-\frac{3}{2}-2\psi\right)\frac{1}{10}$$

or

$$\sigma_z^2 = \frac{12}{5}\psi^2 + \frac{14}{5}\psi + \frac{7}{5}$$

Now one can differentiate through the expression for σ_z^2 and thereby determine the zero-beta portfolio with an expected return of $E(R_z) = 2\frac{1}{2}$ per cent that has the smallest possible variance in the rate of return:

$$\frac{d\sigma_z^2}{d\psi} = \frac{24}{5}\psi + \frac{14}{5} = 0$$

or $\psi = -\frac{7}{12}$. This in turn implies that the portfolio with the proportionate weights given by

$$\underset{\sim}{w} = \begin{pmatrix} \frac{5}{2} \\ -\frac{3}{2} \\ 0 \end{pmatrix} + \psi \begin{pmatrix} 1 \\ -2 \\ 1 \end{pmatrix} = \begin{pmatrix} \frac{5}{2} \\ -\frac{3}{2} \\ 0 \end{pmatrix} - \frac{7}{12}\begin{pmatrix} 1 \\ -2 \\ 1 \end{pmatrix} = \begin{pmatrix} \frac{23}{12} \\ -\frac{1}{3} \\ -\frac{7}{12} \end{pmatrix}$$

will have a return whose variance is

$$\sigma_z^2 = \frac{12}{5}\psi^2 + \frac{14}{5}\psi + \frac{7}{5} = \frac{12}{5}\left(-\frac{7}{12}\right)^2 + \frac{14}{5}\left(-\frac{7}{12}\right) + \frac{7}{5} = \frac{7}{12}$$

and this variance will be lower than the variance of the return on any other portfolio with an expected return of $E(R_z) = 2\frac{1}{2}$ per cent (per annum). Hence, if an investor was obliged to hold one of these zero-beta portfolios, they would opt to hold the zero-beta portfolio with the above proportionate investments, since this minimizes the risk they would have to take in earning the expected return of $E(R_z) = 2\frac{1}{2}$ per cent (per annum) that it promises.

§2-16. Now it can be shown that when a risk-free asset is unavailable in the economy, the expected return, $E(R_j)$, on the jth risky asset comprising the economy can be stated in terms of the following 'two-factor' version of the CAPM:

$$E(R_j) = E(R_z) + [E(R_m) - E(R_z)]\beta_j$$

where, as previously, $E(R_z)$ is the expected return on the minimum-variance zero-beta portfolio as computed in the manner of §2-15 above, $E(R_m)$ is the expected return on the market portfolio and

$$\beta_j = \frac{\text{Cov}(R_j, R_m)}{\sigma_m^2} = \frac{\sigma_{jm}}{\sigma_m^2}$$

is the beta of the jth risky asset computed with respect to the return on the market portfolio. Hence, we can use the minimum-variance zero-beta portfolio with an expected return of $E(R_z) = 2\frac{1}{2}$ per cent as developed in §2-15 in conjunction with the market portfolio with an expected return of $E(R_m) = 15$ per cent as developed in §2-13, to illustrate this 'two-factor' version of the CAPM. From §2-13, we have that the beta of the first risky asset is given by $\beta_1 = \frac{3}{5}$. Hence, substitution shows

$$E(R_1) = E(R_z) + [E(R_m) - E(R_z)]\beta_1 = 0.025 + (0.15 - 0.025) \times \frac{3}{5} = 0.10$$

Note how this expected return is in agreement with the expected return for the first asset as summarized in the expected returns vector $\underset{\sim}{e}$ in §2-13 above. Likewise, the beta for the second risky asset is $\beta_2 = 1$. Substitution then shows

$$E(R_2) = E(R_z) + [E(R_m) - E(R_z)]\beta_2 = 0.025 + (0.15 - 0.025) \times 1 = 0.15$$

This expected return too is in agreement with the expected return for the second asset as summarized in the expected returns vector $\underset{\sim}{e}$. Finally, the beta for the third risky asset is $\beta_3 = \frac{7}{5}$ and so substitution shows

$$E(R_3) = E(R_z) + [E(R_m) - E(R_z)]\beta_3 = 0.025 + (0.15 - 0.025) \times \frac{7}{5} = 0.20$$

Again the expected return is in agreement with the expected return for the third asset as summarized in the expected returns vector $\underset{\sim}{e}$.

§2-17. We introduced this chapter with the observation that historical returns are often used to provide guidance about the likely magnitude of future returns and of the risks that are likely to arise from investing in a given portfolio or security. Given this, our purpose in this chapter has been to summarize the relationships that exist between the returns one can expect from and the risks that arise on a given portfolio or security and of their implications for the pricing of risky assets. Our analysis shows that there will be a quadratic relationship between the return one can expect from a given portfolio of risky assets and the risks (as measured by the variance of the return on the portfolio) that must be taken to obtain them. If, however, a risk-free asset exists then there will always be a linear relationship between the return on a portfolio comprised of a proportionate investment in the risk-free asset and a complementary proportionate investment in an efficient risky portfolio and the risk that must be taken to obtain the expected return. Moreover, when there is a risk-free asset, risky asset prices will evolve in terms of the Capital Asset Pricing Model. When, however, a risk-free asset is not available, then risky asset prices can still be described in terms of a 'two-factor' asset pricing model that is similar to the CAPM but in which the return on the risk-free asset is replaced by the return on the minimum-variance zero-beta portfolio.

Selected references

Breeden, D. (1979) 'An intertemporal asset pricing model with stochastic consumption and investment opportunities' *Journal of Financial Economics*, 7: 265–96.

Fama, E. and French, K. (2004) 'The capital asset pricing model: theory and evidence', *Journal of Economic Perspectives*, 18: 25–46.

Markowitz, H. (1959) *Portfolio Selection*, New York: Wiley.

Ross, S. (1978) 'The current status of the capital asset pricing model (CAPM)', *Journal of Finance*, 33: 885–901.

Rubinstein, M. (1976) 'The valuation of uncertain income streams and the pricing of options', *Bell Journal of Economics*, 7: 407–25.

Sharpe, W. (1970) *Portfolio Theory and Capital Markets*, New York: McGraw-Hill.

van Zijl, T. (1984) 'A new statement of the extended capital asset pricing model', *Australian Journal of Management*, 9: 67–86.

Exercises

1. A two-asset portfolio possesses the following parameters:

	Asset 1		*Asset 2*
Expected return $E(R_j)$	0.05		0.07
Variance σ_j^2	0.10		0.40
Covariance σ_{12}		−0.1	

   Prove that the following is an expression for the Markowitz locus:

$$\sigma_p = \sqrt{1750\mu^2 - 195\mu + 5.475}$$

   where σ_p is the standard deviation of the return on the portfolio and $E(R_p) = \mu$ is the expected return on the portfolio. Suppose that the risk-free rate of interest is $R_f = 0.05$ or 5 per cent (per annum). Determine the composition of the market portfolio, the expected return on the market portfolio and the variance of the market portfolio. Finally, compute the beta of asset 1 and asset 2 and hence confirm the validity of the Capital Asset Pricing Model.

2. In §2-4, we showed that the variance σ_p^2 of a two-asset portfolio is given by

$$\sigma_p^2 = w_1^2\sigma_1^2 + w_2^2\sigma_2^2 + 2w_1w_2\sigma_{12}$$

   where w_1 is the proportionate investment in the first asset, $w_2 = 1 - w_1$ is the proportionate investment in the second asset, σ_1^2 is the variance of the return on the first asset, σ_2^2 is the variance of the return on the second asset and σ_{12} is the covariance of the return on the first asset with the return on the second asset. Use the fact that the covariance can be restated as $\sigma_{12} = \rho_{12}\sigma_1\sigma_2$, where $-1 \leq \rho_{12} \leq 1$ is the correlation coefficient between the returns on the two assets, to determine the proportionate investments w_1 and w_2 that minimize the expression for σ_p^2. What happens when $\rho_{12} = -1$ and what implications does this have for portfolio formation?

3. In §2-13, we considered the three-asset economy with the expected returns vector

$$\underset{\sim}{e} = \begin{pmatrix} 0.10 \\ 0.15 \\ 0.20 \end{pmatrix}$$

Recall that the first element in the above vector indicates that $E(R_1) = 0.1 = 10$ per cent (per annum) is the expected return on the first asset, the second element indicates that $E(R_2) = 0.15 = 15$ per cent (per annum) is the expected return on the second asset and the third element indicates that $E(R_3) = 0.2 = 20$ per cent (per annum) is the expected return on the third asset.

The variance–covariance matrix for this three-asset economy is

$$\Omega = \begin{pmatrix} 0.2 & 0.1 & 0.2 \\ 0.1 & 0.4 & 0.1 \\ 0.2 & 0.1 & 1.0 \end{pmatrix}$$

Hence, the variance of the return for the first asset is $\sigma_{11} = \sigma_1^2 = 0.1$, the variance of the return on the second asset is $\sigma_{22} = \sigma_2^2 = 0.4$ and the variance of the return for the third asset is $\sigma_{33} = \sigma_3^2 = 1.0$. Furthermore, the covariance of the first asset's return with the second asset's return is $\sigma_{21} = 0.1 = \sigma_{12}$. The covariance of the first asset's return with the third asset's return is $\sigma_{13} = 0.2 = \sigma_{31}$. Finally, the covariance of the second asset's return with the third asset's return is $\sigma_{23} = 0.1 = \sigma_{32}$.

Consider portfolios defined by the weighting vector

$$\underset{\sim}{w} = \begin{pmatrix} 3 - 20\mu \\ 20\mu - 2 \\ 0 \end{pmatrix} + \psi \begin{pmatrix} 1 \\ -2 \\ 1 \end{pmatrix}$$

where $w_1 = (3 - 20\mu) + \psi$ is the proportionate investment in the first asset, $w_2 = (20\mu - 2) - 2\psi$ is the proportionate investment in the second asset, $w_3 = \psi$ is the proportionate investment in the third asset and ψ is a parameter that can assume any numerical value. Show that all portfolios defined by these weights will have an expected return of μ (per annum), irrespective of the particular numerical value that ψ assumes. Moreover, use the expression for the variance of the rate of return for a three-asset portfolio (as in §2-15),

$$\sigma_p^2 = w_1^2\sigma_1^2 + w_2^2\sigma_2^2 + w_3^2\sigma_3^2 + 2w_1w_2\sigma_{12} + 2w_1w_3\sigma_{13} + 2w_2w_3\sigma_{23}$$

to show that the Markowitz locus corresponding to the expected returns vector $\underset{\sim}{e}$ and the variance–covariance matrix Ω given above is

$$\sigma_p = \sqrt{\frac{160}{3}\mu^2 - 12\mu + \frac{17}{20}}$$

Use these results to show that the market portfolio, whose expected return is $E(R_m) = \frac{3}{20} = 15$ per cent (per annum), will be comprised of a $w_1 = \frac{1}{4}$ proportionate investment in the first asset, a $w_2 = \frac{1}{2}$ proportionate investment in the second asset and a $w_3 = \frac{1}{4}$ proportionate investment in the third asset.

4. In §2-6, we showed that the global minimum-variance portfolio will have an expected return

$$E(R_0) = -\frac{b}{2a}$$

and a variance

$$\sigma_0 = \sqrt{\frac{4ac - b^2}{4a}}$$

where a, b and c are the parameters of the Markowitz locus. Use the data and calculations of Exercise 3 to show that the expected return $E(R_j)$ on the jth risky asset can be stated in terms of the following Global Minimum-Variance Asset Pricing Model:

$$E(R_j) = E(R_0) + [E(R_m) - R_0]\theta_j$$

where

$$\theta_j = \frac{\beta_j \sigma_m^2 - \sigma_0^2}{\sigma_m^2 - \sigma_0^2}$$

and

$$\beta_j = \frac{\text{Cov}(R_j, R_m)}{\sigma^2(R_m)}$$

is the jth asset's beta under the two-factor version of the Capital Asset Pricing Model. What does this result imply about the uniqueness of both beta as a measure of risk and the Capital Asset Pricing Model as an asset pricing model?

5. In §2-8, we showed that the slope parameter of the Capital Market Line can be expressed as

$$\gamma = \sqrt{\frac{-4(R_f b + R_f^2 a + c)}{b^2 - 4ac}}$$

where a, b and c are the parameters of the Markowitz locus and R_f is the risk-free rate of interest. Use this result to show

$$\frac{d\gamma}{dR_f} = \frac{R_f - E(R_0)}{\gamma \sigma_0^2}$$

Demonstrate how this result can be used to assess the sensitivity of the market price of risk, γ, to changes in the risk-free rate of interest R_f.

3 Alternative approaches to the relationship between return and risk

§3-1. Our purpose in this chapter is to examine alternative ways of modelling the relationship between risk and return to those considered in Chapter 2. We begin by demonstrating how one can build asset pricing models in which factors other than beta might be interpreted as important determinants of asset returns. The procedure is implemented by first selecting what is known as an 'orthogonal' portfolio. The mean and variance of the return on an orthogonal portfolio always fall on the Markowitz locus. The market portfolio on which the Capital Asset Pricing Model (CAPM) is based is but one example of an infinite number of orthogonal portfolios that lie on the Markowitz locus. Moreover, if one computes asset betas with reference to any of these orthogonal portfolios, there will be a perfectly linear relationship between asset average returns and their betas. Hence, if one wishes to develop a model that appears to demonstrate that there is a direct relationship between asset returns and factors other than beta then one will have to base the calculation of betas on a portfolio with a mean and variance of returns that does not lie on the Markowitz locus. Given this, an important focus of the first part of this chapter is to identify the particular inefficient portfolio that leads to a pre-specified and perfectly linear relationship between the vector of average returns for the assets comprising the sample, the vector of betas based on the inefficient portfolio and such other factors as are deemed to be important in the asset pricing process. This is achieved by first specifying an orthogonal portfolio with certain desirable properties (e.g. a given mean return or variance) and then identifying the inefficient portfolio that mimics these desirable properties associated with the orthogonal portfolio. The proportionate investment weights for the inefficient portfolio are then chosen so as to give a perfectly linear relationship between the asset average returns, the betas based on the inefficient portfolio and such other determining variables as the researcher deems to be important in the asset pricing process. This places the largely *ad hoc* nature of the asset pricing formulae that characterize the empirical research of this area of the literature onto a similar footing to the CAPM in the sense that there will be a perfectly linear relationship between asset average returns and the variables selected as important determinants in the asset pricing process.

We then move our focus towards a second and more theoretically plausible approach to asset pricing issues, namely, the Arbitrage Pricing Theory (APT). The basic assumption behind the APT is that it will never be possible to earn a riskless profit from a self-financing (i.e. a zero-cost) investment portfolio. We note how a variety of arbitrage pricing models have arisen out of this basic assumption. Probably the most commonly employed of these models uses what is known as the 'characteristic polynomial' associated with a particular correlation matrix to identify a comparatively small number of 'factors' through which to account for the off-diagonal terms in the given correlation matrix. This captures the essential feature of what is known as a strict factor model, namely, that the correlation matrix can be decomposed into a matrix composed of an underlying set of factors and a second diagonal matrix composed purely of idiosyncratic variance terms. We would also emphasize that our emphasis in this chapter is on the two most commonly encountered alternatives to the CAPM to be found in the literature. There are, however, many other approaches to asset pricing theory that, owing to limitations of space, we are unable treat in this chapter.

§3-2. We begin our analysis by considering a portfolio composed of $j = 1, 2, 3, 4, \ldots, N$ risky assets. Let $\underset{\sim}{e}$ be the $N \times 1$ vector whose elements are the average returns of the N risky assets and Ω be the $N \times N$ matrix summarizing the variances and covariances of the returns on these N risky assets. We emphasize that $\underset{\sim}{e}$ is composed of the historical average returns (and not the expected returns) on the risky assets since our objective is to construct a perfectly linear relationship between the *ex poste* average returns, the betas based on an inefficient portfolio and such other determining variables as are deemed to be important in the asset pricing process. Likewise, Ω is composed of the variances and covariances determined from these historical returns. Now, in §2-5 of Chapter 2, we noted that one can determine the Markowitz locus implied by $\underset{\sim}{e}$ and Ω and that it will take the following form:

$$\sigma_p = \sqrt{a\mu^2 + b\mu + c}$$

where σ_p is the standard deviation of the return on the portfolio, $\mu = E(R_p)$ is the average return on the portfolio, $a > 0, b < 0$ and $c > 0$ are the parameters that characterize the Markowitz locus, and $\mu \geq E(R_0) = -b/2a$ defines the average return on the global minimum-variance portfolio (as in §2-6 of Chapter 2). Now, suppose a chord is drawn from the origin so that it has a point of tangency at the 'orthogonal portfolio' on the Markowitz locus as depicted in Figure 3.1. We should emphasize that it is unlikely that the orthogonal portfolio shown here will be the 'market portfolio' developed in §2-7, because, if it were, this would imply that the risk-free rate of interest R_f is zero. However, assuming a risk-free rate of zero simplifies the algebra associated with the asset pricing model we are about to develop but does not limit the generalizability of the results that we report.

Now, the average return on the orthogonal portfolio will be $\mu_Q = \underset{\sim}{Q}^T \cdot \underset{\sim}{e}$, where $\underset{\sim}{Q}^T$ is the transpose of the vector whose elements are the proportionate investments in the N risky

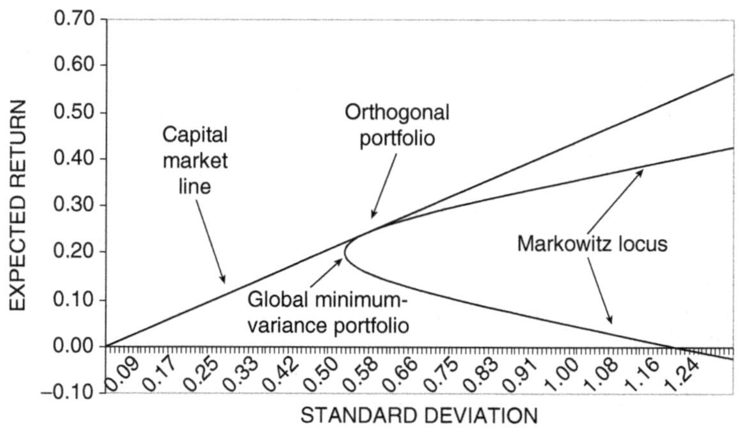

Figure 3.1 Orthogonal portfolio and the capital market line

assets comprising the orthogonal portfolio. We can then compute the vector of asset betas:

$$\underset{\sim}{\beta} = \frac{\Omega \underset{\sim}{Q}}{\underset{\sim}{Q}^T \Omega \underset{\sim}{Q}}$$

relative to the orthogonal portfolio, Q. The numerator in this expression, $\Omega \underset{\sim}{Q}$, is the vector whose elements are the covariances of the return on each of the N risky assets with the return on the orthogonal portfolio, Q. The denominator, $\sigma_Q^2 = \underset{\sim}{Q}^T \Omega \underset{\sim}{Q}$, is the variance of the return on the orthogonal portfolio. Moreover, since the orthogonal portfolio lies on the Markowitz locus, it follows immediately that $\underset{\sim}{e} = \mu_Q \underset{\sim}{\beta}$, or that there is a perfectly linear relationship between the vector of asset average returns $\underset{\sim}{e}$ and the betas $\underset{\sim}{\beta}$ computed relative to the chosen orthogonal portfolio.

§3-3. Now suppose an empirical researcher wishes to construct a pricing formula in which factors other than beta are to be interpreted as instrumental determinants of equity returns. The researcher might wish to argue, for example, that the relative size of the firm or the ratio of the market value of the firm's equity to the book value of its equity has a significant impact on equity prices. The difficulty here is that we have already shown that there is a perfectly linear relationship between the average returns vector $\underset{\sim}{e}$ and the betas $\underset{\sim}{\beta}$ computed relative to the orthogonal portfolio, Q. Of course, the betas based on the orthogonal portfolio are almost certainly not the 'true' betas, since one can only determine these if one knows the composition (i.e. proportionate investment weights) of the market portfolio, M. Unfortunately, it is highly unlikely that one can ever know the composition of the market portfolio, since from §2-7 we know that the market portfolio is composed of all assets in the economy in proportion to their overall market values. Since market prices for many of the assets comprising the market portfolio either do not exist or cannot be observed, this makes it very difficult to quantify the proportionate investment weights associated with the market portfolio. Given the virtual impossibility of observing the market portfolio, it might be thought that choosing a proxy for the market portfolio, such as Q, that lies on the Markowitz locus might be a good idea, since by doing so we maintain the simple linear relationship between the average returns vector $\underset{\sim}{e}$ and the betas $\underset{\sim}{\beta}$ that is the hallmark of the CAPM. But if we do this then these other factors, such as the relative size of the firm and the market-to-book ratio for its equity, which the researcher wishes to interpret as having a significant impact on equity prices, will end up being completely irrelevant to the asset pricing process. Of course, it might be the case that firm size and the market-to-book ratio do have an indirect impact on the asset average returns vector $\underset{\sim}{e}$, through the influence they have on the vector of betas $\underset{\sim}{\beta}$, but this does not provide the direct relationship with the average returns vector that the researcher wishes to demonstrate through their empirical analysis.

Fortunately, there is a solution of a sort to this problem. We say 'of a sort' because, whilst one can specify a procedure that appears to demonstrate a direct relationship between the average returns vector $\underset{\sim}{e}$ and variables like firm size and the market-to-book ratio for equity, in reality the model is 'contrived' because it has no substantive basis in economic theory. We have already noted in this section that it will always be possible to build a more parsimonious CAPM-type model by determining betas relative to an 'orthogonal' portfolio that lies on the Markowitz locus. With these caveats in mind, we now demonstrate how one can build a model in which factors other than beta might be interpreted as instrumental determinants of equity returns.

§3-4. We begin by considering the class of proportionate investment vectors $\underset{\sim}{\alpha}$ that have the same average return as the orthogonal portfolio considered earlier, or $\mu_\alpha \equiv \underset{\sim}{\alpha}^T \cdot \underset{\sim}{e} = \underset{\sim}{Q}^T \cdot \underset{\sim}{e} = \mu_Q$. Here, $\mu_\alpha \equiv \underset{\sim}{\alpha}^T \cdot \underset{\sim}{e}$ is the average return on the portfolio whose proportionate investment weights are the elements of $\underset{\sim}{\alpha}$ and, as previously, $\underset{\sim}{e}$ is the vector whose elements are the average returns on the N assets comprising the portfolio. The proportionate investment vectors $\underset{\sim}{\alpha}$ for these inefficient portfolios are related to the proportionate investment vector for the orthogonal portfolio, $\underset{\sim}{Q}$, through the formula

$$\underset{\sim}{\alpha} = \underset{\sim}{Q} + \sum_{j=1}^{N-2} \psi_j \underset{\sim}{k}_j$$

where the $\underset{\sim}{k}_j$ are self-financing 'kernel' or 'arbitrage' portfolios and the ψ_j are parameters that can take on any numerical value. The arbitrage portfolios $\underset{\sim}{k}_j$ are determined by solving the following system of equations:

$$\begin{pmatrix} e_1 & e_2 & e_3 \dots & e_n \\ 1 & 1 & 1 \dots & 1 \end{pmatrix} \underset{\sim}{k}_j = \underset{\sim}{0}$$

where the $e_1,\ e_2,\ e_3,\ \dots,\ e_n$ are the average returns on the individual risky assets (i.e. i the components of the vector $\underset{\sim}{e}$) and $\underset{\sim}{0} = \begin{pmatrix} 0 \\ 0 \end{pmatrix}$ is the null vector (i.e. the vector both of whose elements are zero). We can solve the above system of equations and thereby show that the arbitrage portfolios take the form

$$\underset{\sim}{k}_1 = \begin{pmatrix} e_3 - e_2 \\ -(e_3 - e_1) \\ e_2 - e_1 \\ 0 \\ 0 \\ \vdots \\ 0 \end{pmatrix}, \quad \underset{\sim}{k}_2 = \begin{pmatrix} e_4 - e_2 \\ -(e_4 - e_1) \\ 0 \\ e_2 - e_1 \\ 0 \\ \vdots \\ 0 \end{pmatrix}, \quad \underset{\sim}{k}_3 = \begin{pmatrix} e_5 - e_2 \\ -(e_5 - e_1) \\ 0 \\ 0 \\ e_2 - e_1 \\ \vdots \\ 0 \end{pmatrix}, \ \dots$$

and so on. Moreover, we can compute the vector of betas based on these inefficient portfolios:

$$\underset{\sim}{b} = \frac{\Omega \underset{\sim}{\alpha}}{\underset{\sim}{\alpha}^T \Omega \underset{\sim}{\alpha}}$$

The numerator, $\Omega \underset{\sim}{\alpha}$, in this expression for $\underset{\sim}{b}$ is the vector whose elements are the covariances of the return on each of the N assets with the return on the inefficient portfolio $\underset{\sim}{\alpha}$. The denominator is the variance of the return on the inefficient portfolio, $\sigma_\alpha^2 = \underset{\sim}{\alpha}^T \Omega \underset{\sim}{\alpha}$. We can then define the vector of errors $\underset{\sim}{\varepsilon}$ in the average returns that arise from basing the calculation of betas on the inefficient portfolio $\underset{\sim}{\alpha}$ instead of the orthogonal portfolio $\underset{\sim}{Q}$ as follows:

$$\underset{\sim}{\varepsilon} = \underset{\sim}{e} - \mu_Q \underset{\sim}{b} = \mu_Q(\underset{\sim}{\beta} - \underset{\sim}{b})$$

where $\underset{\sim}{e} = \mu_Q \underset{\sim}{\beta}$ is the perfectly linear relationship that exists between the vector of asset average returns $\underset{\sim}{e}$ and the betas $\underset{\sim}{\beta}$, computed relative to the chosen orthogonal portfolio $\underset{\sim}{Q}$. Now, if we pre-multiply this latter expression by $\underset{\sim}{Q}^T$ (which, it will be recalled, is the transpose of the vector whose elements are the proportionate investments in the N risky assets comprising the orthogonal portfolio) then it can be shown that the average error from basing the calculation of betas on the inefficient portfolio $\underset{\sim}{\alpha}$ will be

$$\underset{\sim}{Q}^T \cdot \underset{\sim}{\varepsilon} = (1 - R_{\alpha Q}^2)\mu_Q \geq 0$$

where

$$-1 \leqslant R_{\alpha Q} = \sqrt{\frac{\underset{\sim}{Q}^T \Omega \underset{\sim}{Q}}{\underset{\sim}{\alpha}^T \Omega \underset{\sim}{\alpha}}} \leqslant 1$$

is the coefficient of correlation between the return on the orthogonal portfolio $\underset{\sim}{Q}$ and the return on the inefficient portfolio $\underset{\sim}{\alpha}$. Here it will be recalled (as in §3-2) that $\sigma_Q^2 = \underset{\sim}{Q}^T \Omega \underset{\sim}{Q}$ is the variance of the return on the orthogonal (i.e. the Markowitz efficient) portfolio and $\sigma_\alpha^2 = \underset{\sim}{\alpha}^T \Omega \underset{\sim}{\alpha}$ is the variance of the return on the inefficient portfolio. Not surprisingly, the average error is inversely related to the square of the coefficient of correlation between the return on the inefficient portfolio and the return on the orthogonal portfolio, and will always be positive. If, however, we weight the error vector $\underset{\sim}{\varepsilon}$ by the proportionate investments comprising the inefficient portfolio $\underset{\sim}{\alpha}$ then the average error will be identically equal to zero: $\underset{\sim}{\alpha}^T \cdot \underset{\sim}{\varepsilon} = 0$.

§3-5. We can use the above analysis to specify a particular error vector and then determine the inefficient portfolio from which a set of betas may be computed that, when taken in conjunction with the error vector $\underset{\sim}{\varepsilon}$, will have a perfectly linear relationship with the average returns vector $\underset{\sim}{e}$. This in turn means that we can employ the analysis summarized here to determine the inefficient portfolio that leads to a pricing formula in which asset average returns are perfectly correlated with a linear sum of the size of the affected firm, the market-to-book ratio for its equity and/or any other set of variables that the empirical researcher wishes to argue are important determinants of asset prices. We have previously observed that this is of considerable importance in empirical research, where it is often necessary to build pricing formulae in which factors other than beta are interpreted as instrumental determinants of asset prices.

We now demonstrate the principles that lie behind the results summarized in previous sections by considering the five-asset ($N = 5$) portfolio with the following vector of average returns:

$$\underset{\sim}{e} = \begin{pmatrix} 0.10 \\ 0.15 \\ 0.20 \\ 0.25 \\ 0.30 \end{pmatrix}$$

Thus, the average return on the first asset is $e_1 = 0.10$ or 10 per cent. Likewise, the average return on the second asset is $e_2 = 0.15$ or 15 per cent, the average return on the third asset is $e_3 = 0.20$ or 20 per cent, and so on. The remaining entries in $\underset{\sim}{e}$ are to be similarly interpreted.

The matrix of empirical variances and covariances is given by

$$\Omega = \begin{pmatrix} 0.8 & 0.1 & 0.1 & 0.1 & 0.1 \\ 0.1 & 0.8 & 0.1 & 0.1 & 0.1 \\ 0.1 & 0.1 & 0.8 & 0.1 & 0.1 \\ 0.1 & 0.1 & 0.1 & 0.8 & 0.1 \\ 0.1 & 0.1 & 0.1 & 0.1 & 0.8 \end{pmatrix}$$

This shows that the variance of the return on the first asset is $\sigma_1^2 = 0.8$ whilst the covariance between the return on the first and the return on the second asset is $\sigma_{12} = 0.1 = \sigma_{21}$. The remaining entries in Ω are to be similarly interpreted. It is not hard to show that the Markowitz locus implied by the average returns vector $\underset{\sim}{e}$ and the variance–covariance matrix Ω given above is as follows:

$$\sigma_p = \sqrt{28\mu^2 - \frac{56}{5}\mu + \frac{34}{25}}$$

where $a = 28$, $b = -\frac{56}{5}$ and $c = \frac{34}{25}$ are the parameters characterizing the Markowitz locus and

$$\mu \geq E(R_0) = -\frac{b}{2a} = \frac{56}{2 \times 28 \times 5} = 0.2 = 20 \text{ per cent}$$

defines the average return on the global minimum-variance portfolio (as in §2-6 of Chapter 2).

§3-6. Now, using the results summarized in §2-8, we can use the parameters of the Markowitz locus to determine the slope parameter γ of the Capital Market Line:

$$\gamma = \sqrt{\frac{-4(R_f b + R_f^2 a + c)}{b^2 - 4ac}} = \sqrt{\frac{-4 \times \frac{34}{25}}{\left(\frac{56}{5}\right)^2 - 4 \times 28 \times \frac{34}{25}}} = \sqrt{\frac{17}{84}}$$

Note here that we have previously assumed (as in §3-2 above) that, for pedagogical reasons, $R_f = 0$ (i.e. the risk-free rate of interest is zero). These calculations will mean that the Capital Market Line takes the form

$$E(R_p) = \sqrt{\frac{17}{84}}\sigma_p$$

where $E(R_p)$ is the average return on a portfolio with a given proportionate investment in the risk-free asset and a complementary proportionate investment in the orthogonal portfolio, Q. Furthermore, using this result and the procedures summarized in §2-9, it follows that the average return on the orthogonal portfolio, Q, will be

$$\mu_Q = E(R_Q) = \frac{-(b\gamma^2 + 2R_f)}{2(a\gamma^2 - 1)} = \frac{\frac{56}{5} \times \frac{17}{84}}{2(28 \times \frac{17}{84} - 1)} = \frac{17}{70}$$

Finally, we can use the procedures summarized in §2-14 to show that the orthogonal portfolio is composed of the proportionate investments in the risky assets that are given in the following vector:

$$\underset{\sim}{Q} = \frac{1}{35}\begin{pmatrix} 1 \\ 4 \\ 7 \\ 10 \\ 13 \end{pmatrix}$$

This means the orthogonal portfolio is composed of a $Q_1 = \frac{1}{35}$ proportionate investment in the first asset, a $Q_2 = \frac{4}{35}$ proportionate investment in the second asset, a $Q_3 = \frac{7}{35}$ proportionate investment in the third asset, and so on. This in turn means that the variance of the return on the orthogonal will be $\sigma_Q^2 = \underset{\sim}{Q}^T \Omega \underset{\sim}{Q} = \frac{51}{175}$. We can then compute the vector of betas based on this orthogonal portfolio:

$$\underset{\sim}{\beta} = \frac{\Omega \underset{\sim}{Q}}{\underset{\sim}{Q}^T \Omega \underset{\sim}{Q}} = \frac{\frac{1}{50}\begin{pmatrix} 6 \\ 9 \\ 12 \\ 15 \\ 18 \end{pmatrix}}{\frac{51}{175}} = \frac{1}{34}\begin{pmatrix} 14 \\ 21 \\ 28 \\ 35 \\ 42 \end{pmatrix}$$

Hence, the beta for the first asset is $\beta_1 = \frac{14}{34} \approx 0.4118$, the beta for the second asset is $\beta_2 = \frac{21}{34} \approx 0.6176$, the beta for the third asset is $\beta_3 = \frac{28}{34} \approx 0.8235$, and so on. Moreover, the reader will be able to confirm that there is a perfectly linear relationship between the vector of average returns and the vector of betas on which the example is based:

$$\underset{\sim}{e} = \begin{pmatrix} 0.10 \\ 0.15 \\ 0.20 \\ 0.25 \\ 0.30 \end{pmatrix} = \frac{17}{70} \times \frac{1}{34}\begin{pmatrix} 14 \\ 21 \\ 28 \\ 35 \\ 42 \end{pmatrix} = \mu_Q \underset{\sim}{\beta}$$

Hence, if we desire to 'prove' that beta is a 'sufficient statistic' for the determination of risky asset average returns then we can leave the analysis here and go no further. A simple least-squares regression will show that there is a perfectly linear relationship between the average returns and betas based on the orthogonal portfolio. Other factors, such as firm size and the market-to-book ratio for equity, will add nothing to a regression based on these two variables. If, however, we want to build a pricing formula in which firm size, the market-to-book ratio or some other combination of variables can be viewed as instrumental determinants of asset prices then we can do so by basing the calculation of betas on an alternative and generally inefficient portfolio, as is now demonstrated.

§3-7. Consider then the set of generally inefficient portfolios $\underset{\sim}{\alpha}$ that have the same average return $\mu_Q = \underset{\sim}{Q}^T \cdot \underset{\sim}{e} = \frac{17}{70} = \underset{\sim}{\alpha}^T \cdot \underset{\sim}{e} = \mu_\alpha$ as the orthogonal portfolio $\underset{\sim}{Q}$ defined in

§3-6 above, namely,

$$\underset{\sim}{\alpha} = \underset{\sim}{Q} + \sum_{j=1}^{3} \psi_j \underset{\sim}{k_j} = \frac{1}{35}\begin{pmatrix} 1 \\ 4 \\ 7 \\ 10 \\ 13 \end{pmatrix} + \psi_1 \begin{pmatrix} 1 \\ -2 \\ 1 \\ 0 \\ 0 \end{pmatrix} + \psi_2 \begin{pmatrix} 2 \\ -3 \\ 0 \\ 1 \\ 0 \end{pmatrix} + \psi_3 \begin{pmatrix} 3 \\ -4 \\ 0 \\ 0 \\ 1 \end{pmatrix}$$

where ψ_1, ψ_2 and ψ_3 are parameters that can assume any numerical values and the arbitrage portfolios are determined in the manner of §3-4 above. Thus the first arbitrage portfolio in the above expression will be:

$$\underset{\sim}{k_1} = \begin{pmatrix} e_3 - e_2 \\ -(e_3 - e_1) \\ e_2 - e_1 \\ 0 \\ 0 \end{pmatrix} = \begin{pmatrix} 0.20 - 0.15 \\ -(0.20 - 0.10) \\ 0.15 - 0.10 \\ 0 \\ 0 \end{pmatrix} = \begin{pmatrix} 0.05 \\ -0.10 \\ 0.05 \\ 0 \\ 0 \end{pmatrix}$$

However, it facilitates our calculations if we scale the above vector by multiplying all its elements by 20, in which case we take $\underset{\sim}{k_1}$ to be equal to

$$20\begin{pmatrix} 0.05 \\ -0.10 \\ 0.05 \\ 0 \\ 0 \end{pmatrix} = \begin{pmatrix} 1 \\ -2 \\ 1 \\ 0 \\ 0 \end{pmatrix}$$

The arbitrage portfolios $\underset{\sim}{k_2}$ and $\underset{\sim}{k_3}$ are determined in a similar fashion, with both vectors again being scaled by multiplying all elements by 20. We can then use $\underset{\sim}{\alpha}$ in conjunction with the variance–covariance matrix Ω to determine the betas implied by these inefficient portfolios:

$$\underset{\sim}{b} = \frac{\Omega\underset{\sim}{\alpha}}{\underset{\sim}{\alpha}^T\Omega\underset{\sim}{\alpha}} = \frac{\frac{1}{50}\begin{pmatrix} 6 \\ 9 \\ 12 \\ 15 \\ 18 \end{pmatrix} + \psi_1 \begin{pmatrix} 0.7 \\ -1.4 \\ 0.7 \\ 0 \\ 0 \end{pmatrix} + \psi_2 \begin{pmatrix} 1.4 \\ -2.1 \\ 0 \\ 0.7 \\ 0 \end{pmatrix} + \psi_3 \begin{pmatrix} 2.1 \\ -2.8 \\ 0 \\ 0 \\ 0.7 \end{pmatrix}}{\frac{51}{175} + \frac{21}{5}\psi_1^2 + \frac{49}{5}\psi_2^2 + \frac{91}{5}\psi_3^2 + \frac{56}{5}\psi_1\psi_2 + \frac{77}{5}\psi_1\psi_3 + \frac{126}{5}\psi_2\psi_3}$$

Note that if one sets the three parameters ψ_1, ψ_2 and ψ_3 all to zero then the betas will be those obtained in §3-6 above for the orthogonal portfolio $\underset{\sim}{Q}$ and there will be a perfectly linear relationship between the betas and the average returns. When, however, any of ψ_1, ψ_2 and ψ_3 assume values other than zero, there is no longer a perfectly linear relationship between asset betas and their average returns. Moreover, prior analysis (as in §3-4) shows that the relationship between the error vector $\underset{\sim}{\varepsilon}$ and betas based on the orthogonal portfolio, $\underset{\sim}{\beta}$, and the inefficient portfolio, $\underset{\sim}{b}$, will be as follows:

$$\frac{1}{\mu_\alpha}.\underset{\sim}{\varepsilon} = \frac{1}{\mu_Q}.\underset{\sim}{\varepsilon} = \underset{\sim}{\beta} - \underset{\sim}{b}$$

where $\mu_Q = \underset{\sim}{Q}^T \cdot \underset{\sim}{e} = \underset{\sim}{\alpha}^T \cdot \underset{\sim}{e} = \mu_\alpha$ is the common average return on the orthogonal and inefficient portfolios, respectively. One can substitute the expression for $\underset{\sim}{b}$ given above and the expression for $\underset{\sim}{\beta}$ from §3-6 and thereby show that for the five-asset example considered here, the vector of errors

$$\underset{\sim}{\varepsilon} = \begin{pmatrix} \varepsilon_1 \\ \varepsilon_2 \\ \varepsilon_3 \\ \varepsilon_4 \\ \varepsilon_5 \end{pmatrix}$$

that will arise from basing the calculation of betas on the inefficient portfolio $\underset{\sim}{\alpha}$ will be

$$\frac{1}{\mu_\alpha}\underset{\sim}{\varepsilon} = \frac{1}{\mu_Q}\underset{\sim}{\varepsilon} = \underset{\sim}{\beta} - \underset{\sim}{b}$$

$$= \frac{70}{17}\begin{pmatrix} \varepsilon_1 \\ \varepsilon_2 \\ \varepsilon_3 \\ \varepsilon_4 \\ \varepsilon_5 \end{pmatrix} = \frac{1}{34}\begin{pmatrix} 14 \\ 21 \\ 28 \\ 35 \\ 42 \end{pmatrix} \frac{\frac{1}{50}\begin{pmatrix} 6 \\ 9 \\ 12 \\ 15 \\ 18 \end{pmatrix} + \psi_1\begin{pmatrix} 0.7 \\ -1.4 \\ 0.7 \\ 0 \\ 0 \end{pmatrix} + \psi_2\begin{pmatrix} 1.4 \\ -2.1 \\ 0 \\ 0.7 \\ 0 \end{pmatrix} + \psi_3\begin{pmatrix} 2.1 \\ -2.8 \\ 0 \\ 0 \\ 0.7 \end{pmatrix}}{\frac{51}{175} + \frac{21}{5}\psi_1^2 + \frac{49}{5}\psi_2^2 + \frac{91}{5}\psi_3^2 + \frac{56}{5}\psi_1\psi_2 + \frac{77}{5}\psi_1\psi_3 + \frac{126}{5}\psi_2\psi_3}$$

It is important to note that the error expression given here is based on five equations but that there are eight unknowns, namely, the components of the error vector ($\varepsilon_1, \varepsilon_2, \varepsilon_3$, ε_4 and ε_5) and the three parameters ψ_1, ψ_2 and ψ_3 that characterize the inefficient portfolio. Hence, three of these eight variables can be specified so as to satisfy exogenously specified criteria. More generally, if the analysis is based on Nassets then $N-2$ elements of the error vector $\underset{\sim}{\varepsilon}$ can be exogenously specified before the inefficient portfolio on which the asset pricing formula is to be based is determined. If, for example, the researcher determines that firm size and the market-to-book ratio are to be interpreted as important factors in the asset pricing process, then the researcher can specify numerical values for any $N-2$ elements of the error vector so that they accommodate this hypothesis perfectly. There will then be a perfectly linear relationship between the average returns for the $N-2$ firms for which the elements of the error vector have been specified and the factors (beta, firm size, market-to-book ratio, etc.) that the researcher stipulates are to be important in the asset pricing process. Moreover, since large samples typify the empirical research of the area, the two firms for which there will be an inexact relationship can have only a minor impact on the analysis and can safely be excluded from any subsequent work based on the sample.

§3-8. We can further illustrate the principles espoused here by supposing that an empirical researcher wants to determine an asset pricing formula in which a firm's liquidity is viewed as a significant determinant of the return that accrues to its equity holders. Liquidity is measured here by the (natural) logarithm of the firm's current ratio (i.e. the logarithm of current assets divided by current liabilities), and the researcher has specified that the coefficient associated with the liquidity variable in a multivariate average return/risk measures regression equation is to be as close to 5 as possible. The analysis in this chapter shows that the researcher will be able to determine an inefficient portfolio that implies betas that when taken in conjunction with the asset liquidity measures will have a perfectly linear relationship with the average return earned by $N - 2 = 3$ of the $N = 5$ assets on which the analysis is based. We can illustrate the computational procedures by supposing that the empirical researcher determines the logarithm of the current ratio for the third, fourth and fifth firms and summarizes them in the following vector:

$$\underset{\sim}{c} = \begin{pmatrix} c_1 \\ c_2 \\ c_3 \\ c_4 \\ c_5 \end{pmatrix} = \frac{1}{26{,}300} \begin{pmatrix} c_1 \\ c_2 \\ -53 \\ 125 \\ -37 \end{pmatrix}$$

Thus, the logarithms of the current ratio for the third, fourth and fifth firms are specified to be $c_3 = -\frac{53}{26{,}300}$, $c_4 = \frac{125}{26{,}300}$ and $c_5 = -\frac{37}{26{,}300}$, respectively. Now, it will be recalled that the researcher wants a coefficient of 5 to be associated with the logarithm of the current ratio in an empirically determined asset pricing formula that relates betas and the logarithm of the current ratio to asset average returns. Given this, the researcher will need to determine the inefficient portfolio that leads to the following error vector:

$$\underset{\sim}{\varepsilon} = 5\underset{\sim}{c} = \frac{1}{5{,}260} \begin{pmatrix} \varepsilon_1 \\ \varepsilon_2 \\ -53 \\ 125 \\ -37 \end{pmatrix}$$

We can substitute this vector into the expression for

$$\frac{1}{\mu_\alpha}\underset{\sim}{\varepsilon} = \frac{1}{\mu_Q}\underset{\sim}{\varepsilon} = \underset{\sim}{\beta} - \underset{\sim}{b}$$

given earlier (in §3-7) and thereby determine the five unknowns, namely,

$$\psi_1 = \frac{1}{35}, \quad \psi_2 = -\frac{1}{35}, \quad \psi_3 = \frac{1}{35}, \quad \varepsilon_1 = -\frac{154}{5{,}260}, \quad \varepsilon_2 = \frac{279}{5{,}260}$$

that will lead to betas that return an error vector with the desired components. Substituting the computed values for $\psi_1 = \frac{1}{35}$, $\psi_2 = -\frac{1}{35}$ and $\psi_3 = \frac{1}{35}$ into the expression for $\underset{\sim}{\alpha}$ (as given in §3-7) shows that the inefficient portfolio that will lead to betas that are compatible with the desired error vector $\underset{\sim}{\varepsilon}$ will be

$$\underset{\sim}{\alpha} = \frac{1}{35}\begin{pmatrix} 1 \\ 4 \\ 7 \\ 10 \\ 13 \end{pmatrix} + \frac{1}{35}\begin{pmatrix} 1 \\ -2 \\ 1 \\ 0 \\ 0 \end{pmatrix} - \frac{1}{35}\begin{pmatrix} 2 \\ -3 \\ 0 \\ 1 \\ 0 \end{pmatrix} + \frac{1}{35}\begin{pmatrix} 3 \\ -4 \\ 0 \\ 0 \\ 1 \end{pmatrix} = \frac{1}{35}\begin{pmatrix} 3 \\ 1 \\ 8 \\ 9 \\ 14 \end{pmatrix}$$

This in turn means the inefficient portfolio is composed of an $\alpha_1 = \frac{3}{35}$ proportionate investment in the first asset, an $\alpha_2 = \frac{1}{35}$ proportionate investment in the second asset, an $\alpha_3 = \frac{8}{35}$ proportionate investment in the third asset, and so on. This will also mean that the betas for this inefficient portfolio will be

$$\underset{\sim}{b} = \frac{\Omega \underset{\sim}{\alpha}}{\underset{\sim}{\alpha}^T \Omega \underset{\sim}{\alpha}} = \frac{1}{526}\begin{pmatrix} 280 \\ 210 \\ 455 \\ 490 \\ 665 \end{pmatrix}$$

Hence, the beta relative to the inefficient portfolio for the first asset is $b_1 = \frac{280}{526} \approx 0.5323$, the beta for the second asset is $b_2 = \frac{210}{526} \approx 0.3992$, the beta for the third asset is $b_3 = \frac{455}{526} \approx 0.8650$, and so on.

§3-9. As expected, the linear relationship between the average returns and betas predicted by the Capital Asset Pricing Model breaks down when betas are based on the inefficient portfolio detailed here. Indeed, the vector of errors (as in §3-4 and §3-7) that arise from basing the calculation of betas on the inefficient portfolio turns out to be

$$\underset{\sim}{\varepsilon} = \underset{\sim}{e} - \mu_\alpha \underset{\sim}{b} = \begin{pmatrix} 0.10 \\ 0.15 \\ 0.20 \\ 0.25 \\ 0.30 \end{pmatrix} - \frac{17}{70} \times \frac{1}{526}\begin{pmatrix} 280 \\ 210 \\ 455 \\ 490 \\ 665 \end{pmatrix} = \frac{1}{5{,}260}\begin{pmatrix} -154 \\ 279 \\ -53 \\ 125 \\ -37 \end{pmatrix} \neq \underset{\sim}{0}$$

Thus, the error in the Capital Asset Pricing Model associated with the first asset is $\varepsilon_1 = -\frac{154}{5{,}260}$, whilst the error associated with the second asset is $\varepsilon_2 = \frac{279}{5{,}260}$. More important, however, is that the errors associated with the third ($\varepsilon_3 = -\frac{53}{5{,}260}$), fourth ($\varepsilon_4 = \frac{125}{5{,}260}$) and fifth ($\varepsilon_5 = -\frac{37}{5{,}260}$) assets are exactly five times the logarithm of the given firm's current ratio as summarized in the vector $\underset{\sim}{c}$ detailed in §3-8 above. It will be recalled, however, that this is no coincidence, since the portfolio on which the calculation of betas is based was deliberately chosen to return a perfectly linear relationship between the average return, beta and logarithm of the current ratio for all but the first two firms on which the example is based. Thus, one can use the third, fourth and fifth elements of the vector of betas $\underset{\sim}{b}$ and the logarithm of the current ratio $\underset{\sim}{c}$ to confirm that there is a perfectly linear relationship between the average return, beta and the liquidity measure for the firms that appear in our example, namely,

$$\begin{pmatrix}\mu_3\\ \mu_4\\ \mu_5\end{pmatrix} = \begin{pmatrix}0.20\\ 0.25\\ 0.30\end{pmatrix} = \frac{17}{70}\times\frac{1}{526}\begin{pmatrix}455\\ 490\\ 665\end{pmatrix} + 5\times\frac{1}{26{,}300}\begin{pmatrix}-53\\ 125\\ -37\end{pmatrix}$$

$$= \mu_\alpha\begin{pmatrix}b_3\\ b_4\\ b_5\end{pmatrix} + 5\begin{pmatrix}c_3\\ c_4\\ c_5\end{pmatrix}$$

Of course, there is nothing unique about the asset pricing formula determined here. If, for whatever reason, the empirical researcher needs liquidity to play an even more significant role in the returns generating process then they could increase the coefficient associated with the liquidity variable in the error vector $\underset{\sim}{\varepsilon}$ and then determine the inefficient portfolio that returns betas $\underset{\sim}{b}$ that are compatible with the existence of a perfectly linear relationship between the average returns, betas and the revised and more prominent liquidity measures. Alternatively, if the researcher wants to interpret other variables, such as firm size and/or the market-to-book ratio for equity as being important determinants of asset prices then they can fix the coefficients associated with the vectors summarizing these two variables at the desired levels and thereby determine the required error vector $\underset{\sim}{\varepsilon}$. The researcher can then solve the equation (as in §3-4 and §3-7 above)

$$\frac{1}{\mu_\alpha}\underset{\sim}{\varepsilon} = \frac{1}{\mu_Q}\underset{\sim}{\varepsilon} = \underset{\sim}{\beta} - \underset{\sim}{b}$$

and in so doing determine the inefficient portfolio that leads to a set of betas $\underset{\sim}{b}$ that, when taken in conjunction with the vectors summarizing firm size and the market-to-book ratio, will have a perfectly linear relationship with the average returns vector.

The fundamental theorem on which our analysis in this chapter has so far been based is that an inefficient portfolio will always exist that is compatible with a pre-specified pricing formula in which factors other than beta appear to have a significant impact on asset prices. It is important to note, however, that whilst asset pricing formulae determined using procedures similar to this often perform well empirically, they require makeshift specifications of the set of priced factors. Moreover, since the set of potential factors is large, the researcher has considerable discretion over the formulae that may be constructed and investigated. This in turn will mean that tests based on such *ad hoc* assumptions will lack power and it is all but inevitable that there will be over-fitting of the data as well as factor dredging. Our analysis here shows just how easy it can be to construct asset pricing formulae that fit the data well, even though they ignore and often infringe the theoretical restrictions that arise from a properly specified structural model of the asset pricing process.

§3-10. Given this, we now focus our attention on a second and more theoretically plausible approach to asset pricing issues, namely, Arbitrage Pricing Theory (APT) and extensions of that theory. We should note at the beginning, however, that the APT is evocative of a general approach to asset pricing problems; that is, the APT does not involve a single or unique asset pricing formula. The basic assumption behind the APT is that it will never be possible to earn a riskless profit from a self-financing (i.e. a zero-cost) investment portfolio. We can demonstrate this basic principle by employing the arbitrage portfolios identified in

§3-7 above. Recall that the first of the arbitrage portfolios identified in §3-7 takes the form

$$\underset{\sim}{k}_1 = \begin{pmatrix} e_3 - e_2 \\ -(e_3 - e_1) \\ e_2 - e_1 \\ 0 \\ 0 \end{pmatrix}$$

where e_j is the expected return on the jth asset in the economy. This arbitrage portfolio implies that one invests $e_3 - e_2$ in the first asset, 'sells short' (i.e. makes a negative investment of) $e_3 - e_1$ in the second asset, and invests $e_2 - e_1$ in the third asset. Note that the total amount invested is $(e_3 - e_2) - (e_3 - e_1) + (e_2 - e_1) = 0$, in which case the arbitrage portfolio is self-financing and, as such, involves a net investment of zero. Moreover, the expected return on this arbitrage portfolio will be

$$\underset{\sim}{k}_1^T \cdot \underset{\sim}{e} = (e_3 - e_2)e_1 - (e_3 - e_1)e_2 + (e_2 - e_1)e_3 = 0$$

where $\underset{\sim}{k}_1^T$ is the transpose of the vector $\underset{\sim}{k}_1$ and $\underset{\sim}{e}$ is the vector whose elements are the expected returns on the risky assets comprising the economy (as in §3-4 and §3-7 above). Similar calculations show that $\underset{\sim}{k}_2, \underset{\sim}{k}_3$ and all the other arbitrage portfolios developed in §3-7 are self-financing portfolios with an expected return of zero. In other words, our analysis here shows that if one invests nothing, then one can expect to earn nothing in return. Now, a whole variety of arbitrage pricing models have arisen out of this basic assumption. Space limitations mean that we cannot illustrate them all here and so our focus will be on what is probably the most common of the models that appear under the APT rubric.

§3-11. We begin our consideration of APT by recalling from §2-3 of Chapter 2 that the variance of the return on a portfolio composed of N risky assets will be

$$\sigma_p^2 = \sum_{j=1}^{N} \sum_{k=1}^{N} w_j w_k \sigma_{jk}$$

where w_j and w_k are the proportionate investments in the jth and kth assets comprising the portfolio and σ_{jk} is the covariance between the return on the jth asset and the return on the kth asset. Disaggregating the above expression into its variance and covariance components, we have

$$\sigma_p^2 = \sum_{j=1}^{N} w_j^2 \sigma_j^2 + \sum_{\substack{j=1 \\ j \neq k}}^{N} \sum_{k=1}^{N} w_j w_k \sigma_{jk}$$

The first term on the right-hand side of this expression contains only the variances σ_j^2 of the returns on the individual assets comprising the portfolio, whilst the second term contains only the covariances σ_{jk} of the returns between the individual assets. Now, suppose one makes an equal proportionate investment, $w_j = 1/N = w_k$, in each of the N risky assets. Then the variance of the return on this equally weighted portfolio will be

$$\sigma_p^2 = \frac{1}{N^2}\sum_{j=1}^{N}\sigma_j^2 + \frac{1}{N^2}\sum_{\substack{j=1\\ j\neq k}}^{N}\sum_{k=1}^{N}\sigma_{jk}$$

Note, however, that an $N \times N$ variance–covariance matrix will have a total of N^2 variances and covariance terms. There will be N variances down the diagonal of the matrix and $N^2 - N$ covariances in the off-diagonal terms. Hence, the average of the individual asset variances will be

$$\overline{\sigma_j^2} = \frac{1}{N}\sum_{j=1}^{N}\sigma_j^2$$

Likewise, the average of the covariances will be

$$\overline{\sigma_{jk}} = \frac{1}{N^2 - N}\sum_{\substack{j=1\\ j\neq k}}^{N}\sum_{k=1}^{N}\sigma_{jk}$$

Substituting these two averages into the expression for the variance given above shows

$$\sigma_p^2 = \frac{\overline{\sigma_j^2}}{N} + \frac{N^2 - N}{N^2}\overline{\sigma_{jk}} = \overline{\sigma_{jk}} + \frac{\overline{\sigma_j^2} - \overline{\sigma_{jk}}}{N}$$

It thus follows that as we introduce more and more assets into the portfolio, we will have

$$\lim_{N\to\infty}\sigma_p^2 = \overline{\sigma_{jk}}$$

in other words, the variance of the return on the portfolio will depend exclusively on the covariances of the returns between the individual assets. That is, the variances of the returns on the individual assets, σ_j^2, will be diversified away and will play no role in determining the variance of the return on the portfolio as a whole, σ_p^2. Moreover, from §2-3, the average covariance will bear the following relationship to the average correlation coefficient and the average standard deviation of asset returns:

$$\overline{\sigma_{jk}} = \overline{\rho_{jk}}\left(\overline{\sigma_j}\right)\left(\overline{\sigma_k}\right)$$

where

$$\overline{\rho_{jk}} = \frac{1}{N^2 - N}\sum_{\substack{j=1\\ j\neq k}}^{N}\sum_{k=1}^{N}\rho_{jk}$$

is the average correlation coefficient and

$$\overline{\sigma_j} = \frac{1}{N}\sum_{j=1}^{N}\sigma_j = \frac{1}{N}\sum_{k=1}^{N}\sigma_k = \overline{\sigma_k}$$

is the average standard deviation of the returns across the N assets comprising the portfolio. This means that the above result can be restated as

$$\lim_{N\to\infty} \sigma_p^2 = \overline{\rho_{jk}}\left(\overline{\sigma_j}\right)^2$$

and this emphasizes the central role played by the correlation between the returns on the individual assets comprising the portfolio in determining the variance of the rate of return (or risk) on the portfolio as a whole.

§3-12. Given this, consider an economy composed of many assets and for which r_j is the return on the jth asset over a given period of time. Now define the standardized variable z_j, where

$$z_j = \frac{r_j - E(r_j)}{\sigma_j}$$

and $E(r_j)$ and σ_j are the expected return and the standard deviation of the return, respectively, for the jth asset. We can then determine the coefficient of correlation ρ_{jk} between the standardized returns on the jth and kth assets:

$$\rho_{jk} = E(z_j z_k) = \frac{E\{[r_j - E(r_j)][r_k - E(r_k)]\}}{\sigma_j \sigma_k}$$

where $E(\cdot)$ is the expectation operator. Note that when $j = k$, in which case we determine the correlation coefficient of the jth asset's standardized return with its own standardized return, we have

$$\rho_{jj} = E(z_j^2) = \frac{E\{[r_j - E(r_j)]^2\}}{\sigma_j^2} = \frac{\sigma_j^2}{\sigma_j^2} = 1$$

that is, the standardized variables z_j will all have unit variance. This will mean that our analysis is based on a portfolio in which all assets have unit variance, and so, from §3-11 above, the limiting variance of the standardized returns as more and more assets are added to the portfolio will be

$$\lim_{N\to\infty} \sigma_p^2 = \overline{\rho_{jk}}\left(\overline{\sigma_j}\right)^2 = \overline{\rho_{jk}}$$

Hence, once we have standardized the returns on the portfolio we need only concern ourselves with the correlation of the returns between the assets comprising the portfolio. Given this, we now consider a four-asset portfolio with the following correlation matrix:

$$R = \begin{pmatrix} 1 & 0.74 & 0.24 & 0.24 \\ 0.74 & 1 & 0.24 & 0.24 \\ 0.24 & 0.24 & 1 & 0.74 \\ 0.24 & 0.24 & 0.74 & 1 \end{pmatrix}$$

The off-diagonal entries ρ_{jk} for $j \neq k$ give the correlation between the return on the jth asset and the return on the kth asset, whilst, as we have just seen, the diagonal entries ρ_{jj} give the correlation between the *j*th asset's return and its own return and will therefore be equal to unity. Thus, from the above matrix, the correlation between the return on the second asset and the return on the first asset is $\rho_{21} = 0.74 = \rho_{12}$, as summarized in the second row and the first column of the above matrix. This will be the same as the correlation between the return on the first asset and the return on the second asset as given in the first row and second column of the above matrix. Thus, the matrix R is 'symmetric' in the sense that the entries above the diagonal (or unit variance terms) are a mirror image of the entries appearing below the diagonal terms.

Probably the most common approach to the APT is to use what is known as the 'characteristic polynomial' associated with a correlation matrix to identify a comparatively small number of 'factors' through which to account for the off-diagonal terms in the given correlation matrix. It is the off-diagonal terms, or the correlation between the returns of the individual assets comprising the portfolio, that are important, because, as we have just shown in §3-11, the diagonal terms, which encapsulate the variances of the returns on the individual assets, can be diversified away. The characteristic polynomial associated with a given square matrix R is defined by the equation

$$\det(R - \lambda I) = \det\begin{pmatrix} 1-\lambda & 0.74 & 0.24 & 0.24 \\ 0.74 & 1-\lambda & 0.24 & 0.24 \\ 0.24 & 0.24 & 1-\lambda & 0.74 \\ 0.24 & 0.24 & 0.74 & 1-\lambda \end{pmatrix} = 0$$

where $\det(R - \lambda I)$ is the determinant of the matrix $R - \lambda I$,

$$I = \begin{pmatrix} 1 & 0 & 0 & 0 \\ 0 & 1 & 0 & 0 \\ 0 & 0 & 1 & 0 \\ 0 & 0 & 0 & 1 \end{pmatrix}$$

is the identity matrix composed of unit entries down its diagonal and zeroes for all off-diagonal terms, and λ is called an eigenvalue of the matrix R. There are a variety of ways in which one can evaluate this determinant and thereby calculate the characteristic polynomial for an $N \times N$ matrix like this. One of the most computationally efficient of these techniques takes the form

$$\det(R - \lambda I) = (-1)^N(\lambda^N + c_1\lambda^{N-1} + c_2\lambda^{N-2} + c_3\lambda^{N-3} + \cdots + c_N)$$

where $c_1 = -\mathrm{tr}(R)$ and the trace, $\mathrm{tr}(R)$, is the sum of the diagonal elements of the matrix R. The other constants associated with the characteristic polynomial are determined from the following formulae:

$$c_2 = -\frac{c_1\mathrm{tr}(R) + \mathrm{tr}(R^2)}{2}$$

$$c_3 = -\frac{c_2\mathrm{tr}(R) + c_1\mathrm{tr}(R^2) + \mathrm{tr}(R^3)}{3}$$

$$c_4 = -\frac{c_3\text{tr}(R) + c_2\text{tr}(R^2) + c_1\text{tr}(R^3) + \text{tr}(R^4)}{4}$$

$$\vdots$$

$$c_N = -\frac{c_{N-1}\text{tr}(R) + c_{N-2}\text{tr}(R^2) + c_{N-3}\text{tr}(R^3) + \cdots + \text{tr}(R^N)}{N}$$

where again the trace, $\text{tr}(R^k)$, is the sum of the diagonal elements of the matrix R raised to the kth power.

§3-13. Now we can apply this result to the matrix R given in §3-12 above. We begin by noting that the trace of the correlation matrix R is given by the sum of its diagonal elements, $\text{tr}(R) = 1+1+1+1 = 4 \times 1 = 4$, since we have standardized all returns and thus all assets have unit variances. It then follows that the first coefficient associated with the characteristic polynomial for R will be $c_1 = -\text{tr}(R) = -4$. Moreover, we can square the matrix R, in which case we have

$$R^2 = R \times R = \begin{pmatrix} 1 & 0.74 & 0.24 & 0.24 \\ 0.74 & 1 & 0.24 & 0.24 \\ 0.24 & 0.24 & 1 & 0.74 \\ 0.24 & 0.24 & 0.74 & 1 \end{pmatrix} \begin{pmatrix} 1 & 0.74 & 0.24 & 0.24 \\ 0.74 & 1 & 0.24 & 0.24 \\ 0.24 & 0.24 & 1 & 0.74 \\ 0.24 & 0.24 & 0 & 1 \end{pmatrix}$$

or, equivalently,

$$R^2 = \begin{pmatrix} 1.6628 & 1.5952 & 0.8352 & 0.8352 \\ 1.5952 & 1.6628 & 0.8352 & 0.8352 \\ 0.8352 & 0.8352 & 1.6628 & 1.5952 \\ 0.8352 & 0.8352 & 1.5952 & 1.6628 \end{pmatrix}$$

It then follows that the trace of the square of the matrix R is given by $\text{tr}(R^2) = 4 \times 1.6628 = 6.6512$. Using this result, we have that the second coefficient associated with the characteristic polynomial for R will be

$$c_2 = -\frac{c_1\text{tr}(R) + \text{tr}(R^2)}{2} = -\frac{-4 \times 4 + 6.6512}{2} = 4.6744$$

Likewise, we can compute the cube of the matrix R, in which case we have

$$R^3 = R^2 \times R = \begin{pmatrix} 1.6628 & 1.5952 & 0.8352 & 0.8352 \\ 1.5952 & 1.6628 & 0.8352 & 0.8352 \\ 0.8352 & 0.8352 & 1.6628 & 1.5952 \\ 0.8352 & 0.8352 & 1.5952 & 1.6628 \end{pmatrix} \begin{pmatrix} 1 & 0.74 & 0.24 & 0.24 \\ 0.74 & 1 & 0.24 & 0.24 \\ 0.24 & 0.24 & 1 & 0.74 \\ 0.24 & 0.24 & 0.74 & 1 \end{pmatrix}$$

or, equivalently,

$$R^3 = \begin{pmatrix} 3.244144 & 3.226568 & 2.235168 & 2.235168 \\ 3.226568 & 3.244144 & 2.235168 & 2.235168 \\ 2.235168 & 2.235168 & 3.244144 & 3.226568 \\ 2.235168 & 2.235168 & 3.226568 & 3.244144 \end{pmatrix}$$

It then follows that the trace of the cube of R is given by $\text{tr}(R^3) = 4 \times 3.244144 = 12.976576$. We can use this result to show that the third coefficient associated with the characteristic polynomial for R will be

$$c_3 = -\frac{c_2\text{tr}(R) + c_1\text{tr}(R^2) + \text{tr}(R^3)}{3} = -\frac{4.6744 \times 4 - 4 \times 6.6512 + 12.976576}{3}$$
$$= -1.68979$$

To determine the final coefficient for the characteristic polynomial, we first raise R to the fourth power:

$$R^4 = R^3 \times R = \begin{pmatrix} 6.704685 & 6.700115 & 5.442163 & 5.442163 \\ 6.700115 & 6.704685 & 5.442163 & 5.442163 \\ 5.442163 & 5.442163 & 6.704685 & 6.700115 \\ 5.442163 & 5.442163 & 6.700115 & 6.704685 \end{pmatrix}$$

It then follows that $\text{tr}(R^4) = 4 \times 6.704685 = 26.81874$. Using this result shows that the final coefficient associated with the characteristic polynomial for R will be

$$c_4 = -\frac{c_3\text{tr}(R) + c_2\text{tr}(R^2) + c_1\text{tr}(R^3) + \text{tr}(R^4)}{4}$$
$$= -\frac{(-1.68979 \times 4 + 4.6744 \times 6.6512 - 4 \times 12.976576 + 26.81874)}{4} = 0.189089$$

Bringing these results together shows that the characteristic polynomial for the matrix R will be

$$\det(R - \lambda I) = (-1)^N(\lambda^N + c_1\lambda^{N-1} + c_2\lambda^{N-2} + \cdots + c_N)$$
$$= \lambda^4 - 4\lambda^3 + 4.6744\lambda^2 - 1.68979\lambda + 0.189089 = 0$$

Now we can plot this characteristic polynomial and thereby determine its roots, that is, the eigenvalues λ of the matrix R, as portrayed in Figure 3.2. This diagram shows that the roots of the characteristic polynomial, and hence the eigenvalues of R, are $\lambda = 0.26$, $\lambda = 1.26$ and $\lambda = 2.22$, the first of these being a repeated root or eigenvalue. This in turn implies that the characteristic polynomial for R has the following alternative representation:

$$\det(R - \lambda I) = (\lambda - 2.22)(\lambda - 1.26)(\lambda - 0.26)^2 = 0$$

The relative size of the roots (i.e. the eigenvalues) associated with the characteristic polynomial provide a fundamental measure of the importance of a given factor in accounting for the off-diagonal terms in the correlation matrix R. Moreover, the loadings on the individual assets associated with each factor comprising the economy are determined by calculating the eigenvectors associated with each of the eigenvalues.

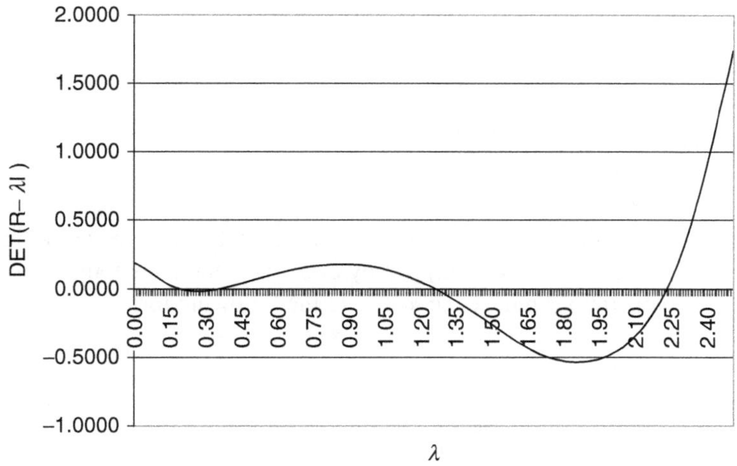

Figure 3.2 Roots of the characteristic polynomial

$$\lambda^4 - 4\lambda^3 + 4.6744\lambda^2 - 1.68979\lambda + 0.189089 = (\lambda - 2.22)(\lambda - 1.26)(\lambda - 0.26)^2 = 0$$

§3-14. We begin with the most important factor; namely, that associated with the largest eigenvalue, $\lambda = 2.22$. Substituting this eigenvalue into the expression from which the characteristic polynomial is derived shows

$$\det(R - \lambda I) = \begin{pmatrix} 1-\lambda & 0.74 & 0.24 & 0.24 \\ 0.74 & 1-\lambda & 0.24 & 0.24 \\ 0.24 & 0.24 & 1-\lambda & 0.74 \\ 0.24 & 0.24 & 0.74 & 1-\lambda \end{pmatrix} = \begin{pmatrix} -1.22 & 0.74 & 0.24 & 0.24 \\ 0.74 & -1.22 & 0.24 & 0.24 \\ 0.24 & 0.24 & -1.22 & 0.74 \\ 0.24 & 0.24 & 0.74 & -1.22 \end{pmatrix}$$

We now determine the eigenvector associated with this eigenvalue by using row operations to reduce the matrix on the right-hand side of the above equation to what is known as its row echelon form. Hence, adding the first row of the matrix on the right-hand side of this equation to the second row of the same matrix gives

$$\begin{pmatrix} -1.22 & 0.74 & 0.24 & 0.24 \\ -0.48 & -0.48 & 0.48 & 0.48 \\ 0.24 & 0.24 & -1.22 & 0.74 \\ 0.24 & 0.24 & 0.74 & -1.22 \end{pmatrix}$$

Next, we add the third row of the matrix on the right-hand side of the equation for $\det(R - \lambda I)$ to the fourth row of the same matrix. This operation reduces the matrix to the following form:

$$\begin{pmatrix} -1.22 & 0.74 & 0.24 & 0.24 \\ -0.48 & -0.48 & 0.48 & 0.48 \\ 0.24 & 0.24 & -1.22 & 0.74 \\ 0.48 & 0.48 & -0.48 & -0.48 \end{pmatrix}$$

We now divide every element of the second and fourth rows of this matrix by 0.48, which then gives

$$\begin{pmatrix} -1.22 & 0.74 & 0.24 & 0.24 \\ -1 & -1 & 1 & 1 \\ 0.24 & 0.24 & -1.22 & 0.74 \\ 1 & 1 & -1 & -1 \end{pmatrix}$$

Now, we subtract 0.24 multiplied by every element in the second row of the above matrix from the first row. We also subtract 0.24 multiplied by every element in the fourth row from the third row. These two operations reduce the matrix to the following form:

$$\begin{pmatrix} -0.98 & 0.98 & 0 & 0 \\ -1 & -1 & 1 & 1 \\ 0 & 0 & -0.98 & 0.98 \\ 1 & 1 & -1 & -1 \end{pmatrix}$$

We can then divide every element of the first and third rows of this matrix by 0.98, in which case we have

$$\begin{pmatrix} -1 & 1 & 0 & 0 \\ -1 & -1 & 1 & 1 \\ 0 & 0 & -1 & 1 \\ 1 & 1 & -1 & -1 \end{pmatrix}$$

Now, we add the second row of this matrix to the fourth row, giving

$$\begin{pmatrix} -1 & 1 & 0 & 0 \\ -1 & -1 & 1 & 1 \\ 0 & 0 & -1 & 1 \\ 0 & 0 & 0 & 0 \end{pmatrix}$$

Next, we subtract the first row of this matrix from the second row and then add the third row to the second row. These two operations reduce the matrix to the following form:

$$\begin{pmatrix} -1 & 1 & 0 & 0 \\ 0 & -2 & 0 & 2 \\ 0 & 0 & -1 & 1 \\ 0 & 0 & 0 & 0 \end{pmatrix}$$

We can then multiply through each row of this matrix by –1 and also divide the second row by 2, thereby giving

$$\begin{pmatrix} 1 & -1 & 0 & 0 \\ 0 & 1 & 0 & -1 \\ 0 & 0 & 1 & -1 \\ 0 & 0 & 0 & 0 \end{pmatrix}$$

Finally, adding the second row to the first row of this matrix gives what is known as the row echelon form of the matrix, namely,

$$\begin{pmatrix} 1 & 0 & 0 & -1 \\ 0 & 1 & 0 & -1 \\ 0 & 0 & 1 & -1 \\ 0 & 0 & 0 & 0 \end{pmatrix}$$

Note that if a matrix is stated in row echelon form, the leading coefficient of a non-zero row is always strictly to the right of the leading coefficient of the row above it. Moreover, the elements of the matrix below the leading coefficient of a non-zero row are all zero.

§3-15. We now let

$$\underset{\sim}{x} = \begin{pmatrix} x_1 \\ x_2 \\ x_3 \\ x_4 \end{pmatrix}$$

be the eigenvector associated with the eigenvalue $\lambda = 2.22$. It then follows that the eigenvector $\underset{\sim}{x}$ will bear the following relationship to the row echelon form of the matrix $R - \lambda I$ developed in the previous section:

$$\begin{pmatrix} 1 & 0 & 0 & -1 \\ 0 & 1 & 0 & -1 \\ 0 & 0 & 1 & -1 \\ 0 & 0 & 0 & 0 \end{pmatrix} \begin{pmatrix} x_1 \\ x_2 \\ x_3 \\ x_4 \end{pmatrix} = \begin{pmatrix} 0 \\ 0 \\ 0 \\ 0 \end{pmatrix}$$

This in turn implies that $x_1 = x_2 = x_3 = x_4$. Hence, if we let $x_4 = 1$ then it follows that, apart from a scaling constant, the eigenvector associated with the eigenvalue $\lambda = 2.22$ will take the following form:

$$\underset{\sim}{x} = \begin{pmatrix} 1 \\ 1 \\ 1 \\ 1 \end{pmatrix}$$

The reader will be able to confirm that similar procedures to those summarized above and in §3-14 show that the eigenvector associated with the eigenvalue $\lambda = 1.26$ turns out to be

$$\underset{\sim}{x} = \begin{pmatrix} 1 \\ 1 \\ -1 \\ -1 \end{pmatrix}$$

Finally, the eigenvalue $\lambda = 0.26$ is a repeated root of the characteristic polynomial associated with the correlation matrix R. There are two eigenvectors associated with this eigenvalue, namely,

$$\underset{\sim}{x} = \begin{pmatrix} -1 \\ 1 \\ 0 \\ 0 \end{pmatrix} \text{ and } \underset{\sim}{x} = \begin{pmatrix} 0 \\ 0 \\ -1 \\ 1 \end{pmatrix}$$

Now, we have previously noted (in §3-13) how the relative magnitudes of the eigenvalues obtained by determining the roots of the characteristic polynomial provide a fundamental measure of the importance of a given factor in accounting for the off-diagonal terms in the correlation matrix R. Given this, suppose that we use the eigenvectors associated with the two largest eigenvalues, $\lambda = 2.22$ and $\lambda = 1.26$, to account for the off-diagonal terms in the correlation matrix R. Here it will be recalled that we have determined all four eigenvalues for R except for a scaling constant. Given this, we multiply each element of the eigenvector associated with the eigenvalue $\lambda = 2.22$ by 0.7, in which case we have

$$0.7\begin{pmatrix} 1 \\ 1 \\ 1 \\ 1 \end{pmatrix} = \begin{pmatrix} 0.7 \\ 0.7 \\ 0.7 \\ 0.7 \end{pmatrix}$$

We also multiply each element of the eigenvector associated with the eigenvalue $\lambda = 1.26$ by 0.5, in which case we have

$$0.5\begin{pmatrix} 1 \\ 1 \\ -1 \\ -1 \end{pmatrix} = \begin{pmatrix} 0.5 \\ 0.5 \\ -0.5 \\ -0.5 \end{pmatrix}$$

We then form the matrix U whose columns are composed of the two scaled eigenvectors:

$$U = \begin{pmatrix} 0.7 & 0.5 \\ 0.7 & 0.5 \\ 0.7 & -0.5 \\ 0.7 & -0.5 \end{pmatrix}$$

Direct calculation then shows

$$R = UU^T + 0.26I$$

or

$$R = \begin{pmatrix} 1 & 0.74 & 0.24 & 0.24 \\ 0.74 & 1 & 0.24 & 0.24 \\ 0.24 & 0.24 & 1 & 0.74 \\ 0.24 & 0.24 & 0.74 & 1 \end{pmatrix}$$

$$= \begin{pmatrix} 0.7 & 0.5 \\ 0.7 & 0.5 \\ 0.7 & -0.5 \\ 0.7 & -0.5 \end{pmatrix} \begin{pmatrix} 0.7 & 0.7 & 0.7 & 0.7 \\ 0.5 & 0.5 & -0.5 & -0.5 \end{pmatrix} + 0.26 \begin{pmatrix} 1 & 0 & 0 & 0 \\ 0 & 1 & 0 & 0 \\ 0 & 0 & 1 & 0 \\ 0 & 0 & 0 & 1 \end{pmatrix}$$

$$= \begin{pmatrix} 0.74 & 0.74 & 0.24 & 0.24 \\ 0.74 & 0.74 & 0.24 & 0.24 \\ 0.24 & 0.24 & 0.74 & 0.74 \\ 0.24 & 0.24 & 0.74 & 0.74 \end{pmatrix} + \begin{pmatrix} 0.26 & 0 & 0 & 0 \\ 0 & 0.26 & 0 & 0 \\ 0 & 0 & 0.26 & 0 \\ 0 & 0 & 0 & 0.26 \end{pmatrix}$$

where, it will be recalled, U^T is the transpose of the matrix U and I is the identity matrix. The important point to be made here is that we have been able to completely account for the off-diagonal terms of the correlation matrix R with just two eigenvectors. We have previously noted (in §3-11 and §3-12) that it is the off-diagonal terms, or the correlation between the returns of the individual assets comprising the portfolio, that are important, because the diagonal terms, which encapsulate the variances of the returns on the individual assets, can always be diversified away. However, identifying the important factors, or eigenvectors, is one thing; interpreting what these eigenvectors might mean is a much more difficult task.

§3-16. Here, we can note that to obtain the above result we had to scale the eigenvalue associated with the eigenvector $\lambda = 2.22$ by 0.7 so that its elements are composed of the following factor loadings:

$$\begin{pmatrix} 0.7 \\ 0.7 \\ 0.7 \\ 0.7 \end{pmatrix}$$

Hence, this first factor encompasses the same loading (0.7) across all four assets comprising the economy. Recall from §3-11 and §3-12 above that as assets are added to an equally weighted portfolio, the variance of the (standardized) rate of return on the portfolio asymptotically declines towards the average correlation coefficient for the portfolio as a whole. Thus, the equal loadings associated with all elements of this factor lead one to interpret it as a 'market' or 'diversification' factor.

The second eigenvector, $\lambda = 1.26$, leads to the following factor loadings:

$$\begin{pmatrix} 0.5 \\ 0.5 \\ -0.5 \\ -0.5 \end{pmatrix}$$

Thus, whilst in absolute terms this factor encompasses equal loadings across all four assets, it draws a clear distinction between the equal loadings for the first two assets and the equal but negative loadings for the last two assets. This suggests that the first two assets are from similar industrial classifications and that the last two assets are also from similar but very different industrial classifications when compared with the first two assets. Thus, one can demonstrate the significance of this factor by supposing that the first two firms are drawn from (say) the Heavy Industries sector (for example, steel and/or forging) whilst the last two firms operate in (say) the Services Industry (for example, tourism or financial services). This factor could then be interpreted as a kind of 'Heavy Industries versus Services Industries' factor, since it distinguishes the very strong correlation between the returns earned by the two firms operating in the Heavy Industries sector and the returns earned by the two firms operating in the Services Industry sector. Moreover, it can be seen from the diagonal entries of the matrix

UU^T in §3-15 that these two factors associated with the eigenvalues $\lambda = 2.22$ and $\lambda = 1.26$, respectively, account for 74 per cent of the variances of the returns of the individual firms comprising the economy. These are the so-called 'communalities' in the factor model and measure the proportion of the variance in the rate of return on the particular asset that is explained by the two factors on which our factor model is based. Low communalities are not necessarily interpreted as evidence of a poorly fitting factor model, but merely as evidence that the returns on the assets comprising the economy have little in common with each other. This captures the essential feature of what is known as a strict factor model, namely, that the correlation matrix can be decomposed into a matrix composed of underlying factors, UU^T, and a second diagonal matrix composed only of idiosyncratic variance terms.

§3-17. We began this chapter by demonstrating how an empirical researcher can determine the inefficient portfolio that yields a set of betas that, when taken in conjunction with such other factors as the researcher stipulates are to be important in the asset pricing process (e.g. firm size, market-to-book ratios, etc.), will be perfectly correlated with the average returns earned by the firms on which the empirical analysis is based. This places the largely makeshift nature of the asset pricing formulae that characterize the empirical research of this area of the literature onto a similar footing to the Capital Asset Pricing Model in the sense that asset average returns have a perfectly linear relationship with the selected risk factors deemed to be important in the asset pricing process. We note, however, that whilst asset pricing formulae determined using procedures similar to this often perform well empirically, they require arbitrary specifications of the set of priced factors. Moreover, since the set of potential factors is large, the researcher has considerable discretion over the model to be investigated. This in turn can lead to tests that lack power, and the possibility exists for over-fitting the data and factor dredging. Our analysis has shown just how easy it can be to construct asset pricing formulae that fit the data well, even though they ignore and often infringe theoretical restrictions that arise from a properly developed structural model of the asset pricing process.

We then shifted our focus towards a second and more theoretically plausible approach to asset pricing issues, namely, the Arbitrage Pricing Theory (APT). The basic assumption behind the APT is that it will never be possible to earn riskless profits from a zero-cost portfolio. We then show how this leads to a general approach to asset pricing problems; that is, the APT does not involve a single or unique asset pricing formula. Probably the most common of the APT models employs what is known as the 'characteristic polynomial' associated with the correlation matrix for a particular portfolio of assets to identify a comparatively small number of 'factors' through which to account for the off-diagonal terms in the given correlation matrix. This captures the essential feature of a strict factor model, namely, that the correlation matrix can be decomposed into a matrix composed of underlying factors and a second diagonal matrix composed only of idiosyncratic variance terms. One can then use this model to distinguish the non-diversifiable (or factor component) of portfolio risk from the diversifiable (or idiosyncratic) component of portfolio risk.

Selected references

Ashton, D. and Tippett, M. (1998) 'Systematic risk and empirical research', *Journal of Business Finance and Accounting*, 25: 1325–56.

Bai, J. and Ng, S. (2002) 'Determining the number of factors in approximate factor models' *Econometrica*, 70: 191–221.

Brisley, W. (1973) *A Basis for Linear Algebra*, Sydney: Wiley.

Chamberlain, G. and Rothschild, M. (1983) 'Arbitrage, factor structure, and mean variance analysis on large asset markets', *Econometrica*, 51: 1281–304.

Connor, G. (1995) 'The three types of factor models: A comparison of their explanatory power', *Financial Analysts Journal*, 51: 42–6.

Davidson, I., Guo, Q., Song, X. and Tippett, M. (2012) 'Determining asset pricing models with specific factor loadings', *Abacus*, 48: 199–213.

Fama, E. and French, K. (1992) 'The cross-section of expected stock returns', *Journal of Finance*, 47: 427–65.

Fama, E. and French, K. (1993) 'Common factors in the returns on stocks and bonds', *Journal of Financial Economics*, 33: 3–56.

Onatski, A. (2009) 'Testing hypotheses about the number of factors in large factor models', *Econometrica*, 77: 1447–79.

Roll, R. (1977) 'A critique of the asset pricing theory's tests – I', *Journal of Financial Economics*, 4: 129–76.

Ross, S. (1976) 'The arbitrage theory of capital asset pricing, *Journal of Economic Theory*, 13: 341–60.

Exercises

1. Let $\underset{\sim}{e}$ be the $N \times 1$ vector whose elements are the average returns on a set of risky assets. Let Ω be the $N \times N$ matrix whose diagonal elements are the variances of the asset returns and whose off-diagonal terms are the covariances of the returns between the assets. Consider the proportionate investments vector

$$\underset{\sim}{\alpha} = \underset{\sim}{Q} + \sum_{j=1}^{N-2} \psi_j \underset{\sim}{k}_j$$

where $\underset{\sim}{Q}$ is the vector of proportionate investments for an orthogonal portfolio that has an average return of $\underset{\sim}{Q}^T \cdot \underset{\sim}{e} = \mu_Q$, the $\underset{\sim}{k}_j$ are the self-financing 'kernel' or 'arbitrage' portfolios defined in §3-4 and the ψ_j are parameters that can take on any numerical value. Use this result to show that

$$\underset{\sim}{\alpha}^T \Omega \underset{\sim}{Q} = \underset{\sim}{Q}^T \Omega \underset{\sim}{Q} = \underset{\sim}{Q}^T \Omega \underset{\sim}{\alpha}$$

and hence that the coefficient of correlation $R_{\alpha Q}$ between the return on the portfolio $\underset{\sim}{\alpha}$ and the return on the orthogonal portfolio $\underset{\sim}{Q}$ will be

$$R_{\alpha Q} = \sqrt{\frac{\underset{\sim}{Q}^T \Omega \underset{\sim}{Q}}{\underset{\sim}{\alpha}^T \Omega \underset{\sim}{\alpha}}}$$

Use this latter result to show that if

$$\underset{\sim}{b} = \frac{\Omega \underset{\sim}{\alpha}}{\underset{\sim}{\alpha}^T \Omega \underset{\sim}{\alpha}}$$

is the vector of betas relative to the portfolio $\underset{\sim}{\alpha}$ then $\underset{\sim}{Q}^T \cdot \underset{\sim}{b} = R^2_{\alpha Q}$. Moreover, use this result to show that the weighted average error from basing the calculation of betas on the inefficient portfolio can be expressed as

$$\underset{\sim}{Q}^T \cdot \underset{\sim}{\varepsilon} = \underset{\sim}{Q}^T \cdot \underset{\sim}{e} - \mu_Q \underset{\sim}{Q}^T \cdot \underset{\sim}{b} = (1 - R^2_{\alpha Q})\mu_Q \geq 0$$

2. The variance–covariance matrix for a three-asset portfolio takes the following form:

$$\Omega = \begin{pmatrix} 0.7 & -0.2 & 0.1 \\ -0.2 & 1.0 & -0.2 \\ 0.1 & -0.2 & 0.7 \end{pmatrix}$$

Moreover, the average returns on the three assets comprising the portfolio are summarized in the following average returns vector:

$$\underset{\sim}{e} = \begin{pmatrix} 0.10 \\ 0.15 \\ 0.20 \end{pmatrix}$$

Consider the vector of proportionate investments defined by

$$\underset{\sim}{\alpha} = \begin{pmatrix} \frac{2}{9} \\ \frac{1}{3} \\ \frac{4}{9} \end{pmatrix} + \psi \begin{pmatrix} 1 \\ -2 \\ 1 \end{pmatrix}$$

where ψ is a parameter that can take on any numerical value. Show that the portfolios defined by $\underset{\sim}{\alpha}$ all have an average return of $E(R_p) = \frac{29}{180} = 16\frac{1}{9}$ per cent. Compute the vector of betas,

$$\underset{\sim}{b} = \frac{\Omega\underset{\sim}{\alpha}}{\underset{\sim}{\alpha}^T \Omega \underset{\sim}{\alpha}}$$

based on these inefficient portfolios. Determine the value of ψ that minimizes the variance of the return on the portfolio $\underset{\sim}{\alpha}$ and hence determine the orthogonal portfolio $\underset{\sim}{Q}$.

3. Determine the characteristic polynomial of the three-asset variance–covariance matrix Ω given in Exercise 2. Use the characteristic polynomial to determine the eigenvalues of Ω. Use the eigenvector

$$\underset{\sim}{x} = \begin{pmatrix} x_1 \\ x_2 \\ x_3 \end{pmatrix}$$

associated with the largest eigenvector to show that Ω can be disaggregated into the following form:

$$\Omega = 0.1\underset{\sim}{x}\underset{\sim}{x}^T + 0.6I$$

where I is the identity matrix. What are the communalities associated with this factor model? Are the communalities to be interpreted as evidence of a poorly fitting factor model?

4. Show that the following result holds for the three-asset variance–covariance matrix Ω given in Exercise 2:

$$G^{-1}\Omega G = G^T\Omega G = P$$

where P is the matrix whose off-diagonal elements are all zero and whose diagonal elements are the eigenvalues of Ω, and

$$G = \begin{pmatrix} \frac{1}{\sqrt{6}} & \frac{1}{\sqrt{2}} & \frac{1}{\sqrt{3}} \\ \frac{-2}{\sqrt{6}} & 0 & \frac{1}{\sqrt{3}} \\ \frac{1}{\sqrt{6}} & \frac{-1}{\sqrt{2}} & \frac{1}{\sqrt{3}} \end{pmatrix}$$

Interpret this result in light of the answer you obtained to Exercise 3.

5. Define the norm of the vector $\underset{\sim}{u}$ as $||\underset{\sim}{u}|| = \sqrt{\underset{\sim}{u}^T \cdot \underset{\sim}{u}}$. Then, from Fourier's Theorem,

$$\left\| \underset{\sim}{e} - \sum_{j=1}^{k} \psi_j \underset{\sim}{x}_j \right\|^2 = \|\underset{\sim}{e}\|^2 - \sum_{j=1}^{k} \psi_j^2$$

where $\underset{\sim}{e}$ is the vector whose elements are the average returns on the $N \geq k$ assets comprising a portfolio, $\psi_j = \underset{\sim}{e}^T \cdot \underset{\sim}{x}_j$ and the $\underset{\sim}{x}_j$ are the eigenvectors associated with the variance–covariance matrix Ω, but scaled so that $\|\underset{\sim}{x}_j\| = \sqrt{\underset{\sim}{x}_j^T \cdot \underset{\sim}{x}_j} = 1$. Use the above result and the variance–covariance matrix employed in Exercises 2–4 to show that

$$\|\underset{\sim}{e}\|^2 = \sum_{j=1}^{3} \psi_j^2$$

a result that is known as Parseval's relation. Explain how Parseval's relation can be used to construct approximate factor models of the asset pricing process.

4 Returns and the capital structure of the firm

§4-1. Previous chapters have examined how returns ought to be calculated and averaged and have summarized the relationships one might expect to find between average returns and the various risk measures encountered in the literature. Our purpose in this chapter is to focus on a risk measure that empirical research has shown to have an instrumental association with equity returns, namely, the ratio of the debt and equity with which firms finance their operating activities. Moreover, company law provides that debt holders receive preferential treatment over equity holders in the payment of income (interest and dividends) and capital. This in turn will mean that an investment in equity is more risky than an investment in debt, and so equity holders will demand a higher return on their investment as compensation for the extra risk they are required to take.

Now, it is often suggested that firms can use the 'wedge' between the lower return on debt and the higher return required by equity holders to minimize the overall cost of financing their productive activities. We can illustrate the reasoning that lies behind this idea by supposing a firm is initially financed completely by equity. If the firm issues a small amount of debt and uses the proceeds to redeem (i.e. retire) some of its equity then the firm's cost of capital will decline because the return it has to pay to its new debt holders will be less than the return it would have had to pay to its former equity holders. The downside to replacing debt with equity is that the firm can always omit dividend payments to its equity holders during times of financial stress. In contrast, it must always pay the interest due to its debt holders – irrespective of how difficult its financial position might become. But since the debt issued by the firm is relatively small in relation to the equity it has on issue, there ought to be no significant increases in the firm's overall risk from this new debt issue. So, we have a marginally lower cost of servicing the firm's capital without any appreciable increase in risk as a result of replacing a small proportion of the firm's equity with this new issue of debt.

We can continue in this vein of substituting small amounts of debt for small amounts of equity, and a similar argument shows that the cost of servicing the firm's capital will continue to decline. However, a point must eventually be reached where so much debt has been issued that the firm will have difficulty meeting the interest payments on its debt should it find itself getting into financial difficulties. At this point, both the debt and equity holders will demand higher rates of return as compensation for the increased risks they are being required to bear and the cost of servicing the firm's capital will begin to rise. These considerations imply that the relationship between the cost of servicing the firm's capital and its debt-to-equity ratio will be as depicted in Figure 4.1. Note how the received theory as summarized in this figure argues that as debt is issued and used to retire equity, the firm's cost capital at first declines, thereby increasing the overall market value of the firm. However, as more and more debt is used to retire equity, a point is eventually reached where the cost of capital reaches

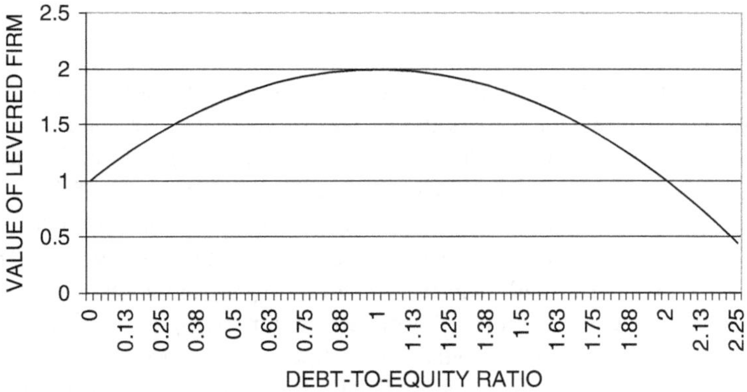

Figure 4.1 Optimal debt-to-equity ratio

a minimum and then begins to rise. Correspondingly, the firm's market value will reach a maximum at this minimum cost of capital and then fall away as the cost of capital increases in response to the risks posed by the increasing levels of debt comprising the firm's capital structure. Thus, received theory argues, the principal function of those responsible for the financial management of the firm is to determine the debt-to-equity ratio which minimizes the cost of capital and correspondingly, maximizes the market value of the firm.

§4-2. This way of thinking about the cost of servicing a firm's capital and of its relationship with the firm's debt-to-equity ratio held sway amongst theorists until the latter half of the twentieth century. Indeed, researchers devoted much time and effort towards searching for rules that would allow firms to identify the mix of debt and equity that would minimize the cost of servicing their capital requirements. However, in the late 1950s and early 1960s, Franco Modigliani and Merton Miller published a series of papers that showed how in a perfect capital market, manipulating a firm's debt-to-equity ratio in search of an optimal capital structure is a pointless exercise. A perfect capital market is one in which there are no transactions costs, personal taxes or bankruptcy costs, where all traders in the market have costless and equal access to any information they desire and where firms and individuals can borrow and lend as much as they want at the same riskless rate of interest.

We can illustrate the important principles behind the Modigliani–Miller analysis by making a few definitions. We thus consider two firms that are identical in every respect with the exception that the first of these firms is financed completely by equity. We call this the unlevered firm. The second firm is financed by a combination of debt and equity. We call this the levered firm. To simplify matters, we also assume that debt and equity are the only sources of finance available to firms. Now, let S_L be the market value of the levered firm's equity and B_L be the market value of its debt. It then follows that $V_L = S_L + B_L$ will be the overall market value of the levered firm. We can also let S_U be the market value of the unlevered firm's equity. It then follows that $V_U = S_U$ will be the unlevered firm's market value since it has no debt on issue. Next, let X be the annual operating profit (before interest and corporation tax) earned by both the levered and unlevered firms, that is, earnings before interest and taxes (EBIT). We emphasize again that the operating profit of the unlevered firm is perfectly correlated with the operating profit of the levered firm so that the only difference between the two firms is in the way their productive activities are financed. Finally, let T_C be the rate of corporation tax.

§4-3. The annual interest charge on the levered firm's debt will be rB_L, where r is the risk-free rate of interest and, as previously, B_L is the market value of its debt. Moreover, this will mean that the levered firm will have a net profit each year (after corporation tax) of $(X - rB_L)(1 - T_C)$. Consider then an investor who buys a fraction $0 \leq \alpha \leq 1$ of the levered firm's equity capital. This will cost αS_L and will entitle the investor to $\alpha(X - rB_L)(1 - T_C)$ of the levered firm's annual net profit. Suppose also that the investor buys $\alpha(1 - T_C)B_L$ of the levered firm's debt. The investor will then receive $r\alpha(1 - T_C)B_L$ in interest income each year. Hence, the total investment in the levered firm will amount to $\alpha S_L + \alpha(1 - T_C)B_L$. The income the investor will receive each year from this investment will be $\alpha(X - rB_L)(1 - T_C) + r\alpha(1 - T_C)B_L = \alpha X(1 - T_C)$. Now, suppose instead that the investor purchases a proportion α of the unlevered firm's equity capital. This would cost αS_U and yield an income each year of $\alpha X(1 - T_C)$, which is exactly the same as the income obtained from purchasing a proportion α of the levered firm's equity and investing $\alpha(1 - T_C)B_L$ in the levered firm's debt. Hence, the income from the investment in the levered firm's debt and equity will be perfectly correlated with and equal to the income obtained from the investment in the unlevered firm's equity stock. By the law of one price, the investment in the levered firm must have the same market value as the investment in the unlevered firm, in which case we have

$$\alpha S_L + \alpha(1 - T_C)B_L = \alpha S_U$$

A little algebra then shows that

$$S_U = S_L + B_L - T_C B_L$$

Using the fact that $V_U = S_U$ and $V_L = S_L + B_L$ and solving for V_L then shows that the market value of the levered firm will bear the following relationship to the market value of the unlevered firm:

$$V_L = V_U + T_C B_L$$

In other words, the market value of the levered firm V_L will be equal to the market value of the unlevered firm V_U plus the corporate tax rate T_C multiplied by the market value of the levered firm's debt B_L. We now draw out some of the important implications of this result.

§4-4. Consider then, two firms, Esther and Hannah, that are perfect substitutes in terms of the industries in which they operate and the technology they utilize, and so their net profits are perfectly correlated over time. Both firms have expected operating profits before interest and taxes of $X = £90{,}000$ (per annum). However, the two firms have chosen to finance their productive activities in different ways. Esther's activities are financed entirely by equity. The current market value of Esther's equity securities is $S_U = £600{,}000$. Hannah has financed its activities by issuing both equity and debt securities. The current market value of Hannah's equity is $S_L = £340{,}000$, whilst the nominal and market value of its $r = 8$ per cent (per annum) irredeemable debt securities is also $B_L = £340{,}000$. Finally, the corporation tax rate is $T_C = \frac{1}{4} = 25$ per cent.

Now, suppose one implements the procedures summarized in §4-3 above by selling Esther's equity stock in its entirety, thereby receiving S_U = £600,000. This also commits one to paying $X(1 - T_C)$ = £90,000 × $\frac{3}{4}$ = £67,500 in future annual income to Esther's new shareholders. We then purchase all of Hannah's equity stock at a cost of S_L = £340,000 and receive a future annual income of $(X - rB_L)(1 - T_C)$ = (£90,000 − 0.08 × £340,000) × $(1 - \frac{1}{4})$ = £47,100 from this investment. Finally, we also purchase $(1 - T_C)B_L = (1 - \frac{1}{4})$ × £340,000 = £255,000 of Hannah's debt thereby receiving annual interest payments of £255,000 × 0.08 = £20,400. A summary of these transactions appears in Table 4.1. The important point to make about this table is that the future income from our investments in Hannah's equity (£47,100) and debt (£20,400) is just sufficient to meet the income due to Esther's equity holders (£67,500). Hence, in undertaking these transactions, we have not committed ourselves to the payment of any future income streams, because the investments we have bought and sold are entirely self-financing in terms of their future cash flows. Yet, we have an immediate (present) net cash inflow of £5,000. We could, of course, conduct the above transactions again and again, making ourselves infinitely wealthy in the process. However, everybody in the economy will be trying to do exactly the same thing. This will mean that everyone in the economy will be trying to sell Esther's equity but no one will want to purchase it. This can only drive down the market value of Esther's equity. Similarly, everyone will be trying to purchase Hannah's equity but no one will be willing to sell it. This will drive up the market value of Hannah's equity. And when will these frenetic investment activities cease? This will be when the immediate (present) cash flow from the investment activities summarized in Table 4.1 has fallen to zero, that is, when $V_L = S_L + B_L$ = £340,000 + £340,000 = £680,000 becomes equal to $V_U + T_C B_L$ = £600,000 + $\frac{1}{4}$ × £340,000 = £685,000. At present, there is a £5,000 difference between these two figures, thereby indicating that there is a fundamental disequilibrium in the values of Esther's equity and Hannah's equity. The arbitrage opportunity implied by this mispricing will not be eliminated until Hannah and Esther's equity securities are priced so that the identity $V_L = V_U + T_C B_L$ given in §4-3 above is satisfied.

§4-5. Note also that the interest paid on Hannah's debt is an allowable deduction for corporation tax purposes. That is, Hannah's net profit before tax will be $X - rB_L$. Hannah's after-tax net profit is thus $(X - rB_L)(1 - T_C)$. This means that the after-tax cost of the interest payment on Hannah's debt is given by $rB_L(1 - T_C)$. In other words, the Inland Revenue reduces the annual interest cost on Hannah's debt by $rT_C B_L$ because they allow the interest payments Hannah makes to its debt holders to be deducted from Hannah's income

Table 4.1 Summary of financial transactions for Esther and Hannah

Investment activity	*Present* £	*Future* £
Sell short equity stock in Esther	600,000	$90{,}000 \times (1 - \frac{1}{4}) = -67{,}500$
Buy equity stock in Hannah	−340,000	$(90{,}000 - 0.08 \times 340{,}000) \times (1 - \frac{1}{4}) = 47{,}100$
Purchase Hannah debt	−255,000	$0.08 \times 255{,}000 = 20{,}400$
TOTAL	£5,000	£0

before determining the taxation Hannah has to pay. The present value of these tax savings is given by

$$\sum_{t=1}^{\infty} \frac{rT_C B_L}{(1+r)^t} = rT_C B_L \sum_{t=1}^{\infty} \frac{1}{(1+r)^t}$$

However, from Exercise 1 of Chapter 1, we know that

$$\sum_{t=1}^{N} \frac{1}{(1+r)^t} = \frac{1}{r}\left[1 - \frac{1}{(1+r)^N}\right]$$

Now, if we assume $r > 0$ and let $N \to \infty$ then it follows that

$$\sum_{t=1}^{\infty} \frac{1}{(1+r)^t} = \frac{1}{r}$$

We then have that the present value of the annual tax savings on Hannah's interest payments will be

$$rT_C B_L \sum_{t=1}^{\infty} \frac{1}{(1+r)^t} = \frac{rT_C B_L}{r} = T_C B_L$$

Hence, the fundamental valuation relationship summarized in §4-3 above, namely, $V_L = V_U + T_C B_L$, implies that the market value of the levered firm (V_L) is equal to the market value of an equivalent unlevered firm (V_U) plus the present value of the future tax savings that accrue to the levered firm as a result of the tax deductibility of the interest payments on its debt ($T_C B_L$). In Hannah's case, the present value of the future tax savings that arise from the tax deductibility of the interest payments on its debt amounts to $T_C B_L = \frac{1}{4} \times £340{,}000 = £85{,}000$.

§4-6. Now, let us suppose that in the previous analysis Esther's equity has been mispriced and that its 'correct' value is $V_U = £595{,}000$. From §4-3 above, this will mean that Hannah's overall market value will have to be $V_L = V_U + T_C B_L = £595{,}000 + \frac{1}{4} \times £340{,}000 = £680{,}000$. From §4-4, however, we have that Hannah's overall market value amounts to $V_L = S_L + B_L = £340{,}000 + £340{,}000 = £680{,}000$. Hence, the market value of Esther's equity is now in equilibrium with the market value of Hannah's debt and equity. Given this, we can define the cost of equity capital, p_L, for Hannah's equity as follows:

$$p_L = \frac{(X - rB_L)(1 - T_C)}{S_L} = \frac{(90{,}000 - 0.08 \times 340{,}000) \times (1 - \frac{1}{4})}{340{,}000} = \frac{471}{3{,}400} \approx 0.1385$$

or $p_L \approx 13.85$ per cent (per annum). The numerator in the above expression is the profit earned for equity after the payment of interest on Hannah's debt and the payment of taxation. The denominator is the market value of Hannah's equity. Now, let us expand this expression for p_L:

$$p_L = \frac{(X - rB_L)(1 - T_C)}{S_L} = \frac{(1 - T_C)X}{S_L} - \frac{(1 - T_C)rB_L}{S_L}$$

We can then multiply and divide the first term on the right-hand side of this expression by $S_U = V_U$ so that

$$p_L = \frac{(1-T_C)X}{V_U}\left(\frac{V_U}{S_L}\right) - \frac{(1-T_C)rB_L}{S_L}$$

Here we can note that

$$p_U = \frac{(1-T_C)X}{V_U} = \frac{(1-T_C)X}{S_U}$$

in the first term on the right-hand side of the above equation is the rate of return on the equity of an unlevered firm, that is, a firm that is financed exclusively through equity. We can then use this definition to restate the expression for p_L as follows:

$$p_L = p_U\frac{V_U}{S_L} - \frac{(1-T_C)rB_L}{S_L}$$

Now if we add and subtract

$$p_U\frac{(1-T_C)B_L}{S_L}$$

from the above expression, we have

$$p_L = p_U\frac{V_U}{S_L} - p_U\frac{(1-T_C)B_L}{S_L} + p_U\frac{(1-T_C)B_L}{S_L} - \frac{(1-T_C)rB_L}{S_L}$$

$$p_L = p_U\left[\frac{V_U}{S_L} - \frac{(1-T_C)B_L}{S_L}\right] + p_U\frac{(1-T_C)B_L}{S_L} - \frac{(1-T_C)rB_L}{S_L}$$

$$p_L = p_U\left[\frac{V_U-(1-T_C)B_L}{S_L}\right] + (1-T_C)\frac{B_L}{S_L}(p_U - r)$$

Recall from §4-3, however, that $V_L = V_U + T_C B_L$. Moreover, since $V_L = S_L + B_L$, this latter result can be restated as $S_L + B_L = V_U + T_C B_L$ or $S_L = V_U - (1-T_C)B_L$. We can substitute this result into the above expression for p_L and thereby show

$$p_L = p_U + (1-T_C)(p_U - r)\frac{B_L}{S_L}$$

This result says that the return on equity for a levered firm, p_L, will be equal to the return on equity of an 'equivalent' unlevered firm, p_U, plus a risk premium given by $(1-T_C)$ $(p_U - r)(B_L/S_L)$. Note how the risk premium hinges on the difference between the return on the equity of the unlevered firm, p_U, the return on risk-free debt, r, and the debt-to-equity ratio B_L/S_L for the levered firm.

Now, Modigliani and Miller collected data for electric utility and oil companies in order to assess whether the relationship between the debt-to-equity ratio and the return on equity is compatible with the result derived above. They defined the return on equity, p_L, as the firm's net profit after interest and taxes divided by the market value of the firm's equity.

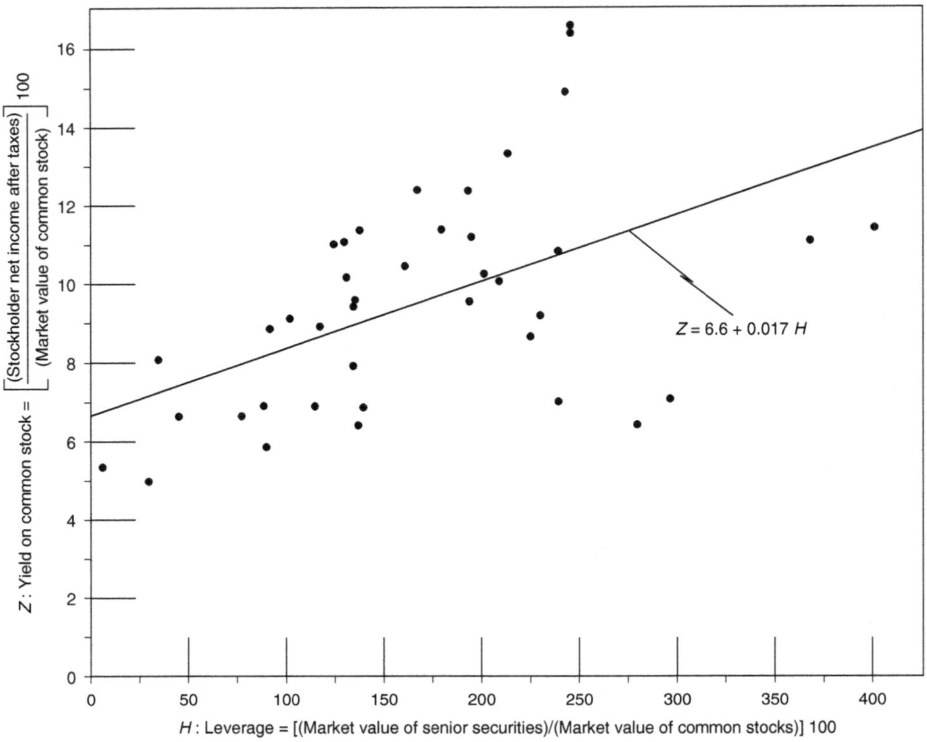

Figure 4.2 Return on equity against debt-to-equity ratio for US electric utility companies

The debt-to-equity ratio B_L/S_L was defined as the market value of the bonds and preference shares the firm has on issue divided by the market value of the firm's equity. The results they obtained for electric utility companies are summarized in Figure 4.2. Note how this graph shows that there is an upward-sloping and broadly linear relationship between the return on equity and the debt-to-equity ratio. Moreover, the regression equation given in Figure 4.2 shows that $p_U \approx 6\frac{3}{4}$ per cent (per annum) is the return one could expect on an electric utility company that is financed purely by equity; that is, where the debt-to-equity ratio $H = B_L/S_L$ is zero in Figure 4.2. It also shows that the financial risk premium for the electric utility industry was comparatively small, namely, $(1 - T_C)(p_U - r) \approx 0.017$ per cent – or about one-fiftieth of one per cent.

Modigliani and Miller obtained similar results for US oil firms, as summarized in Figure 4.3. Again, this graph shows that there is an upward-sloping and broadly linear relationship between the return on equity and the debt-to-equity ratio. However, this time Modigliani and Miller's regression equation shows that $p_U \approx 9$ per cent (per annum) is the return one could expect on an oil company that is financed purely by equity, that is, where the debt-to-equity ratio (H in Figure 4.3) is zero. This is much higher than the return expected from an unlevered electric utility company ($6\frac{3}{4}$ per cent) and reflects the greater business risks associated with the oil industry. Note also how Figure 4.3 shows that the financial risk premium for the oil industry was $(1 - T_C)(p_U - r) \approx 0.051$ per cent – which is three times as large as the financial

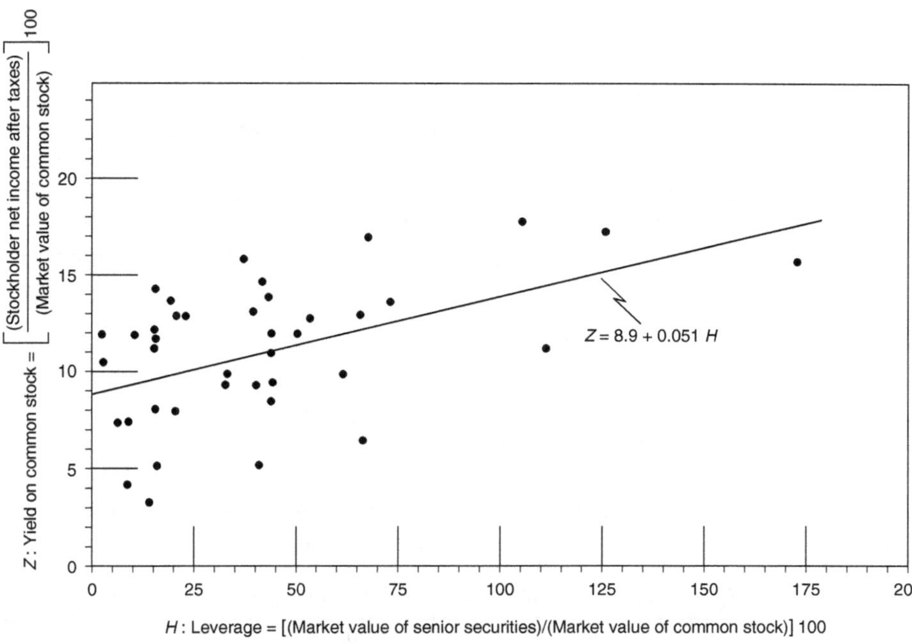

Figure 4.3 Return on equity against debt-to-equity ratio for US oil companies

risk premium for the electric utility industry. This again reflects the generally higher business risks associated with the oil industry in comparison with the electric utility industry. Hence, the empirical results for both the US electric utility industry and the US oil industry are generally compatible with the equity returns formula derived above – although for both industries one might have reservations about the magnitude of the financial risk premium obtained from Modigliani and Miller's empirical analysis.

§4-7. Here, it should be noted that the interest expense that the firm will have to meet each year increases in proportion to the level of debt on the firm's balance sheet. Moreover, the interest expense must always be paid as and when it falls due. Interest payments are not like dividends, which can be reduced or even omitted if the firm finds itself in financial difficulties. The obligatory nature of interest payments will mean that the volatility of the return on the levered firm's equity will increase as the level of the firm's debt rises. Equity investors will respond to the increased volatility (and therefore uncertainty) associated with the income stream available to them by demanding a higher rate of return on their investment. The result summarized in §4-6 captures the trade-off that equity investors will demand between the return they expect and the risk implied by the debt-to-equity ratio. We can further illustrate this point by computing the cost of equity for Esther, which is an unlevered firm. Here, it will be recalled that Esther has an annual operating profit of $X = £90{,}000$. Moreover, we have previously established (in §4-6) that the equilibrium price for Esther's equity is $V_U = £595{,}000$. Finally, the corporation tax rate is $T_C = \frac{1}{4} = 25$ per cent. It then follows that

Esther's cost of equity will be

$$p_U = \frac{X(1-T_C)}{S_U} = \frac{90{,}000 \times (1-\frac{1}{4})}{595{,}000} = \frac{27}{238} \approx 0.1134$$

or $p_U \approx 11.34$ per cent (per annum). Now, we can use Esther's cost of equity capital in conjunction with the result summarized in §4-6 to determine the cost of equity for Hannah. Here it will be recalled that Hannah's equity has a market value of $S_L = £340{,}000$. Likewise, Hannah's debt has a market value of $B_L = £340{,}000$. Finally, the return on risk-free debt is $r = \frac{2}{25} = 8$ per cent (per annum). Substitution then shows that the equilibrium return on Hannah's equity will be

$$p_L = p_U + (1-T_C)(p_U - r)\frac{B_L}{S_L} = \frac{27}{238}$$
$$+\left(1-\frac{1}{4}\right) \times \left(\frac{27}{238} - \frac{2}{25}\right) \times \frac{340{,}000}{340{,}000} = \frac{471}{3{,}400} \approx 0.1385$$

or $p_L \approx 13.85$ per cent (per annum). Note also how this result agrees with the direct calculation of Hannah's cost of equity given earlier (as in §4-6), namely,

$$p_L = \frac{(X - rB_L)(1-T_C)}{S_L} = \frac{(90{,}000 - 0.08 \times 340{,}000) \times (1-\frac{1}{4})}{340{,}000} = \frac{471}{3{,}400} \approx 0.1385$$

What distinguishes the two calculations, however, is that we now have a basis for understanding how risk (as captured by the debt-to-equity ratio) affects the equilibrium return on a firm's equity.

§4-8. In Chapter 2, we demonstrated how the Capital Asset Pricing Model (CAPM) shows that there will be a linear relationship between the expected return on an equity security and the equity security's beta. It will be recalled that beta measures the sensitivity of the equity security's return to variations in the return on the market as a whole – as captured by the return on the market portfolio. We can use the results derived so far in this chapter to determine how the debt-to-equity ratio affects an equity security's sensitivity to variations in market returns. Thus, suppose we let p_M be the return on the market portfolio and $\sigma^2(p_M)$ be its variance. It then follows that the beta β_L of a levered equity security can be computed as

$$\beta_L = \frac{\mathrm{Cov}(p_L, p_M)}{\sigma^2(p_M)}$$

where $\mathrm{Cov}(p_L, p_M)$ is the covariance between the return on the levered firm's equity and the return on the market portfolio (as in §2-11 of Chapter 2). However, from §4-6 above, we have

$$\mathrm{Cov}(p_L, p_M) = \mathrm{Cov}\left(p_U + (1-T_C)(p_U - r)\frac{B_L}{S_L}, p_M\right)$$

Now, this may be broken down into two components:

$$\mathrm{Cov}(p_U, p_M) + \mathrm{Cov}\left((1-T_C)(p_U - r)\frac{B_L}{S_L}, p_M\right)$$

Moreover, the second term here may be further simplified to

$$(1-T_C)\frac{B_L}{S_L}\text{Cov}(p_U - r, p_M) = (1-T_C)\frac{B_L}{S_L}\text{Cov}(p_U, p_M)$$

by virtue of the fact that in the CAPM, the risk-free rate of interest is a constant independent of time. Hence, it follows that

$$\beta_L = \frac{\text{Cov}(p_L, p_M)}{\sigma^2(p_M)} = \frac{\text{Cov}(p_U, p_M)}{\sigma^2(p_M)} + \frac{(1-T_C)\frac{B_L}{S_L}\text{Cov}(p_U, p_M)}{\sigma^2(p_M)}$$

However, here it will be recalled that the beta of an equivalent unlevered firm, β_U, is given by

$$\beta_U = \frac{\text{Cov}(p_U, p_M)}{\sigma^2(p_M)}$$

where $\text{Cov}(p_U, p_M)$ is the covariance between the return on the unlevered firm's equity and the return on the market portfolio. Substituting this expression for β_U into the expression for β_L given above thus shows

$$\beta_L = \beta_U\left[1+(1-T_C)\frac{B_L}{S_L}\right] = \beta_U\left(\frac{S_L + B_L - T_C B_L}{S_L}\right) = \beta_U\left(\frac{V_L - T_C B_L}{S_L}\right)$$

Finally, using §4-3 above, we have $V_U = V_L - T_C B_L$ and also $V_U = S_U$, and so this latter result may be rewritten as

$$\beta_L = \beta_U\left(\frac{S_U}{S_L}\right)$$

This result tells us that a levered firm's beta is comprised of its 'business' or 'operating' risk β_U, grossed up by $1+(1-T_C)(B_L/S_L)$ to reflect the financing risk associated with the debt-to-equity ratio.

§4-9. We can illustrate the importance of the above result by considering a simple numerical example. We suppose that Wombat Brewing Company is considering an investment in the soft drinks industry. Wombat will have to invest £100 in plant and facilities and this will return (after tax) cash flows of £13 (per annum) indefinitely into the future. However, Wombat's management cannot decide on an appropriate discount rate through which to evaluate the profitability of its proposed soft drinks investment. Fortunately, the Lion Brewing Company's equity is listed on the stock exchange and it has very similar markets and technology to that which Wombat is considering adopting for its soft drinks investment. Lion's equity is currently valued at $S_L = £100$ whilst it also has outstanding irredeemable debt with a current market value $B_L = £50$. This means that Lion's market value is $V_L = S_L + B_L = £100 + £50 = £150$. The corporate taxation rate is $T_C = 30$ per cent and the interest rate on Lion's debt is 7 per cent (per annum). Furthermore, Wombat's Finance Department has estimated that Lion's beta (based on a very well-diversified market index with an expected return of $p_M = 0.15$ or 15 per cent) amounts to $\beta_L = 0.9$. We can draw on this information to determine Lion's cost of equity using the CAPM, namely

$$p_L = r + (p_M - r)\beta_L = 0.07 + (0.15 - 0.07) \times 0.9 = 0.142$$

or 14.2 per cent (per annum). Moreover, using §4-6 above, we can determine the cost of equity capital for an equivalent unlevered firm, namely,

$$p_L = p_U + (1 - T_C)(p_U - r)\frac{B_L}{S_L}$$

or

$$0.142 = p_U + (1 - 0.3)(p_U - 0.07)\frac{50}{100}$$

Solving this equation yields $p_U = \frac{37}{300} = 12\frac{1}{3}$ per cent (per annum) as the cost of equity capital Lion would have if its operations were completely financed by equity, that is, if it had no debt at all.

An alternative way of arriving at Lion's cost of equity capital is to note from §4-3 above that if Lion had financed its activities using equity only then the value of its equity would have been $S_U = V_U = V_L - T_C B_L = £150 - 0.3 \times £50 = £135$. It then follows that the beta for the equity of an equivalent unlevered firm would be

$$\beta_L = \beta_U \frac{S_U}{S_L}$$

or

$$0.9 = \frac{135}{100}\beta_U$$

This latter result implies $\beta_U = \frac{2}{3}$. Applying the CAPM, we then have that if Lion were financed purely by equity, its cost of capital would be

$$p_U = r + (p_M - r)\beta_U = 0.07 + (0.15 - 0.07) \times \frac{2}{3} = \frac{37}{300}$$

that is, $12\frac{1}{3}$ per cent (per annum) as obtained above.

We can now use this discount rate to compute the net present value of Wombat's investment opportunity. Recall that Wombat will have to invest £100 in plant and facilities and this will return (after tax) cash flows of £13 (per annum). Hence, the net present value of this investment opportunity will be

$$\sum_{t=1}^{\infty} \frac{13}{(1 + p_U)^t} - 100 = \frac{13}{p_U} - 100 = \frac{13 \times 300}{37} - 100 = \frac{200}{37} \approx £5.41 > 0$$

and so the proposal represents a profitable investment opportunity for Wombat. Note that if Wombat had not stripped out the financing effects implicit in Lion's capital structure then the net present value of Wombat's investment proposal would have been computed as

$$\frac{13}{p_L} - 100 = \frac{13}{0.142} - 100 \approx -£8.45 < 0$$

Using this discount rate, the net present value is negative and so Wombat would not have undertaken the proposed investment. This would have been a serious mistake, since Wombat would have rejected an investment proposal that would have increased its overall market value.

§4-10. When a firm finances its activities through a combination of debt and equity, there are several ways in which one can compute the weighted average cost of the capital it employs. Probably the easiest of these is to apply the formula

$$k^* = \frac{X(1 - T_C)}{V_L}$$

where the numerator in this expression is the firm's operating profit before deducting the interest on its debt (i.e. its earnings before interest and taxes or EBIT) and the denominator is composed of the market value of the firm's equity plus the market value of its debt, that is, $V_L = S_L + B_L$. Now, for the Hannah example employed earlier (in §4-4), we have an operating profit after taxation of $X(1 - T_C) = £90{,}000 \times (1 - \frac{1}{4}) = £67{,}500$, a market value of equity of $S_L = £340{,}000$ and debt with a market value of $B_L = £340{,}000$. Hence, the weighted average cost of capital for Hannah turns out to be

$$k^* = \frac{X(1 - T_C)}{V_L} = \frac{67{,}500}{340{,}000 + 340{,}000} = \frac{27}{272} \approx 0.0993$$

or about 9.93 per cent (per annum). But there are several other potentially more convenient ways in which this figure of 9.93 per cent for the weighted average cost of capital may be computed.

We begin by noting that the market value of a levered firm is determined by capitalising its future operating profit, namely,

$$V_L = \frac{(1 - T_C)X}{k^*}$$

Similar considerations dictate that the market value of an equivalent unlevered firm will be

$$V_U = S_U = \frac{(1 - T_C)X}{p_U}$$

Note how this latter result implies $p_U S_U = (1 - T_C)X$, in which case we can use §4-3 to show that the market value of the levered firm can be restated as

$$V_L = \frac{(1 - T_C)X}{k^*} = \frac{p_U S_U}{k^*} = \frac{p_U(V_L - T_C B_L)}{k^*}.$$

It then follows that the weighted average cost of capital for the levered firm can be restated as

$$k^* = \frac{p_U(V_L - T_C B_L)}{V_L} = p_U\left(1 - \frac{T_C B_L}{S_L + B_L}\right)$$

Now suppose we add and subtract

$$\frac{r(1-T_C)B_L}{B_L+S_L}$$

from the right-hand side of this latter equation. We then have

$$k^* = \frac{r(1-T_C)B_L}{B_L+S_L} - \frac{r(1-T_C)B_L}{B_L+S_L} + p_U - \frac{p_U T_C B_L}{S_L+B_L}$$

Note, however, that

$$p_U = \frac{p_U(B_L+S_L)}{B_L+S_L} = \frac{p_U B_L}{B_L+S_L} + \frac{p_U S_L}{B_L+S_L}$$

and so we have

$$k^* = \frac{r(1-T_C)B_L}{B_L+S_L} - \frac{r(1-T_C)B_L}{B_L+S_L} + \frac{p_U B_L}{B_L+S_L} + \frac{p_U S_L}{B_L+S_L} - \frac{p_U T_C B_L}{S_L+B_L}$$

However, since

$$\frac{p_U B_L}{B_L+S_L} - \frac{p_U T_C B_L}{S_L+B_L} = \frac{p_U B_L(1-T_C)}{B_L+S_L}$$

this reduces to

$$k^* = \frac{r(1-T_C)B_L}{B_L+S_L} + \frac{p_U S_L}{B_L+S_L} + \frac{p_U B_L(1-T_C)}{B_L+S_L} - \frac{r(1-T_C)B_L}{B_L+S_L}$$

If we multiply and divide the last two terms by S_L, this may be restated as

$$k^* = \frac{r(1-T_C)B_L}{B_L+S_L} + \frac{p_U S_L}{B_L+S_L} + p_U(1-T_C)\left(\frac{B_L}{S_L}\right)\frac{S_L}{B_L+S_L} - r(1-T_C)\left(\frac{B_L}{S_L}\right)\frac{S_L}{B_L+S_L}$$

Collecting the last three terms in this expression then gives

$$k^* = \frac{r(1-T_C)B_L}{B_L+S_L} + \left[p_U + p_U(1-T_C)\frac{B_L}{S_L} - r(1-T_C)\frac{B_L}{S_L}\right]\frac{S_L}{B_L+S_L}$$

We can simplify this again by collecting terms involving B_L/S_L inside the square brackets to give

$$k^* = \frac{r(1-T_C)B_L}{B_L+S_L} + \left[p_U + (p_U - r)(1-T_C)\frac{B_L}{S_L}\right]\frac{S_L}{B_L+S_L}$$

From §4-6 above, however, we have

$$p_L = p_U + (1 - T_C)(p_U - r)\frac{B_L}{S_L}$$

and so it follows that the weighted average cost of capital for the levered firm may be restated as

$$k^* = r(1 - T_C)\frac{B_L}{B_L + S_L} + p_L\frac{S_L}{B_L + S_L}$$

or, since $V_L = B_L + S_L$, this is equivalent to

$$k^* = \frac{X(1 - T_C)}{V_L} = r(1 - T_C)\frac{B_L}{V_L} + p_L\frac{S_L}{V_L}$$

We can demonstrate the application of this formula by recalling how in §4-7 we showed that the cost of equity for Hannah is

$$p_L = \frac{(X - rB_L)(1 - T_C)}{S_L} = \frac{(90{,}000 - 0.08 \times 340{,}000) \times (1 - \frac{1}{4})}{340{,}000} = \frac{471}{3{,}400} \approx 0.1385$$

Likewise, the after-tax cost of Hannah's debt is given by

$$r(1 - T_C) = \frac{2}{25}\left(1 - \frac{1}{4}\right) = \frac{3}{50} = 6 \text{ per cent}$$

Hence, Hannah's weighted average cost of capital amounts to

$$\begin{aligned} k^* &= r(1 - T_C)\frac{B_L}{V_L} + p_L\frac{S_L}{V_L} \\ &= \frac{3}{50} \times \frac{340{,}000}{340{,}000 + 340{,}000} + \frac{471}{3{,}400} \times \frac{340{,}000}{340{,}000 + 340{,}000} = \frac{27}{272} \approx 0.0993 \end{aligned}$$

or about 9.93 per cent (per annum). Note that this is the same figure as that obtained in §4-10 above for Hannah's weighted average cost of capital.

§4-11. There are, however, several other ways of determining the weighted average cost of capital for a levered firm. As but one further example, it will be recalled from §4-6 above that the cost of equity for a levered firm can be computed from the formula

$$p_L = p_U + (1 - T_C)(p_U - r)\frac{B_L}{S_L}$$

Furthermore, we have just shown in §4-10 that the weighted average cost of capital is

$$k^* = r(1 - T_C)\frac{B_L}{V_L} + p_L\frac{S_L}{V_L}$$

Hence, substitution shows that the weighted average cost of capital may be restated as

$$k^* = r(1 - T_C)\frac{B_L}{V_L} + \left[p_U + (1 - T_C)(p_U - r)\frac{B_L}{S_L}\right]\frac{S_L}{V_L}$$

Now, expanding out this expression shows

$$k^* = r(1 - T_C)\frac{B_L}{V_L} + p_U\frac{S_L}{V_L} + (1 - T_C)p_U\frac{B_L}{V_L} - r(1 - T_C)\frac{B_L}{V_L}$$

or, equivalently,

$$k^* = p_U\frac{S_L}{V_L} + (1 - T_C)p_U\frac{B_L}{V_L} = p_U\frac{S_L}{V_L} + p_U\frac{B_L}{V_L} - T_C p_U\frac{B_L}{V_L}$$

This in turn will mean

$$k^* = p_U\frac{S_L + B_L}{V_L} - T_C p_U\frac{B_L}{V_L}$$

However, since $S_L + B_L = V_L$, it follows from this last result that

$$k^* = p_U - T_C p_U\frac{B_L}{V_L} = p_U\left(1 - T_C\frac{B_L}{V_L}\right)$$

Now, here it will be recalled from §4-7 above that Esther is an unlevered firm whose cost of equity amounts to

$$p_U = \frac{X(1 - T_C)}{S_U} = \frac{90{,}000 \times (1 - \frac{1}{4})}{595{,}000} = \frac{27}{238} \approx 0.1134$$

where $T_C = \frac{1}{4} = 25$ per cent is the rate of corporation tax. Moreover, Hannah has $S_L =$ £340,000 of equity on issue and $B_L =$ £340,000 of debt on issue. It thus follows from the above result that Hannah's weighted average cost of capital will have to be

$$k^* = p_U\left(1 - T_C\frac{B_L}{V_L}\right) = \frac{27}{238}\left(1 - \frac{1}{4} \times \frac{340{,}000}{680{,}000}\right) = \frac{27}{272} \approx 0.0993$$

or about 9.93 per cent (per annum). Note how this is the same figure as that obtained using the formulae applied in §4-10 above. More important, however, is that this result shows how the weighted average cost of capital k^* continuously declines as the firm's debt-to-equity ratio B_L/S_L grows in magnitude. We can demonstrate this by noting that the above result can be restated in the following way:

$$k^* = p_U\left(1 - T_C\frac{B_L}{V_L}\right) = p_U\left(1 - T_C\frac{B_L}{B_L + S_L}\right) = p_U\left(1 - T_C\frac{\frac{B_L}{S_L}}{1 + \frac{B_L}{S_L}}\right)$$

Moreover, since the corporation tax rate is $T_C = \frac{1}{4} = 25$ per cent and Esther is an unlevered firm whose cost of equity amounts to $p_U = \frac{27}{238}$, it then follows that the weighted average cost of capital for an equivalent levered firm will be

$$k^* = p_U \left(1 - T_C \frac{\frac{B_L}{S_L}}{1 + \frac{B_L}{S_L}} \right) = \frac{27}{238} \left(1 - \frac{1}{4} \frac{\frac{B_L}{S_L}}{1 + \frac{B_L}{S_L}} \right)$$

Figure 4.4 graphs the relationship summarized here between the weighted average cost of servicing the firm's capital and its debt-to-equity ratio. Note in this graph how the weighted average cost of capital k^* decays away as the debt-to-equity ratio grows in magnitude. This in turn implies that the firm should finance its productive activities with as much debt as possible.

The weighted average cost of capital is often used by firms as the discount rate through which to evaluate potential investment projects. However, two very important conditions must be satisfied if the weighted average cost of capital is to be used as a discount factor in capital investment analysis. First, the capital project must be financed in exactly the same way as the firm is currently financed. Thus, if the firm is currently financed two-thirds by equity and one-third by debt then the proposed capital project must be financed in exactly the same way, that is, two-thirds by equity and one-third by debt. Second, the proposed capital project must be a microcosm of the firm's existing productive activities in the sense that its business risk (as in §4-8 above) does not differ from the business risk of the firm's pre-existing productive activities. These two conditions mean that the proposed capital project is a perfect substitute for the firm's existing productive activities and therefore must have the same weighted average cost of capital. If these two important conditions are not satisfied, however, then it is all but inevitable that using the weighted average cost of capital in capital investment decisions will lead to incorrect investment outcomes.

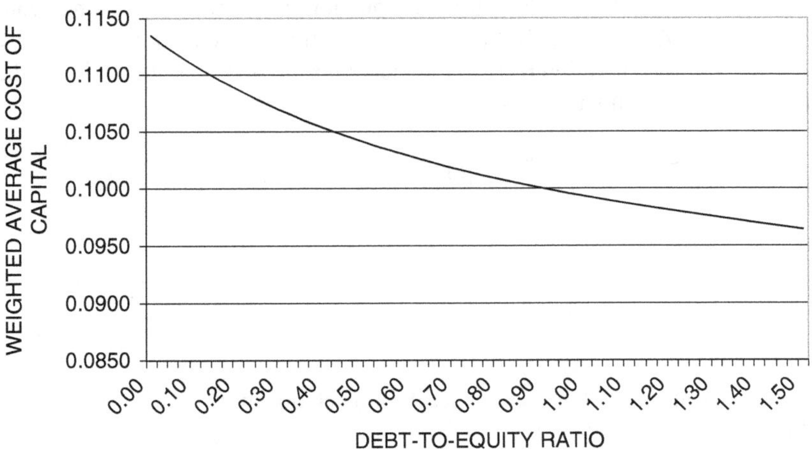

Figure 4.4 Relationship between the weighted average cost of capital and the debt-to-equity ratio

§4-12. In 'real life', apart from corporate tax, investors also pay personal income tax and capital gains taxes. We have previously defined T_C to be the rate of corporation tax. We now define T_P to be the rate of personal taxation and T_G to be rate at which capital gains taxes are levied. In many countries, capital gains taxes are levied at a lower rate than personal taxes and so this implies that $T_G < T_P$. Moreover, it is often possible to delay the payment of capital gains taxes by not selling the asset on which the taxes accrue, and this creates a further 'wedge' between the personal and capital gains tax rate. In the UK, there is also a 'threshold' below which capital gains are exempt from taxation. However, there are no exemptions from tax in the payment of dividends. Hence, in what follows, we assume $T_G < T_P$ and so the investor has an incentive to take all value increases in the form of capital gains.

Now, recall that we have previously defined X to be the firm's annual operating profit (before interest and corporation tax). Hence, the operating profit for an unlevered firm after the payment of taxation will be $(1 - T_C)X$. Moreover, equity holders take their income in the form of capital gains, and so this will mean that the market value of an unlevered firm's equity will have to be

$$V_U = \frac{(1 - T_C)(1 - T_G)X}{k^{**}}$$

where k^{**} is the appropriate discount rate after corporation and capital gains taxes. Similar considerations show that the levered firm's operating profit (after corporation, personal and capital gains taxes) is

$$(1 - T_C)(1 - T_G)(X - rB_L) + (1 - T_P)rB_L$$

This may be restated as

$$(1 - T_C)(1 - T_G)X + rB_L[(1 - T_P) - (1 - T_C)(1 - T_G)]$$

Now, the first component in the above equation, $(1 - T_C)(1 - T_G)X$, is identical to the unlevered firm's operating profit, has the same risk profile and will therefore be discounted at the rate k^{**}. The second component, $rB_L[(1 - T_P) - (1 - T_C)(1 - T_G)]$, is the debt holders' after-tax income, $(1 - T_P)rB_L$, and the after-tax reduction in the firm's operating profit due to borrowing, $rB_L(1 - T_C)(1 - T_G)$. Both these income streams are certain and will thus be discounted at the riskless rate of interest after personal tax, $(1 - T_P)r$. It then follows that the value of the levered firm will have to be

$$V_L = \frac{(1 - T_C)(1 - T_G)X}{k^{**}} + \frac{rB_L}{(1 - T_P)r}[(1 - T_P) - (1 - T_C)(1 - T_G)]$$

or, equivalently,

$$V_L = V_U + B_L\left[1 - \frac{(1 - T_C)(1 - T_G)}{(1 - T_P)}\right]$$

The economic implications of the above equilibrium relationship between the levered and unlevered firm values are as follows:

(i) if $\frac{(1 - T_C)(1 - T_G)}{(1 - T_P)} < 1$, the firm should finance its operations completely from debt;

(ii) if $\dfrac{(1-T_C)(1-T_G)}{(1-T_P)} > 1$, the firm should finance its operations completely from equity; and

(iii) if $\dfrac{(1-T_C)(1-T_G)}{(1-T_P)} = 1$, it makes no difference whether the firm finances its operations using debt or equity.

Note also that if the rate of taxation applied to capital gains (T_G) is the same as the rate of taxation applied to personal income (T_P), then the above result reduces to

$$V_L = V_U + B_L[1-(1-T_C)] = V_U + T_C B_L$$

This is the same result as that obtained in §4-3 above, where it was assumed that there were corporate but no personal taxes. Hence, the results obtained in earlier paragraphs also hold in a world where there are capital gains and personal income taxes but where there is no differential tax treatment between them.

We can illustrate the above results by assuming that the rate of corporate taxation is $T_C = 0.4$, the rate of personal taxation is $T_P = 0.3$ and, owing to investors' ability to defer taxes and threshold differences, the effective rate of capital gains tax is $T_G = 0.2$. Now, we assume also that investors can buy securities in two firms H and Z that, apart from their capital structures, are identical in every respect. Relevant financial information for these two firms is summarized in Table 4.2. From this table, it will be seen that firm Z's debt amounts to $B_L = £100$ with interest payable at the rate of $r = 10$ per cent (per annum). The cost of capital applicable to the equity of firm H is $k^{**} = 20$ per cent (per annum). We thus have the following:

(i) The after-tax cash flows for the equity holders of firm H amount to $(1-T_C)(1-T_G)X = (1-0.4)(1-0.2)200 = £96$, since shareholders will take all profits in the form of capital gains.
(ii) The after-tax cash flows to firm Z's equity holders amount to $(1-T_C)(1-T_G)(X - rB_L) = (1-0.4)(1-0.2)(200-10) = £91.20$.
(iii) The value of firm H will be

$$V_U = \frac{(1-T_C)(1-T_G)X}{k^{**}} = \frac{96}{0.2} = £480$$

Table 4.2 Summary financial information for firm H and firm Z

	H	*Z*
Earnings before interest and taxes	£200	£200
Interest		10
Taxable profit	200	190
Corporate tax	80	76
Net profit	120	114
Personal tax	24	23
Net profit after personal and corporate taxes	£ 96	£ 91

(iv) The value of firm Z will be

$$V_L = V_U + B_L\left[1 - \frac{(1-T_C)(1-T_G)}{(1-T_P)}\right] = 480 + 100\left[1 - \frac{(1-0.4)(1-0.2)}{(1-0.3)}\right] = £511$$

§4-13. An important underlying assumption of our analysis so far is that both individuals and firms can borrow (and lend) as much as they want at the risk-free rate of interest. This implies that the debt concerned has no risk and so it is important to note that this excludes any possibility of bankruptcy or the costs associated with bankruptcy. In the real world, of course, firms and individuals do go bankrupt and significant costs are incurred when they do so. We can illustrate how the incidence of bankruptcy costs invalidates much of the preceding analysis by the following simple example.

Suppose that the corporate tax rate is $T_C = 0.3$ and that the cost of bankruptcy is 20 per cent of the value of the firm's assets at the time of bankruptcy. Define G as the market value of the firm's debt divided by the total value of its assets, or

$$G = \frac{B_L}{V_L} = \frac{B_L}{S_L + B_L}$$

Now, suppose that the probability of the firm entering bankruptcy is G^2. It then follows that the bankruptcy costs will be $0.2V_L$ with probability G^2, whilst the probability that there will be no bankruptcy costs is $1 - G^2$. This in turn means that the market value of the levered firm, V_L, will satisfy the identity

$$V_L = V_U + T_C B_L - [0.2V_L G^2 + 0\cdot(1-G^2)] = V_U + T_C V_L G - 0.2V_L G^2$$

Note here that $V_L = V_U + T_C B_L$ is the value of the firm when there is no possibility of bankruptcy. Moreover, $0.2V_L G^2 + 0\cdot(1-G^2)$ are the expected bankruptcy costs. So the above valuation formula is based on the assumption that the value of the firm is determined by subtracting the expected bankruptcy costs from the value of the firm when there is no possibility of bankruptcy. Now, we can solve this equation for V_L, in which case we have

$$V_L = \frac{V_U}{1 - T_C G + 0.2G^2}$$

Differentiating through this expression with respect to the choice variable G gives

$$\frac{dV_L}{dG} = \frac{-V_U(0.4G - T_C)}{(1 - T_C G + 0.2G^2)^2} = 0$$

for a stationary point. Hence, we must have $0.4G - T_C = 0.4G - 0.3 = 0$ or $G = \frac{3}{4}$. This result implies that

$$G = \frac{B_L}{B_L + S_L} = \frac{3}{4}$$

or that the debt-to-equity ratio that maximizes the market value of the firm will be

$$\frac{B_L}{S_L} = \frac{G}{1-G} = \frac{\frac{3}{4}}{1-\frac{3}{4}} = 3$$

In other words, the firm should finance its productive activities by raising £3 of debt for every £1 of equity it issues, since this financial strategy will maximize the overall market value of the firm. Thus, if we assume that the market value of the unlevered firm is $V_U = £1$, we can then substitute

$$G = \frac{\frac{B_L}{S_L}}{1+\frac{B_L}{S_L}}$$

into the above expression for V_L and show that the relationship between the firm's debt-to-equity ratio and the overall market value of the firm will be

$$V_L = \frac{\left(1+\frac{B_L}{S_L}\right)^2}{0.9\left(\frac{B_L}{S_L}\right)^2 + 1.7\frac{B_L}{S_L} + 1}$$

A graph of the above relationship between the market value of the levered firm V_L and the debt-to-equity ratio B_L/S_L is plotted in Figure 4.5. Note how Figure 4.5 shows that the value of the levered firm is maximized when the debt-to-equity ratio is $B_L/S_L = 3$, beyond which the market value of the firm slowly decays away. The important point to glean from this

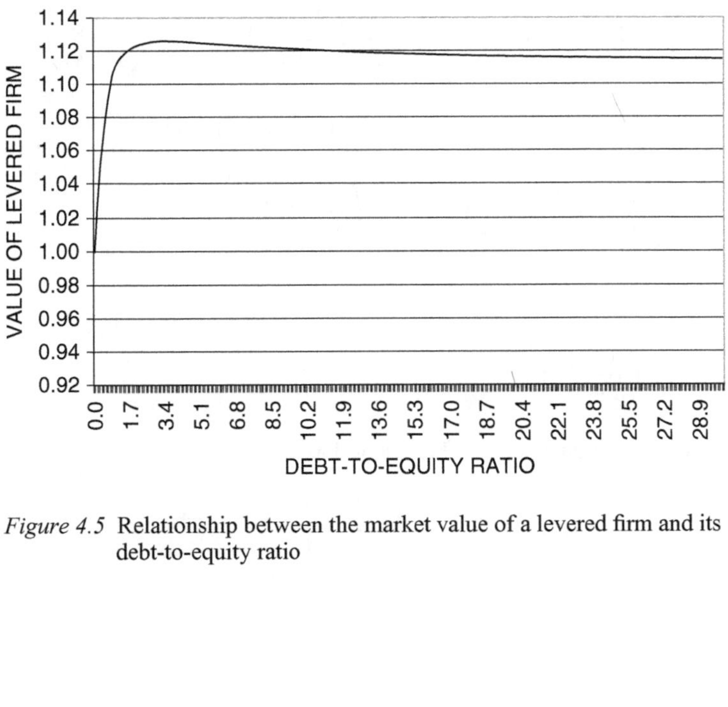

Figure 4.5 Relationship between the market value of a levered firm and its debt-to-equity ratio

simple example is that when there are market imperfections, such as non-trivial bankruptcy costs, it is not hard to envisage how firms will manipulate their debt-to-equity ratios in order to minimize the capital costs associated with the financing of their productive activities. In short, the existence of market imperfections opens up the strong possibility of their being an optimal capital structure for the firm.

§4-14. In Chapter 1, we illustrated several methods for determining the interest rate on debt securities and also for estimating the expected return on equity securities. We now develop a simple but widely used method for estimating the cost of equity capital that we have not previously considered – the so-called constant-growth model. This model assumes that the dividend d_t paid at time t on a given equity security will grow at a constant compound rate of g per annum, or

$$d_t = d_1(1+g)^{t-1}$$

where $t = 0, 1, 2, \ldots, N$ is the time at which the dividends will be paid. We can determine the present value P_0 of the dividends for this constant-growth model as follows:

$$P_0 = \sum_{t=1}^{N} \frac{d_1(1+g)^{t-1}}{(1+k_e)^t}$$

where k_e is the cost of equity capital. Note, however, that the above result can be restated as follows:

$$P_0 = \frac{d_1}{1+g} \sum_{t=1}^{N} \left(\frac{1+g}{1+k_e}\right)^t$$

Expanding out the expression under the summation sign gives

$$S_N = \sum_{t=1}^{N} \left(\frac{1+g}{1+k_e}\right)^t = \left(\frac{1+g}{1+k_e}\right) + \left(\frac{1+g}{1+k_e}\right)^2 + \left(\frac{1+g}{1+k_e}\right)^3 + \cdots + \left(\frac{1+g}{1+k_e}\right)^N$$

Multiplying through the above expansion by $(1+k_e)/(1+g)$, we then have

$$S_N \frac{1+k_e}{1+g} = 1 + \left(\frac{1+g}{1+k_e}\right) + \left(\frac{1+g}{1+k_e}\right)^2 + \cdots + \left(\frac{1+g}{1+k_e}\right)^{N-1}$$

Subtraction then gives

$$S_N \frac{1+k_e}{1+g} - S_N = 1 - \left(\frac{1+g}{1+k_e}\right)^N$$

Now the left-hand side of this equation may be restated as

$$S_N \frac{1+k_e}{1+g} - S_N = S_N \frac{1+k_e}{1+g} - S_N \frac{1+g}{1+g} = S_N \frac{1+k_e-1-g}{1+g} = S_N \frac{k_e-g}{1+g}$$

from which it follows

$$S_N \frac{1+k_e}{1+g} - S_N = S_N \frac{k_e - g}{1+g} = 1 - \left(\frac{1+g}{1+k_e}\right)^N$$

This result in turn implies that

$$S_N = \frac{1+g}{k_e - g}\left[1 - \left(\frac{1+g}{1+k_e}\right)^N\right]$$

Substituting this latter result back into the formula for the present value then gives

$$P_0 = \frac{d_1}{1+g}\sum_{t=1}^{N}\left(\frac{1+g}{1+k_e}\right)^t = \frac{d_1}{1+g} S_N$$

or

$$P_0 = \frac{d_1}{1+g}\left(\frac{1+g}{k_e - g}\right)\left[1 - \left(\frac{1+g}{1+k_e}\right)^N\right] = \frac{d_1}{k_e - g}\left[1 - \left(\frac{1+g}{1+k_e}\right)^N\right]$$

Now, if we suppose that $k_e > g$, then it follows that

$$\lim_{N\to\infty}\left(\frac{1+g}{1+k_e}\right)^N = 0$$

and so we have

$$\lim_{N\to\infty} P_0 = \frac{d_1}{k_e - g}$$

In other words, if we know or can estimate the dividend d_1 that the firm will pay in one year's time, as well as the growth rate g in the dividend over time, then it is a relatively simple matter to work out the cost of equity capital for the firm. In particular, solving this equation for k_e shows that

$$k_e = \frac{d_1}{P_0} + g$$

provides the desired estimate for the cost of the firm's equity capital.

We can illustrate the application of this result by supposing that a firm's equity is currently priced at £10 (per share). Suppose also that the firm has just paid a dividend of $d_0 = £1$ (per share) and that it has a consistent record of increasing its dividend payments by 5 per cent (per annum). Now, we assume dividends grow in accordance with the formula $d_t = d_1(1+g)^{t-1}$, in which case we have $d_0 = d_1(1+g)^{-1}$, or $d_1 = d_0(1+g)$. It thus follows that $d_1 = 1\cdot(1+0.05) = 1.05$, and so we have

$$k_e = \frac{d_1}{P_0} + g = \frac{1.05}{10} + 0.05 = 0.155$$

Hence, using this constant-growth model, we estimate the cost of the firm's equity capital to be 15.5 per cent (per annum).

§4-15. Probably the most widely used interpretation of the constant-growth model developed in §4-14 is the so-called Gordon Growth Model. We can develop this interpretation of the constant-growth model by defining E to be the firm's earnings during the current (first) year, that is, the firm's earnings over the time period from $t = 0$ until $t = 1$. Moreover, suppose the firm re-invests a constant proportion, $0 \leq b \leq 1$, of its earnings in each year, in which case the dividend payment at the end of the first year will be $d_1 = (1 - b)E$. Now assuming that retained earnings are re-invested at the rate R, it then follows that the firm's earnings during the second year will be $E + RbE = E(1 + Rb)$. At the end of the second year, the firm will pay a dividend amounting to $d_2 = (1 - b)E(1 + Rb)$ and re-invest $bE(1 + Rb)$. This means that its earnings during the third year will be $E(1 + Rb) + RbE(1 + Rb) = E(1 + Rb)(1 + Rb) = E(1 + Rb)^2$. The dividend at the end of the third year will thus be $d_3 = (1 - b)E(1 + Rb)^2$, and so on. Generalizing this procedure shows that the dividend payment at time t will be $d_t = (1 - b)E(1 + bR)^{t-1}$. This in turn implies that the present value of the future stream of dividends will be

$$P_0 = \sum_{t=1}^{N} \frac{(1 - b)E(1 + bR)^{t-1}}{(1 + k_e)^t} = \frac{E(1 - b)}{1 + bR} \sum_{t=1}^{N} \left(\frac{1 + bR}{1 + k_e} \right)^t$$

where, as previously, k_e is the cost of equity capital. Now, if we set $d_1 = E(1 - b)$, $g = bR$ and let $N \to \infty$ in the constant-growth model developed in §4-14 then the above equation reduces to

$$\lim_{N \to \infty} P_0 = \frac{E(1 - b)}{1 + bR} \sum_{t=1}^{N} \left(\frac{1 + bR}{1 + k_e} \right)^t = \lim_{N \to \infty} \frac{d_1}{1 + g} \sum_{t=1}^{N} \left(\frac{1 + g}{1 + k_e} \right)^t = \frac{d_1}{k_e - g} = \frac{(1 - b)E}{k_e - bR}$$

In other words, the dividend payment made at time one will be $d_1 = E(1 - b)$, whilst dividends will grow each year by the product of the retention rate for earnings b and the rate R at which retained earnings will be re-invested. That is, $g = bR$ in the constant-growth model formulated in §4-14.

We can demonstrate the application of this result by supposing that a firm's cost of equity capital is $k_e = 20$ per cent (per annum) and that the firm earns $R = 25$ per cent (per annum) on new investments and pays $1 - b = 40$ per cent of its earnings out as dividends at the end of each year. These assumptions will mean that the firm's future earnings will grow at a rate $g = bR = 0.6 \times 0.25 = 0.15$ or 15 per cent (per annum). Hence, since the cost of equity is $k_e = 20$ per cent (per annum), it follows that

$$P_0 = \frac{(1 - b)E}{k_e - bR} = \frac{0.4 \times E}{0.2 - 0.15} = \frac{0.4E}{0.05}$$

or

$$\frac{E}{P_0} = \frac{0.05}{0.4} = 0.125$$

will be the firm's earnings to price ratio.

§4-16. Our main focus in this chapter has been on a risk measure that empirical researchers have shown to have an instrumental association with equity returns, namely, the ratio of the debt and equity with which firms finance their operating activities. Our analysis has been based on the assumption of a perfect capital market in which there are no transactions costs and no personal taxes or bankruptcy costs, where all traders in the market have costless and equal access to any information they need and where firms and individuals can borrow (and lend) as much as they want at the same riskless rate of interest. Under these assumptions, the return on equity for a levered firm will be equal to the return on the equity of an 'equivalent' unlevered firm plus a risk premium that hinges on the ratio of the debt and equity with which the levered firm finances its productive activities. Moreover, in the perfect capital market on which our analysis is based, firms will finance their operating activities with as much debt as possible. This follows from the fact that the weighted average cost of capital continuously declines as the firm's debt-to-equity ratio grows in magnitude. Unfortunately, in the real world, firms and individuals cannot borrow at the riskless rate of interest. And when this assumption is relaxed and other market imperfections are taken into account, it is not hard to show that a firm's weighted average cost of capital will at first decline as debt is substituted for equity in the firm's capital structure. However, a point will eventually be reached where so much debt has been issued that the firm will have difficulty meeting the interest payments on its debt should it find itself getting into financial difficulties. At this point, both the debt and equity holders will demand higher rates of return as compensation for the increased risks they are required to bear and the firm's weighted average cost of capital will begin to rise. Correspondingly, the firm's market value will reach a maximum at this minimum cost of capital and will then fall away as the cost of capital increases in response to the risks posed by the increasing levels of debt comprising the firm's capital structure.

Selected references

Miller, M. (1977) 'Debt and taxes', *Journal of Finance*, 32: 261–75.

Miller, M. (1988) 'The Modigliani–Miller proposition after thirty years', *Journal of Economic Perspectives*, 2: 99–120.

Modigliani, F. and Miller, M. (1958) 'The cost of capital, corporation finance and the theory of investment', *American Economic Review*, 48: 261–97.

Modigliani, F. and Miller, M. (1963) 'Corporate income taxes and the cost of capital: a correction', *American Economic Review*, 53: 433–43.

Myers, S. and Majluf, N. (1984) 'Corporate financing and investment decisions when firms have information that investors do not', *Journal of Financial Economics*, 13: 187–221.

Villamil, A. (2008) 'Modigliani–Miller theorem', in S. Durlauf and L. Blume (eds) *New Palgrave Dictionary of Economics*, Basingstoke: Palgrave Macmillan.

Exercises

1. In §4-10, it was shown that in a capital market where there are no bankruptcy costs, the weighted average cost of capital for a levered firm will be

$$k^* = r(1 - T_C)\frac{B_L}{V_L} + p_L\frac{S_L}{V_L}$$

where

$$k^* = \frac{(1 - T_C)X}{V_L}$$

is the weighted average cost of capital for the levered firm, r is the risk-free rate of interest, T_C is the rate of corporation tax, p_L is the cost of the levered firm's equity, B_L is the market value of the levered firm's debt, S_L is the market value of the levered firm's equity and $V_L = B_L + S_L$ is the overall market value of the levered firm. Now suppose that we let $S_L \to 0$ so that $B_L \to V_L$; that is, in the limit, the firm is completely financed by debt. Explain why it will ***not*** be the case that $k^* \to r(1 - T_C)$.

2. Suppose that the overall market value of the firm is determined by subtracting the expected bankruptcy costs from the market value of the firm when there is no possibility of bankruptcy. In §4-13, it was shown that the market value of the levered firm V_L will then bear the following relationship to the market value V_U of the unlevered firm:

$$V_L = \frac{V_U}{1 - T_C G + \alpha G^2}$$

where T_C is the rate of corporation tax, α is the proportion of the firm's market value that is absorbed in bankruptcy costs should bankruptcy occur and G^2 is the probability of bankruptcy. Here,

$$G = \frac{B_L}{V_L} = \frac{B_L}{S_L + B_L}$$

where B_L is the market value of the levered firm's debt, S_L is the market value of the levered firm's equity and $V_L = S_L + B_L$ is the levered firm's overall market value. Use this result to show that the weighted average cost of capital for a levered firm will bear the following relationship to the cost of equity for the unlevered firm:

$$k^* = p_U(1 - T_C G + \alpha G^2)$$

where

$$p_U = \frac{(1 - T_C)X}{V_U}$$

is the cost of equity for the unlevered firm,

$$k^* = \frac{(1 - T_C)X}{V_L}$$

is the weighted average cost of capital for the levered firm and X is the unlevered firm's operating profit.

3. The cost of equity for the levered firm is given by

$$p_L = \frac{(X - rB_L)(1 - T_C)}{S_L}$$

Use the expression for the weighted average cost of capital k^* obtained in Exercise 2 to show that when there are non-trivial bankruptcy costs, the weighted average cost of capital can still be expressed as

$$k^* = p_L \frac{S_L}{V_L} + r(1 - T_C)\frac{B_L}{V_L}$$

where $r(1 - T_C)$ is the after-tax cost of debt.

4. Use your answer to Exercise 3 to show that in the presence of bankruptcy costs, the cost of equity for the levered firm will be given by

$$p_L = p_U + (p_U - r)(1 - T_C)\frac{B_L}{S_L} + \alpha p_U \left(1 + \frac{B_L}{S_L}\right)\left(\frac{\frac{B_L}{S_L}}{1 + \frac{B_L}{S_L}}\right)^2$$

where, from Exercise 2, α is the proportion of the firm's market value that is absorbed in bankruptcy costs. Show that substituting this result into the expression given for the weighted average cost of capital in Exercise 3 leads to the expression for the weighted average cost of capital given in Exercise 2.

5. In §4-13, it was shown that in the presence of potential bankruptcy costs, the market value of the levered firm V_L will bear the following relationship to the market value V_U of the unlevered firm:

$$V_L = \frac{V_U}{1 - T_C G + \alpha G^2}$$

Differentiate through this expression with respect to $G = B_L/V_L$ and thereby determine the debt-to-equity ratio that maximizes the market value of the firm. Use the result you obtain in conjunction with your answer to Exercise 3 to determine the cost of equity p_L and the weighted average cost of capital k^* at which the market value of the levered firm is maximized.

5 The relationship between equity value, dividends and other cash flow streams

§ 5-1. In 1937, John Burr Williams, one of the founding fathers of what today is known as the fundamental analysis approach to equity valuation, argued that an asset's value should be determined by calculating the present value of its future cash flows. 'A cow', wrote Williams, 'for her milk. A hen for her eggs, and a stock, by heck, for her dividends. An orchard for fruit, bees for their honey, and stocks, besides, for their dividends.' Thus, said Williams, since future dividends are the cash flows one expects to receive from an investment in ordinary shares, it necessarily follows that one should determine the intrinsic, long-term worth of an ordinary share by calculating the present value of the dividends that one expects to receive from it. Nowadays, this approach for determining intrinsic value is widely used in the financial markets, although it is normally applied in conjunction with an asset pricing model, such as the Capital Asset Pricing Model (CAPM), in order to provide a rational basis for determining the cost of equity to be used in the discounting process.

Now, in a seminal article published in 1961, Merton Miller and Franco Modigliani showed that whilst one could always calculate the value of an ordinary share in the way suggested by Williams – that is, by calculating the present value of its future dividend stream – it is not the stream of future dividend payments that is the fundamental determinant of investment (i.e. intrinsic) value. Miller and Modigliani argued, in particular, that if a firm's existing investment opportunity set is applied indefinitely into the future then 'the division' of a firm's earnings 'between cash dividends and retained earnings in any period is a mere detail …'. In particular, 'the dividend payout … determine[s] merely how a given return to stockholders … split[s] as between current dividends and current capital gains and [does] not affect either the size of the total return or the current value of the shares'. In other words, whilst dividend payments reduce the market value of equity on a pound-for-pound basis, the dividend policy invoked by the firm will have no secondary or indirect effects on equity value. Hence, a firm can change its plans about the way it will distribute its future earnings as dividends, but this will have no impact on the current market value of the firm's equity; that is, whether the firm plans to pay niggardly dividends in the immediate future and then generous dividends over the longer term or vice versa will have no effect on the current market value of the firm's equity stock. The fundamental insight that Miller and Modigliani brought to bear on this issue is that dividends must be viewed as part of the firm's financing policies. We can see this by a careful inspection of the original proof presented by Miller and Modigliani.

§ 5-2. Suppose then that one defines the discrete-time return $r(t+1)$ to a share over the period from time t until time $t+1$ as

$$r(t+1)=\frac{div(t+1)+P(t+1)-P(t)}{P(t)}$$

where $P(t)$ is the price (per share) at time t of the firm's equity, $div(t+1)$ is the dividend (per share) paid at time $t+1$ and $P(t+1)$ is the price (per share) at time $t+1$. Now, suppose we define $n(t)$ to be the number of shares the firm has on issue at time t. Then we can multiply the numerator and denominator of the above expression by $n(t)$, in which case we have

$$r(t+1)=\frac{n(t)div(t+1)+n(t)P(t+1)-n(t)P(t)}{n(t)P(t)}$$

But here we can define $Div(t+1)\equiv n(t)div(t+1)$ to be the total value of the dividends paid out by the firm at time $t+1$ and $V(t)\equiv n(t)P(t)$ to be the overall market value of the firm's equity at time t. Using these definitions it follows that the return on equity over the period from time t until time $t+1$ can be restated as

$$r(t+1)=\frac{Div(t+1)+n(t)P(t+1)-V(t)}{V(t)}=\frac{Div(t+1)+n(t)P(t+1)}{V(t)}-1$$

or

$$V(t)=\frac{Div(t+1)+n(t)P(t+1)}{1+r(t+1)}$$

This result says that the market value $V(t)$ of the firm's equity at time t is given by discounting the market value of its shares at time $t+1$,

$$\frac{n(t)P(t+1)}{1+r(t+1)}$$

and adding the discounted value of any dividends that will be paid at time $t+1$,

$$\frac{Div(t+1)}{1+r(t+1)}=\frac{n(t)div(t+1)}{1+r(t+1)}$$

Note that this equation, which is often referred to as the Hamilton–Jacobi–Bellman equation, seems to suggest that a firm's dividend policy does have important implications for the value of the firm's equity, since the total dividend paid by the firm, $Div(t+1)$, is an instrumental variable on the right-hand side of the equation. We now show, however, that this is not the case.

Now suppose the firm issues $m(t+1)$ new shares at time $t+1$ so that the number of shares on issue at time $t+1$ will be $n(t+1)=m(t+1)+n(t)$. Then we may state the 'funds flow' identity:

$$NOI(t+1)+m(t+1)P(t+1)=I(t+1)+Div(t+1)$$

where $NOI(t+1)$ is the firm's net operating income over the period from time t until time $t+1$ and $I(t+1)$ is the investment the firm makes in productive assets (buildings, equipment, etc.)

at time $t+1$. Note that the left-hand side of this equation captures the sources of funds available to the firm, namely, the firm's net operating income plus the proceeds it receives from any new share issues. The right-hand side of this equation captures the way the firm uses these funds, namely, the cash the firm invests in productive assets and the dividend it pays to its shareholders. Now, it is this equation that Miller and Modigliani regard as crucial since it captures the financing aspect of a firm's dividend policy. Furthermore, since, as previously noted, the number of shares on issue at time $t+1$ is given by $n(t+1) = n(t) + m(t+1)$, the funds flow identity may be restated as

$$NOI(t+1) + [n(t+1) - n(t)]P(t+1) = I(t+1) + Div(t+1)$$

or, upon using the fact that $V(t+1) \equiv n(t+1)P(t+1)$ represents the market value of the firm's equity on issue at time $t+1$,

$$Div(t+1) = NOI(t+1) + V(t+1) - n(t)P(t+1) - I(t+1)$$

Substituting this latter expression for $Div(t+1)$ into the Hamilton–Jacobi–Bellman equation then shows

$$V(t) = \frac{Div(t+1) + n(t)P(t+1)}{1 + r(t+1)}$$

or

$$V(t) = \frac{NOI(t+1) + V(t+1) - n(t)P(t+1) - I(t+1) + n(t)P(t+1)}{1 + r(t+1)}$$

which simplifies to

$$V(t) = \frac{NOI(t+1) - I(t+1) + V(t+1)}{1 + r(t+1)}$$

Now, for pedagogical convenience, we assume that the discount rate $r(t+1)$ is constant through time. We then have

$$V(t) = \frac{NOI(t+1) - I(t+1)}{1 + r} + \frac{V(t+1)}{1 + r}$$

where r is the inter-temporally constant discount rate, that is, the cost of the firm's equity capital. This version of the Hamilton–Jacobi–Bellman equation says that the value of the firm's equity at time t, $V(t)$, is given by the present value of its operating cash flows at time $t+1$,

$$\frac{NOI(t+1) - I(t+1)}{1 + r}$$

plus the present value of the firm's equity at time $t+1$,

$$\frac{V(t+1)}{1 + r}$$

Most importantly, note that the dividend $Div(t+1)$ that the firm pays at time t does not appear explicitly in this version of the Hamilton–Jacobi–Bellman equation. We say that it does not 'explicitly' appear because we cannot preclude the possibility that the firm's dividend policy influences $V(t+1)$. To assess whether this might be the case one can replace 't' with $t+1$ in the operating cash flow version of the Hamilton–Jacobi–Bellman equation given above. This will mean that the market value of the firm's equity at time $t+1$ will bear the following relationship to the operating cash flow that accrues to equity at time $t+2$ and the market value of equity at time $t+2$:

$$V(t+1) = \frac{NOI(t+2) - I(t+2)}{1+r} + \frac{V(t+2)}{1+r}$$

Using this result, it follows that we can restate the market value of the firm's equity at time t in the following terms:

$$\begin{aligned} V(t) &= \frac{NOI(t+1) - I(t+1)}{1+r} + \frac{V(t+1)}{1+r} \\ &= \frac{NOI(t+1) - I(t+1)}{1+r} + \frac{NOI(t+2) - I(t+2)}{(1+r)^2} + \frac{V(t+2)}{(1+r)^2} \end{aligned}$$

However, the previous analysis also implies that

$$V(t+2) = \frac{NOI(t+3) - I(t+3) + V(t+3)}{1+r}$$

and so substitution into the above expression shows that

$$V(t) = \frac{NOI(t+1) - I(t+1)}{1+r} + \frac{NOI(t+2) - I(t+2)}{(1+r)^2} + \frac{NOI(t+3) - I(t+3)}{(1+r)^3} + \frac{V(t+3)}{(1+r)^3}$$

will be an alternative and equally valid expression for the market value of the firm's equity at time t. Hence, if we continue with this iterative process, we can show that the market value of the firm's equity will be

$$V(t) = \sum_{j=1}^{N} \frac{NOI(t+j) - I(t+j)}{(1+r)^j} + \frac{V(t+N)}{(1+r)^N}$$

where $V(t+N)$ is the market value of the firm's equity at time $t+N$ and where N can assume any integral value.

Now, assume that $V(t+N) \leq K < \infty$ for all values of N, where K is a finite real number. This is known as a 'transversality condition' and states that the market value of equity will always remain finite – no matter how far into the future one carries the calculations. Moreover, this assumption implies

$$\lim_{N\to\infty} \frac{V(t+N)}{(1+r)^N} \leq \lim_{N\to\infty} \frac{K}{(1+r)^N} = 0$$

since K is a finite number and $\lim_{N\to\infty}(1+r)^N \to \infty$. Hence, when the firm has an infinite life, the market value of its equity will be

$$V(t)=\sum_{j=1}^{\infty}\frac{NOI(t+j)-I(t+j)}{(1+r)^j}$$

Note how this result shows that the market value of a firm's equity depends exclusively on its operating cash flows. In other words, since dividends do not appear in the above valuation expression, it looks as though our analysis proves that dividend payments hold no relevance at all for the valuation of a firm's equity. Here we need to recall, however, that the equity holders in a firm will be the eventual recipients of all the operating cash flows earned by the firm. This in turn will mean that the present value of the dividends paid out over the life of the firm must be equal to the present value of the operating cash flows the firm generates through its investment opportunity set, or

$$V(t)=\sum_{j=1}^{\infty}\frac{NOI(t+j)-I(t+j)}{(1+r)^j}=\sum_{j=1}^{\infty}\frac{D(t+j)}{(1+r)^j}$$

This shows that one can determine equity value either by discounting the future dividends a firm will pay or alternatively, by discounting its future operating cash flows since the present value of its future dividends must adjust to (i.e. be equal to) the present value of its operating cash flows. However, the specific time pattern of dividend payments will be irrelevant to the value of a firm's equity, since every time pattern of dividend payments will have a present value that is equal to the present value of the firm's future operating cash flows. In other words, investors will care little about whether the firm pays niggardly dividends in the immediate future and generous dividends in the longer term or vice versa, since the present value of the dividends it will pay must be equal to the present value of the operating cash flows generated by its investment opportunity set. Thus, whilst one can legitimately determine equity value by discounting the stream of future dividends, the precise dividend policy invoked by the firm will hold no relevance whatsoever for the valuation of a firm's equity.

§ 5-3. We can further clarify the role that dividends play in equity valuation by considering the following simple example. Tai-Leigh is a company financed entirely by equity that has been paying an annual dividend for many years of £0.12 per share on the five million shares it has on issue. It has existing capital projects in place that will enable this policy to continue indefinitely into the future. Tai-Leigh has been offered a contract for a major capital project that would involve an investment of £500,000 in each of the next two years. In all subsequent years, as a result of the contract, earnings are expected to increase by £300,000 per annum. Tai-Leigh's directors plan to obtain the finance necessary for implementing the capital project by withholding dividend payments for each of the next two years. The current market price of Tai-Leigh's shares is £0.60 each. This means that Tai-Leigh's cost of equity capital can be calculated as its annual dividend payment divided by the price of its shares, or $0.12/0.60 = 0.2 = 20$ per cent per annum (as in §4-14 of Chapter 4 with a growth rate in dividends of $g = 0$).

Now, Tai-Leigh effectively has a capital investment opportunity with the following net present value:

$$-\frac{500{,}000}{1.2}-\frac{500{,}000}{1.2^2}+\sum_{t=3}^{\infty}\frac{300{,}000}{1.2^t}$$

Here it will be recalled from Exercise 1 in Chapter 1 that

$$\sum_{t=3}^{\infty}\frac{300{,}000}{1.2^t}=\frac{1}{1.2^2}\sum_{t=1}^{\infty}\frac{300{,}000}{1.2^t}=\frac{300{,}000}{0.2\times 1.2^2}$$

and so the net present value of Tai-Leigh's capital investment opportunity will be

$$-\frac{500{,}000}{1.2}-\frac{500{,}000}{1.2^2}+\frac{300{,}000}{0.2\times 1.2^2}\approx £277{,}777.78$$

Since the capital project has a positive net present value, it ought to be implemented. However, this is not how Tai-Leigh's shareholders will look at it. Rather, they will be concerned with the impact that the capital project will have on the present value of the future dividends they will receive. Note that under its current dividend policy, Tai-Leigh earns a profit of and pays a dividend of 12 pence per share each year. Since Tai-Leigh has five million shares on issue, this will mean that its profit amounts to £0.12 × 5,000,000 = £600,000 per annum. However, under the revised dividend policy, no dividends will be paid at time one or at time two. But from time three and beyond Tai-Leigh, will pay all of its operating cash flows out as dividends. Now, if the proposed capital project is implemented, Tai-Leigh only invests £500,000 at time one and a further £500,000 at time two. Hence, since Tai-Leigh generates £600,000 in cash flows at both these dates, it will have £100,000 left over, which it will be able to invest at its cost of capital. In other words, the £100,000 left over at time one will be invested at Tai-Leigh's cost of capital of 20 per cent per annum and will have grown to £100,000 × 1.2 = £120,000 at time two. At time two, Tai-Leigh receives another £100,000, meaning that over these two years it will have accumulated £220,000 that has not been distributed as dividends. Again it can invest this sum at time two so that it returns £220,000 × 0.2 = £44,000 at time three and beyond, all of which will be paid out as dividends. This means that the extra dividend payments that accrue at time three and beyond as a result of the capital project will be £300,000 + £44,000 = £344,000 per annum. Tai-Leigh's shareholders will compute the net present value of these dividend flows in the following manner:

$$-\frac{600{,}000}{1.2}-\frac{600{,}000}{1.2^2}+\sum_{t=3}^{\infty}\frac{344{,}000}{1.2^t}$$

However, again since

$$\sum_{t=3}^{\infty}\frac{344{,}000}{1.2^t}=\frac{1}{1.2^2}\sum_{t=1}^{\infty}\frac{344{,}000}{1.2^t}=\frac{344{,}000}{0.2\times 1.2^2}$$

this can be restated as

$$-\frac{600{,}000}{1.2}-\frac{600{,}000}{1.2^2}+\frac{344{,}000}{0.2\times 1.2^2}\approx £277{,}777.78$$

Note that the net present value of the extra dividend payments that the firm will make as a result of implementing the capital project is exactly equal to the present value of the capital project calculated earlier. This reflects the fact that the present value of the dividends paid out over the life of the firm must be equal to the present value of the operating cash flows that the firm generates through its investment opportunity set. Moreover, the present value of the dividends that Tai-Leigh will pay under its existing investment opportunity set is given by the number of shares on issue multiplied by the price of each share, or $5{,}000{,}000 \times £0.60 = £3{,}000{,}000$. Hence, if the proposed investment project is implemented, the present value of the dividends that Tai-Leigh will pay out will grow to $£3{,}000{,}000 + £277{,}777.78 = £3{,}277{,}777.78$. This in turn will mean that the market value of each Tai-Leigh share will grow to $£3{,}277{,}777.78/5{,}000{,}000 = 65\frac{5}{9}$ pence once the capital project has been put into place.

§ 5-4. There are, however, a number of objections that have been raised to the Miller and Modigliani dividend policy irrelevance theorem demonstrated here. The first of these says that economic agents will be attracted to firms whose dividend policies are most compatible with the way the agents wish to allocate their consumption expenditure through time. Hence, a firm that changes its dividend policy will be penalized by agents (e.g. by selling their interests in the firm, thereby depressing its equity price) as agents seek to find other firms whose dividend policies are more compatible with their consumption expenditure plans. This is the so-called 'clientele' effect, although, as detailed below, more often than not it is explained in terms of the marginal tax rates facing the economic agents who invest in the firm. This objection is easily rebutted, however, when it is realized that economic agents can 'restore' the dividend policy they prefer by either re-investing the dividends they receive – that is, by buying more equity in the firm (if the dividend pay-out rate is too large) – or by selling some of their equity in the firm (if the dividend pay-out rate is too small). In other words, agents can create what is known as 'home-spun' dividends by such procedures.

A second objection is called the 'bird in the hand argument' and has it that shareholders would prefer dividends now rather than later because of the extra uncertainty that surrounds the payment of future as against current dividends. But the cost of equity, r (as in §5-2 above), already reflects this uncertainty, and so adjusting further for it represents a form of 'double counting'. A dividend to be received in one period's time is discounted by $1/(1+r)$, whereas a dividend to be received in two periods' time is discounted by $1/(1+r)^2$, and so on. To depress the present values of future dividend payments beyond that implied by the cost of capital, r, because of the alleged extra uncertainty associated with them, is clearly a case of double counting.

A legitimate objection relates to taxation. Since dividends attract taxation at the marginal rate of personal taxation, leaving potential dividends in the firm to accumulate as capital gains delays the incidence of the taxation liability. If needed, the economic agent can borrow against the capital value of their equity, thereby effectively receiving a dividend but without the burden of incurring an immediate tax liability. Moreover, when the economic agent does eventually sell their equity securities, they will be liable for capital gains tax on the capital appreciation that has occurred since the original purchase of their equity securities. The rate of capital gains tax is normally much lower than the rate of personal taxation on dividends, and so, when the economic agent does eventually have to pay taxation on the income from their equity investment, it will be much lower than would have been the case had they taken the income from the equity investment as dividends. Hence, when tax rates vary according to the source of income, the dividend policy implemented by the firm can have a significant impact on the value of the firm's equity. Given this, one would expect to see high income earners (with high rates of marginal taxation) to be attracted to firms that pay niggardly dividends in order that they can take most of their gains in the form of capital appreciation on their equity investments and thereby benefit from the favourable tax treatment associated with the capital gains that arise when the shares are eventually sold. This is another aspect of the 'clientele' effect alluded to earlier.

A second legitimate objection to Miller and Modigliani's dividend policy irrelevance theorem relates to the fact that dividends might be used to signal permanent increases in a firm's future cash flows. If a firm's operating cash flows have permanently increased then the firm might increase its dividends to let shareholders know that such is the case. This observation goes back to a seminal study by John Lintner in 1956 (see the 'Selected References' for this chapter), who showed, both by using statistical techniques and by interviewing financial executives in large US firms, that once dividends are increased, managers are very reluctant to see them reduced. Hence, a firm will only increase its dividends if it is convinced that it can at least maintain them into the future. And this will mean that the way a firm plans to distribute its future earnings as dividends can have a significant impact on the current market value of the firm's equity, because reduced dividend payments will be interpreted as a signal for reduced future operating cash flows and vice versa.

§ 5-5. Before 1973, the taxation of dividends in the UK was based on what is known as the 'classical' system of taxation. This system effectively taxes dividends twice. Thus, suppose that a company has earnings of £1 and that the rate of corporation tax on its earnings is 26 per cent. Then, if the company distributes the balance of its earnings after the payment of corporation tax, its equity holders will receive £1 – £0.26 = £0.74 in dividends. Moreover, suppose that the company's shareholders pay income tax at a rate of 20 per cent on the income they receive. Then the shareholders will receive (£1 – £0.20) × 0.74 = £0.592 (59.2 pence) in dividends after the payment of income tax. Thus, since only 59.2 pence of the original £1 in earnings finds its way to the company's shareholders, we have an effective rate of taxation of 1 – 0.592 = 0.408, or 40.8 per cent. The imputation system introduced in 1973 was designed to redress this 'double-taxation' burden. Under the imputation system that operated in the UK from 1973 until 1999, dividends were deemed to be received net of the basic rate of taxation. Hence, if a company paid a dividend of £500,000, the Inland Revenue would 'gross this up' to £625,000 and take £625,000 × 0.2 = £625,000 – £500,000 = £125,000 as being the payment of income tax at the basic rate. The company would then pay the imputed tax to the Inland Revenue when the dividend was paid to its shareholders. However, the company would also receive a tax credit for this amount and it could use this to reduce its corporation tax when it fell due for payment. Hence, the payment of the £500,000 dividend would invoke the following entries in the company's accounting records:

DR	Profit and Loss Appropriation Account	£500,000	
CR	Provision for Dividend		£500,000
DR	Advanced Corporation Taxation	£125,000	
DR	Provision for Dividend	£500,000	
CR	Bank		£625,000

Now if we suppose the firm has earnings (i.e. a profit) of £2,000,000, this will give rise to a corporation tax liability of £2,000,000 × 0.26 = £520,000. However, the Advanced Corporation Tax can be set against the corporation tax liability, thus resulting in the payment of only £520,000 – £125,000 = £395,000 in taxation to the Inland Revenue. The entries in the firm's books would thus be

DR	Profit and Loss	£520,000	
CR	Provision for Income Tax		£520,000
DR	Provision for Income Tax	£520,000	
CR	Advanced Corporation Tax		£125,000
CR	Bank		£395,000

Note that the total amount paid in taxation is the £125,000 in Advanced Corporation Tax plus £395,000 in corporation tax paid through the last journal entry. Thus, the total amount of taxation paid is £125,000 + £395,000 = £520,000, or 26 per cent of the £2,000,000 profit the firm has made. This means that shareholders will have £2,000,000 – £520,000 = £1,480,000 of the original profit left. Under the classical system, however, the amount of the original profit left for shareholders after the payment of taxation would have been nearly £300,000 lower, as demonstrated by the following calculation:

$$(1 - 0.26)(1 - 0.2) \times £2{,}000{,}000 = 0.592 \times £2{,}000{,}000 = £1{,}184{,}000$$

Before concluding this section, we should note that there were many UK companies whose corporation tax was persistently less than their Advanced Corporation Tax. In such circumstances, the companies would have to carry forward this difference on their balance sheets. It was often the case that this 'overhang' of Advanced Corporation Tax would never be recouped and this is one reason given by the UK Government for the abandonment of the dividend imputation system in 1999. Dividends in the UK are now taxed using a combination of the imputation system and the classical system that prevailed before 1973, depending on the shareholder's marginal rate of income tax.

§ 5-6. It will occasionally be the case that the stream of operating cash flows that a firm earns through their investment opportunity set can be approximated by a functional form that leads to a closed-form expression for the value of the firm's equity. The constant-growth model considered in §4-14 of Chapter 4 is a good example of a dividend stream that leads to a closed-form expression for the value of a firm's equity. But there are other cash flow specifications that also lead to closed-form expressions for the valuation of equity. As an example, suppose it is expected that a firm's future operating cash flows will take the following form:

$$C(t) = a + \frac{b}{t!}$$

where a and b are parameters and $t! = t(t-1)(t-2)\cdots 1$ is the factorial function. Note that the opening ($t = 1$) cash flow will be $C(1) = a + b$, but the cash flow will then asymptotically decay away towards a long run cash flow of $C(\infty) = a$. Figure 5.1 is prepared on the assumption that $a = 1$ and $b = 1$ and gives a typical profile for the cash flows associated with this particular cash flow function. One might expect to see a cash flow profile like this when a

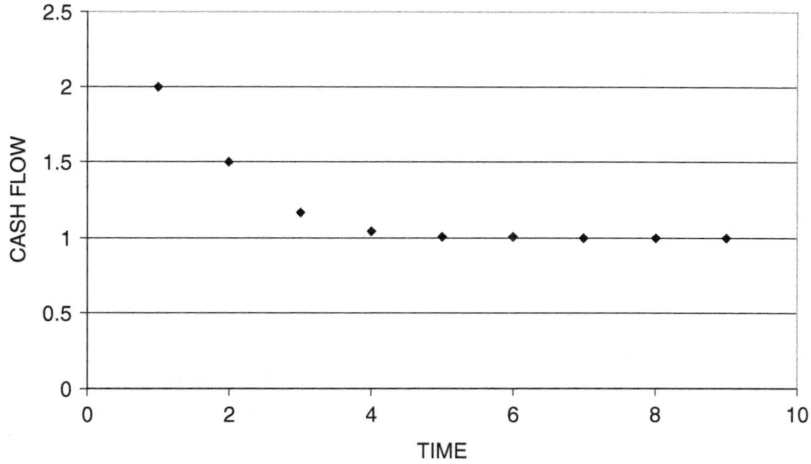

Figure 5.1 The cash flow function $C(t) = 1 + \frac{1}{t!}$

firm is experiencing economic rents that are gradually being eaten away as new firms enter the industry seeking a share of the excessive profits that are available. Moreover, for this cash flow specification, the value of equity $V(0)$ will be

$$V(0) = \sum_{t=1}^{\infty} \frac{C(t)}{(1+r)^t} = \sum_{t=1}^{\infty} \frac{a + \frac{b}{t!}}{(1+r)^t}$$

Now, one can split this expression into two components, namely,

$$V(0) = a \sum_{t=1}^{\infty} \frac{1}{(1+r)^t} + b \sum_{t=1}^{\infty} \frac{1}{t!(1+r)^t}$$

We have previously shown, however, that the first term in this expression can be evaluated as

$$\sum_{t=1}^{\infty} \frac{1}{(1+r)^t} = \frac{1}{r}$$

(as in §5-3 above and Exercise 1 in Chapter 1). For the second term, we note that the Taylor series expansion for the exponential function is

$$\exp(z) = e^z = 1 + z + \frac{1}{2!}z^2 + \frac{1}{3!}z^3 + \frac{1}{4!}z^4 + \cdots$$

and if we let $z = \frac{1}{1+r}$ in this expression then we have

$$\exp\left(\frac{1}{1+r}\right) = 1 + \frac{1}{1+r} + \frac{1}{2!}\frac{1}{(1+r)^2} + \frac{1}{3!}\frac{1}{(1+r)^3} + \cdots = 1 + \sum_{t=1}^{\infty} \frac{1}{t!(1+r)^t}$$

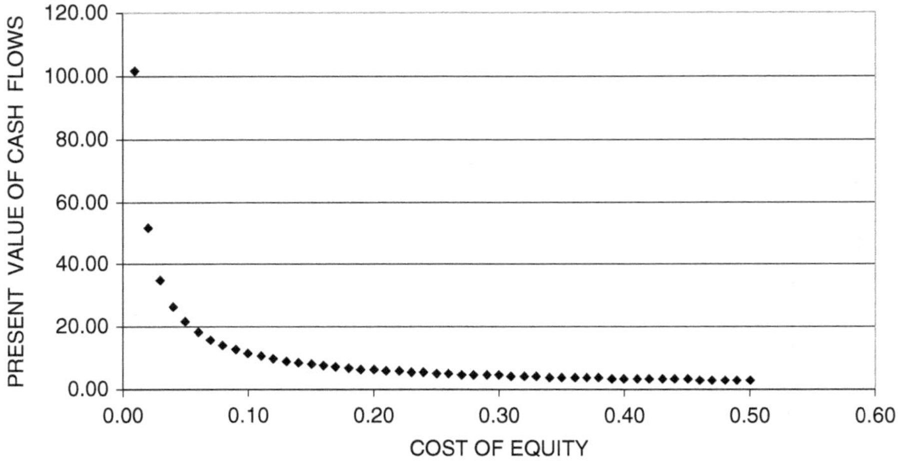

Figure 5.2 Present value of future cash flows for the cash flow function: $C(t) = 1 + \frac{1}{t!}$

It thus follows that the present value of the future cash flows generated by this particular cash flow function must be

$$V(0) = \sum_{t=1}^{\infty} \frac{a + \frac{b}{t!}}{(1+r)^t} = \frac{a}{r} + b\left[\exp\left(\frac{1}{1+r}\right) - 1\right]$$

Again we can let $a = 1$ and $b = 1$ in the above formula, in which case the relationship between the present value of the cash flows $V(0)$ and the cost of equity r is as summarized in Figure 5.2. Note how, under this specification, the present value of the future cash flows falls away as the cost of equity grows in magnitude. Now, an important point to be made here is that we can differentiate across both sides of the expression for $V(0)$ given above with respect to r and thereby determine the present value of the future cash flows associated with alternative cash flow functions. Doing so, shows

$$\begin{aligned}\frac{d}{dr}\left[\sum_{t=1}^{\infty} \frac{a + \frac{b}{t!}}{(1+r)^t}\right] &= \sum_{t=1}^{\infty} \frac{-\left(a + \frac{b}{t!}\right)t}{(1+r)^{t+1}} = \frac{d}{dr}\left\{\frac{a}{r} + b\left[\exp\left(\frac{1}{1+r}\right) - 1\right]\right\} \\ &= -\left[\frac{a}{r^2} + \frac{b}{(1+r)^2}\exp\left(\frac{1}{1+r}\right)\right]\end{aligned}$$

Now if we multiply both sides of the above expression by $1 + r$, we end up with the result that if the firm's cash flows evolve in accordance with the formula

$$C(t) = \left(a + \frac{b}{t!}\right)t = at + \frac{b}{(t-1)!}$$

then the present value of its future cash flows will be

$$V(0) = \sum_{t=1}^{\infty} \frac{at + \frac{b}{(t-1)!}}{(1+r)^t} = a\frac{1+r}{r^2} + b\frac{\exp\left(\frac{1}{1+r}\right)}{1+r}$$

Moreover, the procedure used here can be applied to every 'well-behaved' cash flow function that returns a closed-form expression for the present value of the firm's future cash flows. More important, however, is that it is suggestive of an approximation procedure that can be employed even when the function that describes the evolution of the firm's future cash flows does not lead to a closed-form expression for the present value of the future cash flows.

§ 5-7. We can develop the point being made here by considering the following exponential cash flow function and its associated Taylor series expansion:

$$C(t) = ae^{-\lambda t} = a\left[1 - \lambda t + \tfrac{1}{2}(\lambda t)^2 - \tfrac{1}{6}(\lambda t)^3 + \cdots\right]$$

where a is a parameter and λ captures the rate of decay in the firm's periodic cash flows over time. The series expansion for the cash flow function given here will mean that the present value of the future cash flows the firm expects to earn will be

$$V(0) = \sum_{t=1}^{\infty} \frac{ae^{-\lambda t}}{(1+r)^t} = a\sum_{t=1}^{\infty} \frac{1 - \lambda t + \frac{1}{2}(\lambda t)^2 - \frac{1}{6}(\lambda t)^3 + \cdots}{(1+r)^t}$$

Now, we can break this expression down into its various components, namely,

$$V(0) = a\sum_{t=1}^{\infty} \frac{1}{(1+r)^t} - a\lambda\sum_{t=1}^{\infty} \frac{t}{(1+r)^t} + \frac{1}{2}a\lambda^2\sum_{t=1}^{\infty} \frac{t^2}{(1+r)^t} - \frac{1}{6}a\lambda^3\sum_{t=1}^{\infty} \frac{t^3}{(1+r)^t} + \cdots$$

Recall, however, from previous analysis (as in §5-3 above and Exercise 1 in Chapter 1) that we have

$$\sum_{t=1}^{\infty} \frac{1}{(1+r)^t} = \frac{1}{r}$$

and so the first term in the above expression is easily evaluated. To evaluate the second term, we first differentiate through this latter result with respect to r as follows:

$$\frac{d}{dr}\left[\sum_{t=1}^{\infty} \frac{1}{(1+r)^t}\right] = \sum_{t=1}^{\infty} \frac{-t}{(1+r)^{t+1}} = \frac{d}{dr}\left(\frac{1}{r}\right) = -\frac{1}{r^2}$$

Multiplying both sides of this latter equation by $1+r$ gives

$$\sum_{t=1}^{\infty} \frac{t}{(1+r)^t} = \frac{1+r}{r^2}$$

Now, we can again differentiate through this expression with respect to r:

$$\frac{d}{dr}\left[\sum_{t=1}^{\infty}\frac{t}{(1+r)^t}\right]=\sum_{t=1}^{\infty}\frac{-t^2}{(1+r)^{t+1}}=-\frac{2+r}{r^3}$$

Again multiplying both sides of this equation by $1+r$ gives

$$\sum_{t=1}^{\infty}\frac{t^2}{(1+r)^t}=\frac{(2+r)(1+r)}{r^3}$$

Continuing with this process by differentiating with respect to r a third time, we have

$$\frac{d}{dr}\left[\sum_{t=1}^{\infty}\frac{t^2}{(1+r)^t}\right]=\sum_{t=1}^{\infty}\frac{-t^3}{(1+r)^{t+1}}=-\frac{6+6r+r^2}{r^4}$$

Multiplying both sides of this equation by $1+r$ then gives

$$\sum_{t=1}^{\infty}\frac{t^3}{(1+r)^t}=\frac{1+r}{r^3}+\frac{(3+r)(2+r)(1+r)}{r^4}$$

We could continue with this process *ad infinitum* and thereby obtain closed-form expressions for even higher powers of t, but the results already derived will suffice for our present purposes.

Suppose then that we substitute each of the above results into the series expansion for the present value of the future cash flows. It then follows that

$$\begin{aligned}V(0)&=\sum_{t=1}^{\infty}\frac{ae^{-\lambda t}}{(1+r)^t}=a\sum_{t=1}^{\infty}\frac{1-\lambda t+\frac{1}{2}(\lambda t)^2-\frac{1}{6}(\lambda t)^3+\cdots}{(1+r)^t}\\&=\frac{a}{r}-a\lambda\frac{1+r}{r^2}+\frac{a\lambda^2}{2}\frac{(2+r)(1+r)}{r^3}-\frac{a\lambda^3}{6}\left[\frac{1+r}{r^3}+\frac{(3+r)(2+r)(1+r)}{r^4}\right]+\cdots\end{aligned}$$

provides a fourth-order approximation for the present value of the future cash flows. If we include enough terms in the series expansion for $C(t)$, it can be shown that the estimation procedure illustrated here will always provide a good approximation for the present value of the future cash flows for 'well-behaved' cash flow functions. Unfortunately, there will be occasions when the rate of convergence is extremely slow and the series expansion for $C(t)$ will have to be carried to a large number of terms before a satisfactory approximation for the present value of the future cash flows will be obtained. We can illustrate this point by noting that the present value of the future cash flows for the exponential cash flow function demonstrated here turns out to be

$$V(0)=\sum_{t=1}^{\infty}\frac{ae^{-\lambda t}}{(1+r)^t}=\frac{a}{e^{\lambda}(1+r)-1}$$

Now suppose we let $a=1$ and $\lambda=0.005=\frac{1}{2}$ per cent, so that the firm's cash flows decay away at the rate of one-half of one per cent per annum. Then Table 5.1 summarizes

Table 5.1 Relationship between the actual present value of the future cash flows and the present value of the future cash flows as given by the fourth-order approximation formula when $a = 1$ and $\lambda = 0.005$

Cost of equity r	*Estimated present value*	*Actual present value*
0.01	48.6175	66.3894
0.02	41.9047	39.8204
0.03	29.4763	28.4391
0.04	22.6443	22.1175
0.05	18.3929	18.0952
0.06	15.4942	15.3108
0.07	13.3897	13.2690
0.08	11.7913	11.7077
0.09	10.5354	10.4752
0.10	9.5223	9.4774
0.11	8.6875	8.6532
0.12	7.9877	7.9609
0.13	7.3926	7.3711
0.14	6.8801	6.8627
0.15	6.4342	6.4200
0.16	6.0427	6.0308
0.17	5.6962	5.6862
0.18	5.3873	5.3788
0.19	5.1103	5.1030
0.20	4.8603	4.8540
0.21	4.6337	4.6282
0.22	4.4273	4.4225
0.23	4.2386	4.2343
0.24	4.0652	4.0615
0.25	3.9055	3.9022
0.26	3.7579	3.7549
0.27	3.6211	3.6184
0.28	3.4939	3.4914
0.29	3.3753	3.3731
0.30	3.2645	3.2625

the relationship between the actual present value of the future cash flows as given by the above expression and the present value of the future cash flows as given by the fourth-order approximation formula derived earlier. We can see from this table that, except for very small values of the cost of equity, the estimate of the present value obtained from the fourth-order approximation formula is very close to the actual present value of the future cash flows. However, if we assume instead that $a = 1$ and $\lambda = 0.10$, so that the firm's cash flows decay away at the rate of 10 per cent per annum, then the relationship between the fourth-order approximation and the actual present values of the future cash flows is as summarized in Table 5.2. We can see from this table that the fourth-order formula gives a particularly poor approximation to the actual present value of the future cash flows for all values of the cost of equity. Here, it is important to note that the poor estimates summarized in Table 5.2 can be improved by adding higher-order terms:

$$a\lambda^k \sum_{t=1}^{\infty} \frac{t^k}{(1+r)^t}$$

Table 5.2 Relationship between the actual present value of the future cash flows and the present value of the future cash flows as given by the fourth-order approximation formula when $a = 1$ and $\lambda = 0.10$

Cost of equity r	*Estimated present value*	*Actual present value*
0.01	−582729.60	8.6042
0.02	−35409.80	7.8570
0.03	−6801.72	7.2293
0.04	−2091.15	6.6944
0.05	−830.7200	6.2333
0.06	−387.3407	5.8315
0.07	−201.2382	5.4785
0.08	−112.8406	5.1657
0.09	−66.8371	4.8867
0.10	−41.1600	4.6363
0.11	−26.0158	4.4103
0.12	−16.6796	4.2054
0.13	−10.7129	4.0186
0.14	−6.7853	3.8477
0.15	−4.1363	3.6908
0.16	−2.3139	3.5461
0.17	−1.0398	3.4124
0.18	−0.1378	3.2884
0.19	0.5067	3.1731
0.20	0.9700	3.0656
0.21	1.3039	2.9651
0.22	1.5440	2.8710
0.23	1.7157	2.7827
0.24	1.8367	2.6997
0.25	1.9200	2.6215
0.26	1.9750	2.5477
0.27	2.0088	2.4779
0.28	2.0265	2.4119
0.29	2.0319	2.3492
0.30	2.0281	2.2898

for $k = 4, 5, 6, \ldots$, to the approximation formula until a point is reached where these higher-order terms become insignificantly small and the approximation relatively accurate. But our analysis here shows that the rate of convergence is very slow as extra terms are added and so the power series expansion will have to be carried to a fairly high order if a satisfactory approximation to the present value of the cash flows is to be obtained.

§ 5-8. Much of the subsequent analysis in this book will proceed on the assumption that a firm's operating cash flows evolve continuously in time. Whilst large companies, like those listed on the stock exchange, will normally make dividend payments on only a few fixed dates in any given year, their operating cash flows are typically the outcome of thousands of transactions on any given day and so their operating cash flows will evolve in a way that is closely approximated by the continuous-time assumptions we now invoke. Suppose then that we take $D(s)$ to be the dividend payment a firm makes on an annualized basis over the time period from time s until time $s + ds$. It then follows that the actual dividend payment over this period will be $D(s)ds$. Now, in §5-2 above, it was shown that the present value of the stream of future dividends must be equal to the present value of the firm's operating cash flows, or

$$V(t) = \int_t^\infty e^{-r(s-t)} D(s)ds = \int_t^\infty e^{-r(s-t)} C(s)ds$$

where, as previously, $C(s)$ is the firm's operating cash flow at time s and r is the cost of equity, both measured on an annualized basis. One can demonstrate the application of the above result by assuming that a firm's operating cash flows evolve in accordance with the following function:

$$C(s) = (s-t)e^{-(s-t)}$$

where $s \geq t$. A graph of this cash flow function is depicted in Figure 5.3. One might expect to see a cash flow profile like this when a firm introduces a new product that initially turns out to be very popular but whose profitability decays away once the novelty associated with it begins to wear off. It then follows that the present value of the future cash flows generated by this particular cash flow function must be

$$V(t) = \int_t^\infty e^{-r(s-t)} C(s)ds = \int_t^\infty (s-t)e^{-(1+r)(s-t)} ds = \frac{1}{(1+r)^2}$$

The relationship between the present value of the future cash flows and the cost of equity for this cash flow function is depicted graphically in Figure 5.4. Note how the present value of the future cash flows portrayed in this graph follows the typical pattern of decaying away as the cost of equity grows in magnitude.

We can also differentiate across both sides of the expression for $V(t)$ given above with respect to r and thereby determine the present value of the future cash flows associated with

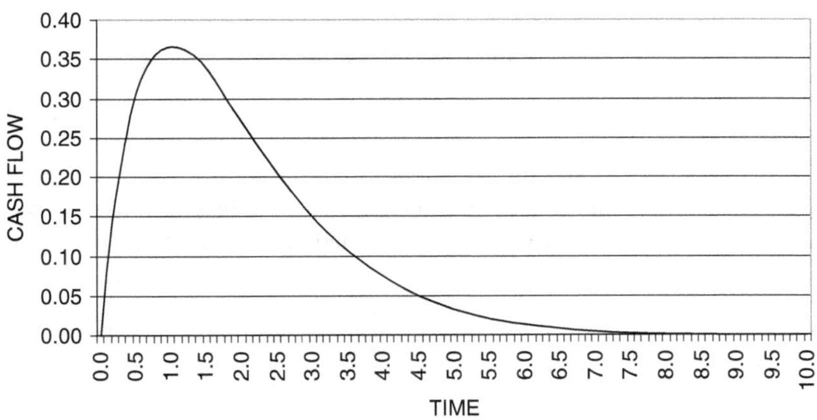

Figure 5.3 The cash flow function $C(s) = (s-t)e^{-(s-t)}$, where $s \geq t$

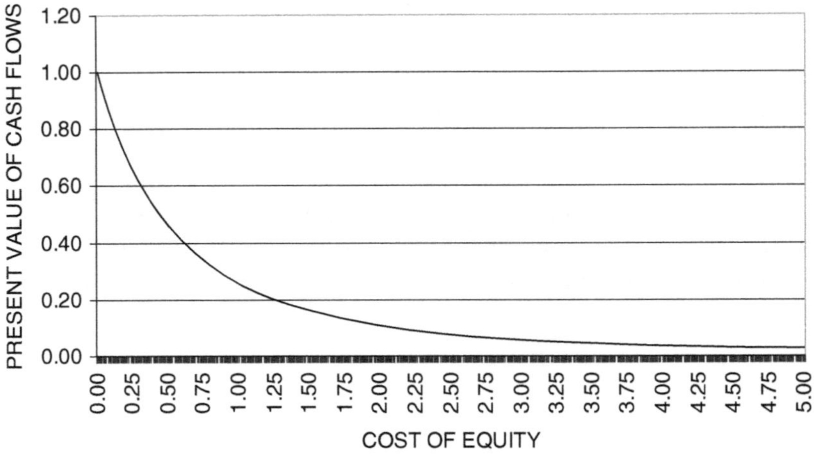

Figure 5.4 Present value of future cash flows for the cash flow function $C(s) = (s-t)e^{-(s-t)}$, where $s \geq t$

alternative cash flow functions. Doing so gives

$$\frac{d}{dr}\left[\int_t^\infty (s-t)e^{-(1+r)(s-t)}ds\right] = -\int_t^\infty (s-t)^2 e^{-(1+r)(s-t)}ds = \frac{d}{dr}\left[\frac{1}{(1+r)^2}\right] = \frac{-2}{(1+r)^3}$$

or

$$\int_t^\infty (s-t)^2 e^{-(1+r)(s-t)}ds = \frac{2}{(1+r)^3}$$

This result shows that if the cash flow function is

$$C(s) = (s-t)^2 e^{-(s-t)}$$

for $s \geq t$, then the present value of the future cash flows will be

$$V(t) = \frac{2}{(1+r)^3}$$

As in §5-7 above, this procedure could be repeated ad infinitum, in which case we can show that the present value of the future cash flows corresponding to the cash flow function

$$C(s) = (s-t)^k e^{-(s-t)}$$

for $s \geq t$ and $k = 1, 2, 3, 4, \ldots$, will be

$$V(t) = \frac{k!}{(1+r)^{k+1}}$$

Table 5.3 Present value as the Laplace transform of the given cash flow function

Cash flow function $C(s)$, for $s \geq t$	*Laplace transform (present value) $V(t) = \int_t^{\infty} e^{-r(s-t)} C(s) ds$*
$(s-t)^k e^{\alpha(s-t)}$	$\dfrac{k!}{(r-\alpha)^{k+1}}$
$\sin[\beta(s-t)]$	$\dfrac{\beta}{r^2+\beta^2}$
$\cos[\beta(s-t)]$	$\dfrac{r}{r^2+\beta^2}$
$e^{\alpha(s-t)} \sin[\beta(s-t)]$	$\dfrac{\beta}{(r-\alpha)^2+\beta^2}$
$e^{\alpha(s-t)} \cos[\beta(s-t)]$	$\dfrac{r-\alpha}{(r-\alpha)^2+\beta^2}$
$\dfrac{1}{\sqrt{\pi[(s-t)+\alpha]}}$	$\dfrac{e^{\alpha r}}{\sqrt{r}}\left[1-\mathrm{erf}\left(\sqrt{\alpha r}\right)\right]$
$\dfrac{\sin\left(2\alpha\sqrt{s-t}\right)}{\pi(s-t)}$	$\mathrm{erf}\left(\dfrac{\alpha}{\sqrt{r}}\right)$

§ 5-9. More generally, the present value of the future cash flows associated with a particular cash flow function is known as the Laplace transform of the given cash flow function. The Laplace transform has been tabulated for a wide variety of functions and in Table 5.3 we summarize some of the more commonly encountered examples.

We can illustrate the application of Table 5.3 by supposing that a capital project's operating cash flows evolve in terms of the function

$$C(s) = (s-t)^k e^{\alpha(s-t)}$$

for $s \geq t$ and integral k, as in the first row, first column of Table 5.3. It then follows that the present value of the future cash flows – or, equivalently, the Laplace transform of $C(s)$ – will be

$$V(t) = \int_t^{\infty} e^{-r(s-t)} C(s) ds = \int_t^{\infty} (s-t)^k e^{(\alpha-r)(s-t)} ds = \frac{k!}{(r-\alpha)^{k+1}}$$

as in the first row, second column of the table. Note that if we let $\alpha = -1$ then the above result reduces to the previously obtained result (as in §5-8 above):

$$V(t) = \int_t^{\infty} (s-t)^k e^{-(s-t)} e^{-r(s-t)} ds = \int_t^{\infty} (s-t)^k e^{-(1+r)(s-t)} ds = \frac{k!}{(1+r)^{k+1}}$$

As a second illustration, suppose the firm's cash flows evolve in terms of the function

$$C(s) = \frac{1}{\sqrt{\pi[(s-t)+\alpha]}}$$

again for for $s \geq t$. Then Table 5.3 shows that the Laplace transform of $C(s)$, or equivalently the present value of the future cash flows, is given by

$$V(t) = \int_t^{\infty} e^{-r(s-t)} C(s) ds = \int_t^{\infty} \frac{e^{-r(s-t)}}{\sqrt{\pi[(s-t)+\alpha]}} ds = \frac{e^{\alpha r}}{\sqrt{r}} [1 - \operatorname{erf}(\sqrt{\alpha r})]$$

where

$$\operatorname{erf}(x) = \frac{2}{\sqrt{\pi}} \int_0^x e^{-z^2} dz$$

is known as the error function. The other entries in Table 5.3 are to be similarly interpreted.

A particular advantage of viewing the present-value relationship in terms of the Laplace transform is that one can always invert the expression for the present value of the future cash flows to determine the underlying cash flow function on which the Laplace transform is based. We can illustrate this by supposing that the present value of the future operating cash flows associated with a particular capital project is given by

$$V(t) = \frac{r-5}{r^2+6}$$

where r is the cost of capital (or discount rate) for the given capital project. Now, this expression for $V(t)$ can be broken down into two rational functions of the discount rate, namely,

$$V(t) = \frac{r}{r^2 + \left(\sqrt{6}\right)^2} - \frac{5}{\sqrt{6}} \frac{\sqrt{6}}{r^2 + \left(\sqrt{6}\right)^2}$$

Now from the third row of Table 5.3, we have that if $\beta = \sqrt{6}$ then

$$\frac{r}{r^2+\beta^2} = \frac{r}{r^2 + \left(\sqrt{6}\right)^2} \text{ is the Laplace transform of } \cos\left(\sqrt{6}t\right)$$

Likewise, from the second row of Table 5.3, we see that

$$\frac{5}{\sqrt{6}} \frac{\sqrt{6}}{r^2 + \left(\sqrt{6}\right)^2} \text{ is the Laplace transform of } \frac{5}{\sqrt{6}} \sin\left(\sqrt{6}t\right)$$

This in turn will mean that the underlying cash flow function on which the Laplace transform is based must be

$$C(s) = \cos\left[\sqrt{6}(s-t)\right] - \frac{5}{\sqrt{6}} \sin\left[\sqrt{6}(s-t)\right]$$

where $s \geq t$. Alternatively, this will mean that the present value of the capital project's future cash flows can be evaluated as

$$V(t) = \int_t^{\infty} e^{-r(s-t)} C(s) ds = \int_t^{\infty} e^{-r(s-t)} \left\{ \cos\left[\sqrt{6}(s-t)\right] - \frac{5}{\sqrt{6}} \sin\left[\sqrt{6}(s-t)\right] \right\} ds = \frac{r-5}{r^2+6}$$

where, as previously, r is the discount rate applied in determining the present value of the future cash flows.

§ 5-10. Of course, it is not always possible to obtain a closed-form expression for the integral describing the present value of the future cash flows. However, even when the present-value integral cannot be found in closed form, one can apply the numerical integration procedure of Gauss–Laguerre quadrature. Under Gauss–Laguerre quadrature, the integral describing the present value of the future cash flows must first be transformed so that it is in the following form:

$$V(t) = \int_t^{\infty} e^{-r(s-t)} C(s) ds = \int_0^{\infty} e^{-z} f(z) dz$$

where, as previously, $C(s)$ is the firm's cash flow function at time s, r is the cost of capital and $f(z)$ is a transform function describing the evolution of the future cash flows. If, for example, we make the substitution $z = r(s-t)$ so that

$$s = \frac{rt+z}{r} \quad \text{and} \quad ds = \frac{dz}{r}$$

we have

$$V(t) = \int_t^{\infty} e^{-r(s-t)} C(s) ds = \frac{1}{r} \int_0^{\infty} e^{-z} C\left(\frac{rt+z}{r}\right) dz$$

so that

$$f(z) = \frac{1}{r} C\left(\frac{rt+z}{r}\right)$$

is the transformed function describing the evolution of the future cash flows. We would emphasize that whilst the transformation employed here will always reduce the present-value integral to the form required for the application of Gauss–Laguerre quadrature, alternative transformations may be more convenient once the precise form of the cash flow function $C(s)$ is known. In any event, the transformed integral is then evaluated using the following quadrature formula:

$$V(t) = \int_0^{\infty} e^{-z} f(z) dz = \sum_{i=0}^{n} w_i f(z_i)$$

where n is known as the order of the quadrature formula, $f(z)$ is the transform of the function describing the evolution of the future cash flows, the z_i are the roots of the Laguerre polynomial of order $n+1$ and the w_i are the weights associated with the roots z_i.

We can illustrate the implementation of the Gauss–Laugerre quadrature integration formula by recalling for the example in §5-8 above that we assume that a firm's cash flows evolve in terms of the function

$$C(s-t)=(s-t)e^{-(s-t)}$$

when $s \geq t$. In §5-8, we also showed that the present value of the future cash flows for this example is given by

$$V(t)=\int_t^\infty e^{-r(s-t)}C(s)ds=\int_t^\infty (s-t)e^{-(1+r)(s-t)}ds=\frac{1}{(1+r)^2}$$

The most convenient way to reduce this integral to the form required for the application of Gauss–Laguerre quadrature is to apply the transformation $z=(1+r)(s-t)$, in which case it follows that

$$s-t=\frac{z}{1+r} \quad \text{and} \quad ds=\frac{dz}{1+r}$$

The present-value integral $V(t)$ given above can be restated as follows:

$$V(t)=\int_t^\infty (s-t)e^{-(1+r)(s-t)}ds=\frac{1}{(1+r)^2}\int_0^\infty e^{-z}zdz$$

where the transformed function describing the evolution of the future cash flows turns out to be:

$$f(z)=\frac{z}{(1+r)^2}$$

Applying the Gauss-Laguerre quadrature formula to the above integral gives

$$V(t)=\frac{1}{(1+r)^2}\int_0^\infty e^{-z}zdz=\frac{1}{(1+r)^2}\sum_{i=0}^{n} w_i z_i$$

Now suppose we apply the four-point quadrarture formula ($n=3$) to the above integral. The roots of the Laguerre polynomial of order 4 and their associated weights are summarized in Table 5.4. Here $z_0=0.322547689619$ is the smallest root of the Laguerre polynomial of order 4 and has an associated weight of $w_0=0.603154104342$. Similarly, $z_1=1.745761101158$ is the next smallest root of the Laguerre polynomial of order 4 and has an associated weight of $w_1=0.357418692438$. Then we have $z_2=4.536620296921$ with an associated weight of

Table 5.4 Roots z_i of the Laguerre polynomial of order 4 and their associated weights w_i

i	*Roots of Laguerre polynomial of order 4* (z_i)	*Weight factors* (w_i)
0	0.322547689619	0.603154104342
1	1.745761101158	0.357418692438
2	4.536620296921	0.038887908515
3	9.395070912301	0.000539294706

$w_2 = 0.038887908515$. Finally, we have $z_3 = 9.395070912301$ with an associated weight of $w_3 = 0.000539294706$. We can then use these roots and their associated weights to show that

$$\begin{aligned}V(t) &= \frac{1}{(1+r)^2}\int_0^\infty ze^{-z}dz = \frac{1}{(1+r)^2}\sum_{i=0}^{3} w_i z_i \\ &= \frac{1}{(1+r)^2}(0.603154104342 \times 0.322547689619 + 0.357418692438 \\ &\quad \times 1.745761101158 + 0.038887908515 \times 4.536620296921 + 0.000539294706 \\ &\quad \times 9.395070912301) \\ &= \frac{1}{(1+r)^2}\end{aligned}$$

will be the estimate of the present value of the future cash flows. This example has the important property that we obtain an exact answer, namely,

$$V(t) = \int_t^\infty (s-t)e^{-(1+r)(s-t)}ds = \frac{1}{(1+r)^2}$$

from using just four carefully chosen and weighted observations of the cash flow function. We should emphasize, however, that it is not always the case that the Gauss–Laguerre quadrature formula returns an exact solution using just four observations of the cash flow function. Given this, one should gradually increase the order of the Gauss–Laguerre quadrature formula applied to a given problem until the solution obtained converges to a given constant value. It is only then that one can be confident that one has obtained the correct numerical value for the problem.

We can demonstrate the procedures involved by assuming that a firm's operating cash flows evolve in terms of the function

$$C(s) = (s-t)^{0.8}$$

for $s \geq t$. It then follows that the present value of the future operating cash flows will be

$$V(t) = \int_t^\infty e^{-r(s-t)}C(s)ds = \int_t^\infty e^{-r(s-t)}(s-t)^{0.8}ds$$

We can then reduce this integral to the form required for the application of Gauss–Laguerre quadrature formula by making the substitution $z = r(s-t)$. It then follows that $s - t = z/r$ and $ds = dz/r$. The present-value integral can then be restated as

$$V(t) = \int_t^{\infty} e^{-r(s-t)} C(s) ds = \int_t^{\infty} (s-t)^{0.8} e^{-r(s-t)} ds = \frac{1}{r^{1.8}} \int_0^{\infty} e^{-z} z^{0.8} dz$$

where the transformed function describing the evolution of the future cash flows turns out to be

$$f(z) = \frac{z^{0.8}}{r^{1.8}}$$

Now if we apply the four-point ($n = 3$) Gauss–Laguerre quadrature formula to this integral, we obtain the following estimate for the present value of the future cash flows:

$$\begin{aligned} V(t) &= \frac{1}{r^{1.8}} \int_0^{\infty} e^{-z} z^{0.8} dz = \frac{1}{r^{1.8}} \sum_{i=0}^{3} w_i z_i^{0.8} \\ &= \frac{1}{r^{1.8}} (0.603154104342 \times 0.322547689619^{0.8} + 0.357418692438 \\ &\quad \times 1.745761101158^{0.8} + 0.038887908515 \times 4.536620296921^{0.8} \\ &\quad + 0.000539294706 \times 9.395070912301^{0.8}) \end{aligned}$$

or

$$V(t) = \frac{1}{r^{1.8}} \int_0^{\infty} e^{-z} z^{0.8} dz = \frac{0.935734}{r^{1.8}}$$

where the roots of the Laguerre polynomial of order 4, z_i, and their associated weights, w_i, are summarized in Table 5.4. However, as we increase the order of the quadrature formula employed, the estimated present value of the future cash flows gradually declines. Hence, for five-point quadrature ($n = 4$), the estimated present value of the future cash flows is $0.934261/r^{1.8}$. The six-point quadrature ($n = 5$) formula returns an estimated present value of $0.933441/r^{1.8}$. Finally, the 20-point quadrature($n = 19$) formula returns an estimated present value of $0.931614/r^{1.8}$. Now, the actual present value of the future cash flows for this cash flow function turns out to be $0.931383/r^{1.8}$. Hence, it is not until 20-point Gauss–Laguerre quadrature is applied that we get a reasonable approximation to the present value of the future cash flows. A selection of the roots of the Laguerre polynomials and their associated weights for the higher-order Gauss–Laguerre quadrature formulae appear in the Appendix to this chapter.

§ 5-11. We have previously noted (in §5-2 above) how the present value of the dividends paid out over the life of a firm must be equal to the present value of the operating cash flows that the firm generates through its investment opportunity set. This means that one can determine the value of a firm's equity by computing the present value of the future dividends it expects to pay or, alternatively, by computing the present value of the stream of cash flows it expects to earn. Both calculations will lead to the same equity value. There is, however, a third way in which the value of a firm's equity can be determined – one that leads to the same value for equity as discounting its future dividends or, equivalently, discounting its future cash flows. We can illustrate this technique by first defining $b(s)$ to be the book value of the firm's equity at time s as recorded in its accounting records. Moreover, we let $x(s)$ be the accounting or book profits on an annualized basis that accrue to equity over the instantaneous period from time s until time $s + ds$. Finally, we assume that all profits and losses are governed by the 'clean surplus identity'. This identity requires that increments in the book value of the firm's equity are composed of the profit (or loss) appearing on the firm's profit and loss account less any provisions that have been made for the payment of dividends. This will mean that the relationship between the book value of the firm's equity, the profits earned by the firm and the dividends paid by the firm will be as follows:

$$db(s) = [x(s) - D(s)]ds$$

Here $db(s) = b(s + ds) - b(s)$ is the increment in the book value of equity over the instantaneous time period from time s until time $s + ds$ and, as previously, $D(s)$ is the dividend payment on an annualized basis made over this same time period (as in §5-8 above). Note how the clean surplus identity implies that dividend payments can be restated in terms of the accounting profits and changes in the book value of equity, or $D(s)ds = x(s)ds - db(s)$. In turn, this will mean that the present value of future dividend payments can be expressed as

$$V(t) = \int_t^\infty e^{-r(s-t)} D(s)ds = \int_t^\infty e^{-r(s-t)} [x(s)ds - db(s)]$$

We now apply integration by parts to the component of the above integral involving the book value of equity:

$$\int_t^\infty e^{-r(s-t)} db(s) = \left[e^{-r(s-t)} b(s)\right]_t^\infty + r \int_t^\infty e^{-r(s-t)} b(s)ds$$

Evaluating the first term on the right-hand side of this expression gives

$$\left[e^{-r(s-t)} b(s)\right]_t^\infty = \lim_{s \to \infty} [e^{-r(s-t)} b(s)] - b(t)$$

Hence, if we are to progress beyond this point, we must ensure that the book value of equity remains finite as the time period over which the present value of the future dividend payments is computed becomes infinitely large. This is known as a 'transversality requirement' (as in §5-2 above) and ensures that the market value of the firm's equity will always remain finite. In the present context, the transversality requirement takes the form

$$\lim_{s \to \infty} [e^{-r(s-t)} b(s)] = 0$$

We can then evaluate the integral defining the present value of the future dividend payments as follows:

$$V(t) = \int_t^\infty e^{-r(s-t)}[x(s)ds - db(s)] = \int_t^\infty e^{-r(s-t)}x(s)ds - \left[r \int_t^\infty e^{-r(s-t)}b(s)ds - b(t) \right]$$

Thus, if we define $a(s) = x(s) - rb(s)$ as the firm's residual or abnormal earnings, it then follows that the present value of the future dividend payments can be restated as

$$V(t) = b(t) + \int_t^\infty e^{-r(s-t)}a(s)ds$$

Note also how the abnormal earnings $a(s)$ are composed of the accounting profit $x(s)$ attributable to equity less a capital charge $rb(s)$ based on the book value of the firm's equity. If the firm records all their assets and liabilities at their market values then one would expect its abnormal earnings to fluctuate around a mean of zero. However, the historical cost conventions on which accounting practices have generally been based will mean that balance sheets seldom fully reflect the market values of the resources available to firms. This in turn will mean that abnormal earnings will typically assume positive values even when firms are earning only 'normal' returns on the resources available to them. The important point to be made here, however, is that the above result shows that the book value of the firm's equity plus the present value of its future abnormal earnings must be equal to the present value of the future dividend payments the firm will make. Moreover, since the present value of the future dividend payments must be equal to the present value of the firm's operating cash flows (as in §5-2 above), we also have the important result that the book value of the firm's equity plus the present value of its future abnormal earnings must be equal to the present value of the firm's operating cash flows. This result will be of considerable importance in later chapters of this book.

§ 5-12. We opened this chapter by demonstrating how the present value of the dividends paid out over the life of a firm must be equal to the present value of the operating cash flows the firm will generate through its investment opportunity set. This in turn means that whilst one can always determine equity value by discounting the future dividends to be paid by a firm, it is the firm's operating cash flows (and not the dividends it pays) that are the instrumental determinants of equity value. This has the important consequence that the specific time pattern of dividend payments invoked by a firm will be irrelevant to the valuation of the firm's equity, since every time pattern of dividend payments will have a present value that is equal to the present value of the firm's future operating cash flows. In other words, investors will care little about whether the firm pays niggardly dividends in the immediate future and generous dividends in the longer term or vice versa, as long as the present value of the dividends it pays is equal to the present value of the operating cash flows generated by its investment opportunity set. That is, the specific dividend policy implemented by a firm will hold no relevance for the valuation of the firm's equity.

This result hinges, however, on the existence of a perfect capital market. Hence, when there is differential tax treatment of income according to source (capital gains as against dividends), it is not hard to show that a firm's dividend policy can become an important determinant of its equity value. Moreover, if economic agents have differential and/or costly access to the information needed to value a firm's equity then the firm can use its dividend policy to convey information about the magnitude of its future operating cash flows. In such circumstances, the firm's dividend policy can again become an instrumental determinant of its equity value.

It will occasionally be the case that the stream of operating cash flows that a firm earns through its investment opportunity set can be approximated by a functional form that leads to a closed-form solution for the value of the firm's equity. We have demonstrated some specific examples of where this will be the case. Importantly, when there is a closed-form solution for the present value of the future cash flows associated with a given discrete-time cash flow function, it is normally possible to differentiate through it to derive closed-form expressions for the present value of alternative discrete-time cash flow functions. However, even when a particular cash flow function does not lead to a closed-form present-value expression, it will still normally be possible to obtain a convergent series expansion for the present value of the future cash flows. We have given examples of some discrete-time cash flow functions where this will be so, although it will often be the case that the affected series expressions will converge very slowly.

An important point to be made here is that the operating cash flows of large firms will typically be composed of thousands of transactions on any given day, and so their cash flows will normally evolve in a way that can be closely approximated by a continuous function of time. When the present-value integral associated with a continuous-time cash flow function cannot be evaluated in closed form, one can apply the numerical integration procedure of Gauss–Laguerre quadrature to estimate the present value of its future cash flows. Several examples of this procedure have been provided in this chapter.

We concluded the chapter by demonstrating how the book value of a firm's equity plus the present value of its future abnormal earnings must be equal to the present value of the future dividend payments that the firm will make. Moreover, since the present value of the future dividend payments must be equal to the present value of the firm's operating cash flows, this leads to the important result that the book value of the firm's equity plus the present value of its future abnormal earnings must be equal to the present value of the future operating cash flows that the firm will earn through its investment opportunity set. This result will be of considerable importance in subsequent chapters of this book.

Selected references

Bernstein, P. (1992) *Capital Ideas: The Improbable Origins of Modern Wall Street*, New York: The Free Press.

Black, F. (1976) 'The dividend puzzle' *Journal of Portfolio Management*, 2: 5–8.

Denis, D. and Osobov, I. (2008) 'Why do firms pay dividends? International evidence on the determinants of dividend policy, *Journal of Financial Economics*, 89: 62–82.

Ferris, S., Sen, N. and Yui, H. (2006) 'God save the queen and her dividends: corporate payouts in the United Kingdom', *Journal of Business*, 79: 1149–73.

Fisher, I. (1930) *The Theory of Interest*, New York: Macmillan.

Graham, B. and Dodd, D. (2009) *Security Analysis*, New York: McGraw-Hill.

Lintner, J. (1956) 'Distribution of incomes of corporations among dividends, retained earnings, and taxes', *American Economic Review*, 46: 97–113.

Miller, M. and Modigliani, F. (1961) 'Dividend policy, growth and the valuation of shares', *Journal of Business*, 34: 411–33.

Williams, J. (1997) *The Theory of Investment Value*, Burlington, VT: Fraser Publishing.

Appendix: Roots and weights of the Gauss–Laguerre quadrature formulae

	Two-Point Formula ($n = 1$)	
i	z_i	w_i
0	0.585786437627	0.853553390593
1	3.414213562370	0.146446609407
	Three-Point Formula ($n = 2$)	
i	z_i	w_i
0	0.415774556783	0.711093009929
1	2.294280360280	0.278517733569
2	6.289945082940	0.010389256502
	Four-Point Formula ($n = 3$)	
i	z_i	w_i
0	0.322547689619	0.603154104342
1	1.745761101160	0.357418692438
2	4.536620296920	0.038887908515
3	9.395070912300	0.000539294706
	Five-Point Formula ($n = 4$)	
i	z_i	w_i
0	0.263560319718	0.521755610583
1	1.413403059110	0.398666811083
2	3.596425771040	0.075942449682
3	7.085810005860	0.003611758680
4	12.640800844300	0.000023369972
	Six-Point Formula ($n = 5$)	
i	z_i	w_i
0	0.222846604179	0.458964673950
1	1.188932101670	0.417000830772
2	2.992736326060	0.113373382074
3	5.775143569100	0.010399197453
4	9.837467418380	0.000261017203
5	15.982873980600	8.98548E-07
	Seven-Point Formula ($n = 6$)	
i	z_i	w_i
0	0.193043676560	0.409318951701
1	1.026664895340	0.421831277862
2	2.567876744950	0.147126348658
3	4.900353084530	0.020633514469
4	8.182153444560	0.001074010143
5	12.734180291800	0.000015865464
6	19.395727862300	3.17032E-08
	Eight-Point Formula ($n = 7$)	
i	z_i	w_i
0	0.170279632305	0.369188589342
1	0.903701776799	0.418786780814
2	2.251086629870	0.175794986637
3	4.266700170290	0.033343492261
4	7.045905402390	0.002794536235
5	10.758516010200	0.000090765088
6	15.740678641300	8.48575E-07
7	22.863131736900	1.048E-09

Continued

Cont'd

	Nine-Point Formula ($n = 8$)	
i	z_i	w_i
0	0.152322227732	0.336126421798
1	0.807220022742	0.411213980424
2	2.005135155620	0.199287525371
3	3.783473973330	0.047460562766
4	6.204956777880	0.005599626611
5	9.372985251690	0.000305249767
6	13.466236911100	6.59212E-06
7	18.833597789000	4.11077E-08
8	26.374071890900	3.29087E-11
	10-Point Formula ($n = 9$)	
i	z_i	w_i
0	0.137793470540	0.308441115765
1	0.729454549503	0.401119929155
2	1.808342901740	0.218068287612
3	3.401433697850	0.062087456099
4	5.552496140060	0.009501516975
5	8.330152746760	0.000753008389
6	11.843785837900	0.000028259233
7	16.279257831400	4.24931E-07
8	21.996585812000	1.83956E-09
9	29.920697012300	9.91183E-13
	11-Point Formula ($n = 10$)	
i	z_i	w_i
0	0.125796442188	0.284933212894
1	0.665418255839	0.389720889528
2	1.647150545870	0.232781831849
3	3.091138143040	0.076564453546
4	5.029284401580	0.014393282767
5	7.509887863810	0.001518880847
6	10.605950999500	0.000085131224
7	14.431613758100	2.2924E-06
8	19.178857403200	2.48635E-08
9	25.217709339700	7.71263E-11
10	33.497192847200	2.88378E-14
	12-Point Formula ($n = 11$)	
i	z_i	w_i
0	0.115722117358	0.264731371055
1	0.611757484515	0.377759275873
2	1.512610269780	0.244082011320
3	2.833751337740	0.090449222212
4	4.599227639420	0.020102381155
5	6.844525453120	0.002663973542
6	9.621316842450	0.000203231593
7	13.006054993300	8.36506E-06
8	17.116855187500	1.66849E-07
9	22.151090379400	1.34239E-09
10	28.487967251000	3.0616E-12
11	37.099121044500	8.14808E-16

Continued

Cont'd

15-Point Formula ($n = 14$)		
i	z_i	w_i
0	0.093307812017	0.218234885940
1	0.492691740302	0.342210177923
2	1.215595412070	0.263027577942
3	2.269949526200	0.126425818106
4	3.667622721750	0.040206864922
5	5.425336627420	0.008563877804
6	7.565916226600	0.001212436147
7	10.120228568000	0.000111674392
8	13.130282482100	6.45993E-06
9	16.654407708500	2.22632E-07
10	20.776478899000	4.22743E-09
11	25.623894227300	3.9219E-11
12	31.407519169400	1.45652E-13
13	38.530683306600	1.48303E-16
14	48.026085572700	1.60059E-20
20-Point Formula ($n = 19$)		
i	z_i	w_i
0	0.070539889692	0.168746801851
1	0.372126818002	0.291254362006
2	0.916582102483	0.266686102867
3	1.707306531030	0.166002453271
4	2.749199255310	0.074826064663
5	4.048925313840	0.024964417315
6	5.615174970870	0.006202550837
7	7.459017453890	0.001144962389
8	9.594392867490	0.000155741772
9	12.038802556600	0.000015401440
10	14.814293415500	1.08649E-06
11	17.948895568600	5.33012E-08
12	21.478788190400	1.75798E-09
13	25.451702809400	3.72551E-11
14	29.932554663400	4.76753E-13
15	35.013434186800	3.37285E-15
16	40.833057097400	1.15501E-17
17	47.619994029900	1.53952E-20
18	55.810795754100	5.28644E-24
19	66.524416525200	1.65646E-28

Exercises

1. In §5-2, we showed that the value of an all-equity-financed firm, $V(0)$, can be determined from the following expression:

$$V(0) = \sum_{t=1}^{\infty} \frac{NOI(t) - I(t)}{(1+p_U)^t}$$

where $NOI(t)$ is the firm's operating income over the period from time $t-1$ until time t, $I(t)$ is the amount expended on productive investments at time t and p_U is the cost of capital for an unlevered firm. Suppose that the firm's operating profit evolves in terms of the equation

$$NOI(t+1) = NOI(t) + h(t)I(t)$$

where $h(t)$ is the rate of return earned on productive investments made at time t. Use the above result to show that

$$V(0) = \frac{NOI(1)}{p_U} + \sum_{t=1}^{\infty} \frac{I(t)[h(t) - p_U]}{p_U(1+p_U)^t}$$

What are the implications of the above formula for the firm's dividend policy and the impact of changing levels of investment on the value of the firm?

2. Suppose that an all-equity-financed firm's operating cash flows $C(t)$ evolve in accordance with the following formula:

$$C(t) = \theta(1-\theta)^{t-1}$$

where $0 < \theta < 1$ is a parameter and t is time. Use this expression to show that the present value of the future operating cash flows will be

$$V(0) = \sum_{t=1}^{\infty} \frac{C(t)}{(1+r)^t} = \frac{\theta}{r+\theta}$$

where r is the cost of equity capital.

3. Use the binomial series approximation

$$(1-\theta)^{t-1} = 1 - (t-1)\theta + \frac{(t-1)(t-2)}{2}\theta^2 + \cdots$$

to show that the present value of the future operating cash flows for the cash flow function defined in Exercise 2 may be expressed in terms of the following series expansion:

$$V(0) = \frac{\theta+\theta^2+\theta^3}{r} - \frac{(\theta^2+\frac{3}{2}\theta^3)(1+r)}{r^2} + \frac{1}{2}\theta^3\left[\frac{1+r}{r^3} + \frac{(3+r)(2+r)(1+r)}{r^4}\right] + \cdots$$

Let $\theta = 0.001$ and then prepare a table that summarizes the difference between the series expansion given here and the exact expression for the present value of the future cash flows as obtained in Exercise 2. Let the cost of capital vary from $r = 0.01$ to $r = 0.30$. Repeat your calculations with $\theta = 0.01$.

4. Differentiate the expression for

$$V(0) = \frac{\theta}{r+\theta}$$

obtained in Exercise 2 with respect to r and thereby show that if the firm's operating cash flow evolves in accordance with the formula

$$C(t) = \theta t(1-\theta)^{t-1}$$

then the present value of its future cash flows will be

$$V(0) = \sum_{t=1}^{\infty} \frac{C(t)}{(1+r)^t} = \sum_{t=1}^{\infty} \frac{\theta t(1-\theta)^{t-1}}{(1+r)^t} = \frac{\theta(1+r)}{(r+\theta)^2}$$

5. A firm's operating cash flow at time s evolves continuously in time according to the formula

$$C(s) = \frac{\exp\left[-\frac{1}{2}(s-t)^2\right]}{\sqrt{2\pi}}$$

where $s > t$. Show that the present value of the future operating cash flows for a firm with this cash flow function are given by

$$V(t) = \exp\left(\tfrac{1}{2}r^2\right)[1 - N(r)]$$

where r is the cost of equity capital and

$$N(r) = \frac{1}{\sqrt{2\pi}} \int_{-\infty}^{r} \exp\left(-\tfrac{1}{2}u^2\right) dz$$

is the accumulated area under the standard normal distribution between $u = -\infty$ and $u = r$.

6 The relationship between book (accounting) rates of return and the cost of capital for firms and capital projects

§6-1. In previous chapters, we have noted how the expected return on an asset is an instrumental determinant of the price at which the asset will sell in the marketplace. We have also observed how the expected return on an asset is often estimated using the past returns it has earned based on the prices it has been selling at in the market. Thus, if one wishes to base the estimate of an asset's expected return on its past monthly returns then one must be able to observe the market prices at which the asset is trading on a monthly basis. There are occasions, however, when the market prices of assets either do not exist or can only be observed infrequently, and this can create difficulties with measuring returns on the given assets. Given this, our purpose in this chapter is to develop a technique for estimating the expected return on a particular asset using only figures provided by a firm's accountants about the past profitability of the asset and of the book values at which the asset has been recorded in the firm's accounting records. That is, we develop a procedure for estimating the expected returns on assets that does not involve the use of information about the prices at which the assets have traded in the market place in previous periods.

§ 6-2. We begin our analysis by considering a capital project that is purchased at a cost of C_0 at time $t = 0$. Let C_t be the periodic operating cash flow at time $t = 1, 2, 3, \ldots, N$ generated by the particular capital project. Moreover, let r be the cost of capital (or discount rate) applicable to the given capital project. Finally, suppose that the firm receives a liquidation (or scrap value) payment of R_N when the capital project is taken out of service and disposed of at time $t = N$. It then follows that the net present value V_0 of the capital project at time $t = 0$ will be

$$V_0 = \sum_{t=1}^{N} v_t C_t + v_N R_N - C_0$$

where $v_t = (1 + r)^{-t}$ is the discount factor applicable to the cash flow received (or paid out) at time t. Now define A_t to be the book value of the asset at time t as recorded in the firm's accounting records. Moreover, suppose that at acquisition the asset is recorded at cost in the firm's accounting records, in which case we have $C_0 = A_0$. Over the intervening period, the asset is written down to its liquidation (or scrap) value, and from this it follows that $A_N = R_N$. We can then define the accounting (or book) profit P_t for the capital project over the period from time $t - 1$ until time t in terms of the following relationship:

$$P_t = C_t - (A_{t-1} - A_t)$$

Note here that $A_{t-1} - A_t$ is the amount by which the accountants have written down the book value of the capital project over the period from time $t-1$ until time t. It is, in other words, the estimate that the accountants have made of the capital project's deprecation over this period. Hence, we can subtract the depreciation from the cash flow C_t generated by the capital project over the period from time $t-1$ until time t to determine the profit P_t that the accountants attribute to the capital project for this period. It then follows that the cash flow can be restated in terms of the capital project's profit and book values as follows:

$$C_t = P_t + (A_{t-1} - A_t)$$

Given this, we can replace the cash flow variable in the expression for V_0 and thereby restate the present value in terms of the capital project's profitability and book values as recorded by the firm's accountants:

$$V_0 = \sum_{t=1}^{N} v_t C_t + v_N R_N - C_0 = \sum_{t=1}^{N} v_t (P_t + A_{t-1} - A_t) + v_N R_N - C_0$$

or

$$V_0 = \sum_{t=1}^{N} v_t P_t + \left(\sum_{t=1}^{N} v_t A_{t-1} - \sum_{t=1}^{N} v_t A_t \right) + v_N R_N - C_0$$

§ 6-3. Now, if we expand the two terms within parentheses in the above expression, we find

$$\sum_{t=1}^{N} v_t A_{t-1} = v_1 A_0 + v_2 A_1 + v_3 A_2 + \ldots + v_N A_{N-1}$$

and

$$\sum_{t=1}^{N} v_t A_t = v_1 A_1 + v_2 A_2 + v_3 A_3 + \ldots + v_{N-1} A_{N-1} + v_N A_N$$

so that

$$\sum_{t=1}^{N} v_t A_{t-1} - \sum_{t=1}^{N} v_t A_t$$
$$= v_1 A_0 + v_2 A_1 - v_1 A_1 + v_3 A_2 - v_2 A_2 + \ldots + v_N A_{N-1} - v_{N-1} A_{N-1} - v_N A_N$$

We now add and subtract $v_0 A_0$ from the above expression, to give

$$\sum_{t=1}^{N} v_t A_{t-1} - \sum_{t=1}^{N} v_t A_t$$
$$= (v_1 A_0 - v_0 A_0) + (v_2 A_1 - v_1 A_1) + (v_3 A_2 - v_2 A_2) + \ldots + (v_N A_{N-1} - v_{N-1} A_{N-1})$$
$$+ v_0 A_0 - v_N A_N$$

But this latter result may also be stated as

$$\sum_{t=1}^{N} v_t A_{t-1} - \sum_{t=1}^{N} v_t A_t = \sum_{t=1}^{N} (v_t - v_{t-1}) A_{t-1} + v_0 A_0 - v_N A_N$$

Note here, however, that the term within parentheses in this expression can be restated as follows:

$$v_t - v_{t-1} = \frac{1}{(1+r)^t} - \frac{1}{(1+r)^{t-1}} = \frac{1-(1+r)}{(1+r)^t} = \frac{-r}{(1+r)^t} = -rv_t$$

It then follows that

$$\sum_{t=1}^{N} v_t A_{t-1} - \sum_{t=1}^{N} v_t A_t = -\sum_{t=1}^{N} r v_t A_{t-1} + v_0 A_0 - v_N A_N$$

Substituting this result into the expression for the present value of the capital project's future cash flows then gives

$$\begin{aligned} V_0 &= \sum_{t=1}^{N} v_t P_t + \left(\sum_{t=1}^{N} v_t A_{t-1} - \sum_{t=1}^{N} v_t A_t \right) + v_N R_N - C_0 \\ &= \sum_{t=1}^{N} v_t P_t - \sum_{t=1}^{N} r v_t A_{t-1} + v_0 A_0 - v_N A_N + v_N R_N - C_0 \end{aligned}$$

Collecting terms and simplifying then leads to the following expression for the present value of the capital project's future cash flows:

$$V_0 = \sum_{t=1}^{N} v_t (P_t - rA_{t-1}) + v_N (R_N - A_N) - (C_0 - v_0 A_0)$$

Now, the variable $P_t - rA_{t-1}$ is the profit attributed to the capital project over the period from time $t-1$ until time t less the cost of capital multiplied by the book value at time $t-1$. Moreover, if one thinks of rA_{t-1} as the profit to be expected from the capital project over the period from time $t-1$ until time t then $P_t - rA_{t-1}$ is the unexpected or abnormal profit that has accrued over this same time period (as in §5-10 of Chapter 5). $P_t - rA_{t-1}$ is normally called the abnormal (or residual) earnings relating to the period, since it represents the profit that remains after paying a normal return to the firm's investment in the capital project as represented by its book value (again as in §5-10 of Chapter 5).

§ 6-4. It is often the case, however, that a capital project's viability is assessed not so much in terms of its stream of abnormal earnings but in terms of its rate of profitability defined as the profit earned over the period from time $t-1$ until time t divided by the book value of the capital project at the beginning of this period:

$$a_t = \frac{P_t}{A_{t-1}}$$

Here a_t is referred to as the accounting rate of return on the capital project for the period from time $t-1$ until time t. Now, since from this definition we have that the capital project's periodic profit may be rewritten as $P_t = a_t A_{t-1}$, it follows that the net present value of the capital project given in §6-3 above can be restated as

$$V_0 = \sum_{t=1}^{N} v_t(P_t - rA_{t-1}) + v_N(R_N - A_N) - (C_0 - v_0 A_0)$$

$$= \sum_{t=1}^{N} v_t(a_t - r)A_{t-1} + v_N(R_N - A_N) - (C_0 - v_0 A_0)$$

Moreover, if we assume that there are no economic rents in this economy (i.e. only normal returns are earned) then the net present value of the capital project V_0 will be zero. It then follows that we can solve the above equation for the cost of capital r:

$$V_0 = 0 = \sum_{t=1}^{N} v_t a_t A_{t-1} - r\sum_{t=1}^{N} v_t A_{t-1} + v_N(R_N - A_N) - (C_0 - v_0 A_0)$$

and hence

$$r = \frac{\sum_{t=1}^{N} v_t a_t A_{t-1} + v_N(R_N - A_N) - (C_0 - v_0 A_0)}{\sum_{t=1}^{N} v_t A_{t-1}}$$

Finally, if, as previously noted (in §6-2 above), the capital project is initially (i.e. at $t = 0$) recorded in the firm's accounting records at its cost then we have

$$C_0 = v_0 A_0 = \frac{A_0}{(1+i)^0} = A_0$$

Furthermore, if the capital project's book value is written down to its scrap value on disposal (again as in §6-2), then we will also have $R_N = A_N$. In these circumstances, we have $C_0 - v_0 A_0 = 0$ and $R_N - A_N = 0$, in which case the above formula simplifies to

$$r = \frac{\sum_{t=1}^{N} v_t a_t A_{t-1}}{\sum_{t=1}^{N} v_t A_{t-1}}$$

We thus have an expression for the capital project's cost of capital r, expressed in terms of the accounting rate of return a_t and the book values of the capital project A_t as recorded by the firm's accountants. Now, it is normally very easy to retrieve the accounting rates of return and the book values necessary to implement the above formula from a firm's accounting records, and so this is a formula that gives the appearance of being relatively easy to implement.

§ 6-5. There remains, however, a significant difficulty with implementing the above formula. This stems from the fact that we know from §6-2 above that $v_t = (1+r)^{-t}$, and so the cost of capital r appears as an argument on both sides of the formula given at the end of §6-4 above. This means that we need to substitute the actual value of r into the right-hand side of the above formula before we can determine r from the formula; in other words, we need to know r before we can determine r through the above formula. Fortunately, there is a fairly simple way around this problem. We can illustrate this by defining the function

$$g(r) = \frac{\sum_{t=1}^{N} v_t a_t A_{t-1}}{\sum_{t=1}^{N} v_t A_{t-1}}$$

in which case our problem is to find the value of r for which

$$r = g(r)$$

Now let r_n be an approximation to the solution r of this latter equation and consider the iteration procedure under which r_n is used to obtain the following updated approximation to this solution:

$$r_{n+1} = g(r_n)$$

We can expand $g(r_n)$ as a Taylor series about the solution r in the above equation, in which case we have

$$r_{n+1} = g(r) + (r_n - r)g'(\xi_n)$$

where ξ_n is a number that lies between r_n and r. Moreover, since $r = g(r)$ is the solution we are looking for, it necessarily follows from the above equation that

$$r_{n+1} - r = (r_n - r)g'(\xi_n)$$

Noting that the error in the approximation at the nth iteration is $e_n = r_n - r$, we can restate the above result in the following equivalent form:

$$e_{n+1} = e_n g'(\xi_n)$$

We now let $n = 0$, in which case the error at the first iteration will be

$$e_1 = e_0 g'(\xi_0)$$

Likewise, when $n = 1$, the error at the second iteration will be

$$e_2 = e_1 g'(\xi_1) = e_0 g'(\xi_0) g'(\xi_1)$$

When $n = 2$, the error at the third iteration will be

$$e_3 = e_2 g'(\xi_2) = e_0 g'(\xi_0) g'(\xi_1) g'(\xi_2)$$

Continuing with this procedure shows that the error at the $(n+1)$th iteration will be

$$e_{n+1} = e_0 \prod_{j=0}^{n} g'(\xi_j)$$

Hence, provided that $|g'(\xi_j)| < 1$ for all j, the error in the above approximation procedure will become progressively smaller as we increase the order of iteration; that is, as we let n become larger and larger, the error in the above approximation procedure will become progressively smaller. Fortunately, it can be shown that the condition $|g'(\xi_j)| < 1$ will normally be satisfied, and so the procedure outlined here will usually provide a convergent approximation to the cost of equity. We can demonstrate the application of this approximation procedure in terms of the following simple example.

§ 6-6. Consider a capital project that has an up-front (time-zero) investment cost of $C_0 = £850$. It has operating cash flows of $C_1 = £500$ at time one, $C_2 = £300$ at time two and $C_3 = £146.35$ at time three. In addition to these operating cash flows, the capital project has a scrap value of $R_3 = £50$ at time three. The firm's accountants have decided to record the capital project in its books at its time zero cost of $C_0 = £850 = A_0$. They have also decided to depreciate (i.e. write down) the book value of the capital project by £250 at time one, by £300 at time two and by £250 at time three. Note that the total of the depreciation charges is $£250 + £300 + £250 = £800$, and so the asset will be written down to its scrap value of $£850 - £800 = £50 = R_3$ at time three.

Now, the net present value of the capital project V_0 will be

$$V_0 = -C_0 + \frac{C_1}{1+r} + \frac{C_2}{(1+r)^2} + \frac{C_3 + R_3}{(1+r)^3} = -850 + \frac{500}{1+r} + \frac{300}{(1+r)^2} + \frac{146.35 + 50}{(1+r)^3}$$

We can use this to graph the relationship between V_0 and r as in Figure 6.1. Note that the graph of V_0 against r cuts the horizontal axis at the point where $r = 0.1$ or 10 per cent. Hence, it is clear from this graph that the cost of capital for the given capital project is $r = 10$ per cent. Suppose, however, that we only have information about the capital project that is released by the firm's accountants. Thus, all we know is that the capital project was recorded in the firm's books at a cost of $C_0 = £850 = A_0$ on acquisition. At the end of the first year of its operations, the capital project's book value was written down to $A_1 = A_0 - £250 = £850 - £250 = £600$. At the end of the second year of its operations, the capital project's book value was written down to $A_2 = A_1 - £300 = £600 - £300 = £300$. Finally, at the end of the third year of its operations, the capital project's book value was written down to $A_3 = A_2 - £250 = £300 - £250 = £50 = R_3$. Note also that this latter figure is equal to the capital project's scrap value at time three. Moreover, the capital project earned a profit of $P_1 = C_1 - (A_0 - A_1) = £500 - £250 = £250$ in the first year of its operations, it earned a profit of $P_2 = C_2 - (A_1 - A_2) = £300 - £300 = £0$ in the second year of its operations, whilst it incurred a loss in the third year of its operations of $P_3 = C_2 - (A_2 - A_3) = £146.35 - £250 = -£103.65$. The profits and losses earned by the capital project imply that the accounting rate of return in the first year of the capital project's operations amounts to $a_1 = P_1/A_0 = £250/£850 \approx 0.2941$. Likewise, the accounting rate of return for the capital project in the second year of its operations amounts to $a_2 = P_2/A_1 = £0/£600 = 0$. Finally, in the third and last year of its operations, the accounting rate of return for the capital project amounts to $a_3 = P_3/A_2 = -£103.65/£300 \approx -0.3455$.

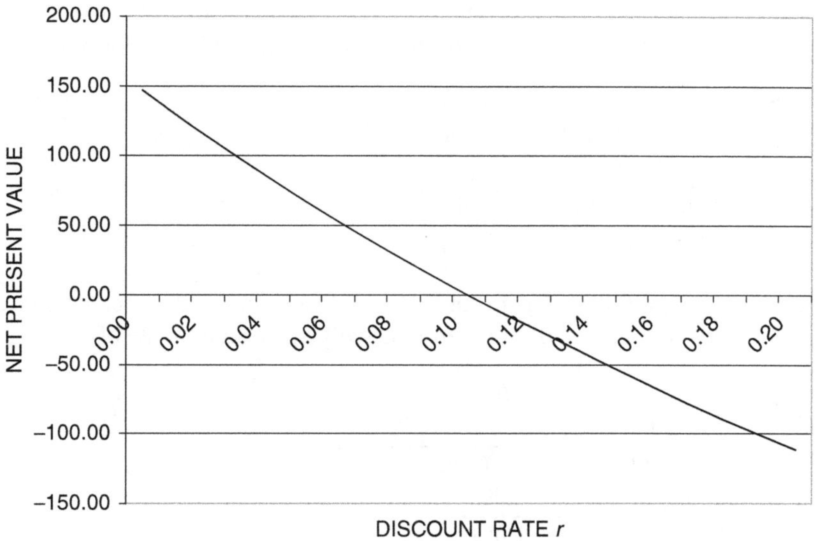

Figure 6.1 Relationship between the net present value V_0 and the discount rate r

§ 6-7. Now, let us apply the formula

$$r = \frac{\sum_{t=1}^{N} v_t a_t A_{t-1}}{\sum_{t=1}^{N} v_t A_{t-1}}$$

(as in §6-5) and see if it returns a cost of capital for the capital project of $r = 10$ per cent (as in §6-6). We first note that our calculations of the book value of equity show

$$\sum_{t=1}^{3} v_t A_{t-1} = \frac{850}{1+r} + \frac{600}{(1+r)^2} + \frac{300}{(1+r)^3}$$

Moreover, our calculations for the accounting rate of return also show

$$\sum_{t=1}^{3} v_t a_t A_{t-1} = \frac{\frac{250}{850} \times 850}{1+r} + \frac{0.0 \times 600}{(1+r)^2} - \frac{\frac{103.65}{300} \times 300}{(1+r)^3}$$

It thus follows that

$$r = \frac{\sum_{t=1}^{3} v_t a_t A_{t-1}}{\sum_{t=1}^{3} v_t A_{t-1}} = \frac{\frac{\frac{250}{850} \times 850}{1+r} + \frac{0.0 \times 600}{(1+r)^2} - \frac{\frac{103.65}{300} \times 300}{(1+r)^3}}{\frac{850}{1+r} + \frac{600}{(1+r)^2} + \frac{300}{(1+r)^3}}$$

Now, suppose that we apply the iteration procedure determined in §6-5 above to estimate the cost of capital for the capital project. It then follows that the $(n+1)$th estimate of the cost of capital r_{n+1}, conditional on the estimate at the nth iteration, r_n, will be as follows:

$$r_{n+1} = \frac{\dfrac{\frac{250}{850} \times 850}{1+r_n} + \dfrac{0.0 \times 600}{(1+r_n)^2} - \dfrac{\frac{103.65}{300} \times 300}{(1+r_n)^3}}{\dfrac{850}{1+r_n} + \dfrac{600}{(1+r_n)^2} + \dfrac{300}{(1+r_n)^3}}$$

Now, suppose we use $r_0 = 0.05 = 5$ per cent as a 'seed' value in the above equation. It then follows that the first iteration $(n = 0)$ of the formula will return an estimate of

$$r_1 = \frac{\dfrac{\frac{250}{850} \times 850}{1.05} + \dfrac{0.0 \times 600}{(1.05)^2} - \dfrac{\frac{103.65}{300} \times 300}{(1.05)^3}}{\dfrac{850}{1.05} + \dfrac{600}{(1.05)^2} + \dfrac{300}{(1.05)^3}}$$

$$= 0.092107$$

or $r_1 = 9.2107$ per cent for the capital project's cost of capital. We can then substitute $r_1 = 0.092107$ into the iteration formula to show

$$r_2 = \frac{\dfrac{\frac{250}{850} \times 850}{1.092107} + \dfrac{0.0 \times 600}{(1.092107)^2} - \dfrac{\frac{103.65}{300} \times 300}{(1.092107)^3}}{\dfrac{850}{1.092107} + \dfrac{600}{(1.092107)^2} + \dfrac{300}{(1.092107)^3}}$$

$$= 0.098791$$

or that $r_2 = 9.8791$ per cent will be the estimate of the capital project's cost of capital at the second $(n = 1)$ iteration. Substituting $r_2 = 0.098791$ into the iteration formula then shows that $r_3 = 0.099816 = 9.9816$ per cent is the capital project's estimated cost of capital at the third $(n = 2)$ iteration. Continuing with this process shows that at the seventh iteration $(n = 6)$, we obtain an estimate of $r_7 = 0.1 = 10$ per cent for the capital project's cost of capital. Hence, we obtain the correct estimate of the capital project's cost of capital after the seventh iteration of the above iteration formula. If we substitute $r_7 = 0.1 = 10$ per cent into the formula again, then we will obtain an estimate of the cost of capital of 10 per cent at all subsequent iterations, that is, $r_8 = r_9 = r_{10} = \ldots = 0.10$ or 10 per cent, thus confirming that we have the correct estimate of the cost of capital. The important point to be made here is that we have obtained this estimate of the cost of capital using only accounting information about the capital project taken from the firm's accounting records. That is, we have not used information about the capital project's market value at any stage of our calculations.

§ 6-8. Now suppose that we have access to a firm's financial statements going back for several years but that its ordinary shares trade only infrequently on the stock market or

Table 6.1 Accounting (book) data for British Petroleum (BP) PLC

Year end	*Book value (per share)*	*Earnings (per share)*	*Accounting rate of return*
1987	0.901	0.124	
1988	0.944	0.100	0.111
1989	1.010	0.159	0.168
1990	1.030	0.156	0.154
1991	0.987	0.038	0.037
1992	0.920	−0.043	−0.044
1993	0.893	0.056	0.061
1994	1.004	0.144	0.161
1995	1.058	0.101	0.101
1996	1.131	0.228	0.216
1997	1.207	0.216	0.191
1998	1.285	0.102	0.085
1999	1.442	0.160	0.125
2000	2.172	0.363	0.252
2001	2.269	0.248	0.114
2002	1.921	0.202	0.089
2003	1.919	0.281	0.146
2004	1.855	0.392	0.204
2005	2.365	0.583	0.314
2006	2.216	0.591	0.250
2007	2.495	0.542	0.245
2008	3.344	0.611	0.245
2009	3.388	0.567	0.170

perhaps, not at all. Then we can apply the above procedures to estimate the cost of capital for its ordinary shares without knowing anything about the prices at which its shares are trading. We can demonstrate the procedures involved by considering the data for British Petroleum (BP) PLC summarized in Table 6.1. The 'Year End' Column in Table 6.1 gives the date of BP's annual financial statements. The book value column is Datastream item WC05476 and is the book value (per share) of equity as recorded in BP's annual financial statements. The earnings column is Datastream item WC05201 and is the earnings (per share), also as summarized in BP's annual financial statements. Thus, BP's ordinary shares have a book value of 90.1 pence at the end of the 1987 fiscal year, whilst the earnings per share as computed by BP's accountants are 12.4 pence per share over the 1987 fiscal year. Finally, the accounting rate of return for the 1988 fiscal year is the earnings (per share) for the 1988 fiscal year divided by the book value (per share) at the end of the 1987 fiscal year, or £0.100/£0.901 = 0.111 = 11.1 per cent and is recorded in the third column of the table. The remaining accounting rates of return summarized in this column are calculated in a similar manner.

Now we can use the procedures developed above and illustrated through the simple example summarized in §6-6 and §6-7 above to estimate the cost of BP's equity capital. Suppose then that we use a seed value of $r_0 = 0.10$, or 10 per cent, as the starting point for the application of our iteration formula. Then, we can summarize the calculations that need to be made in Table 6.2. The first column in Table 6.2 summarizes the fiscal year end. The second and third columns summarize the book value per share at the end of the relevant fiscal year and the earnings per share in the relevant fiscal year, respectively.

Table 6.2 Calculations at first iteration ($n = 0$) for determining the rate of return on British Petroleum (BP) PLC ordinary shares

				$r_0 = 0.1000$	
Year end t	*Book value (per share)*	*Earnings (per share)*	*Accounting rate of return* a_t	$v_t a_t A_{t-1}$	$v_t A_{t-1}$
1987	0.901	0.124			
1988	0.944	0.100	0.111	0.091	0.819
1989	1.010	0.159	0.168	0.131	0.780
1990	1.030	0.156	0.154	0.117	0.759
1991	0.987	0.038	0.037	0.026	0.704
1992	0.920	−0.043	−0.044	−0.027	0.613
1993	0.893	0.056	0.061	0.032	0.519
1994	1.004	0.144	0.161	0.074	0.458
1995	1.058	0.101	0.101	0.047	0.468
1996	1.131	0.228	0.216	0.097	0.449
1997	1.207	0.216	0.191	0.083	0.436
1998	1.285	0.102	0.085	0.036	0.423
1999	1.442	0.160	0.125	0.051	0.409
2000	2.172	0.363	0.252	0.105	0.418
2001	2.269	0.248	0.114	0.065	0.572
2002	1.921	0.202	0.089	0.048	0.543
2003	1.919	0.281	0.146	0.061	0.418
2004	1.855	0.392	0.204	0.078	0.380
2005	2.365	0.583	0.314	0.105	0.334
2006	2.216	0.591	0.250	0.097	0.387
2007	2.495	0.542	0.245	0.081	0.329
2008	3.344	0.611	0.245	0.083	0.337
2009	3.388	0.567	0.170	0.070	0.411
			TOTALS	1.5499	10.9659
				$r_1 = 0.1413$	

The fourth column summarizes the accounting rate of return for the relevant fiscal year. The fifth column calculates $v_t a_t A_{t-1}$ for each year. Thus, for the 1988 fiscal year, we have $t = 1$ and $v_t = v_1 = 1/1.10$, $a_t = a_1 = 0.111$ and $A_{t-1} = A_0 = 0.901$. It thus follows that $v_1 a_1 A_0 = 0.111 \times 0.901/1.10 = 0.091$ as summarized in the fifth column of the 1988 fiscal year in Table 6.2. Likewise, $v_1 A_0 = 0.901/1.10 = 0.819$, as summarized in the sixth column of the 1988 fiscal year in Table 6.2. The remaining calculations in Table 6.2 are similarly conducted. We can then use the calculations in Table 6.2 to obtain the following revised estimate of BP's cost of equity capital:

$$r_1 = \frac{\sum_{t=1}^{22} v_t a_t A_{t-1}}{\sum_{t=1}^{22} v_t A_{t-1}} = \frac{1.5499}{10.9659} = 0.1413$$

or $r_1 = 14.13$ per cent (per annum). Now we can apply the iteration formula again, but this time using $r_1 = 0.1413$ as the seed value. Doing so leads to the following estimate of the cost

Table 6.3 Determining the rate of return on British Petroleum (BP) PLC ordinary shares

Iteration number n	r_{n-1}	$\sum_{t=1}^{22} v_t a_t A_{t-1}$	$\sum_{t=1}^{22} v_t A_{t-1}$	r_n
0	0.1000	1.5499	10.9659	0.1413
1	0.1413	1.0324	7.8028	0.1323
2	0.1323	1.1208	8.3575	0.1341
3	0.1341	1.1023	8.2420	0.1337
4	0.1337	1.1061	8.2653	0.1338
5	0.1338	1.1053	8.2606	0.1338
6	0.1338	1.1055	8.2616	0.1338
7	0.1338	1.1054	8.2614	0.1338
8	0.1338	1.1054	8.2614	0.1338
9	0.1338	1.1054	8.2614	0.1338

of equity at the second application of the iteration formula:

$$r_2 = \frac{\sum_{t=1}^{22} v_t a_t A_{t-1}}{\sum_{t=1}^{22} v_t A_{t-1}} = \frac{1.0324}{7.8028} = 0.1323$$

or $r_2 = 0.13.23$ per cent (per annum). Continuing with this procedure shows that the estimate of BP's cost of equity at each iteration will be as summarized in Table 6.3. This table shows that after just four iterations we have arrived at a convergent estimate of BP's cost of equity capital, namely, $r = 13.38$ per cent (per annum). And note that this estimate of the cost of equity capital is obtained without knowing anything about the prices at which BP's shares have traded over the estimation period.

§ 6-9. There is, however, a potentially serious problem with determining the cost of equity in the manner of the algorithm developed in previous sections. We can illustrate this by considering a capital project with an initial up-front (time-zero) investment cost of $C_0 = -£1{,}000$, a cash inflow at time one of $C_1 = £3{,}450$, a cash outflow at time two of $C_2 = -£3{,}965$ and a cash inflow at time three of $C_3 = £1{,}518$. The capital project will also have a scrap value $R_3 = 0$ at time three. However, as with previous examples, we suppose that we only have information about the capital project that has been provided by the firm's accountants. Thus, all we know is that the capital project was recorded in the firm's books at a cost of $C_0 = £1{,}000 = A_0$ on acquisition. At the end of the first year of its operations, the capital project's book value was written down by £500 to $A_1 = A_0 - £500 = £1000 - £500 = £500$. At the end of the second year of its, operations the capital project's book value was written down by £333 to $A_2 = A_1 - £333 = £500 - £333 = £167$. Finally, at the end of the third year of its operations, the capital project's book value was written down by £167 to $A_3 = A_2 - £167 = £167 - £167 = 0 = R_3$. Note that this latter figure is equal to the capital project's scrap value at time three. Moreover, the capital project earned a profit of $P_1 = C_1 - (A_0 - A_1) = £3{,}450 - £500 = £2{,}950$ in the first year of its operations, incurred a loss of $P_2 = C_2 - (A_1 - A_0) = -£3{,}965 - £333 = -£4{,}298$ in the second year of its operations and earned a profit in the third year of its operations of $P_3 = C_3 - (A_2 - A_3) = £1{,}518 - £167 = £1{,}351$. The profits and losses earned by the firm imply that the accounting rate of return in the first year of the capital project's operations amounts to

$$a_1 = \frac{P_1}{A_0} = \frac{2950}{1000} = 295 \text{ per cent}$$

Likewise, the accounting rate of return for the capital project in the second year of its operations amounts to

$$a_2 = \frac{P_2}{A_1} = \frac{-4298}{500} = -859.6 \text{ per cent}$$

Finally, in the third and last year of its operations, the accounting rate of return for the capital project amounts to

$$a_3 = \frac{P_3}{A_2} = \frac{1351}{167} \approx 808.982 \text{ per cent}$$

Now, suppose we apply the iteration procedure summarized in §6-5 above to estimate the cost of capital for the capital project. It then follows that the $(n+1)$th estimate of the cost of capital r_{n+1}, conditional on knowing the estimate at the nth iteration, r_n, will be as follows:

$$r_{n+1} = \frac{\sum_{t=1}^{3} v_t a_t A_{t-1}}{\sum_{t=1}^{3} v_t A_{t-1}} = \frac{\dfrac{\frac{2950}{1000} \times 1000}{1+r_n} - \dfrac{\frac{4298}{500} \times 500}{(1+r_n)^2} + \dfrac{\frac{1351}{167} \times 167}{(1+r_n)^3}}{\dfrac{1000}{1+r_n} + \dfrac{500}{(1+r_n)^2} + \dfrac{167}{(1+r_n)^3}}$$

Given this, suppose we follow our previous practice of implementing the above iteration formula with a seed value of $r_0 = 0.10$ or 10 per cent (per annum). The reader will be able to confirm by direct calculation that with this seed value we have

$$\sum_{t=1}^{3} v_t a_t A_{t-1} = 144.7784 \quad \text{and} \quad \sum_{t=1}^{3} v_t A_{t-1} = 1447.784$$

It then follows that at the first iteration of our formula, the revised estimate of the cost of equity turns out to be

$$r_1 = \frac{\sum_{t=1}^{3} v_t a_t A_{t-1}}{\sum_{t=1}^{3} v_t A_{t-1}} = \frac{144.7784}{1447.784} = 0.10$$

or 10 per cent (per annum). Note that the estimate obtained at the first iteration is the same as the seed value, $r_0 = 10$ per cent. Moreover, if we substitute this revised estimate, $r_1 = 0.10$, of the cost of equity into the iteration formula then the second iteration of the formula gives $r_2 = 0.10$ or 10 per cent. This again equals the seed value, $r_0 = 10$ per cent, that we started with.

Hence, our iteration formula appears to have quickly converged to what seems to be the actual cost of equity for this example, namely, $r = 0.10$ or 10 per cent (per annum).

However, there is a problem here. Suppose instead that we implement the iteration formula with a seed value of $r_0 = 0.15$, or 15 per cent (per annum). With this seed value, the reader will be able to confirm that we have

$$\sum_{t=1}^{3} v_t a_t A_{t-1} = 203.6163 \quad \text{and} \quad \sum_{t=1}^{3} v_t A_{t-1} = 1357.442$$

It then follows that at the first application of our iteration formula, the revised estimate of the cost of equity turns out to be

$$r_1 = \frac{\sum_{t=1}^{3} v_t a_t A_{t-1}}{\sum_{t=1}^{3} v_t A_{t-1}} = \frac{203.6163}{1357.442} = 0.15$$

or 15 per cent (per annum). Note that the estimate obtained at the first iteration is the same as the seed value, $r_0 = 15$ per cent, that we started with. Moreover, if we substitute this revised estimate, $r_1 = 0.15$, of the cost of equity then the second application of the iteration formula gives $r_2 = 0.15$, or 15 per cent. This again equals the seed value we started with, namely, $r_0 = 15$ per cent. Hence, our iteration formula appears to have quickly converged to a second estimate of the cost of equity for this example, namely, $r = 0.15$, or 15 per cent (per annum). In short, there appear to be at least two solutions to our iteration formula, namely, $r = 10$ per cent and $r = 15$ per cent, and hence at least two potentially valid estimates of the cost of capital for the capital project.

Now, here it will be recalled that the net present value of the future cash flows associated with the capital project is given by

$$V_0 = -C_0 + \frac{C_1}{1+r} + \frac{C_2}{(1+r)^2} + \frac{C_3 + R_3}{(1+r)^3} = -1000 + \frac{3450}{1+r} - \frac{3965}{(1+r)^2} + \frac{1518}{(1+r)^3}$$

A graph of this relationship between the net present value V_0 and the discount rate r for the above present-value equation is depicted in Figure 6.2. Note how the graph for V_0 cuts the horizontal axis in three separate places, namely, at $r = 10$ per cent, at $r = 15$ per cent and at $r = 20$ per cent. This shows that there are three equally valid candidates for the cost of capital and that there is no objective way of choosing between them.

§ 6-10. This example highlights a particular danger with the procedure for estimating the cost of capital that is developed in this chapter – be it for a particular capital project or for the firm as a whole. However, one can always use a result known as Descartes' Rule of Signs to identify the circumstances under which this non-uniqueness problem is likely to arise. Descartes' Rule of Signs says that no polynomial equation can have more positive roots than it has changes of sign from $-$ to $+$ in the ordered sequence of its arguments. We can demonstrate the application of Descartes' Rule of Signs by recourse to the equation representing the net present value of the future cash flows associated with the capital project

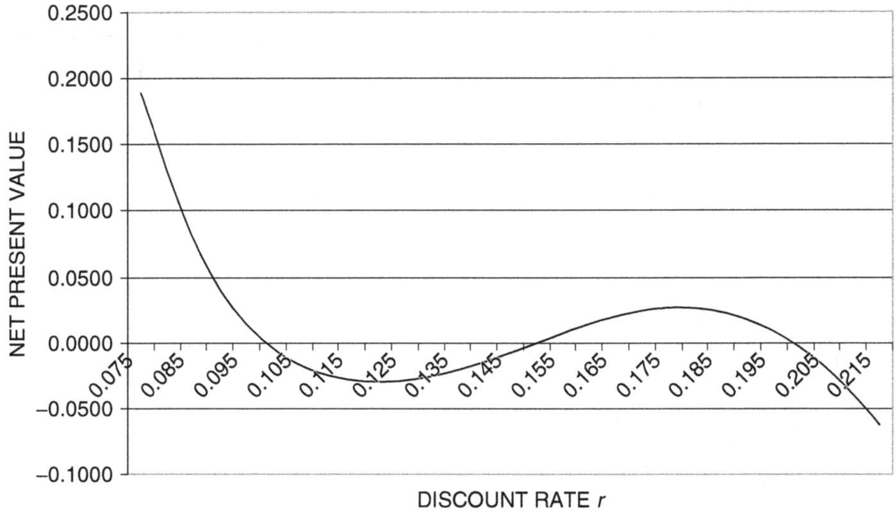

Figure 6.2 Relationship between the net present value V_0 and the discount rate r

developed in §6-9 above, namely:

$$V_0 = -1000 + \frac{3450}{1+r} - \frac{3965}{(1+r)^2} + \frac{1518}{(1+r)^3} = 0$$

Now the first cash flow, $C_0 = -1000$, is negative. However, the second cash flow, $C_1 = 3450$, is positive and so we have our first change of sign. The third cash flow, $C_2 = -3965$, is negative and this gives rise to a second change of sign. Finally, the fourth cash flow, $C_3 = 1518$, is again positive and this gives rise to a third and final change of sign. In summary, the signs of the ordered sequence of cash flows are $- + - +$, giving rise to three changes in sign on working from left to right. Under Descrates' Rule of Signs, this will mean that there are no more than three distinct values of the discount rate r that can be solutions of the equation $V_0 = 0$. We can demonstrate this by applying the following algebraic manipulations to the present value of the capital project's future cash flows:

$$V_0 = 1,000\left[-1 + \frac{\frac{3450}{1000}}{(1+r)} - \frac{\frac{3965}{1000}}{(1+r)^2} + \frac{\frac{1518}{1000}}{(1+r)^3}\right] = 0$$

We can then cancel out the 1,000 and multiply through the above equation by $(1+r)^3$, in which case it follows that

$$(1+r)^3 - \frac{69}{20}(1+r)^2 + \frac{793}{200}(1+r) - \frac{1518}{1000} = 0$$

Hence, if we let $x = 1 + r$ then the above equation can be re-expressed as

$$x^3 - \frac{69}{20}x^2 + \frac{793}{200}x - \frac{1518}{1000} = \left(x - \frac{11}{10}\right)\left(x - \frac{23}{20}\right)\left(x - \frac{6}{5}\right) = 0$$

thereby confirming that there are three discount rates that are solutions of the equation $V_0 = 0$; namely, we have $x = 1 + r = \frac{11}{10}$, or $r = \frac{1}{10} = 10$ per cent, as a first solution, $x = 1 + r = \frac{23}{20}$, or $r = 15$ per cent, as a second solution and $x = 1 + r = \frac{6}{5}$, or $r = 20$ per cent, as a third solution. We would emphasize, however, that whilst Descartes' Rule of Signs guarantees that there can be no more than three positive solutions to the above equation, it does not guarantee that there will be exactly three solutions. We can demonstrate this point by considering a capital project that returns a cash flow of $C_0 = -1$ at time zero, a cash flow of $C_1 = 1$ at time one, a cash flow of $C_2 = -1$ at time two and a cash flow of $C_3 = 1$ at time three. It then follows that the present value of the capital project's stream of cash flows will be

$$V_0 = -1 + \frac{1}{(1+r)} - \frac{1}{(1+r)^2} + \frac{1}{(1+r)^3} = 0$$

This in turn means that the signs of the ordered sequence of cash flows for the capital project will be $- \; + \; - \; +$. There are three changes of sign in this ordered sequence of cash flows and thus up to three positive solutions to the present-value equation given here. We can demonstrate this further by again letting $x = 1 + r$ in the above equation and then multiplying through by $-x^3 = -(1+r)^3$, in which case we have

$$x^3 - x^2 + x - 1 = 0$$

However, the reader will be able to confirm that there is in fact only one positive (real) solution to this equation, namely, $x = 1 + r = 1$ or equivalently $r = 0$. So whilst Descartes' Rule of Signs says that there may be up to three positive solutions to the present-value equation, there is in fact only one positive solution for this particular example.

Two final points need to be made about the analysis summarized in this section. The first is that if there is only one change of sign in the ordered sequence of cash flows then Descartes' Rule of Signs establishes that there will be at most one discount rate r that satisfies the present-value equation $V_0 = 0$. There may of course be no solutions to the present-value equation, but if there is a solution then it will be unique. An important point to be made here, however, is that if one only has access to information about the profits earned by a firm (or capital project) and the book value of its equity as recorded by the firm's accountants then the information on the firm's cash flow data that is necessary to establish the uniqueness or otherwise of the cost of capital will not be available. This is a significant limitation of the procedures summarized in this chapter for estimating the cost of equity.

§ 6-11. We began this chapter with the observation that the return and hence the cost of capital for a given asset is normally computed by reference to the asset's market price at various points in time. There are occasions, however, when the market prices of assets either do not exist or can only be observed infrequently, and this can create difficulties with measuring returns on the given assets. In this chapter, we have demonstrated how one can estimate the cost of capital for a given asset using only figures about the profitability of the asset and the book values at which the asset has been recorded in the firm's accounting records.

This means that one does not have to use information about the asset's market values at any point in the calculations. The principal difficulty with the estimation procedure, however, is that it assumes that an asset's cost of capital is uniquely defined as the discount rate that makes the present value of its future cash flows equal to its cost at acquisition. Unfortunately, this will not always be the case, especially when the asset has a history of returning positive operating cash flows in some years and negative operating cash flows in other years. Although we have identified the circumstances in which this non-uniqueness of the cost of capital might well be a problem, one must be able to identify the stream of cash flows (and not the accountant's profitability figures) associated with the asset before they can be implemented. The difficulty here is that the profitability figures supplied by the accountant will often bear only the most cursory relationship with the original cash flow figures from which they are derived.

Selected References

Chapman, C., Hopwood, A. and Shields, M. (2007) *Handbook of Management Accounting Research*, Volume 2, Oxford: Elsevier.

Edwards, J., Kay, J. and Mayer, C. (1987) *The Economic Analysis of Accounting Profitability*, Oxford: Clarendon Press.

Fisher, F. and McGowan, J. (1983) 'On the misuse of accounting rates of return to infer monopoly profits', *American Economic Review*, 96: 82–97.

Harcourt, G. (1965) 'The accountant in a Golden Age', *Oxford Economic Papers*, 5: 66–80.

Kay, J. (1976) 'Accountants, too, could be happy in a Golden Age: The accountant's rate of profit and the internal rate of return', *Oxford Economic Papers*, 28: 447–60.

McHugh, A. (1976) 'Relationship between accounting and the internal rate of return', *Journal of Accounting Research*, 14: 181–186.

Peasnell, K. (1982) 'Some formal connections between economic values and yields and accounting numbers', *Journal of Business Finance and Accounting*, 9: 361–81.

Steele, A. (1989) 'A note on estimating the internal rate of return from published financial statements', *Journal of Business Finance & Accounting*, 13: 1—13.

Exercises

1 Considering the following data for Unilever PLC

Year end	*Book value (per share)*	*Earnings (per share)*	*Accounting rate of return*
1987	0.992	0.252	
1988	1.048	0.278	0.280
1989	0.889	0.348	0.332
1990	0.932	0.373	0.420
1991	1.131	0.383	0.411
1992	1.488	0.430	0.380
1993	1.527	0.432	0.290
1994	1.731	0.520	0.341
1995	1.823	0.489	0.282
1996	1.683	0.534	0.293
1997	2.453	1.109	0.659
1998	1.093	0.658	0.268

Continued

Year end	Book value (per share)	Earnings (per share)	Accounting rate of return
1999	1.308	0.578	0.529
2000	1.403	0.218	0.167
2001	1.181	0.377	0.269
2002	0.973	0.447	0.378
2003	1.079	0.650	0.668
2004	0.988	0.434	0.402
2005	1.993	0.773	0.782
2006	2.607	0.812	0.407
2007	3.187	0.900	0.345
2008	3.486	1.411	0.443
2009	3.816	1.074	0.308

The year end column gives the date of the firm's annual financial statements. The book value column is Datastream item WC05476 and is the book value (per share) of equity as recorded in Unilever's annual financial statements. The earnings column is Datastream item WC05201 and is the earnings (per share), also as summarized in Unilever's annual financial statements. Thus, Unilever's ordinary shares have a book value of 99.2 pence at the end of the 1987 fiscal year, whilst the earnings per share as computed by Unilever's accountants are 25.2 pence per share over the 1987 fiscal year. Finally, the accounting rate of return for the 1988 fiscal year is the earnings (per share) for the 1988 fiscal year divided by the book value (per share) at the end of the 1987 fiscal year, or £0.278/£0.992 = 0.280 = 28.0 per cent and is recorded in the third column of the above table. The remaining accounting rates of return summarized in this column are calculated in a similar manner. Use the information summarized in the above table in conjunction with the algorithm developed in §6-5 to estimate the cost of equity for Unilever PLC. Use a seed value of $r_0 = 0.1 = 10$ per cent.

2 Suppose that one defines $C(t)$ to be the instantaneous operating cash flow (on an annualized basis) that is generated by a particular capital project at time t. It then follows that the capital project's net present value will be

$$V_0 = \int_0^T e^{-rt} C(t)dt + e^{-rT} R(T) - K(0)$$

where r is the cost of capital, T is the period over which the capital project is maintained in service, $K(0)$ is the capital project's up-front investment and acquisition costs at time zero, and $R(T)$ is the salvage (scrap) value of the capital project when it is taken out of service at time T. Use this result and integration by parts to show that when $V_0 = 0$, one can estimate the cost of capital r by using the following formula:

$$r = \frac{\int_0^T e^{-rt} a(t)A(t)dt + [A(0) - K(0)] - e^{-rT}[A(T) - R(T)]}{\int_0^T e^{-rt} A(t)dt}$$

where $P(t) = C(t) + A'(t)$ is the instantaneous profit earned by the capital project, $A(t)$ is the book value at which the firm's accountants have recorded the capital project at time t, $A'(t) = dA(t)/dt$ is the first derivative of the book value function and $a(t) = P(t)/A(t)$ is the instantaneous accounting rate of return at time t.

3 A capital project's net present value is given by

$$V_0 = \int_0^T e^{-rt} C(t)dt + e^{-rT} R(T) - K(0)$$

where $C(t)$ is the instantaneous operating cash flow at time t, r is the cost of capital, T is the period over which the capital project is maintained in service, $K(0) \geq 0$ is the capital project's up-front investment and acquisition costs at time zero, and $R(T) \geq 0$ is a monotonic non-increasing function that gives the capital project's salvage (scrap) value when it is taken out of service at time T. Show that that the capital project will be kept in service whilst ever

$$C(T) + R'(T) \geq rR(T)$$

Explain the economic intuition that lies behind this result. Use this result to show that if one determines the horizon T so as to maximize the capital project's net present value V_0 then the internal rate of return on the capital project will be unique.

4 A capital project's instantaneous operating cash flow at time t is defined by the function $C(t) = \cos(\pi t)$ whilst its scrap value, if it is taken out of service at time t, is given by $R(t) = \frac{1}{2}e^{-0.05t}$. The capital project's cost of capital is $r = 0.10 = 10$ per cent (per annum). Use the result from Exercise 3 to determine the optimal holding period for the capital project; that is, determine the optimal time before the capital project should be scrapped.

5 Use integration by parts to show that the net present value of the future cash flows for the capital project specified in Exercise 4 will be

$$V_0 = \int_0^T e^{-rt} C(t)dt + e^{-rT} R(T) - K(0)$$

$$= \frac{r}{r^2 + \pi^2} - \frac{e^{-rT}[r\cos(\pi T) - \pi \sin(\pi T)]}{r^2 + \pi^2} - \frac{1}{2}(1 - e^{-(r+0.05)T})$$

where T is the optimal holding period. Plot the net present value of the future cash flows for the capital project V_0 against values of the discount rate that vary from $r = 0$ to $r = 1.75 = 175$ per cent. Use the graph that you have prepared in conjunction with the results obtained in Exercise 3 to show that there is only one r for which $V_0 = 0$.

7 Statistical foundations

First-order stochastic differential equations

§7-1. In previous chapters, we have summarized how returns on assets are computed and how assets will be priced so as to provide an expected return compatible with their inherent risks. However, these models of risk and return have little to say about fundamental supply-side issues; in particular, how the variables comprising a firm's investment opportunity set influence the market value of the firm's equity. Our purpose in this and the next chapter is to lay the foundations for a much fuller treatment of the impact that supply-side considerations can have on equity values as outlined in the second half (Chapters 9–12) of this book. We begin our treatment by considering the Laplace model of accumulated errors. Albert Einstein based his mathematical treatment of the Brownian motion on a limiting form of the Laplace model of accumulated errors. The Brownian motion is the foundation stone on which virtually all of modern asset pricing theory is built, and so the seminal importance of the Laplace model of accumulated errors to asset pricing theory cannot be overemphasized. We then move on to demonstrate how the Laplace model of accumulated errors can be generalized by merely changing the probabilities that Laplace attributed to the positive and negative errors of his model. In particular, we formulate the probabilities associated with the Ornstein–Uhlenbeck process, which leads to one of the most widely employed stochastic differential equations in asset pricing theory. The Ornstein–Uhlenbeck process is then used to illustrate the application of the Fokker–Planck equation. The Fokker–Planck equation allows one to determine the distributional properties of a variable directly from the stochastic differential equation through which it evolves, even when there is no closed-form solution for the underlying stochastic differential equation. The final sections of this chapter deal with the problem of determining the properties of functions of stochastic variables. The market value of a firm's equity hinges, for example, on the firm's profitability as well as the general outlook for the economy in which the firm operates. The firm's profitability and the general economic outlook are both stochastic variables, and so the market value of the firm's equity will be a function of these and many other underlying stochastic variables. Hence, in these final sections of the chapter we introduce a procedure, named for Kiyoshi Itô, which enables one to determine the distributional properties of a stochastic variable that is itself a function of a more primitive set of underlying stochastic variables.

§7-2. Consider then the simple model, first formulated by Pierre-Simon Laplace towards the end of the eighteenth century, in which a measurement error of $\varepsilon > 0$ or $-\varepsilon < 0$ is made each time an observation of a repeated circumstance or event is made. Furthermore, assume that these errors are statistically independent over time. Now, let there be n measurements made in a given (fixed) period of time and let $j \leq n$ of these measurements return positive errors ($+\varepsilon$) whilst the remaining $n-j$ measurements return negative errors ($-\varepsilon$). Define $x(n)$ to be the accumulated (or total measurement) error after making these n observations, in which case we will have

$$x(n) = j\varepsilon - (n-j)\varepsilon = (2j-n)\varepsilon$$

In what follows we make the simple assumption that positive and negative errors have the same probability of occurrence, namely, $\frac{1}{2}$. Now we can take expectations across the expression for $x(n)$ and thereby determine the mean (i.e. average) accumulated measurement error:

$$E[x(n)] = [2E(j) - n]\varepsilon$$

where $E(\cdot)$ is the expectation operator. However, since positive and negative errors occur with equal probabilities, we should expect half of the n errors to be positive and the other half to be negative, in which case it follows that $E(j) = \frac{1}{2}n$. Alternatively, we can use the fact that the number of positive measurement errors, j, is distributed as a binomial variate with a mean $E(j) = np$, where p is the probability of a positive error. Since, by assumption, $p = \frac{1}{2}$, it follows that the expected number of positive errors will be $E(j) = np = \frac{1}{2}n$. Moreover, we can substitute this result into the expression for $E[x(n)]$ given above, in which case the mean accumulated measurement error must be

$$E[x(n)] = [2E(j) - n]\varepsilon = (2 \times \tfrac{1}{2}n - n)\varepsilon = 0$$

Hence, 'on average', the accumulated measurement error will be zero – an unsurprising result given that the probabilities of a negative and positive measurement error are equal to $\frac{1}{2}$.

More interest must therefore lie with the calculation of the variance of the accumulated measurement error. This turns out to be

$$\text{Var}[x(n)] = \text{Var}[(2j-n)\varepsilon] = 4\varepsilon^2\text{Var}(j)$$

where $\text{Var}(\cdot)$ is the variance operator. Now, we can again use the binomial distribution to show that the variance of the number of positive measurement errors will be $\text{Var}(j) = np(1-p)$. Hence, since $p = \frac{1}{2}$ is the probability of a positive measurement error in any given period, it follows that the variance of the number of positive measurement errors will be $\text{Var}(j) = n \times \frac{1}{2} \times \frac{1}{2} = \frac{1}{4}n$. Substitution then shows that the variance of the accumulated measurement error $x(n)$ must be

$$\text{Var}[x(n)] = 4\varepsilon^2\text{Var}(j) = 4\varepsilon^2 \times \frac{n}{4} = n\varepsilon^2$$

This is where Laplace left his model of accumulated errors. It was left to Albert Einstein to develop the model further and, in so doing, to lay the foundations of the stochastic calculus that is now of such importance to modern asset pricing theory.

In one of five landmark papers Einstein published in 1905, he proposed a generalization of the Laplace model of accumulated errors under which the measurement error ε follows a 'square-root' law as the frequency with which observations are made is increased.

In particular, Einstein proposed that as observations are made with increasing frequency over a given fixed interval of time the measurement error will decline in accordance with the following square-root law:

$$\varepsilon = \sigma\sqrt{\Delta t}$$

where σ is a strictly positive parameter (whose meaning will become clear from context) and Δt is the time period between observations. Thus, if the observations are made over a fixed period of time of duration t then this assumption implies that there will be $n = t/\Delta t$ observations in total. Using this result allows us to restate the variance of the accumulated measurement error as

$$\mathrm{Var}[x(n)] = n\varepsilon^2 = \frac{t}{\Delta t}\sigma^2\Delta t = \sigma^2 t = \mathrm{Var}[x(t)]$$

that is, the accumulated measurement error will have a mean of zero and a variance that is proportional to the time period over which the observations are made. We call such a process a 'pure' Brownian motion in honour of the English botanist Robert Brown, who in 1827 first observed that small particles suspended in fluids follow a probability law like the one developed here.

§7-3. We now identify several important properties that are satisfied by the accumulated measurement error $x(t)$ developed in §7-2 above. The first of these is that $x(0) = 0$, or that the accumulated measurement error before any observations are made will have to be zero. Second, the measurement error $\Delta x(t) = x(t + \Delta t) - x(t)$ that arises over the period from time t until time $t + \Delta t$ will be $\Delta x(t) = \varepsilon = \sigma\sqrt{\Delta t}$ with probability $\frac{1}{2}$ or $\Delta x(t) = -\varepsilon = -\sigma\sqrt{\Delta t}$ also with probability $\frac{1}{2}$. It then follows that the expected measurement error over the period from time t until time $t + \Delta t$ will have to be

$$E_t[\Delta x(t)] = \varepsilon \times \frac{1}{2} - \varepsilon \times \frac{1}{2} = \sigma\sqrt{\Delta t} \times \frac{1}{2} - \sigma\sqrt{\Delta t} \times \frac{1}{2} = 0$$

where the subscript t associated with the expectation operator $E_t[\Delta x(t)]$ emphasizes that the expectation is computed at time t; time t being the 'present' time and time $t + \Delta t$ being in the 'immediate future'. Moreover, the variance of the measurement error that arises over the period from time t until time $t + \Delta t$ will be

$$\begin{aligned}\mathrm{Var}_t[\Delta x(t)] &= \frac{1}{2}\{\varepsilon - E_t[\Delta x(t)]\}^2 + \frac{1}{2}\{-\varepsilon - E_t[\Delta x(t)]\}^2 \\ &= \frac{1}{2}(\sigma\sqrt{\Delta t} - 0)^2 + \frac{1}{2}(-\sigma\sqrt{\Delta t} - 0)^2 = \sigma^2\Delta t\end{aligned}$$

where again the subscript t associated with the variance operator $\mathrm{Var}_t[\Delta x(t)]$ emphasizes that the variance is computed at time t. From this result, we also have that the variance of the measurement error will be

$$\frac{\mathrm{Var}_t[\Delta x(t)]}{\Delta t} = \sigma^2$$

when stated on a 'per unit time' basis. Finally, our assumptions in §7-2 will mean that the measurement errors over the contiguous periods $\Delta x(0) = x(\Delta t) - x(0)$, $\Delta x(\Delta t) = x(2\Delta t) - x(\Delta t)$, $\Delta x(2\Delta t) = x(3\Delta t) - x(2\Delta t), \ldots$ will all be statistically independent in time. This in turn means that the covariance between any two measurement errors will be zero; that is, $E_0[\Delta x(j\Delta t)\Delta x(k\Delta t)] = 0$ for integral $j \neq k$. Moreover, and as noted above, when $j = k$ the covariance (or variance) will be $E_0[\{\Delta x(j\Delta t)\}^2] = \sigma^2 \Delta t$.

Now earlier calculations in this section show $[\Delta x(t)]^2 = (\pm\varepsilon)^2 = \sigma^2 \Delta t$; that is, if one squares the measurement error that arises over the period from time t until time $t + \Delta t$ then its sign effectively disappears. Moreover, we have just shown that the variance of the measurement error over this same period will be $\text{Var}_t[\Delta x(t)] = \sigma^2 \Delta t$. Hence, it follows from these two results that the square of the measurement error over the period from time t until time $t + \Delta t$ is equal to the variance of the measurement error over this same period:

$$[\Delta x(t)]^2 = \text{Var}_t[\Delta x(t)] = \sigma^2 \Delta t$$

Moreover, we can define the 'standardized' random variable

$$h(t) = \frac{\Delta x(t)}{\sqrt{\text{Var}_t[\Delta x(t)]}} = \frac{\Delta x(t)}{\sigma\sqrt{\Delta t}}$$

Now, from §7-2 above, $h(t)$ will have a mean of

$$E_t[h(t)] = \frac{E_t[\Delta x(t)]}{\sigma\sqrt{\Delta t}} = 0$$

Also, $h(t)$ will have a variance of

$$\text{Var}_t[h(t)] = \text{Var}_t\left[\frac{\Delta x(t)}{\sigma\sqrt{\Delta t}}\right] = \frac{\text{Var}_t[\Delta x(t)]}{\sigma^2 \Delta t} = \frac{\sigma^2 \Delta t}{\sigma^2 \Delta t} = 1$$

That is, $h(t)$ will be a 'standardized' random variable in the sense that it has a mean of zero and unit variance. Furthermore, we can use $h(t)$ to define a new random variable

$$\Delta z(t) = h(t)\sqrt{\Delta t}$$

We will then obtain what is known as Bernstein's representation of the measurement error over the period from time t until time $t + \Delta t$, namely,

$$\Delta z(t) = h(t)\sqrt{\Delta t} = \frac{\Delta x(t)}{\sigma\sqrt{\Delta t}}\sqrt{\Delta t} = \frac{\Delta x(t)}{\sigma}$$

or, equivalently,

$$\Delta x(t) = \sigma\,\Delta z(t)$$

where $\Delta z(t) = z(t + \Delta t) - z(t)$. It bears emphasizing here that the accumulated measurement error that arises over the period from time $t = 0$ until time $t = n\Delta t$ (as given in §7-2 above) can then be represented as

$$x(t) = x(n\Delta t) = \sum_{j=0}^{n-1} \Delta x(j\Delta t) = \sigma \sum_{j=0}^{n-1} \Delta z(j\Delta t)$$

in which case it follows that

$$x(t) = \sigma \sum_{j=0}^{n-1} \Delta z(j\Delta t) = \sigma \sum_{j=0}^{n-1} [z((j+1)\Delta t) - z(j\Delta t)] = \sigma z(n\Delta t) = \sigma z(t)$$

will be an alternative expression for the total measurement error at time t. Finally, we note also that

$$E_t[\Delta z(t)] = E_t[h(t)]\sqrt{\Delta t} = 0$$

or that $\Delta z(t)$ has a mean of zero and a variance of

$$\mathrm{Var}_t[\Delta z(t)] = \mathrm{Var}_t[h(t)\sqrt{\Delta t}] = \mathrm{Var}_t[h(t)]\Delta t = \Delta t$$

These results will in turn imply that the measurement error over the period from time t until time $t + \Delta t$ will have a mean of

$$E_t[\Delta x(t)] = \sigma E_t[\Delta z(t)] = 0$$

and a variance of

$$\mathrm{Var}_t[\Delta x(t)] = \mathrm{Var}_t[\sigma \Delta z(t)] = \sigma^2 \mathrm{Var}_t[\Delta z(t)] = \sigma^2 \Delta t$$

Hence, the measurement error has a variety of different statistical representations. The important point to remember, however, is that all these representations of the measurement error are equivalent and that, more often than not, the actual statistical representation used for the measurement error is a matter of taste and/or analytical convenience.

§7-4. Often, one will want to know the distributional properties of integral functions of a stochastic variable. As an example, consider the weighted average measurement error over the period from time $t = 0$ until time $t = n\Delta t$, namely,

$$\sum_{j=0}^{n-1} f(j\Delta t)\Delta x(j\Delta t)$$

where $f(j\Delta t)$ is a continuous 'weighting' function of time. We can take expectations through the above expression and use the fact that $E_t[\Delta x(t)] = 0$ (as in §7-3). Doing so shows that the mean of the weighted average measurement error is

$$E_0\left[\sum_{j=0}^{n-1} f(j\Delta t)\Delta x(j\Delta t)\right] = \sum_{j=0}^{n-1} f(j\Delta t)E_0[\Delta x(j\Delta t)] = 0$$

We can also determine the variance of the weighted average measurement error, namely,

$$\mathrm{Var}_0\left[\sum_{j=0}^{n-1} f(j\Delta t)\Delta x(j\Delta t)\right] = E_0\left[\left(\sum_{j=0}^{n-1} f(j\Delta t)\Delta x(j\Delta t)\right)^2\right]$$

$$= \sum_{j=0}^{n-1}\sum_{k=0}^{n-1} f(j\Delta t)f(k\Delta t)E_0[\Delta x(j\Delta t)\Delta x(k\Delta t)]$$

Note, however, that the above result may be broken down into two components, namely,

$$E_0\left[\left(\sum_{j=0}^{n-1} f(j\Delta t)\Delta x(j\Delta t)\right)^2\right] = \sum_{j=0}^{n-1}[f(j\Delta t)]^2 E_0[\{\Delta x(j\Delta t)\}^2]$$

$$+\sum_{\substack{j=0 \\ j\neq k}}^{n-1}\sum_{k=0}^{n-1} f(j\Delta t)f(k\Delta t)E_0[\Delta x(j\Delta t)\Delta x(k\Delta t)]$$

The first component on the right-hand side of this expression includes terms under the double summation sign for which $j = k$ whilst the second component includes terms under the double summation sign for which $j \neq k$. Now, from §7-3 above, we know that $\Delta x(j\Delta t)$ and $\Delta x(k\Delta t)$ are statistically independent and so the covariance between $\Delta x(j\Delta t)$ and $\Delta x(k\Delta t)$ is zero provided $j \neq k$. It follows from this that $E_0[\Delta x(j\Delta t)\Delta x(k\Delta t)] = 0$ when $j \neq k$ and $E_0[\{\Delta x(j\Delta t)\}^2] = \sigma^2\Delta t$ when $j = k$. Substituting these results into the above expression shows that the variance of the weighted average measurement error can be restated as

$$\mathrm{Var}_0\left[\sum_{j=0}^{n-1} f(j\Delta t)\Delta x(j\Delta t)\right] = \sum_{j=0}^{n-1}[f(j\Delta t)]^2 E_0[\{\Delta x(j\Delta t)\}^2]$$

or

$$\mathrm{Var}_0\left[\sum_{j=0}^{n-1} f(j\Delta t)\Delta x(j\Delta t)\right] = \sigma^2\sum_{j=0}^{n-1}[f(j\Delta t)]^2\Delta t$$

Now, a commonly encountered weighting function in many areas of scientific investigation takes the form $f(t) = e^{-\gamma t} = \exp(-\gamma t)$, where $\gamma > 0$ is a parameter. It then follows that the variance of the weighted average measurement error will be

$$\mathrm{Var}_0\left[\sum_{j=0}^{n-1} \exp[-\gamma(j\Delta t)]\Delta x(j\Delta t)\right] = \sigma^2\sum_{j=0}^{n-1}\{\exp[-\gamma(j\Delta t)]\}^2\Delta t$$

Expanding out this series, we obtain

$$\sum_{j=0}^{n-1}\{\exp[-\gamma(j\Delta t)]\}^2 = 1 + e^{-2\gamma\Delta t} + e^{-4\gamma\Delta t} + \ldots + e^{-2\gamma(n-1)\Delta t}$$

Multipying through this expression by $e^{-2\gamma\Delta t}$ shows

$$e^{-2\gamma\Delta t}\sum_{j=0}^{n-1}\{\exp[-\gamma(j\Delta t)]\}^2 = e^{-2\gamma\Delta t}+e^{-4\gamma\Delta t}+e^{-6\gamma\Delta t}+\ldots+e^{-2\gamma n\Delta t}$$

Hence, using term-by-term subtraction, we have

$$\sum_{j=0}^{n-1}\{\exp[-\gamma(j\Delta t)]\}^2 - e^{-2\gamma\Delta t}\sum_{j=0}^{n-1}\{\exp[-\gamma(j\Delta t)]\}^2$$

$$= (1-e^{-2\gamma\Delta t})\sum_{j=0}^{n-1}\{\exp[-\gamma(j\Delta t)]\}^2 = 1-e^{-2\gamma n\Delta t}$$

It will be recalled from §7-2, however, that $t = n\Delta t$, in which case we have

$$\sum_{j=0}^{n-1}\{\exp[-\gamma(j\Delta t)]\}^2 = \frac{1-e^{-2\gamma t}}{1-e^{-2\gamma\Delta t}}$$

Hence, the variance of the weighted average measurement error turns out to be

$$\mathrm{Var}_0\left[\sum_{j=0}^{n-1}\exp[-\gamma(j\Delta t)]\Delta x(j\Delta t)\right] = \sigma^2\sum_{j=0}^{n-1}\{\exp[-\gamma(j\Delta t)]\}^2\Delta t = \frac{\sigma^2(1-e^{-2\gamma t})\Delta t}{1-e^{-2\gamma\Delta t}}$$

§7-5. Now, suppose we apply a Taylor series expansion to the term

$$e^{-2\gamma\Delta t} = 1-2\gamma\Delta t+\frac{1}{2}(2\gamma\Delta t)^2-\frac{1}{6}(2\gamma\Delta t)^3+\ldots$$

in the denominator on the right-hand side of the above expression. It then follows that the variance of the weighted average measurement error can be restated as

$$\mathrm{Var}_0\left[\sum_{j=0}^{n-1}\exp[-\gamma(j\Delta t)]\Delta x(j\Delta t)\right] = \frac{\sigma^2(1-e^{-2\gamma t})\Delta t}{2\gamma\Delta t-2\gamma^2\Delta t^2+\frac{4}{3}\gamma^3\Delta t^3-\ldots}$$

One can thus cancel the Δt term in the numerator and denominator of the above expression and then let $\Delta t \to 0$, in which case it follows that

$$\lim_{\Delta t\to 0}\mathrm{Var}_0\left[\sum_{j=0}^{n-1}\exp[-\gamma(j\Delta t)]\Delta x(j\Delta t)\right]$$

$$= \lim_{\Delta t\to 0}\frac{\sigma^2(1-e^{-2\gamma t})\Delta t}{(2\gamma+2\gamma^2\Delta t-\frac{4}{3}\gamma^3\Delta t^2+\ldots)\Delta t} = \frac{\sigma^2}{2\gamma}(1-e^{-2\gamma t})$$

will be the variance of the weighted average measurement error.

The above analysis leads to a result known as Wiener's Theorem, which will be of considerable importance in subsequent sections of this book. We can formulate Wiener's Theorem by letting

$$\lim_{\Delta t \to 0} \Delta x(t) = x(t + \Delta t) - x(t) = dx(t) = x(t + dt) - x(t)$$

be the measurement error that arises over the instantaneous period from time t until time $t + dt$. From §7-3 above, this will mean that the instantaneous measurement error $dx(t)$ will have a mean $E_t[dx(t)] = 0$ and a variance $\text{Var}_t[dx(t)] = \sigma^2 dt$. Wiener's Theorem then states that the variance of the weighted average measurement error will be

$$\text{Var}_0\left[\int_0^t f(s)dx(s)\right] = \sigma^2 \int_0^t [f(s)]^2 ds$$

We can illustrate the application of Wiener's Theorem by recalling that in §7-4 we used the weighting function $f(t) = e^{-\gamma t} = \exp(-\gamma t)$, where $\gamma > 0$ is a parameter, to determine the variance of the weighted average measurement error. Hence, using this weighting function and Wiener's Theorem, it follows that in continuous time, the variance of the weighted average measurement error will be

$$\text{Var}_0\left[\int_0^t e^{-\gamma s} dx(s)\right] = \sigma^2 \int_0^t e^{-2\gamma s} ds = \frac{\sigma^2}{2\gamma}(1 - e^{-2\gamma t})$$

Note that this result is the same as that obtained by taking limits across the expression for the variance in discrete time as determined earlier in this section. Hence, our analysis in this section shows that

$$\lim_{\Delta t \to 0} \text{Var}_0\left[\sum_{j=0}^{n-1} \exp[-\gamma(j\Delta t)]\Delta x(j\Delta t)\right]$$

$$= \text{Var}_0\left[\int_0^t e^{-\gamma s} dx(s)\right] = \sigma^2 \int_0^t e^{-2\gamma s} ds = \frac{\sigma^2}{2\gamma}(1 - e^{-2\gamma t})$$

§7-6. So far, we have restricted our analysis to what is known as a 'pure' Brownian motion. The distinguishing characteristic of a pure Brownian motion is that it has a mean of zero. Our measurement model can be generalized, however, so as to allow for an upward or downward drift in the accumulated measurement error by merely changing the probabilities associated with a positive and a negative periodic measurement error. To illustrate the procedures involved, let us suppose that the probability of a positive increment ε to the accumulated measurement error is

$$\frac{1}{2}\left(1 + \frac{\mu\sqrt{\Delta t}}{\sigma}\right)$$

Here, μ is an as-yet undefined parameter, but the other symbols (Δt and σ) have the same meanings as previously attributed to them. Furthermore, let the probability of a negative increment, $-\varepsilon$, to the accumulated measurement error be

$$\frac{1}{2}\left(1-\frac{\mu\sqrt{\Delta t}}{\sigma}\right)$$

Note that these probabilities sum to

$$\frac{1}{2}\left(1+\frac{\mu\sqrt{\Delta t}}{\sigma}\right)+\frac{1}{2}\left(1-\frac{\mu\sqrt{\Delta t}}{\sigma}\right)=1$$

as required. Now, these probabilities will mean that the expected measurement error over the period from time t until time $t+\Delta t$ will be

$$E_t[\Delta x(t)]=\frac{1}{2}\left(1+\frac{\mu\sqrt{\Delta t}}{\sigma}\right)\varepsilon-\frac{1}{2}\left(1-\frac{\mu\sqrt{\Delta t}}{\sigma}\right)\varepsilon=\frac{\mu\sqrt{\Delta t}}{\sigma}\varepsilon$$

Thus, if we assume that the measurement error obeys Einstein's 'square-root' law, $\varepsilon=\sigma\sqrt{\Delta t}$ (as in §7-2 above), then the above result simplifies to

$$E_t[\Delta x(t)]=\frac{\mu\sqrt{\Delta t}}{\sigma}\sigma\sqrt{\Delta t}=\mu\Delta t$$

Thus, the expected measurement error over the period from time t until time $(t+\Delta t)$ will have a mean of $\mu\Delta t$. Moreover, this result also implies that the expected measurement error will be

$$\frac{E_t[\Delta x(t)]}{\Delta t}=\mu$$

when stated on a 'per unit time' basis. It is for this reason that μ is normally referred to as a 'drift' parameter.

We can also compute the variance of the measurement error that arises over the period from time t until time $t+\Delta t$ in the usual way, namely,

$$\text{Var}_t[\Delta x(t)]=\frac{1}{2}\{\varepsilon-E_t[\Delta x(t)]\}^2\left(1+\frac{\mu\sqrt{\Delta t}}{\sigma}\right)+\frac{1}{2}\{-\varepsilon-E_t[\Delta x(t)]\}^2\left(1-\frac{\mu\sqrt{\Delta t}}{\sigma}\right)$$

Now we can use the fact that $E_t[\Delta x(t)]=\mu\Delta t$ and $\varepsilon=\sigma\sqrt{\Delta t}$, in which case the above expression for the variance may be restated as

$$\text{Var}_t[\Delta x(t)]=\frac{1}{2}(\sigma\sqrt{\Delta t}-\mu\Delta t)^2\left(1+\frac{\mu\sqrt{\Delta t}}{\sigma}\right)+\frac{1}{2}(-\sigma\sqrt{\Delta t}-\mu\Delta t)^2\left(1-\frac{\mu\sqrt{\Delta t}}{\sigma}\right)$$

The algebra needed to simplify this expression is tedious rather than difficult, but a little perseverance will show the reader that it reduces to

$$\mathrm{Var}_t[\Delta x(t)] = \sigma^2 \Delta t - \mu^2(\Delta t)^2$$

Note that this expression for the variance contains an extra term, $\mu^2(\Delta t)^2$, when compared with the expression for the variance of the pure Brownian motion developed in §7-3 above. If, however, we determine the variance of the instantaneous measurement error, this extra term is of no consequence, since

$$\lim_{\Delta t \to 0} \frac{\mathrm{Var}_t[\Delta x(t)]}{\Delta t} = \lim_{\Delta t \to 0} (\sigma^2 - \mu^2 \Delta t) = \sigma^2$$

Thus, if we work in continuous time then we can safely ignore this extra term $\mu^2(\Delta t)^2$ that arises in the variance term when the measurement error incorporates a drift term μ. Given this, it is normal practice to express the variance of discrete-time increments in a Brownian motion with drift as

$$\mathrm{Var}_t[\Delta x(t)] = \sigma^2 \Delta t + O[(\Delta t)^2]$$

where $O[(\Delta t)^2]$ means that we have omitted terms involving Δt raised to the power of two or more – that is, we have omitted terms involving $(\Delta t)^2$, $(\Delta t)^3$, $(\Delta t)^4$, and so on.

§7-7. The analysis in §7-6 above shows that a Brownian motion with drift has the following representation:

$$\Delta x(t) = \mu \Delta t + \Delta z(t)$$

where μ is the expected increment or 'drift' in the measurement error (stated on a 'per unit time' basis) over the period from time t until time $t + \Delta t$ and $\Delta z(t)$ is the stochastic (error) component of the increment in the measurement error over this period. From §7-2 above, $\Delta z(t) = \varepsilon - \mu \Delta t = \sigma \sqrt{\Delta t} - \mu \Delta t$ when there is a positive measurement error over the period from time t until time $t + \Delta t$, whilst $\Delta z(t) = -\varepsilon - \mu \Delta t = -\sigma \sqrt{\Delta t} - \mu \Delta t$ when there is a negative measurement error over this same period. Note that if we square the stochastic component of the measurement error then we have

$$[\Delta z(t)]^2 = (\sigma \sqrt{\Delta t} - \mu \Delta t)^2 = \sigma^2 \Delta t - 2\sigma \mu \Delta t \sqrt{\Delta t} + \mu^2(\Delta t)^2$$

if there is a positive measurement error over the period from time t until time $t + \Delta t$ and

$$[\Delta z(t)]^2 = (-\sigma \sqrt{\Delta t} - \mu \Delta t)^2 = \sigma^2 \Delta t + 2\sigma \mu \Delta t \sqrt{\Delta t} + \mu^2(\Delta t)^2$$

if there is a negative measurement error over this same period. It thus follows that the square of the stochastic component of the measurement error on a per unit time basis will be

$$\frac{[\Delta z(t)]^2}{\Delta t} = \sigma^2 \pm 2\sigma \mu \sqrt{\Delta t} + \mu^2(\Delta t)$$

with the second term on the right-hand side of the above expression having a − sign if the measurement error is positive and a + sign if the measurement error is negative. This result has the following important consequence:

$$\lim_{\Delta t \to 0} \frac{[\Delta z(t)]^2}{\Delta t} = \frac{[dz(t)]^2}{dt} = \sigma^2$$

where $dz(t) = z(t+dt) - z(t)$ is the increment in the stochastic component of the accumulated measurement error $z(t)$ over the instantaneous period from time t until time $t+dt$.

Now, one can highlight the significance of the above result by recalling from §7-6 that $\frac{1}{2}(1+\mu\sqrt{\Delta t}/\sigma)$ is the probability of a positive measurement error over the period from time t until time $t+\Delta t$, whilst $\frac{1}{2}(1-\mu\sqrt{\Delta t}/\sigma)$ is the probability of a negative measurement error over this same period. It thus follows that the expected value of the stochastic component $\Delta z(t)$, over the period from time t until time $t+\Delta t$ will have to be

$$E_t[\Delta z(t)] = \frac{1}{2}(\sigma\sqrt{\Delta t} - \mu\Delta t)\left(1 + \frac{\mu\sqrt{\Delta t}}{\sigma}\right) + \frac{1}{2}(-\sigma\sqrt{\Delta t} - \mu\Delta t)\left(1 - \frac{\mu\sqrt{\Delta t}}{\sigma}\right) = 0$$

Likewise, we can determine the variance of the stochastic component of the measurement error over this period, namely,

$$\mathrm{Var}_t[\Delta z(t)] = \frac{1}{2}(\sigma\sqrt{\Delta t} - \mu\Delta t)^2\left(1 + \frac{\mu\sqrt{\Delta t}}{\sigma}\right) + \frac{1}{2}(-\sigma\sqrt{\Delta t} - \mu\Delta t)^2\left(1 - \frac{\mu\sqrt{\Delta t}}{\sigma}\right)$$

The algebra here is again tedious rather than difficult, but fortunately we have already shown in §7-6 that this expression reduces to

$$\mathrm{Var}_t[\Delta z(t)] = \sigma^2\Delta t - \mu^2(\Delta t)^2$$

We can thus state the variance of of the measurement error over the period from time t until time $t+\Delta t$ on a per unit time basis, namely,

$$\frac{\mathrm{Var}_t[\Delta z(t)]}{\Delta t} = \sigma^2 - \mu^2\Delta t$$

Hence, upon taking limits, we have

$$\lim_{\Delta t \to 0} \frac{\mathrm{Var}_t[\Delta z(t)]}{\Delta t} = \frac{\mathrm{Var}_t[dz(t)]}{dt} = \sigma^2$$

where, as previously, $dz(t) = z(t+dt) - z(t)$ is the increment in the stochastic component of the measurement error $z(t)$ over the instantaneous period from time t until time $t+dt$. Note how this result shows that

$$\frac{\mathrm{Var}_t[dz(t)]}{dt} = \sigma^2 = \frac{[dz(t)]^2}{dt}$$

that is, if the measurement error evolves in continuous time then the square of the instantaneous measurement error stated on a per unit time basis will be equal to the variance of the measurement error, again stated on a per unit time basis.

§7-8. The sum result of our analysis in §7-6 and §7-7 above is that in continuous time, the instantaneous measurement error may be described by the following stochastic differential equation:

$$\lim_{\Delta t \to 0} \Delta x(t) = \lim_{\Delta t \to 0} [\mu \Delta t + \Delta z(t)] = dx(t) = \mu dt + dz(t)$$

where $x(t)$ is the accumulated measurement error up to and including time t, $dx(t) = x(t + dt) - x(t)$ is the measurement error that arises over the instantaneous period from time t until time $t + dt$, $z(t)$ is the accumulated stochastic (or total unexpected) component of the measurement error up to and including time t, $dz(t) = z(t + dt) - z(t)$ is the stochastic (or unexpected) component of the measurement error that arises over the instantaneous period from time t until time $t + dt$, and μ is the rate at which the accumulated measurement error is expected to drift upwards (if μ is positive) or downwards (if μ is negative), stated on a per unit time basis. Moreover, we can integrate through the expression for $dx(t)$ given above and thereby show that the accumulated measurement error up to and including time t can be stated as follows:

$$x(t) = \int_0^t dx(s) = \int_0^t [\mu ds + dz(s)] = \mu t + z(t)$$

where $z(t) = \int_0^t dz(s)$. Taking expectations through this expression shows

$$E_0[z(t)] = \int_0^t E_0[dz(s)] = 0$$

that is, the accumulated stochastic (or unexpected) component of the measurement error has an expected value of zero. Moreover, it will be recalled from §7-7 that the variance of the stochastic component of the measurement error over the instantaneous period from time t until time $t + dt$ will be $\text{Var}_t[dz(t)] = \sigma^2 dt$. Hence, we can apply Wiener's Theorem (as in §7-5) with the weighting function $f(t) = 1$ to determine the variance of the accumulated stochastic component of the measurement error, namely,

$$\text{Var}_0[z(t)] = \text{Var}_0\left[\int_0^t f(s)dz(s)\right] = \text{Var}_0\left[\int_0^t dz(s)\right] = \sigma^2 \int_0^t ds = \sigma^2 t$$

These results mean that the accumulated measurement error $x(t)$ at time t will have an expected value $E_0[x(t)] = E_0[\mu t + z(t)] = \mu t$ and a variance $\text{Var}_0[x(t)] = \text{Var}_0[\mu t + z(t)] = \text{Var}_0[z(t)] = \sigma^2 t$. Note that the variance for the accumulated measurement error obtained here using Wiener's Theorem is the same as the variance based on the discrete-time development of the accumulated measurement error in §7-2 above. Moreover, since

$$\lim_{\Delta t \to 0} \int_{j=0}^{n-1} \Delta z(j\Delta t) = \int_0^t dz(s) = z(t)$$

it follows that $z(t)$ is the sum of a large number n of small stochastic error terms and will therefore satisfy the requirements for the application of the Central Limit Theorem. This in turn will mean that the probability distribution for the accumulated measurement error $x(t)$ will asymptotically approach that of a normal distribution with a mean $E_0[x(t)] = \mu t$ and a variance $\mathrm{Var}_0[x(t)] = \sigma^2 t$.

§7-9. We can use the procedures developed in previous sections of this chapter to formulate alternative models of the way the measurement error evolves through time. Thus, suppose we continue with the assumption in §7-2 that there are n observations to be made over a given (fixed) period from time $t = 0$ until time $t = b$. The observations are made every $\Delta t = b/n$ units of time and suppose that $m \leq n$ of these observations have already been made. Moreover, $j \leq m$ of these m observations have resulted in a positive measurement error $(+\varepsilon)$ and $m - j$ of these m observations have resulted in a negative measurement error $(-\varepsilon)$. It thus follows that at time $m\Delta t$, the net number of positive measurement errors will be $j - (m - j) = 2j - m$. Now suppose the next observation will be made at time $(m+1)\Delta t \leq n\Delta t = b$. The probability of a positive measurement error at time $(m+1)\Delta t$ will be

$$\frac{1}{2}\left(1 - \frac{2j - m}{n}\right)$$

whilst the probability of a negative measurement error at time $(m+1)\Delta t$ will be

$$\frac{1}{2}\left(1 + \frac{2j - m}{n}\right)$$

Note that if $2j > m$, so that there have been more positive than negative measurement errors up to time $m\Delta t$, then the probability of a negative measurement error at time $(m+1)\Delta t$ will be higher than the probability of a positive measurement error at time $(m+1)\Delta t$. In fact, using these probabilities, it can be shown that the expected measurement error at time $(m+1)\Delta t$ will have to be

$$E_{(m\Delta t)}[\Delta x(m\Delta t)] = \frac{1}{2}\left(1 - \frac{2j - m}{n}\right) \times \varepsilon - \frac{1}{2}\left(1 + \frac{2j - m}{n}\right) \times \varepsilon = -\frac{(2j - m)\varepsilon}{n}$$

where $E_{(m\Delta t)}(\cdot)$ captures the fact that the expectation is taken at time $m\Delta t$. Note here, however, that since $2j - m$ is the net number of positive measurement errors at time $m\Delta t$ then $(2j - m)\varepsilon = x(m\Delta t)$ must be the accumulated measurement error at time $m\Delta t$. It thus follows that the expected measurement error at time $(m+1)\Delta t$ (on a per unit time basis) will have to be

$$\frac{E_{(m\Delta t)}[\Delta x(m\Delta t)]}{\Delta t} = -\frac{x(m\Delta t)}{n\Delta t}$$

Now if we define $t = m\Delta t$ and let $\gamma = (n\Delta t)^{-1} = b^{-1}$, it follows that the expected measurement error at time $t + \Delta t$ will be

$$\frac{E_t[\Delta x(t)]}{\Delta t} = -\gamma x(t)$$

We can then use this result to disaggregate the measurement error into its expected and stochastic components as follows:

$$\Delta x(t) = -\gamma x(t)\Delta t + \Delta z(t)$$

where $\Delta z(t) = \varepsilon + \gamma x(t)\Delta t$ is the stochastic component if there has been a positive measurement error over the period from time $t = m\Delta t$ until time $t + \Delta t = (m+1)\Delta t$ and $\Delta z(t) = -\varepsilon + \gamma x(t)\Delta t$ is the stochastic component if there has been a negative measurement error over this same period. Moreover, we may then compute the variance of the stochastic component of the measurement error over the period from time t until time $t + \Delta t$, namely,

$$\mathrm{Var}_t[\Delta z(t)] = \frac{1}{2}[\varepsilon + \gamma x(t)\Delta t]^2\left(1 - \frac{2j-m}{n}\right) + \frac{1}{2}[-\varepsilon + \gamma x(t)\Delta t]^2\left(1 + \frac{2j-m}{n}\right)$$

Now, here we can again assume that the measurement error obeys Einstein's square-root law, in which case we have $\varepsilon = \sigma\sqrt{\Delta t}$ (as in §7-2 above). Some tedious algebraic calculations then show that the above expression for the variance simplifies to

$$\mathrm{Var}_t[\Delta z(t)] = \sigma^2\Delta t - \gamma^2[x(t)]^2(\Delta t)^2$$

Moreover, stating the variance on a per unit time basis and taking limits shows

$$\lim_{\Delta t \to 0} \frac{\mathrm{Var}_t[\Delta z(t)]}{\Delta t} = \frac{\mathrm{Var}_t[dz(t)]}{dt} = \sigma^2$$

where $dz(t) = z(t+dt) - z(t)$ is the increment in the stochastic component of the accumulated measurement error $z(t)$ over the instantaneous period from time t until time $t + dt$.

§7-10. We can use the analysis in §7-9 to show that in continuous time, the instantaneous measurement error may be described by the following stochastic differential equation:

$$\lim_{\Delta t \to 0} \Delta x(t) = \lim_{\Delta t \to 0}[-\gamma x(t)\Delta t + \Delta z(t)] = dx(t) = -\gamma x(t)dt + dz(t)$$

where $x(t)$ is the accumulated measurement error up to and including time t, $dx(t) = x(t + dt) - x(t)$ is the measurement error that arises over the instantaneous period from time t until time $t + dt$, $z(t)$ is the accumulated stochastic (or total unexpected) component of the measurement error up to and including time t and $dz(t) = z(t + dt) - z(t)$ is the stochastic (or unexpected) component of the measurement error that arises over the instantaneous period from time t until time $t + dt$. Note that if we ignore the stochastic (or unexpected) component of the above differential equation then the accumulated measurement error gravitates toward a mean of zero with a force that hinges on the parameter γ. It is for this reason that the parameter γ is often referred to as the speed-of-adjustment coefficient. Larger values of γ will mean that the accumulated measurement error $x(t)$ is more forcefully constrained to converge towards its long run mean of zero. The stochastic differential equation considered here is named for Leonard Ornstein and George Uhlenbeck, who formulated and published the solution to this particular equation in 1930.

Now, if we divide the above expression for $dx(t)$ by dt and multiply through by $e^{\gamma t}$, it follows that we will have

$$e^{\gamma t}\frac{dx(t)}{dt} = -\gamma e^{\gamma t}x(t) + e^{\gamma t}\frac{dz(t)}{dt}$$

or, equivalently,

$$\frac{d}{dt}[e^{\gamma t}x(t)] = e^{\gamma t}\frac{dx(t)}{dt} + \gamma e^{\gamma t}x(t) = e^{\gamma t}\frac{dz(t)}{dt}$$

We can then integrate across both sides of the above expression and thereby show

$$e^{\gamma t}x(t) = c + \int_0^t e^{\gamma s}\frac{dz(s)}{ds}ds = c + \int_0^t e^{\gamma s}dz(s)$$

where c is a constant of integration. However, setting $t = 0$ in the above expression shows that $c = x(0)$, in which case it follows that

$$e^{\gamma t}x(t) = x(0) + \int_0^t e^{\gamma s}dz(s)$$

We can then divide through the above expression by $e^{\gamma t}$ and thereby show that the general solution to the stochastic differential equation will be

$$x(t) = x(0)e^{-\gamma t} + \int_0^t e^{-\gamma(t-s)}dz(s)$$

Now, applying the expectation operator to the above expression shows that the accumulated measurement error at time t will have a mean of $E_0[x(t)] = x(0)e^{-\gamma t}$. Note how this result implies that in expectations the accumulated measurement error will gradually decay away towards zero. The speed with which it will do so hinges on the speed-of-adjustment parameter $\gamma > 0$. Higher values of γ will mean that the accumulated measurement error will converge towards zero more quickly. Moreover, we can use Wiener's Theorem (as in §7-5) to determine the variance of the accumulated measurement error at time t, namely,

$$\text{Var}_0[x(t)] = \sigma^2\int_0^t e^{-2\gamma(t-s)}ds = \frac{\sigma^2}{2\gamma}(1 - e^{-2\gamma t})$$

Here it is important to note that

$$\lim_{t\to\infty} \text{Var}_0[x(t)] = \frac{\sigma^2}{2\gamma}$$

in which case we say that in the 'steady state' (i.e. as $t \to \infty$), the variance of the accumulated measurement error will be $\sigma^2/2\gamma$.

The variance for the accumulated measurement error obtained here using Wiener's Theorem is the same as the variance based on the discrete-time development of the accumulated measurement error in §7-5 above. Moreover, since

$$\lim_{\Delta t\to 0}\sum_{j=0}^{n-1}\exp[-\gamma(n-j)\Delta t]\Delta z(j\Delta t) = \int_0^t e^{-\gamma(t-s)}dz(s)$$

where $t = n\Delta t$ and $s = j\Delta t$, it follows that the stochastic error term in the expression for $x(t)$ is the sum of a large number n of small stochastic error terms and will therefore satisfy the requirements for the application of the Central Limit Theorem. This in turn will mean that the probability distribution for the accumulated measurement error $x(t)$ will asymptotically approach that of a normal distribution with a mean $E_0[x(t)] = x(0)e^{-\gamma t}$ and a variance

$$\mathrm{Var}_0[x(t)] = \frac{\sigma^2}{2\gamma}(1 - e^{-2\gamma t})$$

§7-11. More often than not, closed-form solutions of stochastic differential equations (as in §7-10) will not exist. When a closed-form solution does not exist for a particular stochastic differential equation, it is often the case in the literature that parameters are estimated by simply taking a discrete-time interpretation of the given equation. As an example, suppose one estimates the parameters of the Ornstein–Uhlenbeck process by taking the discrete-time form of the stochastic differential equation in §7-10, in which case we will have

$$\Delta x(t) = -\gamma x(t)\Delta t + \Delta z(t)$$

where $\Delta x(t) = x(t + \Delta t) - x(t)$ is the increment in the accumulated measurement error $x(t)$ that arises over the period from time t until time $t + \Delta t$. Likewise, $\Delta z(t) = z(t + \Delta t) - z(t)$ is the increment in the stochastic (or unexpected) component of the accumulated measurement error $z(t)$ that arises over the period from time t until time $t + \Delta t$. Now, to determine the biases that arise from following this procedure, we first note from §7-10 that the accumulated measurement error at time $t + \Delta t$ will be

$$x(t + \Delta t) = x(0)e^{-\gamma(t+\Delta t)} + \int_0^{t+\Delta t} e^{-\gamma(t+\Delta t-s)}dz(s)$$

However, we can decompose the integral in the above expression into two components, namely,

$$\int_0^{t+\Delta t} e^{-\gamma(t+\Delta t-s)}dz(s) = \int_0^{t} e^{-\gamma(t+\Delta t-s)}dz(s) + \int_t^{t+\Delta t} e^{-\gamma(t+\Delta t-s)}dz(s)$$

This in turn will mean that the accumulated measurement error at time $t + \Delta t$ can be restated as

$$x(t + \Delta t) = x(0)e^{-\gamma(t+\Delta t)} + \int_0^{t} e^{-\gamma(t+\Delta t-s)}dz(s) + \int_t^{t+\Delta t} e^{-\gamma(t+\Delta t-s)}dz(s)$$

We can then factor out $e^{-\gamma\Delta t}$ from the first two terms of this expression and thereby show

$$x(t + \Delta t) = e^{-\gamma\Delta t}\left[x(0)e^{-\gamma t} + \int_0^{t} e^{-\gamma(t-s)}dz(s)\right] + \int_t^{t+\Delta t} e^{-\gamma(t+\Delta t-s)}dz(s)$$

However, from §7-10, we know that

$$x(t) = x(0)e^{-\gamma t} + \int_0^t e^{-\gamma(t-s)}dz(s)$$

is the solution to the Ornstein–Uhlenbeck differential equation. It then follows that the above result can be restated as

$$x(t+\Delta t) = e^{-\gamma\Delta t}x(t) + \int_t^{t+\Delta t} e^{-\gamma(t+\Delta t-s)}dz(s)$$

We can then subtract $x(t)$ from both sides of the above equation and thereby show

$$\Delta x(t) = -(1-e^{-\gamma\Delta t})x(t) + \int_t^{t+\Delta t} e^{-\gamma(t+\Delta t-s)}dz(s) \neq -\gamma x(t)\Delta t + \Delta z(t)$$

where $\Delta x(t) = x(t+\Delta t) - x(t)$ is the increment in the measurement error over the period from time t until time $t+\Delta t$. This result has several important implications. First, it shows that whilst one might believe that one has obtained an estimate of $-\gamma\Delta t$ by basing one's estimation procedures on the discrete-time interpretation of the Ornstein–Uhlenbeck differential equation, $\Delta x(t) = -\gamma x(t)\Delta t + \Delta z(t)$, what in fact has been obtained is an estimate of $-(1-e^{-\gamma\Delta t})$. Expanding this latter expression as a Taylor series gives

$$-(1-e^{-\gamma\Delta t}) = -\gamma\Delta t + \frac{1}{2}(\gamma\Delta t)^2 - \frac{1}{6}(\gamma\Delta t)^3 + \ldots$$

This shows that basing estimation procedures on a simple discretization of the underlying stochastic differential equation can lead to systematic biases in parameter estimation – and the larger the window Δt over which the estimation procedure is conducted, the more significant the biases are likely to be. Hence, basing estimation procedures on a simple discretization of the underlying stochastic differential equation is something that is best avoided.

§7-12. This raises the important issue of how one might go about parameter estimation when the underlying stochastic differential equation does not possess a closed-form solution. Fortunately, the 'steady-state' probability density (the limit as $t \to \infty$, as in §7-10) of the accumulated measurement error x bears a well-known relationship to the stochastic differential equation describing the evolution of the accumulated measurement error through what is known as the Fokker–Planck equation. We can demonstrate the application of the Fokker–Planck equation by supposing that the stochastic differential equation takes the form

$$dx(t) = \beta(x)dt + \sqrt{\alpha(x)}dz(t)$$

where $\beta(x)$ is the expected measurement error (per unit time) over the instantaneous period from time t until time $t+dt$ and we use Bernstein's representation (as in §7-3 above) for the stochastic (i.e. unexpected) component of the instantaneous measurement error.

Under Bernstein's representation, the stochastic component of the differential equation is given by $\sqrt{\alpha(x)}dz(t)$, where $\alpha(x)$ is the variance (per unit time) of the measurement error over the instantaneous period from time t until time $t+dt$ and $dz(t)$ is a random variable that possesses a mean of zero and a variance of dt. In contrast, our analysis in §7-7 to §7-11 interpreted $dz(t)$ as possessing a mean of zero and variance of $\alpha(x)dt$; that is, the variance is implicitly defined in terms of $dz(t)$ itself rather than being made explicit as in the case of Bernstein's representation. Now, the important point here is that we can use Bernstein's representation of the stochastic component of the underlying differential equation to show that the steady-state probability density $p(x)$ of the accumulated measurement error x will be implicitly defined in terms of the Fokker–Planck equation, namely,

$$\frac{1}{2}\frac{d^2}{dx^2}[\alpha(x)p(x)] = \frac{d}{dx}[\beta(x)p(x)]$$

with the constants of integration being determined so as to ensure that there is a unit area under the probability density curve. We can demonstrate the application of the Fokker–Planck equation by determining the probability density $p(x)$ of the accumulated measurement error for the Ornstein–Uhlenbeck process as formulated in §7-9 and §7-10 above. Here, it will be recalled that the differential equation describing the evolution of the accumulated measurement error for the Ornstein–Uhlenbeck process is given by

$$dx(t) = -\gamma x(t)dt + \sigma dz(t)$$

in which case it follows that $\beta(x) = -\gamma x$ is the expected measurement error (per unit time) over the instantaneous period from time t until time $t+dt$ and we use Bernstein's representation for the stochastic (i.e. unexpected) component of the instantaneous measurement error. It then follows that $\alpha(x) = \sigma^2$ is the variance (per unit time) of the instantaneous measurement error and $dz(t)$ is a random variable that possesses a mean of zero and a variance of dt. Substitution into the Fokker–Planck equation will then imply that the probability density of the accumulated measurement error will satisfy the following differential equation:

$$\frac{1}{2}\sigma^2\frac{d^2p(x)}{dx^2} + \gamma\frac{d}{dx}[xp(x)] = 0$$

Integrating through this equation shows

$$\frac{dp(x)}{dx} + \frac{2\gamma x}{\sigma^2}p(x) = \frac{2c_1}{\sigma^2}$$

where c_1 is a constant of integration. Multiplying through this equation by $\exp(\gamma x^2/\sigma^2)$ then shows

$$\exp\left(\frac{\gamma x^2}{\sigma^2}\right)\frac{dp(x)}{dx} + \frac{2\gamma x}{\sigma^2}\exp\left(\frac{\gamma x^2}{\sigma^2}\right)p(x) = \frac{d}{dx}\left[\exp\left(\frac{\gamma x^2}{\sigma^2}\right)p(x)\right] = \frac{2c_1}{\sigma^2}\exp\left(\frac{\gamma x^2}{\sigma^2}\right)$$

Hence, on integrating a second time, we find

$$\exp\left(\frac{\gamma x^2}{\sigma^2}\right)p(x) = \frac{2c_1}{\sigma^2}\int_{-\infty}^{x}\exp\left(\frac{\gamma y^2}{\sigma^2}\right)dy + c_2$$

where c_2 is a second constant of integration. It follows from this that the steady-state probability density for the Ornstein–Uhlenbeck process will have the general form

$$p(x) = \frac{2c_1}{\sigma^2} \exp\left(-\frac{\gamma x^2}{\sigma^2}\right) \int_{-\infty}^{x} \exp\left(\frac{\gamma y^2}{\sigma^2}\right) dy + c_2 \exp\left(-\frac{\gamma x^2}{\sigma^2}\right)$$

We now consider the probability density at the point $x = 0$, namely,

$$p(0) = \frac{2c_1}{\sigma^2} \int_{-\infty}^{0} \exp\left(\frac{\gamma y^2}{\sigma^2}\right) dy + c_2$$

Note that the integral here is divergent, $\lim_{q \to -\infty} \int_q^0 \exp(\gamma y^2/\sigma^2) dy \to \infty$, and so we must set $c_1 = 0$ if the Ornstein–Uhlenbeck process is to possess a convergent steady-state probability density function. We can then determine c_2 from the requirement that the probability density must have a unit area:

$$c_2 \int_{-\infty}^{\infty} \exp\left(-\frac{\gamma y^2}{\sigma^2}\right) dy = 1$$

Here, we can make the substitution $w = \sqrt{2\gamma/\sigma^2} y$, in which case we have $dw = \sqrt{2\gamma/\sigma^2} dy$, and so the above integral becomes

$$\sqrt{\frac{\sigma^2}{2\gamma}} c_2 \int_{-\infty}^{\infty} \exp(-\tfrac{1}{2}w^2)\, dw = 1$$

Now, it is well known that $\int_{-\infty}^{\infty} \exp(-\frac{1}{2}w^2)\, dw = \sqrt{2\pi}$. It follows from this that we must have

$$\sqrt{\frac{2\pi\sigma^2}{2\gamma}} c_2 = 1, \quad \text{or} \quad c_2 = \sqrt{\frac{\gamma}{\pi\sigma^2}}$$

This in turn will mean that the steady-state probability density for the accumulated measurement error must be

$$p(x) = \sqrt{\frac{\gamma}{\pi\sigma^2}} \exp\left(-\frac{\gamma x^2}{\sigma^2}\right)$$

which is the normal distribution with a mean of $E(x) = 0$ and a variance of $\mathrm{Var}(x) = \sigma^2/2\gamma$. This is compatible with our calculations of the steady-state mean and variance of the Ornstein–Uhlenbeck process as summarized in §7-10 above. This will also mean that we can use the steady-state probability density in conjunction with a set of empirical observations of the measurement error to estimate the parameters σ^2 and γ. There are a variety of techniques that can be used to do this, of which the method of maximum likelihood or the (generalized) method of moments (GMM) are probably the best known and most widely used. However, a detailed consideration of these techniques is beyond the scope of this book.

§7-13. Now, it is often necessary to determine the properties of functions of stochastic variables. For example, the astrophysical measurements on which the Laplace model of accumulated errors is based (as in §7-2) were used by Laplace in the further calculations he made in his work dealing with the asymptotic stability of the solar system. Given this, suppose we let $Y(x, t)$ be some kind of stability measure dependent on the accumulated measurement error $x(t)$ obtained from a set of astrophysical observations. We now expand $Y(x(t+\Delta t), t+\Delta t)$ as a Taylor series about the point $(x(t), t)$, in which case we will have

$$Y(x(t+\Delta t), t+\Delta t) = Y(x(t), t) + \Delta x(t)\frac{\partial Y}{\partial x} + \Delta t\frac{\partial Y}{\partial t} + \frac{1}{2}[\Delta x(t)]^2\frac{\partial^2 Y}{\partial x^2} + [\Delta x(t)\Delta t]\frac{\partial^2 Y}{\partial x \partial t} + \frac{1}{2}(\Delta t)^2\frac{\partial^2 Y}{\partial t^2} + \frac{1}{6}[\Delta x(t)]^3\frac{\partial^3 Y}{\partial x^3} + \ldots$$

where, as previously, $\Delta x(t) = x(t+\Delta t) - x(t)$ is the measurement error that arises over the period from time t until time $t+\Delta t$ and all partial derivatives are evaluated at the point $(x(t), t)$. Now we let $\Delta Y(x(t), t) = Y(x(t+\Delta t), t+\Delta t) - Y(x(t), t)$ be the increment in the stability measure consequent upon the measurement error $\Delta x(t)$ that arises as a result of the observation made at time $t+\Delta t$. It then follows that the increment in the stability measure stated on a per unit time basis, must be

$$\frac{\Delta Y(x(t), t)}{\Delta t} = \frac{\Delta x(t)}{\Delta t}\frac{\partial Y}{\partial x} + \frac{\partial Y}{\partial t} + \frac{1}{2}\frac{[\Delta x(t)]^2}{\Delta t}\frac{\partial^2 Y}{\partial x^2} + \Delta x(t)\frac{\partial^2 Y}{\partial x \partial t} + \frac{1}{2}\Delta t\frac{\partial^2 Y}{\partial t^2} + \frac{1}{6}\frac{[\Delta x(t)]^3}{\Delta t}\frac{\partial^3 Y}{\partial x^3} + \ldots$$

Now, consider the last four terms on the right-hand side of this expression. For the first of these last four terms, it will be recalled that

$$\lim_{\Delta t \to 0}\frac{[\Delta x(t)]^2}{\Delta t} = \lim_{\Delta t \to 0}\frac{[\sigma\sqrt{\Delta t}]^2}{\Delta t} = \sigma^2$$

Hence, this result shows that

$$\lim_{\Delta t \to 0}\frac{1}{2}\frac{[\Delta x(t)]^2}{\Delta t}\frac{\partial^2 Y}{\partial x^2} = \frac{1}{2}\sigma^2\frac{\partial^2 Y}{\partial x^2}$$

For the next term, we first note that $\lim_{\Delta t \to 0}\Delta x(t) = \lim_{\Delta t \to 0}(\pm\sigma\sqrt{\Delta t}) = 0$. Hence, this result shows that

$$\lim_{\Delta t \to 0}\Delta x(t)\frac{\partial^2 Y}{\partial x \partial t} = 0$$

The next term too disappears, since $\lim_{\Delta t \to 0}\frac{1}{2}\Delta t \partial^2 Y/\partial t^2 = 0$. Finally, we can take limits across the coefficient associated with $\partial^3 Y/\partial x^3$, in which case we have

$$\lim_{\Delta t \to 0}\frac{[\Delta x(t)]^3}{\Delta t} = \lim_{\Delta t \to 0}\frac{(\sigma\sqrt{\Delta t})^3}{\Delta t} = \lim_{\Delta t \to 0}\sigma^3\sqrt{\Delta t} = 0$$

This in turn will mean that

$$\lim_{\Delta t\to 0}\frac{1}{6}\frac{[\Delta x(t)]^3}{\Delta t}\frac{\partial^3 Y}{\partial x^3}=0$$

Similar calculations show that all terms involving higher derivatives – that is, $\partial^{i+j}Y/\partial x^i\partial t^j$ for integral i and j and $i+j\geq 3$ – have limiting values of zero. We can use these results to take limits across the expression for the increment in the stability measure as follows:

$$\lim_{\Delta t\to 0}\frac{\Delta Y(x(t),t)}{\Delta t}=\frac{dY(x(t),t)}{dt}=\frac{dx(t)}{dt}\frac{\partial Y}{\partial x}+\frac{\partial Y}{\partial t}+\frac{1}{2}\frac{[dx(t)]^2}{dt}\frac{\partial^2 Y}{\partial x^2}$$

This result was formulated by Kiyoshi Itô in 1951 and is known as Itô's Lemma. Moreover, if we multiply both sides of the above equation by dt then we obtain the form in which Itô's Lemma has traditionally been stated, namely,

$$dY(x(t),t)=dx(t)\frac{\partial Y}{\partial x}+\frac{\partial Y}{\partial t}dt+\frac{1}{2}[dx(t)]^2\frac{\partial^2 Y}{\partial x^2}$$

§7-14. We can demonstrate the application of Itô's Lemma by assuming that the Laplace stability measure (as in §7-13 above) takes the form $Y(x)=x^2$. Differentiation then shows that $\partial Y/\partial x=2x$, $\partial Y/\partial t=0$ and $\partial^2 Y/\partial x^2=2$. Moreover, we assume that the accumulated measurement error x evolves in terms of the Ornstein–Uhlenbeck process developed in §7-9 and §7-10, namely,

$$dx(t)=-\gamma x(t)dt+dz(t)$$

where $\gamma>0$ is the speed-of-adjustment coefficient and $dz(t)$ is a serially uncorrelated error term with a variance of $\mathrm{Var}_t[dz(t)]=[dx(t)]^2=\sigma^2 dt$. Substitution into Itô's Lemma will then imply that the stability measure $Y(x)$ will evolve in accordance with the following stochastic differential equation:

$$dY(x)=dx(t)\frac{\partial Y}{\partial x}+\frac{\partial Y}{\partial t}dt+\frac{1}{2}[dx(t)]^2\frac{\partial^2 Y}{\partial x^2}=2x(-\gamma x dt+dz)+\sigma^2 dt$$

Note, however, that this result simplifies to

$$dY(x)=2\gamma\left(\frac{\sigma^2}{2\gamma}-x^2\right)dt+2x dz(t)$$

Here, it will also be recalled that $Y(x)=x^2$, or $x=\sqrt{Y}$. Hence, the above stochastic differential equation may be restated as

$$dY=2\gamma\left(\frac{\sigma^2}{2\gamma}-Y\right)dt+2\sqrt{Y}dz(t)$$

This shows that, apart from a stochastic term, the stability measure Y gravitates towards a long-term mean of $\sigma^2/2\gamma$ with a speed-of-adjustment coefficient given by 2γ. We can now use the solution to the Ornstein–Uhlenbeck equation as determined in §7-10 to show that the solution of the differential equation describing the Laplace stability measure given above will take the form

$$Y(t) = x^2(t) = \left[x(0)e^{-\gamma t} + \int_0^t e^{-\gamma(t-s)} dz(s) \right]^2$$

Moreover, we can expand out the right-hand side of this expression, take expectations and then let $t \to \infty$, in which case we find

$$\lim_{t\to\infty} E_0[Y] = E_0\left[\left(\int_0^t e^{-\gamma(t-s)} dz(s)\right)^2\right] = \lim_{t\to\infty} \mathrm{Var}_0\left[\int_0^t e^{-\gamma(t-s)} dz(s)\right]$$

Here, we can apply Wiener's Theorem (as in §7-5 above) to evaluate the above expression and thereby show

$$\lim_{t\to\infty} E_0[Y] = \lim_{t\to\infty} \sigma^2 \int_0^t e^{-2\gamma(t-s)} ds = \lim_{t\to\infty} \frac{\sigma^2}{2\gamma}(1 - e^{-2\gamma t}) = \frac{\sigma^2}{2\gamma}$$

This confirms that the Laplace stability measure will gravitate towards a long-term mean of $\sigma^2/2\gamma$ as suggested by the differential equation developed above for Y.

§7-15. Our purpose in this and the next chapter is to lay the foundations for the stochastic analysis of the fundamental supply-side issues that affect the valuation of equity securities. Our analysis began with a consideration of the Laplace model of accumulated errors, which is the foundation stone upon which much of modern asset pricing theory is based. We then moved on to demonstrate how the Laplace model of accumulated errors can be generalized by merely changing the probabilities that Laplace attributed to the positive and negative errors of his model. In particular, we formulated the probabilities that lead to the Ornstein–Uhlenbeck stochastic differential equation. The Ornstein–Uhlenbeck process was then used to illustrate the application of the Fokker–Planck equation. The Fokker–Planck equation allows one to determine the distributional properties of a variable directly from the stochastic differential equation through which it evolves, even when there is no closed-form solution for the given stochastic differential equation. The final sections of this chapter dealt with the problem of determining the properties of functions of stochastic variables, culminating in a procedure, named for Kiyoshi Itô, that enables one to determine the distributional properties of a stochastic variable that is itself a function of more primitive underlying stochastic variables.

Selected references

Arnold, L. (1974) *Stochastic Differential Equations: Theory and Applications*, New York: Wiley.

Cox, D. and Miller, H. (1965) *Theory of Stochastic Processes*, London: Chapman & Hall.

Cox, J., Ingersoll, J. and Ross, S. (1985) 'A theory of the term structure of interest rates', *Econometrica*, 53: 385–408.

Dixit, A. and Pindyck, R. (1994) *Investment under Uncertainty*, Princeton, NJ: Princeton University Press.
Feller, W. (1951) 'Two singular diffusion processes', *Annals of Mathematics*, 54: 173–82.
Hoel, P., Port, S. and Stone, C. (1987) *Introduction to Stochastic Processes*, Long Grove, IL: Waveland Press.
Karlin, S. and Taylor, H. (1981) *A Second Course in Stochastic Processes*, London: Academic Press.
Øksendal, B. (2010) *Stochastic Differential Equations: An Introduction with Applications*, London: Springer.

Exercises

1. Suppose one continues with the assumption in §7-2 and §7-9 that there are n observations to be made over a given period from time $t = 0$ until time $t = b$. The observations are made every $\Delta t = b/n$ units of time and suppose that $m \leq n$ of these observations have already been made. Moreover, $j \leq m$ of these m observations have resulted in a positive measurement error ($+\varepsilon$) and $m - j$ of these m observations have resulted in a negative measurement error ($-\varepsilon$). It thus follows that at time $m\Delta t$, the net number of positive measurement errors will be $j - (m - j) = 2j - m$. Now suppose that the next observation will be made at time $(m+1)\Delta t \leq n\Delta t = b$. The probability of a positive measurement error at time $(m+1)\Delta t$ will be

$$\frac{1}{2}\left(1 - \frac{2j - m}{n - m}\right)$$

whilst the probability of a negative measurement error at time $(m+1)\Delta t$ will be

$$\frac{1}{2}\left(1 + \frac{2j - m}{n - m}\right)$$

Show that these probabilities will be valid if and only if $m - n \leq 2j - m \leq n - m$. Determine the expected measurement error at time $(m+1)\Delta t$. Use these results to write the instantaneous measurement error in terms of a stochastic differential equation. Solve the differential equation and then use it to determine the distributional properties of the accumulated measurement error $x(t)$.

2. Suppose an asset's market value $P(t)$ at time t evolves in accordance with the following process:

$$P(t) = P(0)\exp[(\mu - \tfrac{1}{2}\sigma^2)t + z(t)]$$

where μ is a parameter and $z(t)$ has a normal distribution with a mean $E[z(t)] = 0$ and a variance $\text{Var}[z(t)] = \sigma^2 t$. Use Itô's Lemma (as in §7-13) to determine the distributional properties of instantaneous increments in the asset's market value.

3. Consider the 'square-root' process developed in §7-14, namely,

$$dY = 2\gamma\left(\frac{\sigma^2}{2\gamma} - Y\right)dt + 2\sqrt{Y}dz(t)$$

where $\gamma > 0$, and $dz(t)$ has an instantaneous mean $E_t[dz(t)] = 0$ and an instantaneous variance $\text{Var}_t[dz(t)] = \sigma^2 dt$. Use the Fokker–Planck equation (as in §7-12) to show that the 'steady-state' probability density for the 'square-root' process is given by

$$p(Y) = \frac{1}{\sqrt{\pi\theta Y}} \exp\left(-\frac{Y}{\theta}\right)$$

where $\theta = \sigma^2/\gamma$.

4. Determine a closed-form expression for the increment $\Delta Y(t) = Y(t+\Delta t) - Y(t)$ over the period from time t until time $t+\Delta t$ in the 'square-root' process developed in §7-14. Show that on letting $\Delta t \to 0$, the expression obtained goes over to the stochastic differential equation for $Y(t)$ as developed in §7-14.
5. Suppose the balance on a firm's bank account evolves in accordance with the following stochastic process:

$$C(t) = \frac{2re^{\sqrt{2r}z(t)} - k^2 e^{-\sqrt{2r}z(t)}}{4r}$$

where $r > 0$ and k^2 are parameters and $z(t)$ possesses a normal distribution with a mean $E[z(t)] = 0$ and a variance $\text{Var}[z(t)] = t$. Solve the above equation for $z(t)$ and thereby show that the variate

$$\frac{\Delta z(t)}{\sqrt{\Delta t}} = \frac{z(t+\Delta t) - z(t)}{\sqrt{\Delta t}} = \frac{1}{\sqrt{2r\Delta t}} \log\left[\frac{C(t+\Delta t) + \sqrt{C^2(t+\Delta t) + \frac{k2}{2r}}}{C(t) + \sqrt{C^2(t) + \frac{k2}{2r}}}\right]$$

possesses a standard normal distribution (with zero mean and unit variance). Moreover, use Itô's Lemma (as in §7-13) to determine the distributional properties of increments in the firm's bank account.

8 Statistical foundations

Systems of and higher-order stochastic differential equations

§8-1. This chapter continues with our consideration of the impact that supply-side issues can have on the valuation of a firm's equity. We begin our analysis by using the concepts and techniques developed in Chapter 7 to model the factors comprising a firm's investment opportunity set in terms of a first-order vector system of stochastic differential equations. This makes it possible to capture many of the important interdependences that exist between the factors that most directly influence the value of a firm's equity. Moreover, we demonstrate how to obtain the solution of a first-order vector system of stochastic differential equations. This in turn allows us to determine the distributional properties of the individual factors comprising the firm's investment opportunity set. However, stating the evolution of the factors comprising a firm's investment opportunity set in terms of a first-order vector system of stochastic differential equations does have its limitations. In particular, if the momentum and acceleration of factors is to be part of a firm's investment opportunity set then it will be necessary to consider higher-order systems of stochastic differential equations. Recall that a factor's acceleration is defined in terms of its second derivative. However, if a firm's investment opportunity set is stated in terms of a first-order system of stochastic differential equations then, by definition, it will not include the second or higher derivatives of the factors comprising the firm's investment opportunity set. Given this, in this chapter, we develop the theory behind the formulation and solution of the simplest (or canonical) forms of second- (and higher-) order vector systems of stochastic differential equations. We will see in subsequent chapters that that this is an area of considerable importance in equity valuation. In particular, it can be shown that a model based on a vector system of nth-order stochastic differential equations (where n can assume any positive integral value) can be reduced to an equivalent vector system of nth-order autoregressive (difference) equations in discrete time. Discrete-time autoregressive models are widely used in the accounting and finance literature to model corporate earnings and the other bookkeeping variables that typically comprise a firm's investment opportunity set. The chapter concludes by considering the difficulties that arise with parameter estimation when the variables comprising a firm's investment opportunity set evolve in terms of a second- (or higher-) order system of stochastic differential equations. In particular, we show that a simple discretization of the underlying vector system of stochastic differential equations can lead to systematic biases in parameter estimation – and the larger the window over which the estimation procedure is conducted, the more significant the biases are likely to be. We demonstrate how one can develop methods for differencing data that lead to consistent estimates of the parameters comprising the particular vector system of stochastic differential equations that is under investigation.

§8-2. We begin our analysis by supposing that a firm's investment opportunity set is composed of three interacting variables. These variables might, for example, be the general economic outlook $u_1(t)$, the cost of the firm's primary inputs $u_2(t)$ and the demand for the firm's outputs $u_3(t)$, all observed at time t. Now, suppose that the relationship between the instantaneous increments in these variables is defined by the following vector system of stochastic differential equations:

$$\begin{pmatrix} du_1(t) \\ du_2(t) \\ du_3(t) \end{pmatrix} = \begin{pmatrix} -2 & 1 & 2 \\ -4 & 3 & 2 \\ -5 & 1 & 5 \end{pmatrix} \begin{pmatrix} u_1(t) \\ u_2(t) \\ u_3(t) \end{pmatrix} dt + \begin{pmatrix} dz_1(t) \\ dz_2(t) \\ dz_3(t) \end{pmatrix}$$

Thus the increment $du_1(t) = u_1(t+dt) - u_1(t)$ in the general economic outlook over the instantaneous period from time t until time $t+dt$ will be

$$du_1(t) = [-2u_1(t) + u_2(t) + 2u_3(t)]dt + dz_1(t)$$

where $dz_1(t) = z_1(t+dt) - z_1(t)$ is the increment in the unexpected component of the general economic outlook. Note that $dz_1(t)$ has an instantaneous mean $E_t[dz_1(t)] = 0$ and an instantaneous variance $\text{Var}_t[dz_1(t)] = \sigma_1^2 dt$ (as in §7-7 and §7-8 of Chapter 7). Likewise, the increment in the cost of the firm's primary inputs over the instantaneous period from time t until time $t+dt$ will be

$$du_2(t) = [-4u_1(t) + 3u_2(t) + 2u_3(t)]dt + dz_2(t)$$

where $dz_2(t)$ is the increment in the unexpected component of the cost of the firm's primary inputs and has an instantaneous mean $E_t[dz_2(t)] = 0$ and an instantaneous variance $\text{Var}_t[dz_2(t)] = \sigma_2^2 dt$. Finally, the increment in the demand for the firm's outputs over the instantaneous period from time t until time $t+dt$ will be

$$du_3(t) = [-5u_1(t) + u_2(t) + 5u_3(t)]dt + dz_3(t)$$

where $dz_3(t)$ is the increment in the unexpected component of the demand for the firm's outputs and has an instantaneous mean $E_t[dz_3(t)] = 0$ and an instantaneous variance $Var_t[dz_3(t)] = \sigma_3^2 dt$. Moreover, we allow matters to be as simple as possible by assuming that increments in the unexpected components of the three interacting variables – that is, $dz_1(t), dz_2(t)$ and $dz_3(t)$ – are completely uncorrelated. This will mean that the covariances between the unexpected components will all be zero; that is,

$$E_t[dz_1(t)dz_2(t)] = E_t[dz_1(t)dz_3(t)] = E_t[dz_2(t)dz_3(t)] = 0$$

where $E_t(\cdot)$ is the expectation operator taken at time t (as in §7-3 of chapter 7).

We can illustrate how to obtain a solution for the above vector system of stochastic differential equations by defining

$$d\underset{\sim}{u}(t) = \begin{pmatrix} du_1(t) \\ du_2(t) \\ du_3(t) \end{pmatrix}$$

to be the vector containing the increments in the three variables that characterize the firm's investment opportunity set:

$$Q = \begin{pmatrix} -2 & 1 & 2 \\ -4 & 3 & 2 \\ -5 & 1 & 5 \end{pmatrix}$$

as the matrix of 'structural coefficients',

$$\underset{\sim}{u}(t) = \begin{pmatrix} u_1(t) \\ u_2(t) \\ u_3(t) \end{pmatrix}$$

as the vector containing the levels of the three variables comprising the firm's investment opportunity set and

$$d\underset{\sim}{z}(t) = \begin{pmatrix} dz_1(t) \\ dz_2(t) \\ dz_3(t) \end{pmatrix}$$

as the vector containing the unexpected components of the increments in the variables comprising the firm's investment opportunity set. With these definitions, we can define the vector system of stochastic differential equations describing the evolution of the variables comprising the firm's investment opportunity set in the following terms:

$$d\underset{\sim}{u}(t) = Q\underset{\sim}{u}(t)dt + d\underset{\sim}{z}(t)$$

Now, if we divide all terms on both sides of this expression by *dt*, we can restate this vector system of differential equations in the following form:

$$\underset{\sim}{u}'(t) = Q\underset{\sim}{u}(t) + \underset{\sim}{z}'(t)$$

where

$$\underset{\sim}{u}'(t) = \begin{pmatrix} \dfrac{du_1(t)}{dt} \\ \dfrac{du_2(t)}{dt} \\ \dfrac{du_3(t)}{dt} \end{pmatrix}$$

is the vector containing the derivatives of the variables comprising the firm's investment opportunity set and

$$\underset{\sim}{z}'(t) = \begin{pmatrix} \dfrac{dz_1(t)}{dt} \\ \dfrac{dz_2(t)}{dt} \\ \dfrac{dz_3(t)}{dt} \end{pmatrix}$$

is the vector containing the derivatives of the unexpected components of the variables comprising the firm's investment opportunity set. The components of the vector $\underset{\sim}{z}'(t)$ are often referred to as 'white noise' processes; when this is so, $dz_1(t)/dt$ will be referred to as a white noise process with variance parameter σ_1^2, $dz_2(t)/dt$ will be referred to as a white noise process with variance parameter σ_2^2 and $dz_3(t)/dt$ will be referred to as a white noise process with variance parameter σ_3^2.

§8-3. Now, suppose we determine the eigenvectors for the matrix Q (as in §3-12 to §3-16 of Chapter 3) and stack them into columns to form the matrix M. Then we can define a new set of variables

$$\underset{\sim}{y}(t) = \begin{pmatrix} y_1(t) \\ y_2(t) \\ y_3(t) \end{pmatrix}$$

that are related to the variables comprising the firm's investment opportunity set through the transformation

$$\underset{\sim}{u}(t) = M\underset{\sim}{y}(t)$$

We can then differentiate through this expression to give $\underset{\sim}{u}'(t) = M\underset{\sim}{y}'(t)$, where

$$\underset{\sim}{y}'(t) = \begin{pmatrix} \dfrac{dy_1(t)}{dt} \\ \dfrac{dy_2(t)}{dt} \\ \dfrac{dy_3(t)}{dt} \end{pmatrix}$$

is the vector containing the derivatives of the transforming variables. Substitution will then show

$$\underset{\sim}{u}'(t) = M\underset{\sim}{y}'(t) = Q\underset{\sim}{u}(t) + \underset{\sim}{z}'(t) = QM\underset{\sim}{y}(t) + \underset{\sim}{z}'(t)$$

Moreover, we can premultiply both sides of the above equation by M^{-1} to show

$$\underset{\sim}{y}'(t) = M^{-1}QM\underset{\sim}{y}(t) + M^{-1}\underset{\sim}{z}'(t)$$

However, from Exercise 4 in Chapter 3, we know that when the columns of M are composed of the eigenvectors of Q then, provided certain regularity conditions are satisfied, we will have $D = M^{-1}QM$, where D is the matrix whose off-diagonal elements are all zero and whose diagonal elements are composed of the eigenvalues of Q. This will mean that the above equation simplifies to

$$\underset{\sim}{y}'(t) = D\underset{\sim}{y}(t) + M^{-1}\underset{\sim}{z}'(t)$$

We can demonstrate the significance of this result by first noting that the eigenvalues of the structural matrix

$$Q = \begin{pmatrix} -2 & 1 & 2 \\ -4 & 3 & 2 \\ -5 & 1 & 5 \end{pmatrix}$$

are $\lambda = 1, \lambda = 2$ and $\lambda = 3$. Moreover, the eigenvector associated with the eigenvalue $\lambda = 1$ turns out to be

$$\underset{\sim}{x} = \begin{pmatrix} 1 \\ 1 \\ 1 \end{pmatrix}$$

The eigenvector associated with the eigenvalue $\lambda = 2$ turns out to be

$$\underset{\sim}{x} = \begin{pmatrix} 1 \\ 2 \\ 1 \end{pmatrix}$$

Finally, the eigenvector associated with the eigenvalue $\lambda = 3$ is

$$\underset{\sim}{x} = \begin{pmatrix} 1 \\ 1 \\ 2 \end{pmatrix}$$

Moreover, letting the eigenvectors be the columns of the matrix M will mean that

$$M = \begin{pmatrix} 1 & 1 & 1 \\ 1 & 2 & 1 \\ 1 & 1 & 2 \end{pmatrix}$$

We can then determine the inverse of this matrix, namely,

$$M^{-1} = \begin{pmatrix} 3 & -1 & -1 \\ -1 & 1 & 0 \\ -1 & 0 & 1 \end{pmatrix}$$

This, in turn, will lead to the following calculations:

$$M^{-1}Q = \begin{pmatrix} 3 & -1 & -1 \\ -1 & 1 & 0 \\ -1 & 0 & 1 \end{pmatrix} \begin{pmatrix} -2 & 1 & 2 \\ -4 & 3 & 2 \\ -5 & 1 & 5 \end{pmatrix} = \begin{pmatrix} 3 & -1 & -1 \\ -2 & 2 & 0 \\ -3 & 0 & 3 \end{pmatrix}$$

and

$$D = M^{-1}QM = \begin{pmatrix} 3 & -1 & -1 \\ -2 & 2 & 0 \\ -3 & 0 & 3 \end{pmatrix} \begin{pmatrix} 1 & 1 & 1 \\ 1 & 2 & 1 \\ 1 & 1 & 2 \end{pmatrix} = \begin{pmatrix} 1 & 0 & 0 \\ 0 & 2 & 0 \\ 0 & 0 & 3 \end{pmatrix}$$

Note how all the off-diagonal elements of the matrix D are zero and that the diagonal elements of D are the eigenvalues of the structural matrix Q, namely, $\lambda = 1, \lambda = 2$ and $\lambda = 3$.

These calculations show that the system of differential equations describing the evolution of the vector containing the transformed variables, $\underset{\sim}{y}(t)$, can be restated as

$$\underset{\sim}{y}'(t) = D\underset{\sim}{y}(t) + M^{-1}\underset{\sim}{z}'(t)$$

or

$$\begin{pmatrix} \dfrac{dy_1(t)}{dt} \\ \dfrac{dy_2(t)}{dt} \\ \dfrac{dy_3(t)}{dt} \end{pmatrix} = \begin{pmatrix} 1 & 0 & 0 \\ 0 & 2 & 0 \\ 0 & 0 & 3 \end{pmatrix} \begin{pmatrix} y_1(t) \\ y_2(t) \\ y_3(t) \end{pmatrix} + \begin{pmatrix} 3 & -1 & -1 \\ -1 & 1 & 0 \\ -1 & 0 & 1 \end{pmatrix} \begin{pmatrix} \dfrac{dz_1(t)}{dt} \\ \dfrac{dz_2(t)}{dt} \\ \dfrac{dz_3(t)}{dt} \end{pmatrix}$$

Note how this equation implies that the increment $dy_1(t)$ in the variable $y_1(t)$ over the instantaneous period from time t until time $t+dt$ will be

$$\frac{dy_1(t)}{dt} = y_1(t) + 3\frac{dz_1(t)}{dt} - \frac{dz_2(t)}{dt} - \frac{dz_3(t)}{dt}$$

Now, we can multiply both sides of this equation by e^{-t}, in which case it follows that

$$e^{-t}\frac{dy_1(t)}{dt} - e^{-t}y_1(t) = \frac{d}{dt}[e^{-t}y_1(t)] = e^{-t}\left[3\frac{dz_1(t)}{dt} - \frac{dz_2(t)}{dt} - \frac{dz_3(t)}{dt}\right]$$

Integrating through both sides of this expression then gives

$$e^{-t}y_1(t) = c_1 + \int_0^t e^{-s}\left[3\frac{dz_1(s)}{ds} - \frac{dz_2(s)}{ds} - \frac{dz_3(s)}{ds}\right]ds$$

or equivalently

$$e^{-t}y_1(t) = c_1 + \int_0^t e^{-s}[3dz_1(s) - dz_2(s) - dz_3(s)]$$

where c_1 is a constant of integration. Multiplying through this equation by e^t shows that the general solution of the differential equation describing the evolution of the variable $y_1(t)$ will be

$$y_1(t) = c_1 e^t + \int_0^t e^{(t-s)}[3dz_1(s) - dz_2(s) - dz_3(s)]$$

§8-4. We can apply similar procedures to the differential equation describing the evolution of the variable $y_2(t)$, in which case it follows that

$$y_2(t) = c_2 e^{2t} + \int_0^t e^{2(t-s)}[dz_2(s) - dz_1(s)]$$

where, as before, c_2 is a constant of integration. Likewise, from the differential equation for the variable $y_3(t)$, we have

$$y_3(t) = c_3 e^{3t} + \int_0^t e^{3(t-s)}[dz_3(s) - dz_1(s)]$$

where, again, c_3 is a constant of integration. Moreover, having obtained solutions for each of the transformed variables, we are now in a position to determine the solution to our original vector system of differential equations, namely,

$$\underset{\sim}{u}(t) = M\underset{\sim}{y}(t)$$

or

$$\begin{pmatrix} u_1(t) \\ u_2(t) \\ u_3(t) \end{pmatrix} = \begin{pmatrix} 1 & 1 & 1 \\ 1 & 2 & 1 \\ 1 & 1 & 2 \end{pmatrix} \begin{pmatrix} c_1 e^t + \int_0^t e^{t-s}[3dz_1(s) - dz_2(s) - dz_3(s)] \\ c_2 e^{2t} + \int_0^t e^{2(t-s)}[dz_2(s) - dz_1(s)] \\ c_3 e^{3t} + \int_0^t e^{3(t-s)}[dz_3(s) - dz_1(s)] \end{pmatrix}$$

Evaluating this transformation equation will therefore show that the variable describing the general economic outlook, $u_1(t)$, will evolve in accordance with the following process:

$$\begin{aligned} u_1(t) &= c_1 e^t + c_2 e^{2t} + c_3 e^{3t} \\ &\quad + \int_0^t (3e^{(t-s)} - e^{2(t-s)} - e^{3(t-s)})dz_1(s) + \int_0^t (e^{2(t-s)} - e^{(t-s)})dz_2(s) \\ &\quad + \int_0^t (e^{3(t-s)} - e^{(t-s)})dz_3(s) \end{aligned}$$

Likewise, the variable describing the cost of the firm's primary inputs, $u_2(t)$, will evolve in accordance with the following process:

$$\begin{aligned} u_2(t) &= c_1 e^t + 2c_2 e^{2t} + c_3 e^{3t} \\ &\quad + \int_0^t (3e^{(t-s)} - 2e^{2(t-s)} - e^{3(t-s)})dz_1(s) + \int_0^t (2e^{2(t-s)} - e^{(t-s)})dz_2(s) \\ &\quad + \int_0^t (e^{3(t-s)} - e^{(t-s)})dz_3(s) \end{aligned}$$

Finally, the variable describing the demand for the firm's outputs, $u_3(t)$, will evolve in accordance with the following process:

$$u_3(t) = c_1e^t + c_2e^{2t} + 2c_3e^{3t}$$
$$+ \int_0^t (3e^{(t-s)} - e^{2(t-s)} - 2e^{3(t-s)})dz_1(s) + \int_0^t (e^{2(t-s)} - e^{(t-s)})dz_2(s)$$
$$+ \int_0^t (2e^{3(t-s)} - e^{(t-s)})dz_3(s)$$

Note also that if we set $t = 0$ in the above transformation matrix it follows that

$$\underset{\sim}{u}(0) = \begin{pmatrix} u_1(0) \\ u_2(0) \\ u_3(0) \end{pmatrix} = \begin{pmatrix} 1 & 1 & 1 \\ 1 & 2 & 1 \\ 1 & 1 & 2 \end{pmatrix} \begin{pmatrix} c_1 \\ c_2 \\ c_3 \end{pmatrix} = M\underset{\sim}{y}(0)$$

or

$$\begin{pmatrix} c_1 \\ c_2 \\ c_3 \end{pmatrix} = \begin{pmatrix} 1 & 1 & 1 \\ 1 & 2 & 1 \\ 1 & 1 & 2 \end{pmatrix}^{-1} \begin{pmatrix} u_1(0) \\ u_2(0) \\ u_3(0) \end{pmatrix} = \begin{pmatrix} 3 & -1 & -1 \\ -1 & 1 & 0 \\ -1 & 0 & 1 \end{pmatrix} \begin{pmatrix} u_1(0) \\ u_2(0) \\ u_3(0) \end{pmatrix} = M^{-1}\underset{\sim}{u}(0)$$

This in turn will mean that the integration constants in the above expression for the variables comprising the firm's investment opportunity set will turn out to be

$$c_1 = 3u_1(0) - u_2(0) - u_3(0),\ c_2 = u_2(0) - u_1(0) \text{ and } c_3 = u_3(0) - u_1(0)$$

We can use these results to determine the distributional properties of the variables comprising the firm's investment opportunity set. Thus, if we use the expressions for the integrating constants given here, it follows that for the first variable, the general economic outlook $u_1(t)$, we have

$$u_1(t) = [3u_1(0) - u_2(0) - u_3(0)]e^t + [u_2(0) - u_1(0)]e^{2t} + [u_3(0) - u_1(0)]e^{3t}$$
$$+ \int_0^t (3e^{(t-s)} - e^{2(t-s)} - e^{3(t-s)})dz_1(s) + \int_0^t (e^{2(t-s)} - e^{(t-s)})dz_2(s)$$
$$+ \int_0^t (e^{3(t-s)} - e^{(t-s)})dz_3(s)$$

We can take expectations across this expression and thereby show that the variable describing the general economic outlook will be normally distributed with a mean

$$E_0[u_1(t)] = [3u_1(0) - u_2(0) - u_3(0)]e^t + [u_2(0) - u_1(0)]e^{2t} + [u_3(0) - u_1(0)]e^{3t}$$

Moreover, we can apply Wiener's Theorem (as in §7-5 of Chapter 7) in conjunction with the fact that $dz_1(t), dz_2(t)$ and $dz_3(t)$ are mutually uncorrelated (as in §8-2 above) to show that the variance of the general economic outlook variable will be

$$\mathrm{Var}_0[u_1(t)] =$$

$$\sigma_1^2 \int_0^t (3e^{(t-s)} - e^{2(t-s)} - e^{3(t-s)})^2 ds + \sigma_2^2 \int_0^t (e^{2(t-s)} - e^{(t-s)})^2 ds$$

$$+ \sigma_3^2 \int_0^t (e^{3(t-s)} - e^{(t-s)})^2 ds$$

Similar calculations can be applied to determine the distributional properties of the other two variables, $u_2(t)$ and $u_3(t)$.

§8-5. The above analysis formulates a firm's investment opportunity set in terms of a first-order vector system of stochastic differential equations. If, however, the momentum and acceleration of productive factors is to be part of a firm's investment opportunity set then it will be necessary to consider higher-order systems of stochastic differential equations. Recall here that a variable's acceleration is defined in terms of its second derivative. However, our analysis to date is exclusively based on first-order systems of stochastic differential equations and by definition these will not include the second or higher derivatives of the variables comprising the firm's investment opportunity set. Given this, we now develop the theory behind the formulation and solution of the simplest (or canonical) forms of second-order vector systems of stochastic differential equations. We begin by supposing as in §8-2 to §8-4 above that there are three interacting variables comprising the firm's investment opportunity set and that these variables evolve in accordance with the following second-order system of stochastic differential equations:

$$\underset{\sim}{u}''(t) = Q\underset{\sim}{u}(t) + \underset{\sim}{z}'(t)$$

where

$$\underset{\sim}{u}(t) = \begin{pmatrix} u_1(t) \\ u_2(t) \\ u_3(t) \end{pmatrix}$$

is the vector whose elements are the levels of the variables comprising the firm's investment opportunity set,

$$\underset{\sim}{u}''(t) = \begin{pmatrix} \dfrac{d^2u_1(t)}{dt^2} \\ \dfrac{d^2u_2(t)}{dt^2} \\ \dfrac{d^2u_3(t)}{dt^2} \end{pmatrix}$$

is the vector containing the second derivatives of the variables comprising the firm's investment opportunity set and

$$\underset{\sim}{z}'(t) = \begin{pmatrix} \dfrac{dz_1(t)}{dt} \\ \dfrac{dz_2(t)}{dt} \\ \dfrac{dz_3(t)}{dt} \end{pmatrix}$$

is the vector containing the white noise terms associated with these variables. Now, suppose that we determine the eigenvectors for the matrix Q (as in §3-12 to §3-16 of Chapter 3) and stack them into columns to form the matrix M. Then we can define a new set of variables

$$\underset{\sim}{y}(t) = \begin{pmatrix} y_1(t) \\ y_2(t) \\ y_3(t) \end{pmatrix}$$

that are related to the variables comprising the firm's investment opportunity set through the transformation equation

$$\underset{\sim}{u}(t) = M\underset{\sim}{y}(t)$$

We can then differentiate through this expression to give $\underset{\sim}{u}''(t) = M\underset{\sim}{y}''(t)$, where

$$\underset{\sim}{y}''(t) = \begin{pmatrix} \dfrac{d^2y_1(t)}{dt^2} \\ \dfrac{d^2y_2(t)}{dt^2} \\ \dfrac{d^2y_3(t)}{dt^2} \end{pmatrix}$$

is the vector whose elements are the second derivatives of the transforming variables. Substitution will then show

$$\underset{\sim}{u}''(t) = M\underset{\sim}{y}''(t) = Q\underset{\sim}{u}(t) + \underset{\sim}{z}'(t) = QM\underset{\sim}{y}(t) + \underset{\sim}{z}'(t)$$

We can then premultiply both sides of the above equation by M^{-1} to give

$$\underset{\sim}{y}''(t) = M^{-1}QM\underset{\sim}{y}(t) + M^{-1}\underset{\sim}{z}'(t)$$

However, from Exercise 4 in Chapter 3, we know that when the columns of M are composed of the eigenvectors of Q then, provided certain regularity conditions are satisfied, we will have $D = M^{-1}QM$, where D is the matrix whose off-diagonal elements are all zero and whose diagonal elements are composed of the eigenvalues of Q. This means that the above equation simplifies to

$$\underset{\sim}{y}''(t) = D\underset{\sim}{y}(t) + M^{-1}\underset{\sim}{z}'(t)$$

Now, we can demonstrate the application of this result by supposing that the matix of structural coefficients for the second-order vector system of stochastic differential equations given here is defined by

$$Q = \begin{pmatrix} 1 & 1 & -2 \\ -1 & 2 & 1 \\ 0 & 1 & -1 \end{pmatrix}$$

The eigenvalues of Q are are $\lambda = -1, \lambda = 1$ and $\lambda = 2$. Moreover, the eigenvector associated with the eigenvalue $\lambda = -1$ turns out to be

$$\underset{\sim}{x} = \begin{pmatrix} 1 \\ 0 \\ 1 \end{pmatrix}$$

The eigenvector associated with the eigenvalue $\lambda = 1$ turns out to be

$$\underset{\sim}{x} = \begin{pmatrix} 3 \\ 2 \\ 1 \end{pmatrix}$$

Finally, the eigenvector associated with the eigenvalue $\lambda = 2$ is

$$\underset{\sim}{x} = \begin{pmatrix} 1 \\ 3 \\ 1 \end{pmatrix}$$

Letting the eigenvectors be the columns of the matrix M will then mean that

$$M = \begin{pmatrix} 1 & 3 & 1 \\ 0 & 2 & 3 \\ 1 & 1 & 1 \end{pmatrix}$$

Moreover, we can determine the inverse of this matrix, namely,

$$M^{-1} = \begin{pmatrix} -\frac{1}{6} & -\frac{1}{3} & \frac{7}{6} \\ \frac{1}{2} & 0 & -\frac{1}{2} \\ -\frac{1}{3} & \frac{1}{3} & \frac{1}{3} \end{pmatrix}$$

We can then undertake the following calculations:

$$M^{-1}Q = \begin{pmatrix} -\frac{1}{6} & -\frac{1}{3} & \frac{7}{6} \\ \frac{1}{2} & 0 & -\frac{1}{2} \\ -\frac{1}{3} & \frac{1}{3} & \frac{1}{3} \end{pmatrix} \begin{pmatrix} 1 & 1 & -2 \\ -1 & 2 & 1 \\ 0 & 1 & -1 \end{pmatrix} = \begin{pmatrix} \frac{1}{6} & \frac{1}{3} & -\frac{7}{6} \\ \frac{1}{2} & 0 & -\frac{1}{2} \\ -\frac{2}{3} & \frac{2}{3} & \frac{2}{3} \end{pmatrix}$$

and

$$D = M^{-1}QM = \begin{pmatrix} \frac{1}{6} & \frac{1}{3} & -\frac{7}{6} \\ \frac{1}{2} & 0 & -\frac{1}{2} \\ -\frac{2}{3} & \frac{2}{3} & \frac{2}{3} \end{pmatrix} \begin{pmatrix} 1 & 3 & 1 \\ 0 & 2 & 3 \\ 1 & 1 & 1 \end{pmatrix} = \begin{pmatrix} -1 & 0 & 0 \\ 0 & 1 & 0 \\ 0 & 0 & 2 \end{pmatrix}$$

Note how all off-diagonal elements of the matrix D are zero and that the diagonal elements of D are composed of the eigenvalues of the structural matrix Q. These calculations will thus imply that the differential equation describing the evolution of the vector $\underset{\sim}{y}(t)$ containing the transformed variables can be restated as

$$\underset{\sim}{y}''(t) = D\underset{\sim}{y}(t) + M^{-1}\underset{\sim}{z}'(t)$$

or

$$\begin{pmatrix} \frac{d^2y_1(t)}{dt^2} \\ \frac{d^2y_2(t)}{dt^2} \\ \frac{d^2y_3(t)}{dt^2} \end{pmatrix} = \begin{pmatrix} -1 & 0 & 0 \\ 0 & 1 & 0 \\ 0 & 0 & 2 \end{pmatrix} \begin{pmatrix} y_1(t) \\ y_2(t) \\ y_3(t) \end{pmatrix} + \begin{pmatrix} -\frac{1}{6} & -\frac{1}{3} & \frac{7}{6} \\ \frac{1}{2} & 0 & -\frac{1}{2} \\ -\frac{1}{3} & \frac{1}{3} & \frac{1}{3} \end{pmatrix} \begin{pmatrix} \frac{dz_1(t)}{dt} \\ \frac{dz_2(t)}{dt} \\ \frac{dz_3(t)}{dt} \end{pmatrix}$$

Thus, the differential equation describing the evolution of the first transformed variable $y_1(t)$ is as follows

$$\frac{d^2y_1(t)}{dt^2} + y_1(t) = \frac{7}{6}\frac{dz_3(t)}{dt} - \frac{1}{3}\frac{dz_2(t)}{dt} - \frac{1}{6}\frac{dz_1(t)}{dt}$$

Now, the general solution to this second-order stochastic differential equation takes the form

$$y_1(t) = k_1 \sin t + k_2 \cos t + \int_0^t \sin(t-s)[\tfrac{7}{6}dz_3(s) - \tfrac{1}{3}dz_2(s) - \tfrac{1}{6}dz_1(s)]$$

where k_1 and k_2 are constants that must be determined from a given set of initial conditions. We can demonstrate that this is the general solution of the above stochastic differential equation by initially considering the first two terms on the right-hand side of the above expression. Now, from the 'Useful Formulae' appended to this chapter, we have

$$\frac{d^2}{dt^2}(\sin t) = \frac{d}{dt}(\cos t) = -\sin t$$

It follows from this that if $y_1(t) = \sin t$ then we have

$$\frac{d^2 y_1(t)}{dt^2} + y_1(t) = -\sin t + \sin t = 0$$

Likewise, for the second term in the solution for $y_1(t)$, we have

$$\frac{d^2}{dt^2}(\cos t) = \frac{d}{dt}(-\sin t) = -\cos t$$

Again it follows that if $y_1(t) = \cos t$ then we have

$$\frac{d^2 y_1(t)}{dt^2} + y_1(t) = -\cos t + \cos t = 0$$

§8-6. To determine the derivative of the third and final term on the right-hand side of the solution for $y_1(t)$, we first let

$$W'(t) = \frac{dW(t)}{dt} = \frac{7}{6}\frac{dz_3(t)}{dt} - \frac{1}{3}\frac{dz_2(t)}{dt} - \frac{1}{6}\frac{dz_1(t)}{dt}$$

We can then state the third term of the solution as

$$y_1(t) = \int_0^t \sin(t-s)W'(s)ds$$

Now, suppose we let $x = t$ and $y = -s$ in the expression for $\sin(x+y)$ in the 'Useful Formulae' appended to this chapter. Doing so, we have

$$\sin(t-s) = \sin t \cos(-s) + \cos t \sin(-s)$$

However, since the 'Useful Formulae' also show that $\cos(-s) = \cos s$ and $\sin(-s) = -\sin s$, this result may be restated as

$$\sin(t-s) = \sin t \cos s - \cos t \sin s$$

It follows from this that the third and final term in the solution for $y_1(t)$ can be restated as

$$y_1(t) = \int_0^t \sin(t-s)W'(s)ds = (\sin t)\int_0^t (\cos s)W'(s)ds - (\cos t)\int_0^t (\sin s)W'(s)ds$$

Taking the first derivative through this expression shows:

$$\frac{dy_1(t)}{dt} = (\cos t)\int_0^t (\cos s)W'(s)ds + (\sin t\cos t)W'(t)$$

$$+ (\sin t)\int_0^t (\sin s)W'(s)ds - (\cos t\sin t)W'(t)$$

or

$$\frac{dy_1(t)}{dt} = (\cos t)\int_0^t (\cos s)W'(s)ds + (\sin t)\int_0^t (\sin s)W'(s)ds$$

Moreover, we can differentiate through this expression and thereby show that

$$\frac{d^2y_1(t)}{dt^2} = -(\sin t)\int_0^t (\cos s)W'(s)ds + (\cos t)\int_0^t (\sin s)W'(s)ds + (\sin^2 t + \cos^2 t)W'(t)$$

Note, however, from the 'Useful Formulae' appended to this chapter that $\sin^2 t + \cos^2 t = 1$. Hence, the above result may be restated as

$$\frac{d^2y_1(t)}{dt^2} = -(\sin t)\int_0^t (\cos s)W'(s)ds + (\cos t)\int_0^t (\sin s)W'(s)ds + W'(t)$$

It then follows that $y_1(t) = \int_0^t \sin(t-s)W'(s)ds$ must satisfy the differential equation, since

$$\frac{d^2y_1(t)}{dt^2} + y_1(t) = -(\sin t)\int_0^t (\cos s)W'(s)ds + (\cos t)\int_0^t (\sin s)W'(s)ds + W'(t)$$

$$+ (\sin t)\int_0^t (\cos s)W'(s)ds - (\cos t)\int_0^t (\sin s)W'(s)ds = W'(t)$$

or

$$\frac{d^2y_1(t)}{dt^2} + y_1(t) = W'(t)$$

Likewise, it will be recalled from §8-5 above that $y_1(t) = \sin t$ and $y_1(t) = \cos t$ will both satisfy the differential equation

$$\frac{d^2y_1(t)}{dt^2} + y_1(t) = 0$$

Hence, these calculations show that if

$$y_1(t) = k_1 \sin t + k_2 \cos t + \int_0^t \sin(t-s)W'(s)ds$$

equivalently

$$y_1(t) = k_1 \sin t + k_2 \cos t + \int_0^t \sin(t-s)[\tfrac{7}{6}dz_3(s) - \tfrac{1}{3}dz_2(s) - \tfrac{1}{6}dz_1(s)]$$

then $y_1(t)$ will satisfy the differential equation

$$\frac{d^2 y_1(t)}{dt^2} + y_1(t) = W'(t) = \frac{7}{6}\frac{dz_3(t)}{dt} - \frac{1}{3}\frac{dz_2(t)}{dt} - \frac{1}{6}\frac{dz_1(t)}{dt}$$

Moreover, it will be recalled from §8-5 above that k_1 and k_2 are constants that must be determined from a set of initial conditions.

§8-7. From §8-5 above, it also follows that the second transformed variable, $y_2(t)$, will satisfy the differential equation

$$\frac{d^2 y_2(t)}{dt^2} - y_2(t) = \frac{1}{2}\left[\frac{dz_1(t)}{dt} - \frac{dz_3(t)}{dt}\right]$$

The general solution to this differential equation takes the form

$$y_2(t) = k_3 \sinh t + k_4 \cosh t + \frac{1}{2}\int_0^t \sinh(t-s)[dz_1(s) - dz_3(s)]$$

where k_3 and k_4 are constants, $\sinh t = \frac{1}{2}(e^t - e^{-t})$ is known as the hyperbolic sine function and $\cosh t = \frac{1}{2}(e^t + e^{-t})$ is known as the hyperbolic cosine function. Moreover, this result may be restated as

$$y_2(t) = k_3 \sinh t + k_4 \cosh t + \int_0^t \sinh(t-s)W'(s)ds$$

where

$$W'(t) = \frac{dW(t)}{dt} = \frac{1}{2}\left[\frac{dz_1(t)}{dt} - \frac{dz_3(t)}{dt}\right]$$

Now, from the 'Useful Formulae' appended to this chapter, we have for the first term on the right-hand side of the general solution that

$$\frac{d^2}{dt^2}(\sinh t) = \frac{d}{dt}(\cosh t) = \sinh t$$

It follows from this that if $y_2(t) = \sinh t$ then we have

$$\frac{d^2y_2(t)}{dt^2} - y_2(t) = \sinh t - \sinh t = 0$$

Likewise, for the second term in the solution, we have

$$\frac{d^2}{dt^2}(\cosh t) = \frac{d}{dt}(\sinh t) = \cosh t$$

Again it follows that if $y_2(t) = \cosh t$ then we have

$$\frac{d^2y_2(t)}{dt^2} - y_2(t) = \cosh t - \cosh t = 0$$

Moreover, we can let $x = t$ and $y = -s$ in the expression for $\sinh(x+y)$ summarized in the 'Useful Formulae' appended to this chapter, in which case we have

$$\sinh(t-s) = \sinh(t)\cosh(-s) + \cosh(t)\sinh(-s)$$

However, from the 'Useful Formulae', we also have $\cosh(-s) = \cosh s$ and $\sinh(-s) = -\sinh s$, and so the above result may be restated as

$$\sinh(t-s) = \sinh t \cosh s - \cosh t \sinh s$$

We can use this result to restate the final term in the solution for $y_2(t)$ as follows:

$$y_2(t) = \int_0^t \sinh(t-s)W'(s)ds = (\sinh t)\int_0^t (\cosh s)W'(s)ds - (\cosh t)\int_0^t (\sinh s)W'(s)ds$$

Moreover, taking the first derivative through this expression shows

$$\frac{dy_2(t)}{dt} = (\cosh t)\int_0^t (\cosh s)W'(s)ds + (\sinh t \cosh t)W'(t)$$

$$- (\sinh t)\int_0^t (\sinh s)W'(s)ds - (\cosh t \sinh t)W'(t)$$

or

$$\frac{dy_2(t)}{dt} = (\cosh t)\int_0^t (\cosh s)W'(s)ds - (\sinh t)\int_0^t (\sinh s)W'(s)ds$$

Also, we can differentiate through the above expression and thereby show that

$$\frac{d^2y_2(t)}{dt^2} = (\sinh t)\int_0^t (\cosh s)W'(s)ds - (\cosh t)\int_0^t (\sinh s)W'(s)ds + (\cosh^2 t - \sinh^2 t)W'(t)$$

Note, however, from the 'Useful Formulae' appended to this chapter that $\cosh^2 t - \sinh^2 t = 1$, and so the above result may be restated as

$$\frac{d^2y_2(t)}{dt^2} = (\sinh t)\int_0^t (\cosh s)W'(s)ds - (\cosh t)\int_0^t (\sinh s)W'(s)ds + W'(t)$$

It then follows that $y_2(t) = \int_0^t \sinh(t-s)W'(s)ds$ will satisfy the differential equation, since

$$\frac{d^2y_2(t)}{dt^2} - y_2(t) = (\sinh t)\int_0^t (\cosh s)W'(s)ds - (\cosh t)\int_0^t (\sinh s)W'(s)ds + W'(t)$$
$$- \left[(\sinh t)\int_0^t (\cosh s)W'(s)ds - (\cosh t)\int_0^t (\sinh s)W'(s)ds\right] = W'(t)$$

or

$$\frac{d^2y_2(t)}{dt^2} - y_2(t) = W'(t)$$

Likewise, it will be recalled from earlier in this section that $y_2(t) = \sinh t$ and $y_2(t) = \cosh t$ both satisfy the differential equation

$$\frac{d^2y_2(t)}{dt^2} - y_2(t) = 0$$

Hence, these calculations show that if

$$y_2(t) = k_3 \sinh t + k_4 \cosh t + \int_0^t \sinh(t-s)W'(s)ds$$

or equivalently

$$y_2(t) = k_3 \sinh t + k_4 \cosh t + \frac{1}{2}\int_0^t \sinh(t-s)[dz_1(s) - dz_3(s)]$$

then $y_2(t)$ will satify the differential equation

$$\frac{d^2y_2(t)}{dt^2} - y_2(t) = W'(t) = \frac{1}{2}\left[\frac{dz_1(t)}{dt} - \frac{dz_3(t)}{dt}\right]$$

Here it will also be recalled that k_3 and k_4 are constants that must be determined from a set of initial conditions.

§8-8. We can apply procedures similar to those employed in §8-5 to §8-7 above and thereby show that the variable $y_3(t)$ will evolve in accordance with the following process:

$$y_3(t) = k_5 \sinh(\sqrt{2}t) + k_6 \cosh(\sqrt{2}t) + \frac{1}{3\sqrt{2}} \int_0^t \sinh[\sqrt{2}(t-s)][dz_3(t) + dz_2(t) - dz_1(t)]$$

where, as before, k_5 and k_6 are constants of integration determined from a set of initial conditions. Moreover, having obtained solutions for each of the transformed variables, we are now in a position to determine the solution to our original vector system of differential equations, namely,

$$\begin{pmatrix} u_1(t) \\ u_2(t) \\ u_3(t) \end{pmatrix} = \underset{\sim}{u}(t) = M\underset{\sim}{y}(t) = \begin{pmatrix} 1 & 3 & 1 \\ 0 & 2 & 3 \\ 1 & 1 & 1 \end{pmatrix} \begin{pmatrix} y_1(t) \\ y_2(t) \\ y_3(t) \end{pmatrix}$$

where

$$\begin{pmatrix} y_1(t) \\ y_2(t) \\ y_3(t) \end{pmatrix} =$$

$$\begin{pmatrix} k_1 \sin t + k_2 \cos t + \int_0^t \sin(t-s)[\frac{7}{6}dz_3(s) - \frac{1}{3}dz_2(s) - \frac{1}{6}dz_1(s)] \\ k_3 \sinh t + k_4 \cosh t + \frac{1}{2}\int_0^t \sinh(t-s)[dz_1(s) - dz_3(s)] \\ k_5 \sinh(\sqrt{2}t) + k_6 \cosh(\sqrt{2}t) + \frac{1}{3\sqrt{2}}\int_0^t \sinh[\sqrt{2}(t-s)][dz_3(s) + dz_2(s) - dz_1(s)] \end{pmatrix}$$

Thus, the first of our original variables, $u_1(t)$, will evolve in accordance with the following process:

$$\begin{aligned} u_1(t) &= (k_1 \sin t + k_2 \cos t) + 3(k_3 \sinh t + k_4 \cosh t) + [k_5 \sinh(\sqrt{2}t) + k_6 \cosh(\sqrt{2}t)] \\ &\quad + \int_0^t \sin(t-s)[\tfrac{7}{6}dz_3(s) - \tfrac{1}{3}dz_2(s) - \tfrac{1}{6}dz_1(s)] + \frac{3}{2}\int_0^t \sinh(t-s)[dz_1(s) - dz_3(s)] \\ &\quad + \frac{1}{3\sqrt{2}}\int_0^t \sinh[\sqrt{2}(t-s)][dz_3(s) + dz_2(s) - dz_1(s)] \end{aligned}$$

Similar calculations show that the second of the original variables, $u_2(t)$, will evolve in accordance with the following process:

$$\begin{aligned} u_2(t) &= 2(k_3 \sinh t + k_4 \cosh t) + 3[k_5 \sinh(\sqrt{2}t) + k_6 \cosh(\sqrt{2}t)] \\ &\quad + \int_0^t \sinh(t-s)[dz_1(s) - dz_3(s)] + \frac{1}{\sqrt{2}}\int_0^t \sinh[\sqrt{2}(t-s)][dz_3(s) + dz_2(s) - dz_1(s)] \end{aligned}$$

Finally, the third of the original variables, $u_3(t)$, will evolve in accordance with the following process:

$$u_3(t) = (k_1 \sin t + k_2 \cos t) + (k_3 \sinh t + k_4 \cosh t) + [k_5 \sinh(\sqrt{2}t) + k_6 \cosh(\sqrt{2}t)]$$
$$+ \int_0^t \sin(t-s)[\tfrac{7}{6}dz_3(s) - \tfrac{1}{3}dz_2(s) - \tfrac{1}{6}dz_1(s)] + \frac{1}{2}\int_0^t \sinh(t-s)[dz_1(s) - dz_3(s)]$$
$$+ \frac{1}{3\sqrt{2}}\int_0^t \sinh[\sqrt{2}(t-s)][dz_3(s) + dz_2(s) - dz_1(s)]$$

We have also previously noted (in §8-5) that the exact values of the constants in the solutions for $u_1(t), u_2(t)$ and $u_3(t)$ are determined from a given set of initial conditions. Given this, suppose we set $t = 0$ in the above transformation matrix, in which case it follows that

$$\underset{\sim}{u}(0) = \begin{pmatrix} u_1(0) \\ u_2(0) \\ u_3(0) \end{pmatrix} = \begin{pmatrix} 1 & 3 & 1 \\ 0 & 2 & 3 \\ 1 & 1 & 1 \end{pmatrix} \begin{pmatrix} k_2 \\ k_4 \\ k_6 \end{pmatrix} = M\underset{\sim}{y}(0)$$

Now, we can solve the above system of equations for the given constants as follows:

$$\begin{pmatrix} k_2 \\ k_4 \\ k_6 \end{pmatrix} = \begin{pmatrix} 1 & 3 & 1 \\ 0 & 2 & 3 \\ 1 & 1 & 1 \end{pmatrix}^{-1} \begin{pmatrix} u_1(0) \\ u_2(0) \\ u_3(0) \end{pmatrix} = \begin{pmatrix} -\frac{1}{6} & -\frac{1}{3} & \frac{7}{6} \\ \frac{1}{2} & 0 & -\frac{1}{2} \\ -\frac{1}{3} & \frac{1}{3} & \frac{1}{3} \end{pmatrix} \begin{pmatrix} u_1(0) \\ u_2(0) \\ u_3(0) \end{pmatrix} = M^{-1}\underset{\sim}{u}(0)$$

in which case we have

$$k_2 = \frac{7u_3(0) - 2u_2(0) - u_1(0)}{6}, \; k_4 = \frac{u_1(0) - u_3(0)}{2}$$

and

$$k_6 = \frac{u_3(0) + u_2(0) - u_1(0)}{3}$$

There are, however, three other constants for which we do not yet have values. To determine these constants, we can differentiate through the expression for the transformed variables and thereby obtain

$$\underset{\sim}{u}'(t) = M\underset{\sim}{y}'(t)$$

or

$$\begin{pmatrix} \dfrac{du_1(t)}{dt} \\ \dfrac{du_2(t)}{dt} \\ \dfrac{du_3(t)}{dt} \end{pmatrix} = \begin{pmatrix} 1 & 3 & 1 \\ 0 & 2 & 3 \\ 1 & 1 & 1 \end{pmatrix} \begin{pmatrix} \dfrac{dy_1(t)}{dt} \\ \dfrac{dy_2(t)}{dt} \\ \dfrac{dy_3(t)}{dt} \end{pmatrix}$$

We can then use the results summarized earlier in this section and those summarized in §8-5 to §8-7 above to determine the vector $\underset{\sim}{y}'(t)$ as follows:

$$\begin{pmatrix} \dfrac{du_1(t)}{dt} \\ \dfrac{du_2(t)}{dt} \\ \dfrac{du_3(t)}{dt} \end{pmatrix} = \begin{pmatrix} 1 & 3 & 1 \\ 0 & 2 & 3 \\ 1 & 1 & 1 \end{pmatrix} \times$$

$$\begin{pmatrix} k_1 \cos t - k_2 \sin t + \frac{1}{6}\int_0^t (\cos t \cos s + \sin t \sin s)[7dz_3(s) - 2dz_2(s) - dz_1(s)] \\ k_3 \cosh t + k_4 \sinh t + \frac{1}{2}\int_0^t (\cosh t \cosh s - \sinh t \sinh s)[dz_1(s) - dz_3(s)] \\ \sqrt{2}k_5 \cosh(\sqrt{2t}) + \sqrt{2}k_6 \sinh(\sqrt{2t}) + \frac{1}{3}\int_0^t [\cosh(\sqrt{2t})\cosh(\sqrt{2s}) - \\ \sinh(\sqrt{2t})\sinh(\sqrt{2s})] \times [dz_3(s) + dz_2(s) - dz_1(s)] \end{pmatrix}$$

Hence, if we again set $t = 0$ in the above transformation matrix then it follows that

$$\begin{pmatrix} \dfrac{du_1(0)}{dt} \\ \dfrac{du_2(0)}{dt} \\ \dfrac{du_3(0)}{dt} \end{pmatrix} = \begin{pmatrix} 1 & 3 & 1 \\ 0 & 2 & 3 \\ 1 & 1 & 1 \end{pmatrix} \begin{pmatrix} k_1 \\ k_3 \\ \sqrt{2}k_5 \end{pmatrix}$$

We can again solve the above system of equations for the given constants as follows:

$$\begin{pmatrix} k_1 \\ k_3 \\ \sqrt{2}k_5 \end{pmatrix} = \begin{pmatrix} 1 & 3 & 1 \\ 0 & 2 & 3 \\ 1 & 1 & 1 \end{pmatrix}^{-1} \begin{pmatrix} \dfrac{du_1(0)}{dt} \\ \dfrac{du_2(0)}{dt} \\ \dfrac{du_3(0)}{dt} \end{pmatrix} = \begin{pmatrix} -\frac{1}{6} & -\frac{1}{3} & \frac{7}{6} \\ \frac{1}{2} & 0 & -\frac{1}{2} \\ -\frac{1}{3} & \frac{1}{3} & \frac{1}{3} \end{pmatrix} \begin{pmatrix} \dfrac{du_1(0)}{dt} \\ \dfrac{du_2(0)}{dt} \\ \dfrac{du_3(0)}{dt} \end{pmatrix} = M^{-1}\underset{\sim}{u}'(0)$$

in which case we have

$$k_1 = \frac{7}{6}\frac{du_3(0)}{dt} - \frac{1}{3}\frac{du_2(0)}{dt} - \frac{1}{6}\frac{du_1(0)}{dt}$$

$$k_3 = \frac{1}{2}\frac{du_1(0)}{dt} - \frac{1}{2}\frac{du_3(0)}{dt}$$

and:

$$k_5 = \frac{1}{3\sqrt{2}}\frac{du_3(0)}{dt} + \frac{1}{3\sqrt{2}}\frac{du_2(0)}{dt} - \frac{1}{3\sqrt{2}}\frac{du_1(0)}{dt}$$

Note that we have now specified values for all six constants comprising the solution to our second-order system of stochastic differential equations. This in turn will mean that with these specific values for the constants, the solutions for $u_1(t), u_2(t)$ and $u_3(t)$ will be unique.

§8-9. One cannot, of course, observe any of the variables comprising the firm's investment opportunity set on a continuous basis. Rather, one will observe these variables at discretely sampled points in time. Given this, we now demonstrate how it is possible to use discretely sampled data to obtain consistent estimates of the parameters comprising a second-order system of stochastic differential equations. In particular, we demonstrate the fundamental principles associated with estimating the parameters of a continuous-time process by considering the variable $y_2(t)$ as determined in §8-7, namely,

$$y_2(t) = k_3 \sinh t + k_4 \cosh t + \frac{1}{2}\int_0^t \sinh(t-s)[dz_1(s) - dz_3(s)]$$

Now suppose that $y_2(t)$ is observed at the equally spaced (but discretely sampled) points t, $t+\Delta t$ and $t+2\Delta t$, where Δt represents the time between sampled observations. Simple but somewhat tedious algebraic manipulations employing the 'Useful Formulae' for the hyperbolic functions appended to this chapter will then show that

$$\begin{aligned} &y_2(t+2\Delta t) - 2\cosh(\Delta t)y_2(t+\Delta t) + y_2(t) \\ &= \frac{1}{2}\left\{\int_{t+\Delta t}^{t+2\Delta t} \sinh(t+2\Delta t - s)[dz_1(s) - dz_3(s)] - \int_t^{t+\Delta t} \sinh(t-s)[dz_1(s) - dz_3(s)]\right\} \end{aligned}$$

Now, it is not hard to show that

$$E_t[y_2(t+2\Delta t) - 2\cosh(\Delta t)y_2(t+\Delta t) + y_2(t)] = 0$$

where, as in previous sections, $E_t[\cdot]$ is the expectation operator taken at time t (as in Exercise 4 at the end of this chapter). Moreover, a simple application of Wiener's Theorem (as in §7-5 of Chapter 7) shows that

$$\mathrm{Var}_t\left[\int_{t+\Delta t}^{t+2\Delta t} \sinh(t+2\Delta t - s)[dz_1(s) - dz_3(s)]\right] = \frac{\sigma_1^2 + \sigma_3^2}{4}[\sinh(2\Delta t) - 2\Delta t]$$

where (from §8-2 and §8-5 above) σ_1^2 is the variance parameter associated with $dz_1(t)$ and σ_3^2 is the variance parameter associated with $dz_3(t)$. Similarly, Wiener's Theorem also shows that

$$\mathrm{Var}_t\left[\int_t^{t+\Delta t} \sinh(t-s)[dz_1(s) - dz_3(s)]\right] = \frac{\sigma_1^2 + \sigma_3^2}{4}[\sinh(2\Delta t) - 2\Delta t]$$

Now since the above integrals are defined in terms of non-overlapping periods of time the covariance between them will be zero:

$$E_t\left[\int_{t+\Delta t}^{t+2\Delta t} \sinh(t+2\Delta t-s)[dz_1(s)-dz_3(s)]\int_t^{t+\Delta t} \sinh(t-s)[dz_1(s)-dz_3(s)]\right]=0$$

When this condition is satisfied, the two integral expressions are uncorrelated and it then follows that the variance of this modified second difference formula will be

$$\begin{aligned}
&\mathrm{Var}_t[y_2(t+2\Delta t)-2\cosh(\Delta t)y_2(t+\Delta t)+y_2(t)]\\
&=\mathrm{Var}_t\left[\frac{1}{2}\left\{\int_{t+\Delta t}^{t+2\Delta t} \sinh(t+2\Delta t-s)[dz_1(s)-dz_3(s)]-\int_t^{t+\Delta t} \sinh(t-s)[dz_1(s)-dz_3(s)]\right\}\right]\\
&=\frac{1}{4}\mathrm{Var}_t\left[\int_{t+\Delta t}^{t+2\Delta t} \sinh(t+2\Delta t-s)[dz_1(s)-dz_3(s)]\right]\\
&\quad+\frac{1}{4}\mathrm{Var}_t\left[\int_t^{t+\Delta t} \sinh(t-s)[dz_1(s)-dz_3(s)]\right]
\end{aligned}$$

This taken in conjunction with our earlier results enables us to compute the variance of the modified second difference formula as follows:

$$\begin{aligned}
&\mathrm{Var}_t[y_2(t+2\Delta t)-2\cosh(\Delta t)y_2(t+\Delta t)+y_2(t)]\\
&=\frac{1}{4}\left\{\frac{2(\sigma_1^2+\sigma_3^2)}{4}[\sinh(2\Delta t)-2\Delta t]\right\}=\frac{\sigma_1^2+\sigma_3^2}{8}[\sinh(2\Delta t)-2\Delta t]
\end{aligned}$$

Here, however, we can use the 'Useful Formulae' for the hyperbolic functions appended to this chapter to show that $\sinh(2\Delta t)=2\sinh(\Delta t)\cosh(\Delta t)$. It then follows that the variance of the modified second difference formula can be stated in the alternative form

$$\mathrm{Var}_t[y_2(t+2\Delta t)-2\cosh(\Delta t)y_2(t+\Delta t)+y_2(t)]=\frac{\sigma_1^2+\sigma_3^2}{4}[\sinh(\Delta t)\cosh(\Delta t)-\Delta t]$$

Note that both the mean and variance of this modified second difference formula are stationary in time; that is, neither the expression for the mean nor the expression for the variance depends on the points in time when the variable $y_2(t)$ is observed. Moreover, we can use the expressions for the variance given above to estimate the variance parameter associated with the white noise term (as in §8-7 above):

$$\frac{dW(t)}{dt}=\frac{1}{2}\left[\frac{dz_1(t)}{dt}-\frac{dz_3(t)}{dt}\right]$$

Thus, suppose we have a long time series of observations $y_2(j\Delta t)$ for $j=0,1,2,\ldots,2n$, where, as previously, Δt represents the time between sampled observations. It then follows from the above result that

$$\sum_{j=1}^{n} \text{Var}_t[y_2(2j\Delta t) - 2\cosh(\Delta t)y_2((2j-1)\Delta t) + y_2(2(j-1)\Delta t)]$$

$$= \frac{n(\sigma_1^2 + \sigma_3^2)}{8}[\sinh(2\Delta t) - 2\Delta t]$$

Moreover, we can solve this equation to provide the following estimate of the variance associated with the white noise term $dW(t)/dt$, namely,

$$\frac{8}{n[\sinh(2\Delta t) - 2\Delta t]} \sum_{j=1}^{n} \text{Var}_t[y_2(2j\Delta t) - 2\cosh(\Delta t)y_2((2j-1)\Delta t) + y_2(2(j-1)\Delta t)]$$

$$= \sigma_1^2 + \sigma_3^2$$

Similar procedures may be applied to estimate the variance parameters associated with the other two variables, namely, $y_1(t)$ and $y_3(t)$, comprising the second-order system of stochastic differential equations as developed in §8-5 above. This, in turn, allows separate estimates of the variance parameters σ_1^2, σ_2^2 and σ_3^2 to be obtained.

§8-10. There is, of course, no reason why a firm's investment opportunity set cannot be stated in terms of the higher derivatives of its constituent variables. It might be, for example, that the jerk (third derivative) of the underlying variables are important components of a firm's investment opportunity set. It will then be necessary to summarize the firm's investment opportunity set in terms of a third-order system of stochastic differential equations. Fortunately, it is possible to generalize the procedures summarized in §8-5 to §8-9 above in order to determine solutions for third- (or even higher-) order systems of stochastic differential equations. Thus, suppose that a firm's investment opportunity set evolves in accordance with the following canonical interpretation of a third-order system of stochastic differential equations:

$$\underset{\sim}{u}'''(t) = Q\underset{\sim}{u}(t) + \underset{\sim}{z}'(t)$$

where

$$\underset{\sim}{u}(t) = \begin{pmatrix} u_1(t) \\ u_2(t) \\ u_3(t) \end{pmatrix}$$

is the vector whose elements are the levels of the variables comprising the firm's investment opportunity set,

$$\underset{\sim}{u}'''(t) = \begin{pmatrix} \dfrac{d^3u_1(t)}{dt^3} \\ \dfrac{d^3u_2(t)}{dt^3} \\ \dfrac{d^3u_3(t)}{dt^3} \end{pmatrix}$$

is the vector containing the third derivatives of the variables comprising the firm's investment opportunity set and

$$\underset{\sim}{z}'(t) = \begin{pmatrix} \dfrac{dz_1(t)}{dt} \\ \dfrac{dz_2(t)}{dt} \\ \dfrac{dz_3(t)}{dt} \end{pmatrix}$$

is the vector containing the white noise terms associated with the variables comprising the firm's investment opportunity set. Now, suppose that we determine the eigenvectors for the matrix Q (as in §3-12 to §3-16 of Chapter 3) and stack them into columns to form the matrix M. Then we can follow our previous procedures in defining a new set of variables

$$\underset{\sim}{y}(t) = \begin{pmatrix} y_1(t) \\ y_2(t) \\ y_3(t) \end{pmatrix}$$

that are related to the variables comprising the firm's investment opportunity set through the transformation equation

$$\underset{\sim}{u}(t) = M\underset{\sim}{y}(t)$$

We can then differentiate through this expression to give $\underset{\sim}{u}'''(t) = M\underset{\sim}{y}'''(t)$, where:

$$\underset{\sim}{y}'''(t) = \begin{pmatrix} \dfrac{d^3y_1(t)}{dt^3} \\ \dfrac{d^3y_2(t)}{dt^3} \\ \dfrac{d^3y_3(t)}{dt^3} \end{pmatrix}$$

is the vector containing the third derivatives of the transforming variables. Substitution then gives

$$\underset{\sim}{u}'''(t) = M\underset{\sim}{y}'''(t) = Q\underset{\sim}{u}(t) + \underset{\sim}{z}'(t) = QM\underset{\sim}{y}(t) + \underset{\sim}{z}'(t)$$

We can then premultiply both sides of this equation by M^{-1} to give

$$\underset{\sim}{y}'''(t) = M^{-1}QM\underset{\sim}{y}(t) + M^{-1}\underset{\sim}{z}'(t)$$

However, from our previous analysis, we know that when the columns of M are composed of the eigenvectors of Q then we will have $D = M^{-1}QM$, where, provided certain regularity conditions are satisfied, D is the matrix whose off-diagonal elements are all zero and whose diagonal elements are composed of the eigenvalues of Q. This will mean that the above equation simplifies to

$$\underset{\sim}{y}'''(t) = D\underset{\sim}{y}(t) + M^{-1}\underset{\sim}{z}'(t)$$

We can then follow procedures similar to those developed in previous sections to determine the solution of the above third-order system of stochastic differential equations and hence the particular form of the firm's investment opportunity set.

§8-11. We began this chapter by modelling the variables comprising a firm's investment opportunity set in terms of a first-order system of stochastic differential equations. This allows us to capture the important interdependences between the factors that most directly influence the value of a firm's equity. If, however, the momentum and acceleration of factors comprising the firm's investment opportunity set are instrumental determinants of the firm's equity value then it will be necessary to model the firm's investment opportunity set using higher-order systems of stochastic differential equations. Recall that a variable's acceleration is defined in terms of its second derivative. However, if a firm's investment opportunity set is stated in terms of a first-order system of stochastic differential equations then, by definition, it will not include the second- or higher-order derivatives of the variables comprising the investment opportunity set. Hence, in this chapter, we have provided an introduction to the theory behind the formulation and solution of second-order vector systems of stochastic differential equations. We would emphasize, however, that our analysis in this chapter has embraced only the simplest (or canonical) forms of first- and higher-order systems of stochastic differential equations. As such, our analysis provides only the most elementary of introductions to this important area of the literature. Yet, as will be seen in subsequent chapters, this is an area of considerable importance in equity valuation. In particular, it can be shown that a model based on a vector system of nth-order stochastic differential equations (where n can assume any positive integral value) can be reduced to an equivalent vector system of nth-order autoregressive (difference) equations in discrete time. Discrete-time autoregressive processes are widely applied in the accounting and finance literature to model corporate earnings and the other bookkeeping variables that typically comprise a firm's investment opportunity set. This chapter concluded by considering the difficulties that arise with parameter estimation when the variables comprising a firm's investment opportunity set evolve in terms of a second-order system of stochastic differential equations. In particular, we showed that a simple discretization of the underlying system of stochastic differential equations can lead to systematic biases in parameter estimation; and the larger the window over which the estimation procedure is conducted, the more significant the biases are likely to be. Hence, basing estimation procedures on a simple discretization of the underlying system of stochastic differential equations is something that is best avoided.

Selected references

Brisley, W. (1973) *A Basis for Linear Algebra*, Sydney: Wiley.
Friedman, A. (1975) *Stochastic Differential Equations and Applications*, New York: Academic Press.
Hoel, P., Port, S. and Stone, C. (1987) *Introduction to Stochastic Processes*, Long Grove, IL: Waveland Press.

Wymer, R. (1972) 'Econometric estimation of stochastic differential equation systems', *Econometrica*, 40: 565–77.

Appendix: Useful Formulae

Trigonometric Functions

$$\sin(x+y) = \sin x \cos y + \cos x \sin y$$

$$\cos(x+y) = \cos x \cos y - \sin x \sin y$$

$$\sin^2 x + \cos^2 x = 1$$

$$\frac{d}{dx}[\sin(\lambda x)] = \lambda \cos(\lambda x)$$

$$\frac{d}{dx}[\cos(\lambda x)] = -\lambda \sin(\lambda x)$$

where λ is a given parameter.

$$\cos(-x) = \cos x$$

$$\sin(-x) = -\sin x$$

Hyperbolic Functions

$$\sinh(x+y) = \sinh x \cosh y + \cosh x \sinh y$$

$$\cosh(x+y) = \cosh x \cosh y + \sinh x \sinh y$$

$$\cosh^2 x - \sinh^2 x = 1$$

$$\frac{d}{dx}[\sinh(\lambda x)] = \lambda \cosh(\lambda x)$$

$$\frac{d}{dx}[\cosh(\lambda x)] = \lambda \sinh(\lambda x)$$

where λ is a given parameter.

$$\cosh(-x) = \cosh x$$

$$\sinh(-x) = -\sinh x$$

Taylor Series Expansions

$$\sin x = x - \frac{x^3}{3!} + \frac{x^5}{5!} - \frac{x^7}{7!} + \dots$$

$$\cos x = 1 - \frac{x^2}{2!} + \frac{x^4}{4!} - \frac{x^6}{6!} + \dots$$

$$\sinh x = x + \frac{x^3}{3!} + \frac{x^5}{5!} + \frac{x^7}{7!} + \ldots$$

$$\cosh x = 1 + \frac{x^2}{2!} + \frac{x^4}{4!} + \frac{x^6}{6!} + \ldots$$

Exercises

1. Consider the second-order stochastic differential equation:

$$\frac{d^2u(s)}{ds^2} = -\gamma \frac{du(s)}{ds} + \frac{dz(s)}{ds}$$

where $\gamma > 0$ is a parameter and $dz(s)/ds$ is a white noise process with variance parameter σ^2. Show that by letting $x(s) = du(s)/ds$, one obtains the Ornstein–Uhlenbeck differential equation as given in §7-10 of Chapter 7. Use the solution of the Ornstein–Uhlenbeck differential equation to show that

$$x(s) = \frac{du(s)}{ds} = ce^{-\gamma s} + \int_0^s e^{-\gamma(s-\tau)} dz(\tau)$$

where c is a constant of integration. Integrate the above expression and use appropriate initial conditions to determine the general solution for $u(s)$. Finally, use Wiener's Theorem (as in §7-5 of Chapter 7) to determine the distributional properties of $u(s)$.

2. Suppose that a firm's investment opportunity set is defined by the following first-order system of stochastic differential equations:

$$\underset{\sim}{u}'(t) = Q\underset{\sim}{u}(t) + \underset{\sim}{z}'(t)$$

where

$$\underset{\sim}{u}(t) = \begin{pmatrix} u_1(t) \\ u_2(t) \\ u_3(t) \end{pmatrix}$$

is the vector whose elements are the levels of the variables comprising the firm's investment opportunity set,

$$\underset{\sim}{u}'(t) = \begin{pmatrix} \frac{du_1(t)}{dt} \\ \frac{du_2(t)}{dt} \\ \frac{du_3(t)}{dt} \end{pmatrix}$$

is the vector containing the derivatives of the variables comprising the firm's investment opportunity set and

$$\underset{\sim}{z}'(t) = \begin{pmatrix} \dfrac{dz_1(t)}{dt} \\ \dfrac{dz_2(t)}{dt} \\ \dfrac{dz_3(t)}{dt} \end{pmatrix}$$

is the vector of white noise terms associated with these variables. You may assume that all white noise terms are uncorrelated, with constant variances. Now, suppose the matrix of structural coefficients is given by

$$Q = \begin{pmatrix} 1 & 2 & 2 \\ 1 & 2 & -1 \\ -1 & 1 & 4 \end{pmatrix}$$

Use the procedures summarized in §8-2 to §8-4 of this chapter in conjunction with the procedures summarised in §3-12 to §3-15 of Chapter 3 to determine the solution of the vector system of stochastic differential equations given here.

3. In §8-5 and §8-6, we considered the second-order stochastic differential equation

$$\frac{d^2y_1(t)}{dt^2} + y_1(t) = \frac{7}{6}\frac{dz_3(t)}{dt} - \frac{1}{3}\frac{dz_2(t)}{dt} - \frac{1}{6}\frac{dz_1(t)}{dt}$$

where $dz_1(t)/dt$ is a white noise process with variance parameter $\sigma_1^2, dz_2(t)/dt$ is a white noise process with variance parameter σ_2^2 and $dz_3(t)/dt$ is a white noise process with variance parameter σ_3^2. We showed that the general solution to this differential equation is

$$y_1(t) = k_1 \sin t + k_2 \cos t + \int_0^t \sin(t-s)[\tfrac{7}{6}dz_3(s) - \tfrac{1}{3}dz_2(s) - \tfrac{1}{6}dz_1(s)]$$

where k_1 and k_2 are constants of integration. Use this latter result to show that

$$E_t[y_1(t+2\Delta t) - 2\cos(\Delta t)y_1(t+\Delta t) + y_1(t)] = 0$$

where $E_t[\cdot]$ is the expectation operator taken at time t.

4. In §8-7, we considered the second-order stochastic differential equation

$$\frac{d^2y_2(t)}{dt^2} - y_2(t) = \frac{1}{2}\left[\frac{dz_1(t)}{dt} - \frac{dz_3(t)}{dt}\right]$$

where $dz_1(t)/dt$ and $dz_3(t)/dt$ are the white noise processes defined in Exercise 3. We also showed that the general solution to this differential equation is

$$y_2(t) = k_3 \sinh t + k_4 \cosh t + \frac{1}{2}\int_0^t \sinh(t-s)[dz_1(s) - dz_3(s)]$$

where k_3 and k_4 are constants of integration. Use this latter result to show that

$$E_t[y_2(t+2\Delta t) - 2\cosh(\Delta t)y_2(t+\Delta t) + y_2(t)] = 0$$

where $E_t[\cdot]$ is the expectation operator taken at time t.

5. Refer to the second-order stochastic differential equation summarized in Exercise 4. Use Wiener's Theorem (as in §7-5 of Chapter 7) and thereby show that

$$\mathrm{Var}_t\left[\int_{t+\Delta t}^{t+2\Delta t} \sinh(t+2\Delta t - s)[dz_1(s) - dz_3(s)]\right] = \frac{\sigma_1^2+\sigma_3^2}{4}[\sinh(2\Delta t) - 2\Delta t]$$

Use the Taylor series expansion for $\sinh x$ summarized in the 'Useful Formulae' appended to this chapter to show that

$$\mathrm{Var}_t\left[\int_{t+\Delta t}^{t+2\Delta t} \sinh(t+2\Delta t - s)[dz_1(s) - dz_3(s)]\right] \approx \frac{\sigma_1^2+\sigma_3^2}{3}(\Delta t)^3$$

when Δt is relatively small.

9 Equity valuation

A canonical model

§9-1. In the previous two chapters, we have demonstrated how the variables comprising a firm's investment opportunity set can be summarized in terms of a vector system of stochastic differential equations. Our purpose in the present chapter is to use the analysis in those chapters to determine the relationships which exist between a firm's investment opportunity set and the market value of its equity. We follow what has become the conventional practice of characterizing a firm's investment opportunity set in terms of its abnormal earnings and the book values appearing on its balance sheet (as in §5-10 of Chapter 5) as well as an 'information' variable $\nu(t)$ that captures all the information relevant to the value of a firm's equity that has not, as yet, been incorporated into the firm's accounting records. As such, $\nu(t)$ captures information that will affect the future abnormal earnings and book values such as new patents, regulatory approval of new drugs for pharmaceutical companies, new long-lived contracts and order backlogs but that has not, as yet, been fully reflected in the firm's accounting records. It will be recalled from §5-10 that a firm's abnormal earnings are the difference between the earnings attributable to equity as reported on its profit and loss account and the cost of equity capital multiplied by the book value of the firm's equity as reported on its balance sheet. Specifying a firm's investment opportunity set as a vector system of differential equations stated in terms of its abnormal earnings, the book values appearing on its balance sheet and the information variable shows that there are two complementary aspects to the valuation of the firm's equity. The first of these is determined by discounting the stream of expected future operating cash flows (as in §5-2) under the assumption that the firm will apply its existing investment opportunity set indefinitely into the future. This is usually referred to as the 'recursion value' of equity. The second element of equity value arises out of the fact that the firm will normally have the option to change or modify its investment opportunity set in order that it can use its resources in alternative and potentially more profitable ways. There are a variety of ways in which the firm can exercise this option to change its investment opportunity set, including liquidations, sell-offs, spin-offs, divestitures, CEO changes, mergers, takeovers, bankruptcies, restructurings and new capital investments. The potential to make changes like these gives rise to what is known as the 'adaptation value' of equity.

We begin our analysis by recalling from §5-10 that the present value of the future cash flows a firm expects to make under its existing investment opportunity set – that is, the recursion value of the firm's equity – will be equal to the book value of its equity plus the expected present value of its stream of future abnormal earnings. This in turn will mean that if one states the firm's investment opportunity set in terms of a vector system of stochastic differential equations, it will normally be a relatively simple matter to determine the recursion value of its equity in terms of its current book value, its current abnormal earnings and the current value of the information variable. Moreover, our analysis also shows that the adaptation value of a firm's equity is functionally proportional to the recursion value of its equity. This has the important implication that once the recursion value of equity is known, it will normally be a relatively simple matter to determine the adaptation value of the firm's equity. Furthermore, since the market value of a firm's equity is the sum of its recursion value and its adaptation value, our analysis also shows that there will be a highly convex and non-linear relationship between the market value of the firm's equity on the one hand and the variables comprising its investment opportunity set on the other.

§9-2. We commence our analysis by defining r to be the cost of capital (per unit time) for the firm's equity, $b(t)$ to be the book value of its equity at time t, $x(t)$ to be the instantaneous earnings (per unit time) attributable to equity at time t and $a(t) = x(t) - rb(t)$ to be the instantaneous abnormal earnings (per unit time) attributable to equity at time t. It then follows from §5-10 that the present value of the future cash flows that the firm expects to make, or equivalently the present value of the dividends that the firm expects to pay over its lifetime, must be equal to the book value of equity plus the expected present value of the stream of future abnormal earnings:

$$\eta(t) = b(t) + E_t\left[\int_t^{\infty} e^{-r(s-t)} a(s)ds\right]$$

where $E_t[\cdot]$ is the expectation operator taken at time t, conditional on the firm applying its existing investment opportunity set indefinitely into the future. Now, suppose that the firm's investment opportunity set can be summarized in terms of the following vector system of stochastic differential equations:

$$\begin{pmatrix} \frac{da(t)}{dt} \\ \frac{dv(t)}{dt} \end{pmatrix} = \begin{pmatrix} c_{11} & c_{12} \\ c_{21} & c_{22} \end{pmatrix}\begin{pmatrix} a(t) \\ v(t) \end{pmatrix} + \eta^{\delta}(t)\begin{pmatrix} k_1 & 0 \\ 0 & k_2 \end{pmatrix}\begin{pmatrix} \frac{dz_1(t)}{dt} \\ \frac{dz_2(t)}{dt} \end{pmatrix}$$

or, in matrix notation,

$$\underset{\sim}{u}'(t) = Q\underset{\sim}{u}(t) + \eta^{\delta}(t)K\underset{\sim}{z}'(t)$$

Here

$$\underset{\sim}{u}(t) = \begin{pmatrix} a(t) \\ v(t) \end{pmatrix}$$

is the vector whose elements are the instantaneous abnormal earnings $a(t)$ attributable to equity and the information variable $v(t)$ that captures information that is relevant to the value of the firm's equity but that has not, as yet, been incorporated into the firm's accounting records. The elements of the vector

$$\underset{\sim}{u}'(t) = \begin{pmatrix} \frac{da(t)}{dt} \\ \frac{dv(t)}{dt} \end{pmatrix}$$

are the derivatives of the variables comprising the firm's investment opportunity set. The elements of the matrix

$$Q = \begin{pmatrix} c_{11} & c_{12} \\ c_{21} & c_{22} \end{pmatrix}$$

are the structural coefficients associated with the firm's investment opportunity set. The structural coefficients capture the sensitivity of increments in the variables comprising the firm's investment opportunity set to the existing levels of these variables. K is a matrix whose diagonal elements are a set of 'normalizing' constants

$$k_1 = \frac{(r - c_{11})(r - c_{22}) - c_{21}c_{12}}{(r - c_{22})} \quad \text{and} \quad k_2 = \frac{(r - c_{11})(r - c_{22}) - c_{21}c_{12}}{c_{12}}$$

and whose off-diagonal terms are all zero. These normalizing constants simplify the algebra associated with manipulating the firm's investment opportunity set but otherwise have no substantive role to play in the valuation of the firm's equity. The final term in the system of stochastic differential equations is the vector

$$\underset{\sim}{z}'(t) = \begin{pmatrix} \dfrac{dz_1(t)}{dt} \\ \dfrac{dz_2(t)}{dt} \end{pmatrix}$$

whose elements are the white noise terms associated with the variables comprising the firm's investment opportunity set. Thus, $dz_1(t)/dt$ is a white noise process with variance parameter σ_1^2. Likewise, $dz_2(t)/dt$ is a white noise process with variance parameter σ_2^2. We assume, without loss of generality (as in §8-9), that the two white noise processes are uncorrelated. Finally, $0 \leq \delta \leq \frac{1}{2}$ is a real number that ensures that the market value of the firm's equity remains finite as the recursion value approaches a limiting value of zero. This parameter δ also encapsulates the requirement that the variance associated with instantaneous changes in the variables comprising the firm's investment opportunity set becomes larger as the recursion value of equity grows in magnitude. This assumption reflects the commonly held belief that variations in an economic variable will become more pronounced as the economic variable grows in magnitude.

§9-3. There are several points about the firm's investment opportunity set that require detailed consideration. First amongst these is that simple algebraic manipulation shows how the firm's abnormal earnings evolve in terms of the following process:

$$\frac{da(t)}{dt} = -c_{11}\left[\frac{-c_{12}}{c_{11}}v(t) - a(t)\right] + k_1\eta^{\delta}(t)\frac{dz_1(t)}{dt}$$

This means that, apart from a stochastic component, the firm's abnormal earnings will gravitate towards a long-run mean of $(-c_{12}/c_{11})v(t)$. Moreover, the force with which the abnormal earnings will converge towards this long-run mean is proportional to the difference between the long-run mean and the current abnormal earnings, with the constant of proportionality, or speed-of-adjustment coefficient, being given by $-c_{11} > 0$. Larger values of the speed-of-adjustment coefficient imply that abnormal earnings will be more forcefully constrained to gravitate towards its long-run mean of $(-c_{12}/c_{11})\nu(t)$. Note also that the uncertainty with which the abnormal earnings variable gravitates towards its long-run mean hinges on the recursion value of equity $\eta(t)$ and reflects the commonly held belief that variations in an economic variable will become more pronounced as the economic variable grows in magnitude.

Similar considerations show that the differential equation for the information variable can be stated as

$$\frac{d\nu(t)}{dt} = -c_{22}\left[\frac{-c_{21}}{c_{22}}a(t) - \nu(t)\right] + k_2\eta^{\delta}(t)\frac{dz_2(t)}{dt}$$

This means that, apart from a stochastic component, the information variable $\nu(t)$ will gravitate towards a long-run mean of $(-c_{21}/c_{22})a(t)$. Again, the force with which it will do so is proportional to the difference between this long-run mean and the current value of the information variable, with the speed-of-adjustment coefficient being $-c_{22} > 0$. We have, however, previously noted (in §9-1) that $\nu(t)$ captures all value-relevant information that has not, as yet, found its way into the firm's accounting records. It thus follows that $\nu(t)$ is prospective in nature, and, because of this, it is unlikely that the abnormal earnings variable $a(t)$, which is generally retrospective in nature, can adequately reflect or capture movements in the information variable's long-run mean value. Given this, one would expect c_{22} to be much larger than c_{21} in absolute terms, and it follows from this that c_{21}/c_{22} will have to be close to zero.

§9-4. We can now use integration by parts to show that the present value of the stream of future abnormal earnings will be

$$\int_t^{\infty} e^{-r(s-t)}a(s)ds = \left[\frac{-e^{-r(s-t)}}{r}a(s)\right]_t^{\infty} + \frac{1}{r}\int_t^{\infty} e^{-r(s-t)}\frac{da(s)}{ds}ds$$

Evaluating the first term on the right-hand side of this expression shows

$$\left[\frac{-e^{-r(s-t)}}{r}a(s)\right]_t^{\infty} = \frac{a(t)}{r} - \lim_{s\to\infty}\frac{e^{-r(s-t)}a(s)}{r}$$

Hence, if we are to progress beyond this point then we must ensure that in expectations the present value of the future abnormal earnings remains finite as the time period over which the present value is computed becomes infinitely large. This is known as a 'transversality requirement' (as in §5-2 and §5-10 of Chapter 5) and encapsulates the requirement that the market value of the firm's equity will always remain finite. In the present context, the transversality requirement takes the form

$$\lim_{s\to\infty} e^{-r(s-t)}E_t[a(s)] = 0$$

where $E_t[\cdot]$ is the expectation operator, taken at time t. We can then take expectations across the integral defining the present value of the future abnormal earnings stream and thereby show

$$E_t\left[\int_t^{\infty} e^{-r(s-t)}a(s)ds\right] = \frac{a(t)}{r} + \frac{1}{r}E_t\left[\int_t^{\infty} e^{-r(s-t)}\frac{da(s)}{ds}ds\right]$$

Now, we recall from the system of stochastic differential equations describing the firm's investment opportunity set (as in §9-3) that the abnormal earnings variable will evolve in terms of the following differential equation:

$$\frac{da(s)}{ds} = [c_{11}a(s) + c_{12}\nu(s)] + k_1\eta^{\delta}(s)\frac{dz_1(s)}{ds}$$

Thus, we can substitute this result into the expression for the present value of the firm's abnormal earnings stream, in which case it follows that

$$E_t\left[\int_t^{\infty} e^{-r(s-t)}a(s)ds\right] = \frac{a(t)}{r} + E_t\left[\frac{1}{r}\int_t^{\infty} e^{-r(s-t)}\left(c_{11}a(s) + c_{12}\nu(s) + k_1\eta^{\delta}(s)\frac{dz_1(s)}{ds}\right)ds\right]$$

However, since $E_t[dz_1(s)/ds] = 0$ for all $s > t$, it necessarily follows that the above result can be restated as

$$E_t\left[\int_t^{\infty} e^{-r(s-t)}a(s)ds\right] = \frac{a(t)}{r} + \frac{c_{11}}{r}E_t\left[\int_t^{\infty} e^{-r(s-t)}a(s)ds\right] + \frac{c_{12}}{r}E_t\left[\int_t e^{-r(s-t)}\nu(s)\right]$$

We can then collect terms in the above expression and thereby show

$$\left(1 - \frac{c_{11}}{r}\right)E_t\left[\int_t^{\infty} e^{-r(s-t)}a(s)ds\right] = \frac{a(t)}{r} + \frac{c_{12}}{r}E_t\left[\int_t^{\infty} e^{-r(s-t)}\nu(s)ds\right]$$

or equivalently

$$E_t\left[\int_t^{\infty} e^{-r(s-t)}a(s)ds\right] = \frac{a(t)}{r - c_{11}} + \frac{c_{12}}{r - c_{11}}E_t\left[\int_t^{\infty} e^{-r(s-t)}\nu(s)ds\right]$$

Hence, if we are to make progress towards determining the expected present value of the firm's future abnormal earnings stream then we must evaluate the integral

$$\int_t^{\infty} e^{-r(s-t)}\nu(s)ds = \left[\frac{-e^{-r(s-t)}}{r}\nu(s)\right]_t^{\infty} + \frac{1}{r}\int_t^{\infty} e^{-r(s-t)}\frac{d\nu(s)}{ds}ds$$

We can again apply the transversality requirement

$$\lim_{s\to\infty} e^{-r(s-t)}E_0[\nu(s)] = 0$$

in which case it follows that

$$E_t\left[\int_t^{\infty} e^{-r(s-t)}\nu(s)ds\right] = \frac{\nu(t)}{r} + E_t\left[\frac{1}{r}\int_t^{\infty} e^{-r(s-t)}\frac{d\nu(s)}{ds}ds\right]$$

Now it will be recalled from the system of stochastic differential equations representing the firm's investment opportunity set (as in §9-3) that the information variable will evolve in terms of the following differential equation:

$$\frac{d\nu(s)}{ds} = [c_{21}a(s) + c_{22}\nu(s)] + k_2\eta^{\delta}(s)\frac{dz_2(s)}{ds}$$

We can substitute this result into the above expression and use the fact that $E_t[dz_2(s)/ds] = 0$ for all $s > t$, in which case it follows that

$$E_t\left[\int_t^{\infty} e^{-r(s-t)}\nu(s)ds\right] = \frac{\nu(t)}{r} + \frac{c_{21}}{r}E_t\left[\int_t^{\infty} e^{-r(s-t)}a(s)ds\right] + \frac{c_{22}}{r}E_t\left[\int_t e^{-r(s-t)}\nu(s)\right]$$

Collecting terms in the above equation shows

$$\left(1 - \frac{c_{22}}{r}\right)E_t\left[\int_t^{\infty} e^{-r(s-t)}\nu(s)ds\right] = \frac{\nu(t)}{r} + \frac{c_{21}}{r}E_t\left[\int_t^{\infty} e^{-r(s-t)}a(s)ds\right]$$

or equivalently

$$E_t\left[\int_t^{\infty} e^{-r(s-t)}\nu(s)ds\right] = \frac{\nu(t)}{r - c_{22}} + \frac{c_{21}}{r - c_{22}}E_t\left[\int_t^{\infty} e^{-r(s-t)}a(s)ds\right]$$

Now, we have previously shown in this section that the present value of the expected stream of abnormal earnings will be

$$E_t\left[\int_t^{\infty} e^{-r(s-t)}a(s)ds\right] = \frac{a(t)}{r - c_{11}} + \frac{c_{12}}{r - c_{11}}E_t\left[\int_t^{\infty} e^{-r(s-t)}\nu(s)ds\right]$$

Thus, we can use these latter two results to show that the present value of the stream of expected future abnormal earnings will be

$$E_t\left[\int_t^{\infty} e^{-r(s-t)}a(s)ds\right] = \frac{a(t)}{r - c_{11}} + \frac{c_{12}\nu(t)}{(r - c_{11})(r - c_{22})} + \frac{c_{12}c_{21}}{(r - c_{11})(r - c_{22})}E_t\left[\int_t^{\infty} e^{-r(s-t)}a(s)ds\right]$$

or equivalently

$$E_t\left[\int_t^{\infty} e^{-r(s-t)}a(s)ds\right] = \frac{(r - c_{22})a(t)}{(r - c_{11})(r - c_{22}) - c_{12}c_{21}} + \frac{c_{12}\nu(t)}{(r - c_{11})(r - c_{22}) - c_{12}c_{21}}$$

Note how this result shows that the present value of the stream of expected future abnormal earnings can be stated in terms of the firm's current abnormal earnings $a(t)$ and the current value of the information variable, $\nu(t)$.

§9-5. It will be recalled from §9-2 above that the recursion value of equity is determined by discounting the stream of future cash flows that the firm expects to earn, or equivalently the present value of the dividends that it expects to pay over the life of the firm. In §5-10 of Chapter 5, we showed that this in turn must be equal to the current book value of the firm's equity $b(t)$ plus the present value of the future expected abnormal earnings stream, or

$$\eta(t) = b(t) + E_t\left[\int_t^\infty e^{-r(s-t)}a(s)ds\right]$$

Here, however, we can use the expression for the stream of expected future abnormal earnings obtained above in §9-4 to restate the recursion value of the firm's equity in terms of the current book value of its equity, its current abnormal earnings and the current value of the information variable, or

$$\eta(t) = b(t) + \frac{(r-c_{22})a(t)}{(r-c_{11})(r-c_{22})-c_{12}c_{21}} + \frac{c_{12}\nu(t)}{(r-c_{11})(r-c_{22})-c_{12}c_{21}}$$

Moreover, we can determine the time series properties of the recursion value of equity by differentiating through the above expression. Doing so shows

$$\frac{d\eta(t)}{dt} = \frac{db(t)}{dt} + \frac{(r-c_{22})\dfrac{da(t)}{dt}}{(r-c_{11})(r-c_{22})-c_{12}c_{21}} + \frac{c_{12}\dfrac{d\nu(t)}{dt}}{(r-c_{11})(r-c_{22})-c_{12}c_{21}}$$

Now, suppose that the firm records all its revenues and all its expenses in its profit and loss account; that is, there are no revenues and expenses that do not appear on the firm's profit and loss account. This is called the 'clean surplus' requirement (as in §5-10 of Chapter 5) and it means that changes in the book value of equity are composed exclusively of the profits and losses recorded on the firm's profit and loss account. Thus, if $x(t)$ is the profit (on a per unit time basis) attributable to the firm's equity over the instantaneous period from time t until time $t+dt$ and the firm does not pay any dividends over this period then the increment in the book value of equity will be $db(t)=x(t)dt$. However, we know from §5-10 that the abnormal earnings attributable to equity over the instantaneous period from time t until time $t+dt$ will be $a(t)=x(t)-rb(t)$, where, as previously, r is the cost of the firm's equity capital. This in turn will mean that the increment in the book value of equity over this period can be restated as $db(t)=x(t)dt=[a(t)+rb(t)]dt$, or

$$\frac{db(t)}{dt} = a(t) + rb(t)$$

given that the increment in the book value of equity is stated on a per unit time basis. Now we can take the expression given here for $db(t)/dt$ in conjunction with the expressions summarized in §9-3 for $da(t)/dt$ and $d\nu(t)/dt$ and substitute them into the expression for

$d\eta(t)/dt$ given above. This will show that the increment in the recursion value of the firm's equity over the instantaneous period from time t until time $t+dt$ will be

$$\frac{d\eta(t)}{dt} = a(t) + rb(t) + \frac{(r-c_{22})\left[c_{11}a(t) + c_{12}\nu(t) + k_1\eta^{\delta}(t)\frac{dz_1(t)}{dt}\right]}{(r-c_{11})(r-c_{22}) - c_{12}c_{21}} + \frac{c_{12}\left[c_{21}a(t) + c_{22}\nu(t) + k_2\eta^{\delta}(t)\frac{dz_2(t)}{dt}\right]}{(r-c_{11})(r-c_{22}) - c_{12}c_{21}}$$

But it will be recalled from §9-2 above that the firm's investment opportunity set incorporates two normalizing constants, namely,

$$k_1 = \frac{(r-c_{11})(r-c_{22}) - c_{21}c_{12}}{(r-c_{22})} \quad \text{and} \quad k_2 = \frac{(r-c_{11})(r-c_{22}) - c_{21}c_{12}}{c_{12}}$$

This in turn will mean that the elements associated with the white noise terms in the above expression for $d\eta(t)/dt$ simplify to

$$\frac{(r-c_{22})k_1\eta^{\delta}(t)\frac{dz_1(t)}{dt}}{(r-c_{11})(r-c_{22}) - c_{12}c_{21}} = \eta^{\delta}(t)\frac{dz_1(t)}{dt}$$

and

$$\frac{c_{12}k_2\eta^{\delta}(t)\frac{dz_2(t)}{dt}}{(r-c_{11})(r-c_{22}) - c_{12}c_{21}} = \eta^{\delta}(t)\frac{dz_2(t)}{dt}$$

respectively. Moreover, if we use the fact that

$$a(t) = \frac{(r-c_{11})(r-c_{22}) - c_{12}c_{21}}{(r-c_{11})(r-c_{22}) - c_{12}c_{21}}a(t)$$

then the increment in the recursion value of equity can be restated as

$$\begin{aligned}\frac{d\eta(t)}{dt} &= rb(t) + \frac{(r-c_{11})(r-c_{22}) - c_{12}c_{21}}{(r-c_{11})(r-c_{22}) - c_{12}c_{21}}a(t) \\ &\quad + \frac{(r-c_{22})[c_{11}a(t) + c_{12}\nu(t)]}{(r-c_{11})(r-c_{22}) - c_{12}c_{21}} + \frac{c_{12}[c_{21}a(t) + c_{22}\nu(t)]}{(r-c_{11})(r-c_{22}) - c_{12}c_{21}} \\ &\quad + \eta^{\delta}(t)\left[\frac{dz_1(t)}{dt} + \frac{dz_2(t)}{dt}\right]\end{aligned}$$

If we now collect terms in the above expression for $d\eta(t)/dt$ involving the abnormal earnings variable $a(t)$ then we find

$$\frac{[(r-c_{22})(r-c_{11}+c_{11}) - c_{12}c_{21} + c_{12}c_{21}]a(t)}{(r-c_{11})(r-c_{22}) - c_{12}c_{21}} = \frac{r(r-c_{22})a(t)}{(r-c_{11})(r-c_{22}) - c_{12}c_{21}}$$

Similarly, if we collect terms in the expression for $d\eta(t)/dt$ involving the information variable $\nu(t)$ then we find

$$\frac{[(r-c_{22})c_{12}+c_{12}c_{22}]\nu(t)}{(r-c_{11})(r-c_{22})-c_{12}c_{21}} = \frac{rc_{12}\nu(t)}{(r-c_{11})(r-c_{22})-c_{12}c_{21}}$$

Bringing these results together shows that the increment in the recursion value of equity can be restated as:

$$\frac{d\eta(t)}{dt} = r\left[b(t) + \frac{(r-c_{22})a(t)}{(r-c_{11})(r-c_{22})-c_{12}c_{21}} + \frac{c_{12}\nu(t)}{(r-c_{11})(r-c_{22})-c_{12}c_{21}}\right] + \eta^{\delta}(t)\left[\frac{dz_1(t)}{dt} + \frac{dz_2(t)}{dt}\right]$$

Hence, if we define

$$\frac{dq(t)}{dt} = \frac{dz_1(t)}{dt} + \frac{dz_2(t)}{dt}$$

as a white noise process with variance parameter $\zeta^2 = \sigma_1^2 + \sigma_2^2$ and use the fact that our calculations at the beginning of this section show that the recursion value is given by

$$\eta(t) = b(t) + \frac{(r-c_{22})a(t)}{(r-c_{11})(r-c_{22})-c_{12}c_{21}} + \frac{c_{12}\nu(t)}{(r-c_{11})(r-c_{22})-c_{12}c_{21}}$$

then it follows that the increment in the recursion value of the firm's equity over the instantaneous period from time t until time $t+dt$ will be

$$\frac{d\eta(t)}{dt} = r\eta(t) + \eta^{\delta}(t)\frac{dq(t)}{dt}$$

This result shows that the recursion value of equity will grow at a rate in line with its cost of capital r, but there will also be stochastic perturbations arising from the white noise term $dq(t)/dt$. Moreover, the magnitude of these stochastic perturbations will grow in proportion to η^{δ}, reflecting the commonly held belief that variations in an economic variable will become more pronounced as the economic variable grows in magnitude.

§9-6. The evolution of the recursion value of equity will hinge on the parameter $0 \leq \delta \leq \frac{1}{2}$ (as in §9-2 above). There are two interpretations of this parameter that are commonly employed in the literature. The simplest (and most commonly applied) of these sets $\delta = 0$, in which case the recursion value evolves in terms of the following Ornstein–Uhlenbeck process:

$$\frac{d\eta(t)}{dt} = r\eta(t) + \frac{dq(t)}{dt}$$

Now, we can identify the distributional properties of the recursion value under the above specification by following the procedures in §7-10 of Chapter 7 in order to obtain the solution of the above differential equation. Hence, multiplying both sides of the differential equation by e^{-rt} shows that it can be restated as

$$\frac{d}{dt}[e^{-rt}\eta(t)] = e^{-rt}\frac{d\eta(t)}{dt} - re^{-rt}\eta(t) = e^{-rt}\frac{dq(t)}{dt}$$

We can then integrate across both sides of this expression and thereby show

$$e^{-rt}\eta(t) = c + \int_0^t e^{-rs}\frac{dq(s)}{ds}ds = c + \int_0^t e^{-rs}dq(s)$$

where c is a constant of integration. However, setting $t = 0$ in this expression shows $c = \eta(0)$, in which case it follows that the general solution to this particular interpretation of the Ornstein–Uhlenbeck process will be

$$\eta(t) = \eta(0)e^{rt} + \int_0^t e^{r(t-s)}dq(s)$$

We can then take expectations through the above expression and thereby show that the recursion value of equity at time t will be normally distributed and have a mean of

$$E_0[\eta(t)] = \eta(0)e^{rt}$$

Note how this result implies that in expectations the recursion value of equity will grow in line with its cost of capital r. Moreover, we can use Wiener's Theorem (as in §7-5) to determine the variance associated with the recursion value of equity at time t, namely,

$$\mathrm{Var}_0[\eta(t)] = \mathrm{Var}_0\left[\int_0^t e^{r(t-s)}dq(s)\right] = \zeta^2\int_0^t e^{2r(t-s)}ds = \frac{\zeta^2}{2r}(e^{2rt} - 1)$$

where it will be recalled from §9-5 that $dq(t)/dt$ is a white noise process with variance parameter ζ^2. Given the simplicity of this interpretation of the Ornstein–Uhlenbeck process, it is somewhat unfortunate that it has significant limitations. Probably the most obvious of these is that the variance associated with instantaneous increments in recursion value – that is, $\mathrm{Var}_t[d\eta(t)] = \zeta^2 dt$ – is an inter-temporal constant that is independent of the current level of the recursion value $\eta(t)$ itself. Thus, although the discrete-time equivalent of the Ornstein–Uhlenbeck process developed here is widely applied by empirical researchers (as in §7-11), it runs counter to the commonly held belief that the variance associated with increments in an economic variable must become larger as the variable grows in magnitude (as in §9-2 and §9-3 above).

Given this, a second and more plausible interpretation of the differential equation describing the evolution of recursion value sets $\delta = \frac{1}{2}$, in which case the recursion value evolves in terms of the following process:

$$\frac{d\eta(t)}{dt} = r\eta(t) + \sqrt{\eta(t)}\frac{dq(t)}{dt}$$

This is the differential equation of a continuous-time 'branching process'. Branching processes arise in population dynamics and a number of other areas. Note that the branching process given here maintains our previous requirement that the recursion value of equity grows through time in line with its cost of capital r. However, the variance associated with increments in recursion value is now $\text{Var}_t[d\eta(t)] = \zeta^2\eta(t)dt$. This reflects the requirement that the variance associated with increments in the recursion value of equity ought to become larger as the recursion value grows in magnitude. The downside is that there is no closed-form solution for the stochastic differential equation on which the branching process is based. Fortunately, the moment-generating function of the conditional probability density function for the branching process is well known, namely,

$$E_0[e^{\varphi\eta(t)}] = \exp\left[\frac{2r\eta(0)e^{rt}\varphi}{2r - \zeta^2(e^{rt} - 1)\varphi}\right]$$

where $E_0[\cdot]$ is the expectation operator and φ is an arbitrary parameter. Hence, if we differentiate through this expression with respect to φ, we obtain

$$\frac{dE_0[e^{\varphi\eta(t)}]}{d\varphi} = \frac{2r\eta(0)e^{rt}[2r - \zeta^2(e^{rt} - 1)\varphi] + \zeta^2(e^{rt} - 1)2r\eta(0)e^{rt}\varphi}{[2r - \zeta^2(e^{rt} - 1)\varphi]^2}\exp\left[\frac{2r\eta(0)e^{rt}\varphi}{2r - \zeta^2(e^{rt} - 1)\varphi}\right]$$

or equivalently

$$\frac{dE_0[e^{\varphi\eta(t)}]}{d\varphi} = \frac{4r^2\eta(0)e^{rt}}{[2r - \zeta^2(e^{rt} - 1)\varphi]^2}\exp\left[\frac{2r\eta(0)e^{rt}\varphi}{2r - \zeta^2(e^{rt} - 1)\varphi}\right]$$

Setting $\varphi = 0$ in the above expression then shows

$$\left.\frac{dE_0(e^{\varphi\eta(t)})}{d\varphi}\right|_{\varphi=0} = \frac{4r^2\eta(0)e^{rt}}{4r^2} = \eta(0)e^{rt}$$

Thus, if the recursion value of equity evolves in terms of a continuous-time branching process then in expectations it will grow in line with the cost of equity capital:

$$E_0[\eta(t)] = \eta(0)e^{rt}$$

We can also determine the second derivative for the moment-generating function and then again set $\varphi = 0$, in which case it follows that the variance associated with the recursion value of equity at time t will be

$$\text{Var}_0[\eta(t)] = \frac{\zeta^2}{r}\eta(0)e^{rt}(e^{rt} - 1)$$

Higher moments may be determined by applying similar procedures to the higher derivatives of the moment-generating function given above (as in Exercise 4 at the end of this chapter). Moreover, since the branching process provides a more realistic basis for modelling the evolution of recursion value, it is this process that will be the focus of our attention in subsequent sections of this chapter.

§9-7. Our analysis to date assumes that the firm is constrained to apply its existing investment opportunity set indefinitely into the future. We have previously noted, however, that firms will normally have the option of changing or modifying their investment opportunity sets in order to use the resources available to them in alternative and potentially more profitable ways. There are a variety of ways in which firms can exercise the option to change their investment opportunity sets, including liquidations, sell-offs, spin-offs, divestitures, CEO changes, mergers, takeovers, bankruptcies, restructurings and new capital investments. We have also previously noted (as in §9-1 above) that the potential to make changes like these gives rise to a second element of equity value, which is known as the adaptation value of equity. We now demonstrate the procedures that are used to determine the adaptation value of a firm's equity. We begin by defining $P(\eta(t))$ to be the market value of the firm's equity at time t in terms of its recursion value $\eta(t)$. It will be recalled from §9-5 above that the recursion value of the firm's equity at time t is given by

$$\eta(t) = b(t) + \frac{(r - c_{22})a(t)}{(r - c_{11})(r - c_{22}) - c_{12}c_{21}} + \frac{c_{12}\nu(t)}{(r - c_{11})(r - c_{22}) - c_{12}c_{21}}$$

where $b(t)$ is the book value of the firm's equity, $a(t)$ is the abnormal earnings associated with the firm's equity and $\nu(t)$ is an information variable that captures all the information that is relevant to the value of the firm's equity but that has not, as yet, been incorporated into the firm's accounting records. Moreover, r is the cost of equity capital and c_{11}, c_{12}, c_{21} and c_{22} are the structural coefficients associated with the firm's investment opportunity set.

Now, over the period from time t until time $t + dt$, the market value of the firm's equity will satisfy the following 'no-arbitrage' condition:

$$P(\eta(t)) = e^{-rdt}E_t[P(\eta(t + dt))]$$

where, as in previous sections, $E_t[\cdot]$ is the expectation operator taken at time t. This requirement says nothing more than an investment in the firm's equity will earn (in expectations) a rate of return equal to the cost of the firm's equity r. Now we can expand $P(\eta(t + dt))$ as a Taylor series about the point $\eta(t)$, in which case we have

$$P(\eta(t + dt)) = P(\eta(t)) + d\eta(t)\frac{dP}{d\eta} + \frac{1}{2}[d\eta(t)]^2\frac{d^2P}{d\eta^2} + \ldots$$

where $d\eta(t) = \eta(t + dt) - \eta(t)$ is the increment in the recursion value of equity over the period from time t until time $t + dt$. Taking expectations through the above Taylor series expansion shows

$$E_t[P(\eta(t + dt))] = P(\eta(t)) + E_t[d\eta(t)]\frac{dP}{d\eta} + \frac{1}{2}E_t[(d\eta(t))^2]\frac{d^2P}{d\eta^2} + \ldots$$

Furthermore, standard results tell us that the variance of the increment in the recursion value of equity over the period from time t until time $t + dt$ will be

$$\text{Var}_t[d\eta(t)] = E_t[\{d\eta(t)\}^2] - \{E_t[d\eta(t)]\}^2$$

where $\text{Var}_t[\cdot]$ is the variance operator, again taken at time t. However, our analysis in §9-5 shows that the recursion value of equity will grow in expectations at a rate in line with the firm's cost of capital r; that is, $E_t[d\eta(t)] = r\eta(t)dt$. Moreover, we have shown in §9-6 that the variance associated with increments in recursion value amounts to $\text{Var}_t[d\eta(t)] = \zeta^2\eta(t)dt$. Substituting these results into the expression for the variance of the increment in the recursion value of equity as given above, we have

$$\zeta^2\eta(t)dt = E_t[\{d\eta(t)\}^2] - [r\eta(t)dt]^2$$

or

$$E_t[\{d\eta(t)\}^2] = \zeta^2\eta(t)dt + [r\eta(t)dt]^2$$

Bringing these results together allows us to simplify the expression for the expected value of the firm's equity at time $t + dt$, namely,

$$E_t[P(\eta(t+dt))] = P(\eta(t)) + r\eta(t)\frac{dP}{d\eta}dt + \frac{1}{2}\zeta^2\eta(t)\frac{d^2P}{d\eta^2}dt + \frac{1}{2}[r\eta(t)]^2\frac{d^2P}{d\eta^2}(dt)^2 + \ldots$$

We can then substitute this latter result into the no-arbitrage condition,

$$P(\eta(t)) = e^{-rdt}E_t[P(\eta(t+dt))]$$

in which case it follows that

$$P(\eta(t)) = e^{-rdt}\left\{P(\eta(t)) + r\eta(t)\frac{dP}{d\eta}dt + \frac{1}{2}\zeta^2\eta(t)\frac{d^2P}{d\eta^2}dt + \frac{1}{2}[r\eta(t)]^2\frac{d^2P}{d\eta^2}(dt)^2 + \ldots\right\}$$

Now, here we can use a Taylor series expansion for the exponential term involving the cost of equity in the above expression, namely,

$$e^{-rdt} = 1 - rdt + \frac{1}{2}(rdt)^2 + \ldots$$

This in turn will mean that the no-arbitrage condition can be restated as

$$P(\eta) = \left[1 - rdt + \frac{1}{2}(rdt)^2 + \ldots\right]\left[P(\eta) + r\eta\frac{dP}{d\eta}dt + \frac{1}{2}\zeta^2\eta\frac{d^2P}{d\eta^2}dt + \frac{1}{2}(r\eta)^2\frac{d^2P}{d\eta^2}(dt)^2 + \ldots\right]$$

Cancelling terms where appropriate and then collecting terms involving dt and $(dt)^2$ then gives

$$0 = \left[\frac{1}{2}\zeta^2\eta\frac{d^2P}{d\eta^2} + r\eta\frac{dP}{d\eta} - rP(\eta)\right]dt$$
$$+ \left[\frac{1}{2}(r\eta)^2\frac{d^2P}{d\eta^2} - r^2\eta\frac{dP}{d\eta} - \frac{1}{2}r\zeta^2\eta\frac{d^2P}{d\eta^2} + \frac{1}{2}r^2P(\eta)\right](dt)^2 + \ldots$$

Finally, we can divide both sides of this equation by dt and then take limits in such a way as to let $dt \to 0$. The no-arbitrage condition then implies that the market value of the firm's equity will have to satisfy the following version of what is known as the Hamilton–Jacobi–Bellman equation:

$$\frac{1}{2}\zeta^2\eta\frac{d^2P}{d\eta^2}+r\eta\frac{dP}{d\eta}-rP(\eta)=0$$

This is a second-order linear differential equation with non-constant coefficients. Such equations can be very difficult to solve. Fortunately, the solutions to this version of the Hamilton–Jacobi–Bellman equation are well known.

§9-8. Now, there are two boundary conditions that the Hamilton–Jacobi–Bellman equation given above will have to satisfy. The first requires that when the recursion value of equity falls away to nothing, the firm will exchange its current investment opportunity set for a suite of assets and/or capital projects that have an adaptation (i.e. market) value of $P(0)$. This means that the Hamilton–Jacobi–Bellman equation satisfies the boundary condition

$$\lim_{\eta\to 0} P(\eta)=P(0)$$

The most obvious (but not the only) interpretation of this boundary condition is that $P(0)$ will be the liquidation value of the firm's assets (net of any liabilities that have to be paid). Moreover, the firm will be less and less inclined to exercise the option it possesses to change its existing investment opportunity set as the recursion value of its equity grows in magnitude. This in turn means that the option value associated with changing the firm's investment opportunity set will gradually decay away as the recursion value of its equity grows in magnitude. The Hamilton–Jacobi–Bellman equation will then satisfy the following boundary condition:

$$\lim_{\eta\to\infty} P(\eta)=\eta$$

or that, in the limit, the market value of the firm's equity is comprised exclusively of its recursion value. Now, the unique solution of the Hamilton–Jacobi–Bellman equation under the two boundary conditions given here turns out to be

$$P(\eta)=\eta+\frac{P(0)}{2}\int_{-1}^{1}\exp\left(-\frac{2\theta\eta}{1+z}\right)dz$$

where (as we shall see in §9-10 below) $\theta=2r/\zeta^2$ is a measure of the relative stability with which the recursion value of equity grows over time. We would also emphasize that whilst the differing circumstances that affect firms might lead to slightly different boundary conditions to those on which the above solution is based, all solutions to the Hamilton–Jacobi–Bellman equation must be stated as a linear combination of the two terms appearing on the right-hand side of the above expression for $P(\eta)$.

We can demonstrate that the expression for $P(\eta)$ given above is the unique solution of the Hamilton–Jacobi–Bellman boundary-value problem given here by considering the first term on the right-hand side of the above expression, namely, $P_1(\eta) = \eta$. Note that

$$\frac{dP_1(\eta)}{d\eta} = 1 \text{ and } \frac{d^2P_1(\eta)}{d\eta^2} = 0$$

and so substitution shows

$$\frac{1}{2}\zeta^2\eta\frac{d^2P_1(\eta)}{d\eta^2} + r\eta\frac{dP_1(\eta)}{d\eta} - rP_1(\eta) = r\eta - r\eta = 0$$

This confirms that $P_1(\eta) = \eta$ is a solution of the Hamilton–Jacobi–Bellman equation. We can apply similar procedures to the second term on the right-hand side of the above solution, namely,

$$P_2(\eta) = \frac{1}{2}\int_{-1}^{1} \exp\left(-\frac{2\theta\eta}{1+z}\right)dz$$

Thus, differentiation shows

$$\frac{dP_2(\eta)}{d\eta} = -\theta\int_{-1}^{1} \exp\left(-\frac{2\theta\eta}{1+z}\right)\frac{1+z}{(1+z)^2}dz = \frac{-e^{-\theta\eta}}{2\eta} - \frac{2r}{\zeta^2}\int_{-1}^{1} \exp\left(-\frac{2\theta\eta}{1+z}\right)\frac{zdz}{(1+z)^2}$$

and

$$\frac{d^2P_2(\eta)}{d\eta^2} = 2\theta^2\int_{-1}^{1} \exp\left(-\frac{2\theta\eta}{1+z}\right)\frac{dz}{(1+z)^2} = \frac{8r^2}{\zeta^4}\int_{-1}^{1} \exp\left(-\frac{2\theta\eta}{1+z}\right)\frac{dz}{(1+z)^2} = \frac{2re^{-\theta\eta}}{\zeta^2\eta}$$
$$= \frac{\theta e^{-\theta\eta}}{\eta}$$

Furthermore, we can apply integration by parts and thereby show

$$P_2(\eta) = \frac{1}{2}\int_{-1}^{1} \exp\left(-\frac{2\theta\eta}{1+z}\right)dz = \frac{e^{-\theta\eta}}{2} - \frac{2r\eta}{\zeta^2}\int_{-1}^{1} \exp\left(-\frac{2\theta\eta}{1+z}\right)\frac{zdz}{(1+z)^2}$$

Substituting these results into the Hamilton–Jacobi–Bellman equation then shows

$$\frac{1}{2}\zeta^2\eta\frac{d^2P}{d\eta^2} + r\eta\frac{dP}{d\eta} - rP(\eta)$$
$$= re^{-\theta\eta} - \frac{re^{-\theta\eta}}{2} - \frac{2r^2\eta}{\zeta^2}\int_{-1}^{1} \exp\left(-\frac{2\theta\eta}{1+z}\right)\frac{zdz}{(1+z)^2} - \frac{re^{-\theta\eta}}{2}$$
$$+ \frac{2r^2\eta}{\zeta^2}\int_{-1}^{1} \exp\left(-\frac{2\theta\eta}{1+z}\right)\frac{zdz}{(1+z)^2} = 0$$

This in turn shows that

$$P_2(\eta) = \frac{1}{2}\int_{-1}^{1} \exp\left(-\frac{2\theta\eta}{1+z}\right) dz$$

is a second linearly independent solution of the Hamilton–Jacobi–Bellman equation.

Our analysis to date shows that the market value of the firm's equity is composed of two elements. First, there is the recursion value of equity η, which is the present value of the stream of expected future cash flows attributable to equity given that the firm is indefinitely constrained to operate within its existing investment opportunity set. In addition to this, however, there is the adaptation value of equity, as given by the integral expression in the above solution to the Hamilton–Jacobi–Bellman equation. Note that the adaptation value of equity asymptotically approaches zero as the recursion value grows in magnitude:

$$\lim_{\eta \to \infty} P(\eta) = \eta$$

as required by the second boundary condition specified above. In other words, if the firm is highly profitable under its existing investment opportunity set, it is unlikely that it will exercise the option it possesses to change its investment opportunity set in the foreseeable future. This, in turn, will mean that the adaptation value of equity will be relatively small when compared with the recursion value of equity.

§9-9. A potential difficulty associated with implementing the equity valuation formula developed in §9-7 and §9-8, however, is that the integral

$$P_2(\eta) = \frac{1}{2}\int_{-1}^{1} \exp\left(-\frac{2\theta\eta}{1+z}\right) dz$$

cannot be evaluated in closed form. Fortunately, this integral can be evaluated using numerical procedures similar to those that have been used to tabulate values for the area under the standard normal distribution of mathematical statistics. Thus, if we let $y = \theta\eta$ then we can tabulate the values of the integral

$$P_2(y) = \frac{1}{2}\int_{-1}^{1} \exp\left(-\frac{2y}{1+z}\right) dz$$

as summarized in Table 9.1. We can illustrate the application of this table by supposing that the risk (stability) parameter is $\theta = 2$ and that the recursion value of equity amounts to $\eta = 0.28$. It then follows that $y = \theta\eta = 2 \times 0.28 = 0.56$. We can then read from the table that

$$P_2(y) = \frac{1}{2}\int_{-1}^{1} \exp\left(-\frac{2y}{1+z}\right) dz = \frac{1}{2}\int_{-1}^{1} \exp\left(-\frac{2 \times 0.56}{1+z}\right) dz = 0.2951$$

Table 9.1 Values of the integral $\frac{1}{2}\int_{-1}^{1}\exp\left(-\frac{2y}{1+z}\right)dz$, where $y=\theta\eta$

$y=\theta\eta$	*0.00*	*0.01*	*0.02*	*0.03*	*0.04*	*0.05*	*0.06*	*0.07*	*0.08*	*0.09*
0.00	1.0000	0.9492	0.9128	0.8817	0.8537	0.8280	0.8041	0.7819	0.7610	0.7412
0.10	0.7225	0.7047	0.6877	0.6715	0.6560	0.6410	0.6267	0.6128	0.5995	0.5866
0.20	0.5742	0.5622	0.5505	0.5393	0.5283	0.5177	0.5074	0.4975	0.4877	0.4783
0.30	0.4691	0.4602	0.4515	0.4430	0.4348	0.4267	0.4189	0.4112	0.4038	0.3965
0.40	0.3894	0.3824	0.3756	0.3690	0.3626	0.3562	0.3500	0.3440	0.3381	0.3323
0.50	0.3266	0.3211	0.3157	0.3104	0.3052	0.3001	0.2951	0.2902	0.2855	0.2808
0.60	0.2762	0.2717	0.2673	0.2630	0.2587	0.2546	0.2505	0.2465	0.2426	0.2387
0.70	0.2349	0.2312	0.2276	0.2240	0.2205	0.2171	0.2137	0.2104	0.2072	0.2040
0.80	0.2009	0.1978	0.1948	0.1918	0.1889	0.1860	0.1832	0.1804	0.1777	0.1750
0.90	0.1724	0.1698	0.1673	0.1648	0.1623	0.1599	0.1576	0.1552	0.1530	0.1507
1.00	0.1485	0.1463	0.1442	0.1421	0.1400	0.1380	0.1360	0.1340	0.1321	0.1302
1.10	0.1283	0.1264	0.1246	0.1228	0.1211	0.1193	0.1176	0.1160	0.1143	0.1127
1.20	0.1111	0.1095	0.1080	0.1065	0.1050	0.1035	0.1020	0.1006	0.0992	0.0978
1.30	0.0964	0.0951	0.0938	0.0925	0.0912	0.0899	0.0887	0.0875	0.0862	0.0851
1.40	0.0839	0.0827	0.0816	0.0805	0.0794	0.0783	0.0772	0.0762	0.0751	0.0741
1.50	0.0731	0.0721	0.0711	0.0702	0.0692	0.0683	0.0674	0.0665	0.0656	0.0647
1.60	0.0638	0.0629	0.0621	0.0613	0.0604	0.0596	0.0588	0.0581	0.0573	0.0565
1.70	0.0558	0.0550	0.0543	0.0536	0.0529	0.0522	0.0515	0.0508	0.0501	0.0495
1.80	0.0488	0.0482	0.0475	0.0469	0.0463	0.0457	0.0451	0.0445	0.0439	0.0433
1.90	0.0428	0.0422	0.0417	0.0411	0.0406	0.0401	0.0395	0.0390	0.0385	0.0380
2.00	0.0375	0.0370	0.0366	0.0361	0.0356	0.0352	0.0347	0.0343	0.0338	0.0334
2.10	0.0330	0.0325	0.0321	0.0317	0.0313	0.0309	0.0305	0.0301	0.0297	0.0294
2.20	0.0290	0.0286	0.0282	0.0279	0.0275	0.0272	0.0268	0.0265	0.0262	0.0258
2.30	0.0255	0.0252	0.0249	0.0245	0.0242	0.0239	0.0236	0.0233	0.0230	0.0227
2.40	0.0225	0.0222	0.0219	0.0216	0.0214	0.0211	0.0208	0.0206	0.0203	0.0200
2.50	0.0198	0.0196	0.0193	0.0191	0.0188	0.0186	0.0184	0.0181	0.0179	0.0177
2.60	0.0175	0.0172	0.0170	0.0168	0.0166	0.0164	0.0162	0.0160	0.0158	0.0156
2.70	0.0154	0.0152	0.0150	0.0149	0.0147	0.0145	0.0143	0.0141	0.0140	0.0138
2.80	0.0136	0.0134	0.0133	0.0131	0.0130	0.0128	0.0126	0.0125	0.0123	0.0122
2.90	0.0120	0.0119	0.0117	0.0116	0.0115	0.0113	0.0112	0.0110	0.0109	0.0108
3.00	0.0106	0.0105	0.0104	0.0103	0.0101	0.0100	0.0099	0.0098	0.0096	0.0095
3.10	0.0094	0.0093	0.0092	0.0091	0.0090	0.0089	0.0088	0.0086	0.0085	0.0084
3.20	0.0083	0.0082	0.0081	0.0080	0.0079	0.0078	0.0078	0.0077	0.0076	0.0075
3.30	0.0074	0.0073	0.0072	0.0071	0.0070	0.0070	0.0069	0.0068	0.0067	0.0066
3.40	0.0065	0.0065	0.0064	0.0063	0.0062	0.0062	0.0061	0.0060	0.0059	0.0059
3.50	0.0058	0.0057	0.0057	0.0056	0.0055	0.0055	0.0054	0.0053	0.0053	0.0052
3.60	0.0051	0.0051	0.0050	0.0050	0.0049	0.0048	0.0048	0.0047	0.0047	0.0046
3.70	0.0046	0.0045	0.0045	0.0044	0.0044	0.0043	0.0043	0.0042	0.0042	0.0041
3.80	0.0041	0.0040	0.0040	0.0039	0.0039	0.0038	0.0038	0.0037	0.0037	0.0036
3.90	0.0036	0.0036	0.0035	0.0035	0.0034	0.0034	0.0034	0.0033	0.0033	0.0032
4.00	0.0032	0.0032	0.0031	0.0031	0.0031	0.0030	0.0030	0.0029	0.0029	0.0029
4.10	0.0028	0.0028	0.0028	0.0027	0.0027	0.0027	0.0026	0.0026	0.0026	0.0026
4.20	0.0025	0.0025	0.0025	0.0024	0.0024	0.0024	0.0024	0.0023	0.0023	0.0023
4.30	0.0022	0.0022	0.0022	0.0022	0.0021	0.0021	0.0021	0.0021	0.0020	0.0020
4.40	0.0020	0.0020	0.0020	0.0019	0.0019	0.0019	0.0019	0.0018	0.0018	0.0018
4.50	0.0018	0.0018	0.0017	0.0017	0.0017	0.0017	0.0017	0.0016	0.0016	0.0016

Moreover, let us suppose for convenience that $P(0) = 1$. It then follows that the overall market value of the firm's equity will be

$$P(\eta) = \eta + \frac{P(0)}{2} \int_{-1}^{1} \exp\left(-\frac{2\theta\eta}{1+z}\right) dz = 0.28 + 0.2951 = 0.5751$$

or about 57.51 pence.

§9-10. There are several important points that need to be made about the equity valuation formula developed in §9-7 and §9-8 above. First, $P(0)$ represents the adaptation value of the firm's equity when its recursion value η falls away to nothing. Empirical researchers normally approximate $P(0)$ by the book value of equity as recorded in the firm's accounting records. This approximation procedure is normally justified on the grounds that the impairment testing procedures summarized in accounting standards issued by the Accounting Standards Board in the UK such as *FRS 10: Goodwill and Intangible Assets*, *FRS 11: Impairment of Fixed Assets and Goodwill*, *FRS 15: Tangible Fixed Assets* and the Fourth Schedule of the Companies Act require that assets appearing on a firm's balance sheet are to be carried at no more than their 'recoverable amounts'. Similar reporting requirements have been issued by the Financial Accounting Standards Board in the USA. In particular, *SFAS 157: Fair Value Measurements* summarizes reporting requirements under which assets appearing on a firm's balance sheet are to be carried at their 'fair values'. *SFAS 157* defines an asset's fair value as the price that would be received from selling the asset in an orderly market. Thus, the reporting requirements in the UK and the USA, and indeed most other advanced industrialized countries, mean that it is highly likely that for short periods of time around a firm's balance sheet date, the book value of equity will constitute a reasonable approximation to the firm's current adaptation value $P(0)$, should its recursion value fall away to nothing.

It is also important to note that our analysis in §9-8 and §9-9 shows that $\theta = 2r/\zeta^2$ is a crucial parameter in determining the magnitude of an equity security's adaptation value. Note that θ is twice the cost of equity capital r, divided by the variance parameter ζ^2 associated with the white noise process $dq(t)/dt$ on which the stochastic component of instantaneous changes in the recursion value of equity depends (as in §9-5). As such, θ is a measure of the relative stability with which the recursion value of equity grows over time. Thus, as the variance parameter ζ^2 increases relative to the cost of equity, the parameter θ declines and

$$P_2(\eta) = \frac{1}{2} \int_{-1}^{1} \exp\left(-\frac{2\theta\eta}{1+z}\right) dz$$

grows in magnitude, in which case the adaptation value of equity becomes larger. Similarly, the adaptation value of equity falls as the variability of its recursion value ζ^2 decreases relative to the cost of its equity capital r. And this is as one would expect it to be. For when the growth in recursion value clusters closely around the cost of equity r, it is unlikely that the catastrophic events that will require the firm to change its investment opportunity set will arise. Hence, the small probability associated with the firm's adaptation option being exercised will mean that the adaptation value implied by it will also have to be relatively small.

We can also use the moment-generating function for the probability density of the recursion value of equity, as given in §9-6 above, to develop a further important property of the adaptation value of equity. Thus, if we take expectations through the integral expression for the adaptation value of equity, we find

$$E_0\left[\int_{-1}^{1}\exp\left(-\frac{2\theta\eta(t)}{1+z}\right)dz\right]=\int_{-1}^{1}E_0\left[\exp\left(\frac{-2\theta\eta(t)}{1+z}\right)\right]dz$$

Now, we can evaluate this integral by letting $\varphi=-2\theta/(1+z)$ in the expression for the moment-generating function as given in §9-6. Doing so, we have

$$E_0(e^{\varphi\eta(t)})=E_0\left[\exp\left(-\frac{2\theta\eta(t)}{1+z}\right)\right]=\exp\left[\frac{-\dfrac{4r\theta\eta(0)e^{rt}}{1+z}}{2r+\dfrac{2\theta\varsigma^2(e^{rt}-1)}{1+z}}\right]$$

$$=\exp\left[\frac{-4r\theta\eta(0)e^{rt}}{2r(1+z)+2\theta\varsigma^2(e^{rt}-1)}\right]$$

We can then multiply the numerator and denominator in this expression by e^{-rt}, in which case it follows that

$$\lim_{t\to\infty}E_0\left[\exp\left(-\frac{2\theta\eta(t)}{1+z}\right)\right]=\lim_{t\to\infty}\exp\left[\frac{-4r\theta\eta(0)}{2r(1+z)e^{-rt}+2\theta\varsigma^2(1-e^{-rt})}\right]=e^{-\theta\eta(0)}$$

This result implies that in the steady state (i.e. as $t\to\infty$), the expected adaptation value of the firm's equity will be

$$\lim_{t\to\infty}E_0\left[\frac{P(0)}{2}\int_{-1}^{1}\exp\left(-\frac{2\theta\eta(t)}{1+z}\right)dz\right]=\frac{P(0)e^{-\theta\eta(0)}}{2}\int_{-1}^{1}dz=P(0)e^{-\theta\eta(0)}$$

Here, it can also be shown that

$$\lim_{t\to\infty}\text{Prob}\,[\eta(t)=0]=e^{-\theta\eta(0)}$$

that is, the probability of the recursion value of equity eventually falling away to nothing is $e^{-\theta\eta(0)}$. It thus follows that in expectations the adaptation value of the firm's equity is equal to the adaptation value $P(0)$ should the recursion value of equity fall away to nothing multiplied by the probability $e^{-\theta\eta(0)}$ that the recursion value will indeed eventually fall away to nothing.

Note also that the analysis in §9-8 above shows that the overall market value of the firm's equity is the sum of its recursion value and its adaptation value. Given this, Figure 9.1 depicts the relationship between the recursion value η and the market value of equity $P(\eta)$ for a risk parameter $\theta=2$ and where we let $P(0)=1$ for computational convenience. In this diagram, the upward-sloping line emanating from the origin at a 45-degree angle is the recursion value of equity η. The downward-sloping curve that asymptotes towards the recursion value axis is the adaptation value of equity, namely,

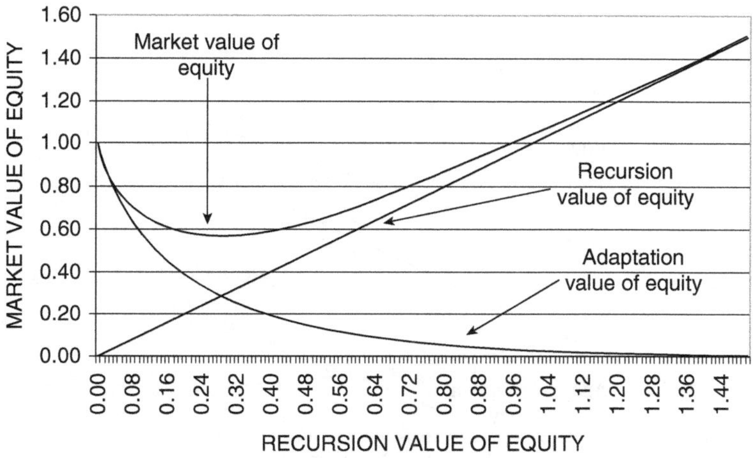

Figure 9.1 Relationship between recursion value η and market value of equity $P(\eta)$ for a risk parameter $\theta = 2$ and where $P(0) = 1$

$$\frac{1}{2}\int_{-1}^{1} \exp\left(-\frac{4\eta}{1+z}\right)dz$$

The sum of the recursion and adaptation values is the market value of equity,

$$P(\eta) = \eta + \frac{1}{2}\int_{-1}^{1} \exp\left(-\frac{4\eta}{1+z}\right)dz$$

and is represented by the convex curve that asymptotes towards the 45-degree line representing the recursion value of equity. Now, here it is important to observe that as the recursion value increases in magnitude, the market value of equity at first declines before reaching a minimum (of £0.5751 as computed in §9-9) and then slowly increases in magnitude. This arises because at small recursion values the decline in the adaptation value of equity will be much larger than the increase in the recursion value itself. This poses an interesting question, namely, why, if the market value of the firm's equity declines to this minimum value as the recursion value of equity grows in magnitude, does the management of the firm simply not exercise the option it possesses to change the firm's investment opportunity set? In doing so, it will instantaneously increase the market value of the firm's equity from a potentially minimum value (of £0.5751) back up to $P(0) = £1$. The answer to this question lies with the fact that if management exercises its option to change the firm's investment opportunity set then it forgoes the possibility that, at some point in the immediate future, the market value of equity will rise to a level well beyond the $P(0) = £1$ that it can obtain from exercising the adaptation option available to it. We elaborate further on this point in §9-12 below.

§9-11. We have previously noted (in §9-8 and §9-10 above) that the parameter $\theta = 2r/\zeta^2$ is a measure of the relative stability with which the recursion value of equity grows over time. When the variance parameter ζ^2 associated with the white noise process $dq(t)/dt$ (as in §9-5)

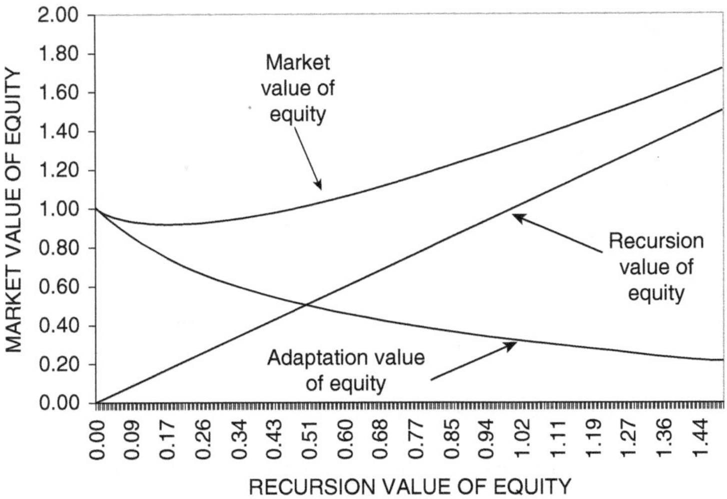

Figure 9.2 Relationship between recursion value η and market value of equity $P(\eta)$ for a risk parameter $\theta = \frac{1}{2}$ and where $P(0) = 1$

is large relative to the cost of equity r, the stability parameter θ will have a relatively small value and the adaptation value of equity

$$\frac{P(0)}{2}\int_{-1}^{1}\exp\left(-\frac{2\theta\eta}{1+z}\right)dz$$

will be relatively large. In contrast, when the variance parameter is small relative to the cost of equity then θ will have a relatively large value and the adaptation value of equity will be relatively small. We can demonstrate the point being made here from Figure 9.2, which graphs the relationship between the recursion value of equity and the market value of equity when the risk parameter $\theta = \frac{1}{2}$. Figure 9.3 also graphs the relationship between the recursion value of equity and the market value of equity, but this time when the risk parameter $\theta = 4$. For both graphs, we assume that the adaptation value of the firm's equity, should its recursion value fall away to nothing, is given by $P(0) = 1$. Note from these two graphs that as the variability parameter grows in magnitude from $\theta = \frac{1}{2}$ to $\theta = 4$, the adaptation value of equity falls more quickly away and the market value of the firm's equity is increasingly composed of its recursion value only.

§9-12. This latter result has important implications for the impact that variables appearing in the firm's investment opportunity set can have on the value of the firm's equity. We can demonstrate this by recalling that when the investment opportunity set is based on the branching process developed in §9-6 above, it leads to a model for which the recursion value of equity will take the following form:

$$\eta(t) = b(t) + \frac{(r - c_{22})a(t)}{(r - c_{11})(r - c_{22}) - c_{21}c_{12}} + \frac{c_{12}\nu(t)}{(r - c_{11})(r - c_{22}) - c_{21}c_{12}}$$

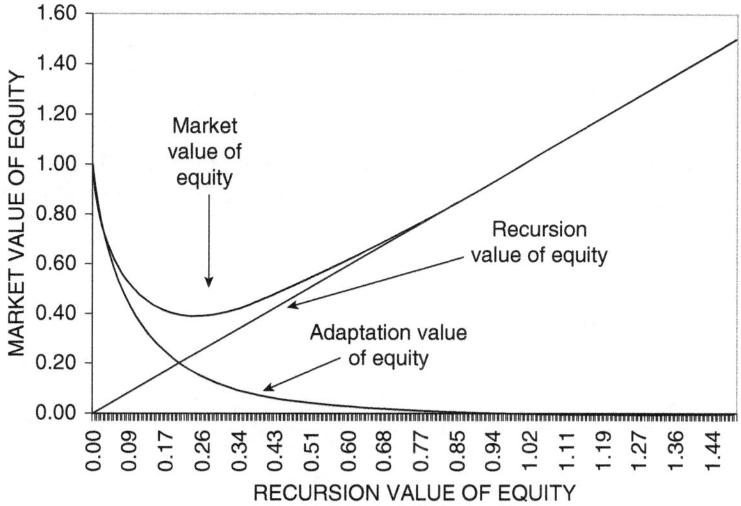

Figure 9.3 Relationship between recursion value η and market value of equity $P(\eta)$ for a risk parameter $\theta = 4$ and where $P(0) = 1$

where $b(t)$ is the book value of the firm's equity, $a(t)$ is the abnormal earnings associated with the firm's equity and $\nu(t)$ is an information variable that captures all the information that is relevant to the value of a firm's equity but that has not, as yet, been incorporated into the firm's accounting records. Moreover, r is the cost of equity capital and c_{11}, c_{12}, c_{21} and c_{22} are the structural coefficients associated with the firm's investment opportunity set (as in §9-2). Now, under the clean surplus identity, book or accounting earnings are related to the book value of equity and abnormal earnings through the formula $a(t) = x(t) - rb(t)$, where $x(t)$ is the instantaneous accounting earnings. Using this definition of the clean surplus identity and a little algebra shows that the recursion value of equity can then be restated in terms of the earnings attributable to equity, as follows:

$$\eta(t) = \frac{(r - c_{22})x(t) - [c_{11}(r - c_{22}) + c_{21}c_{12}]b(t) + c_{12}\nu(t)}{(r - c_{11})(r - c_{22}) - c_{21}c_{12}}$$

Now, we have previously established (in §9-3) that $c_{22} < 0$, and so, if the recursion value of equity is to be a positive function of earnings $x(t)$, then it must be the case that $(r - c_{11})(r - c_{22}) - c_{21}c_{12} > 0$. Moreover, if we takes the derivative of $P(\eta)$ with respect to earnings, we will find

$$\frac{\partial P}{\partial x} = \frac{dP}{d\eta}\frac{\partial \eta}{\partial x} = \frac{r - c_{22}}{(r - c_{11})(r - c_{22}) - c_{21}c_{12}}\frac{dP}{d\eta}$$

However, from the Hamilton–Jacobi–Bellman equation in §9-7 and the results summarized in §9-8, we have

$$\frac{dP}{d\eta} = \frac{P(\eta)}{\eta} - \frac{1}{\theta}\frac{d^2P}{d\eta^2} = 1 + \frac{P(0)}{2\eta}\int_{-1}^{1} \exp\left(-\frac{2\theta\eta}{1+z}\right)dz - \frac{e^{-\theta\eta}}{\eta}$$

From this, it thus follows that

$$\frac{\partial P}{\partial x} = \frac{r - c_{22}}{(r - c_{11})(r - c_{22}) - c_{21}c_{12}} \left[1 + \frac{P(0)}{2\eta} \int_{-1}^{1} \exp\left(-\frac{2\theta\eta}{1+z} \right) dz - \frac{e^{-\theta\eta}}{\eta} \right]$$

This has the important implication that the impact that a change in earnings will have on the value of the firm's equity hinges on the current level of the recursion value of equity. In particular, if

$$1 + \frac{P(0)}{2\eta} \int_{-1}^{1} \exp\left(-\frac{2\theta\eta}{1+z} \right) dz - \frac{e^{-\theta\eta}}{\eta} < 0$$

then an increase in earnings will result in a decrease in the overall market value of the firm's equity. However, if

$$1 + \frac{P(0)}{2\eta} \int_{-1}^{1} \exp\left(-\frac{2\theta\eta}{1+z} \right) dz - \frac{e^{-\theta\eta}}{\eta} > 0$$

then an increase in earnings will result in an increase in the overall market value of the firm's equity. Hence, one cannot predict the impact that variations in a firm's accounting earnings will have on the market value of its equity without first conditioning one's expectations on the current level of the recursion value of equity.

It may appear to be counter-intuitive that a firm's earnings can increase and yet the market value of its equity decline. However, our analysis at the beginning of this section shows that marginal increases in earnings x can lead to only marginal increases in the recursion value of equity η. Moreover, in §9-10, we have noted that the probability of the recursion value eventually falling away to nothing is $e^{-\theta\eta}$. This in turn means that when the recursion value of equity is hovering just above zero, it is all but inevitable that the recursion value will eventually fall away to nothing. It also means that marginal increases in earnings can lead to only marginal decreases in the probability of the recursion value falling away to nothing. Hence, when the recursion value of equity is hovering just above zero, marginal increases in earnings will be seen as doing little more than delaying the inevitable march of the firm's recursion value towards its lower bound of zero. However, this delay in recursion value falling away to nothing will also mean that the firm will have to postpone exchanging its current investment opportunity set for the suite of assets and/or capital projects (as in §9-8 above) that have an adaptation (i.e. market) value of $P(0)$. This in turn will mean that the present (discounted) value of the suite of assets and/or capital projects will be lower than it would otherwise have been if implemented immediately. Thus, a marginal increase in earnings will lead to a reduction in the market value of the firm's equity because of the delay it causes in adapting the firm's resources to alternative and potentially more profitable uses. A similar observation applies to the other variables comprising the firm's investment opportunity set and in particular the information variable ν.

§9-13. Our analysis in this chapter has shown that the market value of a firm's equity will be a complex non-linear function of the variables that characterize the firm's investment opportunity set, including the firm's earnings, the book values appearing on its balance sheet, an information variable that captures all the information relevant to the value of a firm's equity that has not, as yet, been incorporated into the firm's accounting records, and perhaps other contextual and economic variables as well. It is unfortunate that analytical developments in this area have lagged far behind the burgeoning volume of empirical work – so much so that there must be strong suspicions that the empirical results appearing in the literature are based on inappropriate theoretical and econometric methodologies and therefore can have little credibility. In particular, in this chapter, we have formulated a set of procedures that enable one to determine the value of a firm's equity when all the components of the firm's investment opportunity set evolve stochastically and continuously through time. It turns out that our modelling procedures return a closed-form solution for the value of equity and that this is potentially a highly convex function of equity's recursion and adaptation values.

Our analysis also has shown that the recursion value of equity is functionally proportional to its adaptation value. Here, it is well known that the recursion value of equity is equal to its book value plus the expected present value of its abnormal earnings, given that the firm applies its existing investment opportunity set indefinitely into the future. Thus, once the stochastic processes on which a firm's earnings depend have been identified, it is normally a relatively simple matter to compute the recursion value of its equity. Moreover, in the worst-case scenario, the adaptation value of equity will have to be determined using numerical techniques. However, when earnings evolve in terms of the standard stochastic processes encountered in the literature, it will normally be possible for the adaptation value of a firm's equity to be expressed in closed form. Thus, both the Ornstein–Uhlenbeck process and the branching process treated in this chapter lead to closed-form expressions for the adaptation value and overall market values of a firm's equity.

Selected references

Ashton, D., Cooke, T. and Tippett, M. (2003) 'An aggregation theorem for the valuation of equity under linear information dynamics', *Journal of Business Finance and Accounting*, 30: 413–40.

Berger, P., Ofek, E. and Swary, I. (1996) 'Investor valuation of the abandonment option', *Journal of Financial Economics*, 42: 257–81.

Burgstahler, D. and Dichev, I. (1997) 'Earnings, adaptation and equity value', *Accounting Review*, 72: 187–215.

Cox, D. and Miller, H. (1965) *Theory of Stochastic Processes*, London: Chapman & Hall.

Ohlson, J. (1995) 'Earnings, book values, and dividends in security valuation', *Contemporary Accounting Research*, 11: 661–87.

Yee, K. (2000) 'Opportunities knocking: residual income valuation of an adaptive firm', *Journal of Accounting, Auditing and Finance*, 15: 225–66.

Zhang, G. (2000) 'Accounting information, capital investment decisions, and equity valuation: theory and empirical implications', *Journal of Accounting Research*, 38: 271–95.

Exercises

1. In §9-6, it was assumed that the recursion value of equity $\eta(t)$ evolves in terms of the Ornstein–Uhlenbeck process

$$\frac{d\eta(t)}{dt} = r\eta(t) + \frac{dq(t)}{dt}$$

where r is the cost of equity and $dq(t)/dt$ is a white noise process with variance parameter ζ^2. The no-arbitrage condition specified in §9-7 will then mean that the market value of the firm's equity $P(\eta)$ will satisfy the following version of the Hamilton–Jacobi–Bellman equation:

$$\frac{1}{2}\zeta^2\frac{d^2P}{d\eta^2}+r\eta\frac{dP}{d\eta}-rP(\eta)=0$$

where $P_1(\eta)=\eta$ is known to be a solution of this equation. Show that the substitution $P_2(\eta)=u(\eta)P_1(\eta)=u(\eta)\eta$, where $u(\eta)$ is a twice-differentiable function of η, will lead to a second linearly independent solution of the given Hamilton–Jacobi–Bellman equation. Express the market value of the firm's equity in terms of $P_1(\eta)$ and $P_2(\eta)$.

2. In §9-6 to §9-8, it was shown that if the recursion value of equity evolves in terms of a branching process then the adaptation value of the firm's equity will be proportional to

$$P_2(\eta)=\frac{1}{2}\int_{-1}^{1}\exp\left(-\frac{2\theta\eta}{1+z}\right)dz$$

Apply Itô's Lemma to the above expression (as in §7-14 of Chapter 7) and thereby determine the distributional properties of instantaneous increments in the adaptation value of the firm's equity.

3. For the branching process developed in §9-6 to §9-8, show that the market value of the firm's equity is minimized at the recursion value η for which

$$\eta=e^{-\theta\eta}-\frac{P(0)}{2}\int_{-1}^{1}\exp\left(-\frac{2\theta\eta}{1+z}\right)dz$$

Use the above formula and the technique developed in §6-5 of Chapter 6 to determine the recursion value of equity at which the market value of the firm is minimized when $\theta=2$ and $P(0)=1$ (as in §9-10 above). Use a seed value of $\eta_0=1$.

4. One can differentiate the moment-generating function as given in §9-6 to show that the conditional skewness measure for the branching process is

$$\text{Skew}_0[\eta(t)]=\frac{3\zeta^4}{2r^2}\eta(0)e^{rt}(e^{rt}-1)^2$$

One can also use the moment-generating function to show that the conditional kurtosis measure for the branching process is

$$\text{Kurt}_0[\eta(t)]=\frac{3\zeta^6}{2r^3}\eta(0)e^{rt}(e^{rt}-1)^3+\frac{3\zeta^4}{r^2}\eta^2(0)e^{2rt}(e^{rt}-1)^2$$

Use these results and the expression for the variance of the branching process as given in §9-6 and thereby show

$$\lim_{\eta(0)\to\infty}\frac{\text{Skew}_0[\eta(t)]}{\{\sqrt{\text{Var}_0[\eta(t)]}\}^3}=0$$

and

$$\lim_{\eta(0)\to\infty} \frac{\text{Kurt}_0[\eta(t)]}{\{\text{Var}_0[\eta(t)]\}^2} = 3$$

that is, the standardized conditional skewness measure for the branching process has a limiting value of zero and the standardized conditional kurtosis measure has a limiting value of 3. Explain the circumstances in which these results can be used to justify approximating the conditional probability density for the branching process by a normal distribution.

5. The expected present value of the future cash flows $\eta(t)$ for a given capital project evolves in accordance with the following mean reversion process:

$$\frac{d\eta(t)}{dt} = \zeta^2 - r\eta(t) + \sqrt{\eta(t)}\frac{dq(t)}{dt}$$

where $dq(t)/dt$ is a white noise process with variance parameter ζ^2 and r is the cost of capital. Use the analysis in §9-7 to show that the Hamilton–Jacobi–Bellman equation for the given mean reversion process is

$$\frac{1}{2}\zeta^2\eta\frac{d^2P}{d\eta^2} + (\zeta^2 - r\eta)\frac{dP}{d\eta} - rP(\eta) = 0$$

where $P(\eta)$ is the value of an option to implement (or abandon) the given capital project. Show that

$$P(\eta) = \frac{\zeta^2\left[\exp\left(\frac{2r\eta}{\zeta^2}\right) - 1\right]}{2r\eta}$$

is a solution of the Hamilton–Jacobi–Bellman equation and explain how it can be used to value the option to implement the given capital project. Show that the substitution

$$P(\eta) = u(\eta)\frac{\zeta^2\left[\exp\left(\frac{2r\eta}{\zeta^2}\right) - 1\right]}{2r\eta}$$

where $u(\eta)$ is a twice-differentiable function of η, will lead to a second linearly independent solution of the given Hamilton–Jacobi–Bellman equation. Explain how this second solution can be used to value the option to abandon the given capital project.

10 Equity valuation

Non-linearities and scaling

§10-1. Previous analysis (as in Chapter 9) shows that adaptation options can play a significant role in the valuation of a firm's equity. If a firm has the option of abandoning poorly performing capital projects, it can increase the market value of its equity well beyond the traditional benchmark as given by the expected present value of its future cash flows under its existing investment opportunity set. Moreover, one can use the fact that the market value of a firm's equity is the sum of its recursion value and its adaptation value to show that there will be a highly convex and non-linear relationship between the market value of the firm's equity on the one hand and the variables comprising its investment opportunity set on the other. Given this, it is somewhat surprising that both empirical and analytical work on the relationship between equity value and its determining variables continues to be based on models that establish the value of a firm's equity exclusively in terms of the present value of its future cash flows, since this ignores the adaptation option effects associated with the firm's ability to modify or even abandon its existing investment opportunity set. Hence, in the present chapter, our first task is to use the equity valuation procedures developed in Chapter 9 to determine the likely form and magnitude of the biases that arise when researchers assume that the market value of a firm's equity is composed exclusively of its recursion value and therefore is linear in its determining variables. We analyse the biases that arise from assuming that the market value of a firm's equity is composed exclusively of its recursion value by employing an orthogonal polynomial fitting procedure for identifying the relative contribution that the linear and non-linear components of the relationship between equity value and its determining variables make towards overall equity value. The evidence from this procedure is that the non-linearities in equity valuation can be large and significant, particularly for firms where the recursion value of equity is comparatively small. Moreover, empirical work conducted in the area is invariably based on market and/or accounting (book) variables that have been scaled or deflated in order to facilitate comparisons between firms of different size. Given this, it is important that one appreciates how these deflation procedures might alter or even distort the underlying levels relationships that exist between the market value of equity and its determining variables. In particular, our analysis of this issue shows that deflating data before regression procedures are applied can lead to a form of spurious correlation between the regression variables. This in turn can lead a researcher to the conclusion that a non-trivial relationship exists between the regression variables when in fact the data on which the regression analysis is based are completely unrelated. Examples of spurious correlations arising out of the deflation procedures demonstrated here are not difficult to find in the literature and several illustrations are provided in the later sections of this chapter.

§10-2. Our analysis in Chapter 9 shows that the market value of a firm's equity is comprised of two components. The first is called the recursion value of equity and is the present value of the future cash flows that the firm expects to earn, or equivalently the present value of the dividends that the firm expects to pay over its lifetime (as in §5-2 of Chapter 5), given that it is indefinitely constrained to operate within its existing investment opportunity set. There is, however, a second component of equity value, namely, the adaptation (or real option) value of equity. This is the option value that arises out of a firm's ability to change its existing investment opportunity set by (for example) fundamentally changing the nature of its operating activities. Now suppose one follows the analysis of Chapter 9 in assuming that the recursion value of equity $\eta(t)$ evolves in terms of a continuous-time branching process, namely,

$$\frac{d\eta(t)}{dt} = r\eta(t) + \sqrt{\eta(t)}\frac{dq(t)}{dt}$$

where r is the cost of equity capital and $dq(t)/dt$ is a white noise process with variance parameter ς^2. It will be recalled (as in §9-6) that under this process the recursion value of equity will grow at a rate equal to the cost of equity capital r, but that there will also be stochastic perturbations in the growth rate arising from the white noise process $dq(t)/dt$. Moreover, the variance associated with the stochastic component, $\text{Var}_t[\sqrt{\eta(t)}dq(t)] = \eta\varsigma^2 dt$, will grow in line with the recursion value itself. This reflects the commonly held belief that the variance associated with increments in the recursion value of equity will become larger as the recursion value grows in magnitude.

In the previous chapter, we used the branching process articulated above to develop a quasi-supply-side model of the firm that, when taken in conjunction with standard no-arbitrage conditions, showed that the market value of the firm's equity $P(\eta)$ will have to be

$$P(\eta) = \eta + \frac{P(0)}{2}\int_{-1}^{1} \exp\left(-\frac{2\theta\eta}{1+z}\right) dz$$

The first term on the right-hand side of this expression is the recursion value of the firm's equity, namely,

$$\eta(t) = b(t) + \frac{(r - c_{22})a(t)}{(r - c_{11})(r - c_{22}) - c_{21}c_{12}} + \frac{c_{12}\nu(t)}{(r - c_{11})(r - c_{22}) - c_{21}c_{12}}$$

where $b(t)$ is the book value of the firm's equity at time t, $a(t)$ is the instantaneous abnormal earnings associated with the firm's equity and $\nu(t)$ is an information variable that captures all the information that is relevant to the value of a firm's equity but that has not, as yet, been incorporated into the firm's accounting records. Moreover, r is the cost of equity capital and c_{11}, c_{12}, c_{21} and c_{22} are the structural coefficients associated with the firm's investment opportunity set. The second term, involving the integral on the right-hand side of the expression for $P(\eta)$, gives the adaptation value of equity. Here $P(0) > 0$ denotes the value of the firm's adaptation options when the recursion value of equity falls away to nothing and $\theta = 2r/\varsigma^2$ is a risk parameter that captures the relative stability with which the recursion value of equity evolves over time (as in §9-10). Thus, when the risk parameter is $\theta = 2$ and $P(0) = 1$ is the value of the firm's adaptation options when the recursion value of equity

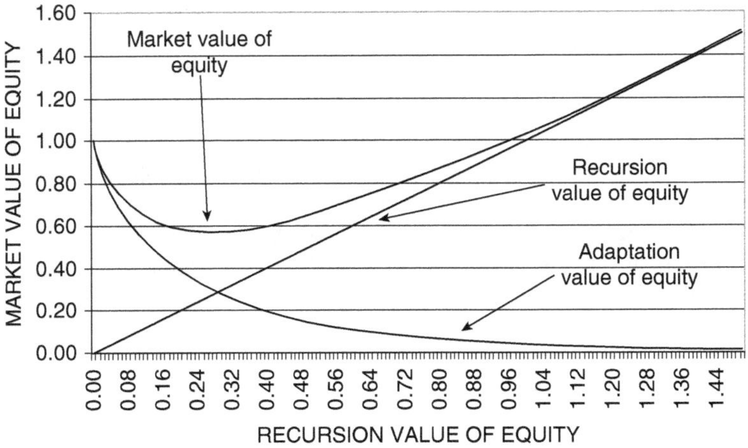

Figure 10.1 Relationship between recursion value η and the equity valuation function $P(\eta)$, for a risk parameter $\theta = 2$ and where $P(0) = 1$

falls away to nothing ($\eta = 0$), there will be a highly convex relationship between the market value of equity, the recursion value of equity and the adaptation value of the firm's equity, as depicted in Figure 10.1. In this diagram, the upward-sloping line emanating from the origin at a 45-degree angle is the recursion value of equity η. The downward-sloping curve that asymptotes towards the recursion value axis is the adaptation value of equity. The sum of the recursion value and adaptation value is the market value of equity and is represented by the convex curve that asymptotes towards the 45-degree line representing the recursion value of equity. Now, suppose that one wants to know the impact that a particular variable (such as earnings or the book value of equity) has on the market value of the firm's equity, or that one wants to know the relative contributions that recursion value and adaptation value make towards the overall market value of the firm's equity. To do this, one will need to know precise numerical values for the structural coefficients c_{11}, c_{12}, c_{21} and c_{22}, the cost of equity r, and the variance parameter associated with the white noise process $dq(t)/dt$, which is ζ^2. It is unlikely that these parameters will be known, and so they will have to be estimated using empirical observations of the variables comprising the firm's investment opportunity set, namely, $b(t)$, $a(t)$ and $v(t)$. This raises the important issue of how one might go about obtaining reliable estimates of the required parameters.

§10-3. Empirical researchers in this area will invariably estimate the parameters they need by assuming that there is a linear relationship between the market value of equity and its determining variables. Here it will be noted that if one sets $P(0) = 0$ in the equity valuation equation summarized in §10-2 above then the following linear relationship will exist between the market value of the firm's equity and its determining variables:

$$P(\eta) = \eta = b(t) + \frac{(r - c_{22})a(t)}{(r - c_{11})(r - c_{22}) - c_{21}c_{12}} + \frac{c_{12}v(t)}{(r - c_{11})(r - c_{22}) - c_{21}c_{12}}$$

where $b(t)$ is the book value of equity, $a(t)$ is the abnormal earnings, $v(t)$ is the information variable, and the parameters c_{11}, c_{12}, c_{21}, c_{22} and r have the meanings attributed to them in §10-2 above. However, by setting $P(0) = 0$, one is invoking the assumption that the market value of a firm's equity is composed exclusively of recursion value or that the real options generally available to firms have no role to play in the equity valuation process. If, as one would normally expect, this is a false assumption then it is all but inevitable that there will be systematic differences between the actual market values and those predicted by the linear model based purely on the recursion value of the firm's equity. We can illustrate the dangers that arise from ignoring the non-linear nature of the relationship between the market value of equity and its determining variables by expanding the equity valuation function $P(\eta)$ as an infinite power series. A significant difficulty here, however, is that the Taylor series expansion for $P(\eta)$ is non-convergent; that is, it will not in general converge to the correct value for $P(\eta)$. Given this, we adopt the alternative procedure of expanding the equity valuation function in terms of an infinite power series based on the Laguerre polynomials, namely,

$$P(\eta) = \sum_{m=0}^{\infty} \alpha_m L_m(\eta)$$

where α_m is known as the Fourier–Laguerre coefficient associated with the mth-order Laguerre polynomial $L_m(\eta)$. The first two Laguerre polynomials are $L_0(\eta) = 1$ and $L_1(\eta) = 1 - \eta$. Higher-order Laguerre polynomials may be determined from the first two Laguerre polynomials by implementing the following recursion formula:

$$mL_m(\eta) = (2m - 1 - \eta)L_{m-1}(\eta) - (m-1)L_{m-2}(\eta)$$

where $L_m(\eta)$ is the Laguerre polynomial of order $m \geq 2$. Thus, we can determine the Laguerre polynomial of order $m = 2$ by noting that the above recursion formula implies

$$2L_2(\eta) = (3 - \eta)L_1(\eta) - L_0(\eta) = (3 - \eta)(1 - \eta) - 1$$

Expanding out the above expression and collecting terms shows that the Laguerre polynomial of order $m = 2$ is

$$L_2(\eta) = \frac{1}{2}(\eta^2 - 4\eta + 2)$$

Similar calculations using $L_1(\eta)$, $L_2(\eta)$ and the above recursion formula shows that the Laguerre polynomial of order $m = 3$ is

$$L_3(\eta) = \frac{1}{6}(-\eta^3 + 9\eta^2 - 18\eta + 6)$$

Continuing this process *ad infinitum* enables one to determine the Laguerre polynomial of any desired order. Moreover, the Riesz Representation Theorem guarantees that the power series expansion for $P(\eta)$ based on the Laguerre polynomials will always converge to the correct value for $P(\eta)$.

We now demonstrate the procedures associated with determining the power series expansion for $P(\eta)$ by assuming (without loss of generality) that $P(0) = 1$ is the value of the firm's adaptation options when the recursion value of equity falls away to nothing. It then follows that the Fourier–Laguerre coefficients α_m are determined by minimizing the weighted least squares integral

$$\int_0^{\infty} e^{-\eta} \left[P(\eta) - \sum_{m=0}^{\infty} \alpha_m L_m(\eta) \right]^2 d\eta$$

This in turn implies that the Fourier coefficient α_0 for the equity valuation function with respect to the Laguerre polynomial of order zero, $L_0(\eta)$, is

$$\alpha_0 = \int_0^\infty e^{-\eta} P(\eta) L_0(\eta) d\eta = \theta \log\left(\frac{\theta}{1+\theta}\right) + 2$$

Similarly, the Fourier coefficient α_1 for the equity valuation function with respect to the Laguerre polynomial of order one, $L_1(\eta)$, turns out to be

$$\alpha_1 = \int_0^\infty e^{-\eta} P(\eta) L_1(\eta) d\eta = -1 - \frac{\theta}{1+\theta} - \theta \log\left(\frac{\theta}{1+\theta}\right)$$

Moreover, the Fourier coefficient α_m for the equity valuation function with respect to the Laguerre polynomial of order $m \geq 2$, $L_m(\eta)$, is

$$\alpha_m = \int_0^\infty e^{-\eta} P(\eta) L_m(\eta) d\eta = \frac{\theta(1+\theta)^m - (m+\theta)\theta^m}{m(m-1)(1+\theta)^m}$$

Thus, substituting $m = 2$ into the right-hand side of this expression shows that the Fourier coefficient α_2 for the equity valuation function with respect to the Laguerre polynomial of order two, $L_2(\eta)$, is

$$\alpha_2 = \frac{\theta(1+\theta)^2 - (2+\theta)\theta^2}{2(2-1)(1+\theta)^2} = \frac{1}{2}\frac{\theta}{(1+\theta)^2}$$

Similar calculations can be applied to determine the Fourier coefficients for the equity valuation function with respect to the higher-order Laguerre polynomials.

§10-4. Using the procedures based on the Laguerre polynomials summarized in §10-3, we can show that the value of a firm's equity $P(\eta)$ can be represented in terms of the following infinite power series expansion:

$$P(\eta) = \eta + \frac{1}{2}\int_{-1}^{1} \exp\left(-\frac{2\theta\eta}{1+z}\right) dz = \sum_{m=0}^{\infty} \alpha_m L_m(\eta)$$

$$= \alpha_0 + \alpha_1(1-\eta) + \frac{\alpha_2}{2}(\eta^2 - 4\eta + 2) + \frac{\alpha_3}{6}(6 - 18\eta + 9\eta^2 - \eta^3) + \ldots$$

or, upon substituting the expressions for the Fourier–Laguerre coefficients specified in §10-3 above,

$$P(\eta) = \eta + \frac{1}{2}\int_{-1}^{1} \exp\left(-\frac{2\theta\eta}{1+z}\right) dz = \sum_{m=0}^{\infty} \alpha_m L_m(\eta)$$

$$= \left[\theta \log\left(\frac{\theta}{1+\theta}\right) + 2\right] - \left[1 + \frac{\theta}{1+\theta} + \theta \log\left(\frac{\theta}{1+\theta}\right)\right](1-\eta)$$

$$+ \frac{1}{4}\frac{\theta}{(1+\theta)^2}(\eta^2 - 4\eta + 2) + \ldots$$

Now, the important issue that arises here is the degree to which the above power series expansion must be carried in order to obtain a good approximation to the equity valuation function $P(\eta)$ over its entire domain. This, in fact, will depend on the magnitude of the risk parameter θ. Larger values of θ will generally require the inclusion of higher-order power series terms before a satisfactory approximation to the equity valuation function can be obtained. Here, we can follow the analysis of §10-2 above and §9-10 of Chapter 9 in letting the risk parameter be $\theta = 2$ and $P(0) = 1$ be the value of the firm's adaptation options when the recursion value of equity falls away to nothing. We can then determine the best linear approximation to the equity valuation function $P(\eta)$ by taking the first two terms of the Laguerre power series expansion given above:

$$P(\eta) = \eta + \frac{1}{2}\int_{-1}^{1} \exp\left(-\frac{2\theta\eta}{1+z}\right) dz \approx \left[\theta \log\left(\frac{\theta}{1+\theta}\right) + 2\right]$$

$$- \left[1 + \frac{\theta}{1+\theta} + \theta \log\left(\frac{\theta}{1+\theta}\right)\right](1-\eta)$$

Now, substituting $\theta = 2$ into the above expression and collecting terms shows that the best linear approximation to the equity valuation function will be

$$P(\eta) = \eta + \frac{1}{2}\int_{-1}^{1} \exp\left(-\frac{4\eta}{1+z}\right) dz \approx 0.3333 + 0.8557\eta$$

Figure 10.2 graphs the relationship between the recursion value of equity η the market value of equity $P(\eta)$ and the best linear approximation to the market value of equity as given by the above expression. In Figure 10.2, the recursion value of equity is defined by the equation $P(\eta) = \eta$, that is, the 45-degree line emanating from the origin. The market value of equity is defined by the equation

$$P(\eta) = \eta + \frac{1}{2}\int_{-1}^{1} \exp\left(-\frac{4\eta}{1+z}\right) dz$$

which is the downward-sloping curve emanating from the point $P(0) = 1$ on the vertical axis that eventually turns upwards and asymptotes towards the 45-degree line describing the recursion value of equity. The best linear approximation to the market value of equity is

$$P(\eta) \approx 0.3333 + 0.8557\eta$$

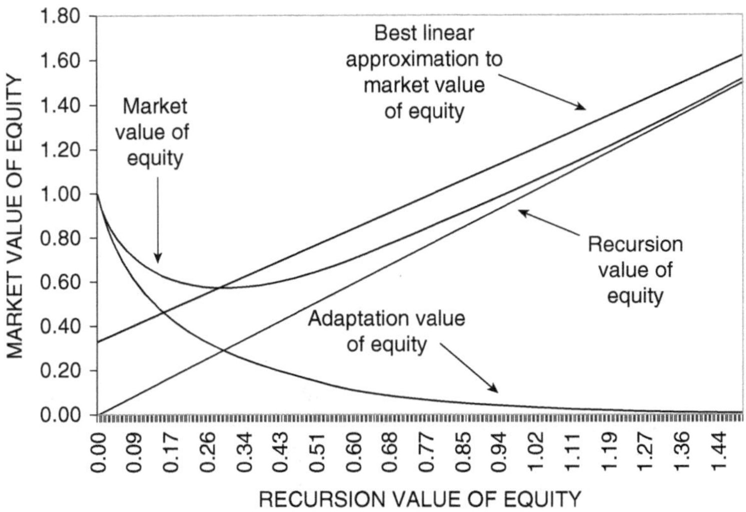

Figure 10.2 Relationship between the recursion value η, the equity valuation function $P(\eta)$ and the best linear approximation to the equity valuation function for a risk parameter $\theta = 2$ and where $P(0) = 1$

and is the upward-sloping line emanating from the point $P(0) = 0.3333$ on the vertical axis. Note how this graph shows that the linear approximation provides both systematically biased estimates of the market value of the firm's equity and particularly poor approximations to the market value of the firm's equity at small recursion values. In short, it is highly unlikely that the linear models so widely employed by empirical researchers can provide a satisfactory basis for determining the relationships between the market value of equity and its determining variables.

§10-5. The problematic nature of the linear models employed in the literature raises the important question as to whether one can obtain better approximations of the relationship between the market value of equity and its determining variables by using higher-order terms from the Laguerre power series expansion for the market value of equity. Here we can again follow the analysis in §10-4 above by letting $\theta = 2$ and $P(0) = 1$ (as also in §9-10), in which case the fifth-order Laguerre power series approximation to the equity valuation function will take the form

$$P(\eta) = \eta + \frac{1}{2}\int_{-1}^{1} \exp\left(-\frac{2\theta\eta}{1+z}\right) dz \approx \sum_{m=0}^{m=5} \alpha_m L_m(\eta)$$

where α_m is the Fourier coefficient associated with the mth-order Laguerre polynomial $L_m(\eta)$, as determined in §10-3 above. Figure 10.3 plots the equity valuation function $P(\eta)$ together with its fifth-order ($m = 5$) Laguerre power series approximation. Note that whilst this fifth-order Laguerre approximation represents a significant improvement on the linear (first-degree) approximating procedures examined in §10-4 above, it nonetheless continues to provide systematically biased estimates of the market value of equity. Moreover, the

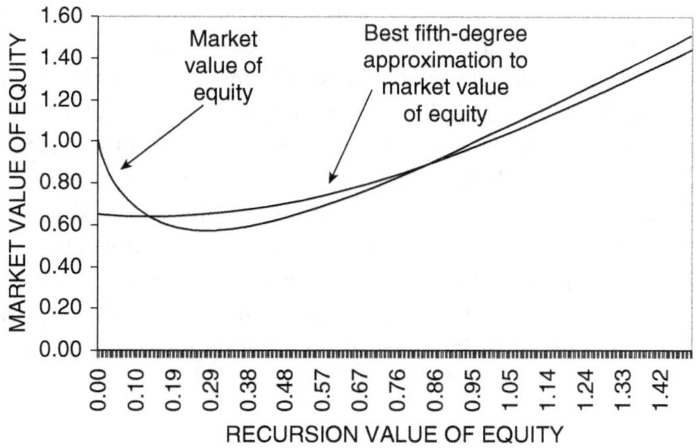

Figure 10.3 Relationship between the equity valuation function $P(\eta)$ and its fifth-order ($m = 5$) Laguerre power series approximation for a risk parameter $\theta = 2$ and where $P(0) = 1$

approximations that the fifth-degree Laguerre power series expansion provides to the market value of equity are also particularly poor when the recursion value of equity is relatively small, that is, near the origin or, equivalently, when the firm is experiencing financial difficulties. Thus, it appears unlikely that a fifth-order power series approximation can provide a satisfactory basis for determining the relationships between the market value of a firm's equity and its determining variables. A similar conclusion applies to the 10th-order ($m = 10$) and 15th-order ($m = 15$) Laguerre approximations to the equity valuation formula $P(\eta)$. The relationship between the equity valuation function and its 10th-order ($m = 10$). Laguerre power series approximation is depicted in Figure 10.4. Likewise, the relationship between the equity valuation function and its 15th-order ($m = 15$) Laguerre approximation is depicted in Figure 10.5. Note how these graphs show that both the 10th- and 15th-order

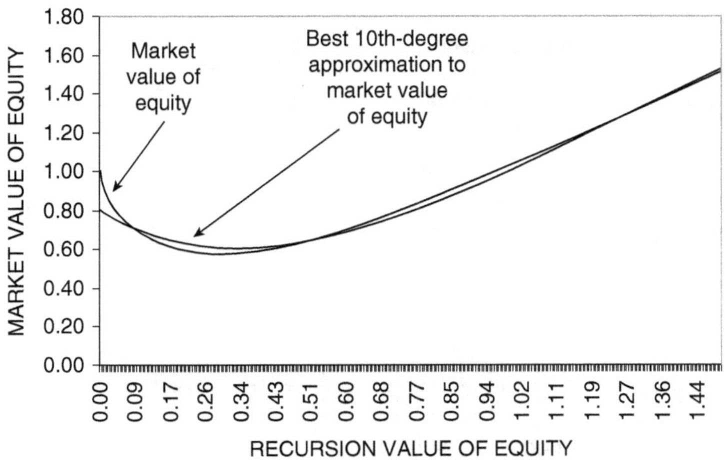

Figure 10.4 Relationship between the equity valuation function $P(\eta)$ and its 10th-order ($m = 10$) Laguerre power series approximation for a risk parameter $\theta = 2$ and where $P(0) = 1$

Laguerre power series approximations continue to provide systematically biased estimates of the market value of the firm's equity and that the two approximations are particularly poor when the recursion value of equity is relatively small, that is, near the origin or when the firm is experiencing financial stress. Thus, it also appears that neither the 10th- nor the 15th-order Laguerre approximations can provide a satisfactory basis for determining the valuation relationships in this area. Indeed, it is not until one employs a 20th-order ($m = 20$) or even a 30th-order ($m = 30$) Laguerre power series expansion that one obtains a satisfactory approximation to the equity valuation function $P(\eta)$. The relationship between the equity valuation function and its 30th-order Laguerre approximation is as depicted in Figure 10.6. The principal conclusion that one can draw from the analysis in this and previous sections of this chapter is that the market value of equity is a highly non-linear function of

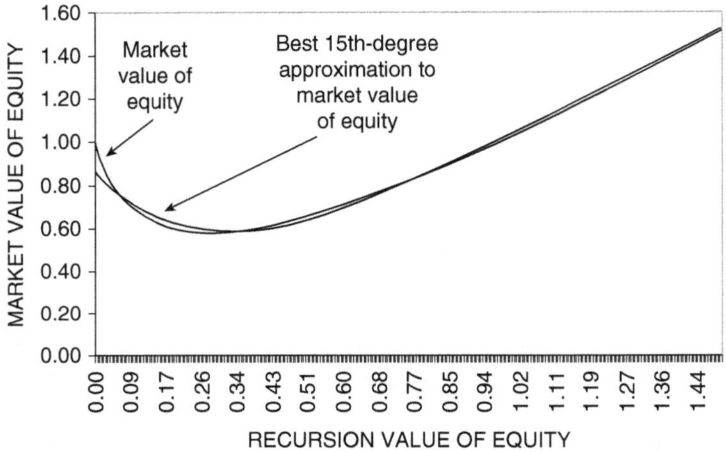

Figure 10.5 Relationship between the equity valuation function $P(\eta)$ and its 15th-order ($m = 15$) Laguerre power series approximation for a risk parameter $\theta = 2$ and where $P(0) = 1$

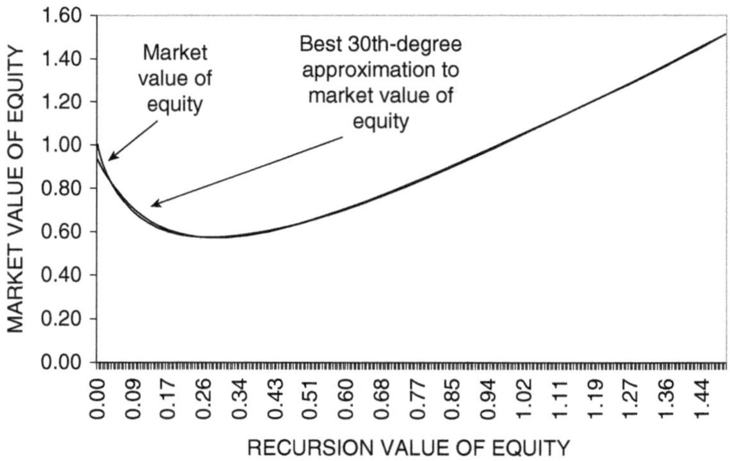

Figure 10.6 Relationship between the equity valuation function $P(\eta)$ and its 30th-order ($m = 30$) Laguerre power series approximation for a risk parameter $\theta = 2$ and where $P(0) = 1$

its determining variables. The non-linearities are most acute around the origin, where the recursion value is relatively low and the adaptation value makes a significant contribution to the overall market value of equity, that is, when the firm is experiencing financial stress. At high recursion values, the adaptation value of equity makes a relatively small contribution to overall equity value and there is a greater likelihood that the linear models so widely employed by empirical researchers will provide a satisfactory basis for determining the relationship between the market value of equity and its determining variables.

§10-6. An important point that needs to be made here, however, is that empirical work in this area is invariably based on market and/or accounting (book) variables that have been normalized or deflated in order to facilitate comparisons between firms of different size. Given this, suppose that we define the normalized recursion value of equity as $h(t) = \eta(t)/\Theta$, where Θ is some kind of normalizing or deflation factor. We can then apply Itô's Lemma (as in §7-13 of Chapter 7) and thereby show that the normalized recursion value will evolve in terms of the following stochastic differential equation:

$$\begin{aligned}\frac{dh(t)}{dt} &= \frac{d\eta(t)}{dt}\frac{\partial h}{\partial \eta} + \frac{\partial h}{\partial t} + \frac{1}{2}\frac{[d\eta(t)]^2}{dt}\frac{\partial^2 h}{\partial \eta^2} \\ &= \frac{1}{\Theta}\left[r\eta(t) + \sqrt{\eta(t)}\frac{dq(t)}{dt}\right] = rh(t) + \sqrt{h(t)}\frac{dv(t)}{dt}\end{aligned}$$

where

$$\frac{dv(t)}{dt} = \frac{1}{\sqrt{\Theta}}\frac{dq(t)}{dt}$$

is a white noise process with variance parameter ς^2/Θ. Note that increments in the normalized recursion value $h(t)$ will have a mean of

$$E_t[dh(t)] = rh(t)dt$$

where $E_t[\cdot]$ is the expectation operator taken at time t. Likewise, the variance of increments in the normalized recursion value will be

$$\text{Var}_t[dh(t)] = h(t)\text{Var}_t[dv(t)] = h(t)\frac{\varsigma^2}{\Theta}dt$$

where $\text{Var}_t[\cdot]$ is the variance operator, again taken at time t. It will also be recalled from §10-2 that the risk (or stability) parameter for this model is twice the expected return on equity, $2r$, divided by the variance ς^2/Θ associated with the white noise term $dv(t)/dt$. This in turn means that the risk parameter for the normalized recursion value will be

$$\frac{2r}{\varsigma^2/\Theta} = \frac{2r\Theta}{\varsigma^2} = \theta\Theta$$

Furthermore, if we work in terms of the normalized recursion value of equity $h(t)$, rather than levels $\eta(t)$, then it follows from §10-2 that the value of equity will be

$$P(h) = h + \frac{P(0)}{2\Theta} \int_{-1}^{1} \exp\left(-\frac{2\theta\Theta h}{1+z}\right) dz$$

where $P(0)/\Theta$ denotes the normalized value of the firm's adaptation options when the normalized recursion value h falls away to nothing. Now, it is important here to note that $\eta(t) = \Theta h(t)$, and so the normalized value of equity will satisfy the following important property:

$$\Theta P(h) = \eta + \frac{P(0)}{2} \int_{-1}^{1} \exp\left(-\frac{2\theta\eta}{1+z}\right) dz = P(\eta)$$

Formally, this result means that the equity valuation model summarized in §10-2 (and Chapter 9) is scale-invariant. In particular, if for all real η, λ and some Δ, a function $P(\cdot)$ satisfies the property $\lambda^{\Delta} P(\eta) = P(\lambda\eta)$ then it is said to be scale-invariant for all dilations λ, with a scaling dimension of Δ. Hence, since the analysis above shows that the equity valuation function satisfies the condition

$$\Theta P\left(\frac{\eta}{\Theta}\right) = P(\eta)$$

it necessarily follows that one can let $\lambda = 1/\Theta$ and $\Delta = 1$. This in turn will mean that the equity valuation formula $P(\eta)$ is scale-invariant under the dilation $\lambda = 1/\Theta$ with a scaling dimension of $\Delta = 1$. In the present context, the scale-invariance property will mean that one can determine the overall market value of a firm's equity simply by multiplying the market value of its equity $P(h)$, computed in terms of the deflated variable h, by the deflation factor Θ.

We can illustrate the importance of this scale-invariance property by considering a firm for which all variables have been deflated by the book value of its equity at some *fixed* point in time (as in §9-10 of Chapter 9). It then follows that Θ will be the book value of the firm's equity at this fixed point in time and $h(t) = \eta(t)/\Theta$ will be the normalized (or scaled) recursion value of equity at time t. Moreover, this will also mean that the market value of equity (per unit of book value) will evolve in terms of the following formula:

$$\frac{P(\eta)}{\Theta} = h + \frac{P(0)}{2\Theta} \int_{-1}^{1} \exp\left(-\frac{2\theta\Theta h}{1+z}\right) dz = P(h) = P\left(\frac{\eta}{\Theta}\right)$$

where $P(\eta)/\Theta$ is the ratio of the market value of equity to the book value of equity on the given fixed date (commonly referred to as the market-to-book ratio). This result shows that if an empirical researcher deflates the market value of a firm's equity by its book value in order to facilitate comparisons between firms of different size (as is often the case with empirical work conducted in this area) then the researcher will also need to deflate the variables of which the recursion value is composed by the book value of equity as well. It is only then that valid comparisons can be made across firms of the relationship between the deflated market value of equity and the variables comprising the recursion value of equity for the different firms.

Thus, if an empirical researcher deflates the market value of a firm's equity by its book value, they will also need to deflate the information variable $v(t)$ and the abnormal earnings variable $a(t)$ by the book value of equity as well if valid comparisons of the relationships between these variables are to be made across firms.

§10-7. The analysis in §10-6 assumes that the deflation factor employed by an empirical researcher is a constant that is not revised (i.e. not updated) through time. More often than not, however, the deflation factor is updated with the same frequency as the other variables employed in the given empirical analysis. The revised (i.e. updated) deflated variables are then invariably used in some form of (time series or cross-sectional) regression analysis. There are, however, significant problems with regression procedures where the denominator of deflated variables is updated with the same frequency as the other variables employed in the regression analysis. We can demonstrate the dangers that can arise with this deflation procedure by considering the three *uncorrelated* variables, x_1, x_2 and x_3. Now, suppose that the third of these variables, x_3, is used to deflate the other two variables before they are used in empirical work. The first deflated variable will thus take the form

$$\frac{x_1}{x_3} = \frac{m_1 + \varepsilon_1}{m_3 + \varepsilon_3} = \frac{m_1}{m_3} \frac{1 + \dfrac{\varepsilon_1}{m_1}}{1 + \dfrac{\varepsilon_3}{m_3}}$$

where $E(x_1) = m_1$ is the mean of the variable x_1, $\varepsilon_1 = x_1 - m_1$ is the difference between the observed value of x_1 and its mean, $E(x_3) = m_3$ is the mean of the variable x_3 and $\varepsilon_3 = x_3 - m_3$ is the difference between the observed value of x_3 and its mean. We can then apply a Taylor series expansion to the denominator on the far right-hand side of the above expression, in which case it follows that

$$\left(1 + \frac{\varepsilon_3}{m_3}\right)^{-1} = 1 - \frac{\varepsilon_3}{m_3} + \left(\frac{\varepsilon_3}{m_3}\right)^2 + \ldots$$

Appropriate substitution will then imply

$$\frac{x_1}{x_3} = \frac{m_1}{m_3}\left(1 + \frac{\varepsilon_1}{m_1}\right)\left[1 - \frac{\varepsilon_3}{m_3} + \left(\frac{\varepsilon_3}{m_3}\right)^2 + \ldots\right]$$

or, equivalently,

$$\frac{x_1}{x_3} = \frac{m_1}{m_3}\left[1 + \frac{\varepsilon_1}{m_1} - \frac{\varepsilon_3}{m_3} + \left(\frac{\varepsilon_3}{m_3}\right)^2 - \frac{\varepsilon_1}{m_1}\frac{\varepsilon_3}{m_3} + \frac{\varepsilon_1}{m_1}\left(\frac{\varepsilon_3}{m_3}\right)^3 + \ldots\right]$$

Note here, however, that $E(\varepsilon_1) = E(x_1) - m_1 = 0$ and $E(\varepsilon_3) = E(x_3) - m_3 = 0$. Moreover, $\text{Cov}(\varepsilon_1, \varepsilon_3) = E(\varepsilon_1\varepsilon_3) - E(\varepsilon_1)E(\varepsilon_3) = E(\varepsilon_1\varepsilon_3)$ will be the covariance between ε_1 and ε_3. However, since by hypothesis ε_1 and ε_3 are uncorrelated, it necessarily follows that $E(\varepsilon_1\varepsilon_3) = E(\varepsilon_1)E(\varepsilon_3) = 0$. Moreover, it may also be shown that this latter result implies $E(\varepsilon_1^j\varepsilon_3^k) = E(\varepsilon_1^j)E(\varepsilon_3^k)$ for all integral j and k. This in turn will mean $E(\varepsilon_1\varepsilon_3^2) = E(\varepsilon_1)E(\varepsilon_3^2) = 0$.

Hence, we can take expectations across the expression for the first deflated variable, x_1/x_3, and thereby obtain the following result:

$$E\left(\frac{x_1}{x_3}\right) = \frac{m_1}{m_3}\left(1 + \frac{\sigma_3^2}{m_3^2} + \ldots\right)$$

where $\sigma_3^2 = E(\varepsilon_3^2)$ is the variance of the variable ε_3. Likewise, we can determine the second moment about the origin for this first deflated variable, namely,

$$E\left[\left(\frac{x_1}{x_3}\right)^2\right] = \frac{m_1^2}{m_3^2}E\left[\left(1 + \frac{\varepsilon_1}{m_1}\right)^2\left\{1 - \frac{\varepsilon_3}{m_3} + \left(\frac{\varepsilon_3}{m_3}\right)^2 + \ldots\right\}^2\right]$$

or, equivalently,

$$E\left[\left(\frac{x_1}{x_3}\right)^2\right] = \frac{m_1^2}{m_3^2}E\left[1 + 2\frac{\varepsilon_1}{m_1} - 2\frac{\varepsilon_3}{m_3} + \left(\frac{\varepsilon_1}{m_1}\right)^2 + 3\left(\frac{\varepsilon_3}{m_3}\right)^2 + 4\frac{\varepsilon_1}{m_1}\frac{\varepsilon_3}{m_3} + \ldots\right]$$

Evaluating this latter expression shows

$$E\left[\left(\frac{x_1}{x_3}\right)^2\right] = \frac{m_1^2}{m_3^2}\left(1 + \frac{\sigma_1^2}{m_1^2} + \frac{3\sigma_3^2}{m_3^2} + \ldots\right)$$

where $\sigma_1^2 = E(\varepsilon_1^2)$ is the variance of the variable ε_1. It then follows that the variance of this first deflated variable is given by

$$\begin{aligned}\mathrm{Var}\left(\frac{x_1}{x_3}\right) = E\left[\left(\frac{x_1}{x_3}\right)^2\right] - \left[E\left(\frac{x_1}{x_3}\right)\right]^2 = \frac{m_1^2}{m_3^2}\left(1 + \frac{\sigma_1^2}{m_1^2} + \frac{3\sigma_3^2}{m_3^2} + \ldots\right) \\ - \frac{m_1^2}{m_3^2}\left(1 + \frac{2\sigma_3^2}{m_3^2} + \frac{\sigma_3^4}{m_2^4} + \ldots\right)\end{aligned}$$

where Var(·) is the variance operator. Simplifying the above expression then shows

$$\mathrm{Var}\left(\frac{x_1}{x_3}\right) = \frac{m_1^2}{m_3^2}\left(\frac{\sigma_1^2}{m_1^2} + \frac{\sigma_3^2}{m_3^2} + \ldots\right)$$

Similar calculations can be applied to the second deflated variable, in which case we have

$$\frac{x_2}{x_3} = \frac{m_2 + \varepsilon_2}{m_3 + \varepsilon_3} = \frac{m_2}{m_3}\frac{1 + \dfrac{\varepsilon_2}{m_2}}{1 + \dfrac{\varepsilon_3}{m_3}} = \frac{m_2}{m_3}\left(1 + \frac{\varepsilon_2}{m_2}\right)\left[1 - \frac{\varepsilon_3}{m_3} + \left(\frac{\varepsilon_3}{m_3}\right)^2 + \ldots\right]$$

or, equivalently,

$$\frac{x_2}{x_3} = \frac{m_2}{m_3}\left[1 + \frac{\varepsilon_2}{m_2} - \frac{\varepsilon_3}{m_3} + \left(\frac{\varepsilon_3}{m_3}\right)^2 - \frac{\varepsilon_2}{m_2}\frac{\varepsilon_3}{m_3} + \frac{\varepsilon_2}{m_2}\left(\frac{\varepsilon_3}{m_3}\right)^2 + \ldots\right]$$

where $E(x_2) = m_2$ is the mean of the variable x_2 and $\varepsilon_2 = x_2 - m_2$. Taking expectations across the above expression then shows

$$E\left(\frac{x_2}{x_3}\right) = \frac{m_2}{m_3}\left(1 + \frac{\sigma_3^2}{m_3^2} + \ldots\right)$$

Moreover, we can use similar procedures to those applied to the first deflated variable in order to show that the variance of this second deflated variable will be

$$\text{Var}\left(\frac{x_2}{x_3}\right) = \frac{m_2^2}{m_3^2}\left(\frac{\sigma_2^2}{m_2^2} + \frac{\sigma_3^2}{m_3^2} + \ldots\right)$$

where $\sigma_2^2 = E(\varepsilon_2^2)$ is the variance of the variable ε_2. Finally, we can determine the covariance between the first deflated variable, x_1/x_3, and the second deflated variable, x_2/x_3, as follows:

$$\text{Cov}\left(\frac{x_1}{x_3}, \frac{x_2}{x_3}\right) = \text{Cov}\left(\frac{m_1}{m_3}\left[1 + \frac{\varepsilon_1}{m_1} - \frac{\varepsilon_3}{m_3} + \left(\frac{\varepsilon_3}{m_3}\right)^2 + \ldots\right],\right.$$
$$\left.\frac{m_2}{m_3}\left[1 + \frac{\varepsilon_2}{m_2} - \frac{\varepsilon_3}{m_3} + \left(\frac{\varepsilon_3}{m_3}\right)^2 + \ldots\right]\right)$$

Evaluating this expression gives

$$\text{Cov}\left(\frac{x_1}{x_3}, \frac{x_2}{x_3}\right) = 3\frac{m_1 m_2}{m_3^2}\frac{\sigma_3^2}{m_3^2} + \ldots$$

The important point to make here is that above result shows that there will in general be a non-trivial covariance between the deflated variables x_1/x_3 and x_2/x_3, even though, in levels, x_1 and x_2 are uncorrelated, that is, $\text{Cov}(x_1, x_2) = 0$.

§10-8. Now, suppose we run a simple least squares regression of the first deflated variable, x_1/x_3, against the second deflated variable, x_2/x_3, namely,

$$\frac{x_1}{x_3} = \delta_0 + \delta_1\frac{x_2}{x_3}$$

where

$$\delta_0 = E\left(\frac{x_1}{x_3}\right) - \delta_1 E\left(\frac{x_2}{x_3}\right)$$

is the constant in the regression equation and

$$\delta_1 = \frac{\text{Cov}\left(\frac{x_1}{x_3}, \frac{x_2}{x_3}\right)}{\text{Var}\left(\frac{x_2}{x_3}\right)} \approx \frac{3\frac{m_1}{m_2}}{1 + \frac{\sigma_2^2}{\sigma_3^2}\frac{m_3^2}{m_2^2}} \neq 0$$

is the slope parameter. Likewise, the coefficient of determination associated with the least squares regression between the two deflated variables will be

$$R^2\left(\frac{x_1}{x_3}, \frac{x_2}{x_3}\right) = \frac{\left[\text{Cov}\left(\frac{x_1}{x_3}, \frac{x_2}{x_3}\right)\right]^2}{\text{Var}\left(\frac{x_1}{x_3}\right)\text{Var}\left(\frac{x_2}{x_3}\right)} \approx \frac{9}{\left(1+\frac{\sigma_1^2}{m_1^2}\frac{m_3^2}{\sigma_3^2}\right)\left(1+\frac{\sigma_2^2}{m_2^2}\frac{m_3^2}{\sigma_3^2}\right)} \neq 0$$

The important point to take from this regression procedure is that there is a non-trivial relationship between the two deflated variables; both the $R^2(x_1/x_3, x_2/x_3)$ statistic and the slope parameter δ_1 are different from zero. One might be tempted to conclude from this that there is a non-trivial relationship between x_1 and x_2. Unfortunately, this would be a totally incorrect inference.

We can further emphasize the point being made here by conducting the regression in levels rather than in the deflated variables. Thus, a regression conducted in the levels of x_1 and x_2 will take the following form:

$$x_1 = \delta_0 + \delta_1 . x_2$$

It will then be the case that $\delta_0 = m_1 - \delta_1 m_2$ will be the constant in the regression equation and

$$\delta_1 = \frac{\text{Cov}(x_1, x_2)}{\text{Var}(x_2)} = \frac{0}{\sigma_2^2} = 0$$

will be the slope parameter since, by assumption, the variables x_1 and x_2 are uncorrelated (as in §10-7 above). Moreover, the coefficient of determination associated with the least squares regression between the levels of the two variables will be

$$R^2(x_1, x_2) = \frac{[\text{Cov}(x_1, x_2)]^2}{\text{Var}(x_1)\text{Var}(x_2)} = \frac{0}{\sigma_1^2\sigma_2^2} = 0$$

Hence, not surprisingly, a regression conducted in the levels of the two variables shows that they are completely unrelated – in a linear sense at least.

This simple example should alert the reader to the dangers that can arise when conducting empirical work with scaled or deflated data. In this simple example a least squares regression based on the deflated variables indicates that there is a non-trivial correlation between the two variables, even though the equivalent regression procedure conducted in levels confirms our initial assumption in §10-7 that the two variables are completely unrelated. In other words, deflating data before the regression procedure is applied has induced a form of spurious correlation between the regression variables. This in turn can lead the researcher to the conclusion that there is a non-trivial relationship between the regression variables when in fact the data on which the regression procedure is based are completely unrelated.

Examples of spurious correlations arising out of the deflation procedure demonstrated here are not difficult to find in the literature. Probably the most commonly encountered example is where the return on a firm's equity is regressed against its earnings deflated by the market price of its equity. We can illustrate this in terms of the notation employed earlier by letting $x_3 = P(t)$ be the price of an equity security at time t. It then follows that $x_1 = \Delta P(t) = P(t+\Delta t) - P(t)$ is the increment in the market price of the firm's equity over the period from time t until time $t+\Delta t$. Moreover, we can let $x_2 = E(t)$ be the firm's earnings over the period from time t until time $t+\Delta t$. It then follows that

$$\frac{x_1}{x_3} = \frac{\Delta P(t)}{P(t)}$$

will be the return on the firm's equity and

$$\frac{x_2}{x_3} = \frac{E(t)}{P(t)}$$

will be the firm's deflated earnings, both over the period from time t until time $t+\Delta t$. The regression equation will then take the form

$$\frac{x_1}{x_3} = \delta_0 + \delta_1 \frac{x_2}{x_3}$$

where δ_0 and δ_1 are the regression parameters defined earlier. Note that since the return on a firm's equity,

$$\frac{x_1}{x_3} = \frac{\Delta P(t)}{P(t)}$$

is merely the increment in the market price of the firm's equity over the given period divided by the opening market price of its equity, it necessarily follows that the opening market price $x_3 = P(t)$ is nothing more than a deflation factor applied to both sides of the regression equation. This will mean that even when the increment $x_1 = \Delta P(t)$ in the market price of a firm's equity is uncorrelated with the firm's earnings $x_2 = E(t)$, there will still be a spurious and non-trivial correlation between the return on the firm's equity and its deflated earnings.

§10-9. There is a further issue of considerable importance that arises out of the deflation (or scaling) procedures analysed in §10-6 to §10-8 above. This stems from the fact that researchers invariably assume that the variables on which their empirical analysis is based are normally distributed. We can demonstrate the importance of this assumption by considering the *uncorrelated* variables x_1 and x_2, both of which are assumed to be distributed as standard normal variates. We would emphasize here that the case of correlated variables is more complicated, but essentially the same results as we are about to report go through. Now, suppose that an empirical researcher uses the variable x_2 as a deflation factor, in which case the empirical analysis will be conducted in terms of the deflated variable $z = x_1/x_2$. It is well known that the probability density function of the ratio z of two uncorrelated standard normal variates is given by

$$f(z) = \frac{1}{\pi(1+z^2)}$$

This is the Cauchy–Lorentz probability density function of mathematical statistics, otherwise known as Student's 't' with one degree of freedom. Suppose we seek to determine the expected value (i.e. the mean) of the deflated variable $z = x_1/x_2$ by evaluating the integral

$$E(z) = \int_{-\infty}^{\infty} zf(z)dz = \frac{1}{\pi}\int_{-\infty}^{\infty} \frac{zdz}{1+z^2}$$

Now, we can split the above integral into two components, namely,

$$E(z) = \frac{1}{\pi}\int_{-\infty}^{0} \frac{zdz}{1+z^2} + \frac{1}{\pi}\int_{0}^{\infty} \frac{zdz}{1+z^2}$$

We can then evaluate the second of the integrals on the right-hand side of this expression by making the substitution $y = \log(1+z^2)$. It follows from this that

$$\frac{1}{2}dy = \frac{zdz}{1+z^2}$$

Substituting these latter two expressions into the affected integral then gives

$$\frac{1}{\pi}\int_{0}^{\infty} \frac{zdz}{1+z^2} = \frac{1}{2\pi}\int_{0}^{\infty} dy = \frac{1}{2\pi}[y]_0^{\infty} = \lim_{y\to\infty} \frac{y}{2\pi}$$

Unfortunately, this is a divergent integral, in which case $E(z)$ is undefined. This has the important implication that none of the moments for the Cauchy–Lorentz probability density function are well defined. This in turn means that determining the significance of the regression coefficients associated with deflated variables on the assumption that the deflated variables are normally distributed has the potential to lead to seriously misleading inferences about the significance of the affected coefficients and the empirical validity of the underlying model.

§10-10. Empirical work dealing with the relationship between the market value of a firm's equity and its determining variables is normally based on some form of linear model that neglects the adaptations options associated with the firm's ability to modify or even abandon its existing operating activities. It is well known, however, that firms typically possesses adaptation options and that these options induce a convex and highly non-linear relationship between the market value of equity and its determining variables. Given this, it is all but inevitable that when adaptation options do impact on equity values, systematic biases will arise in empirical work based on linear valuation models that assume that the market value of a firm's equity is exclusively composed of its recursion value. We have analysed the biases that arise from assuming that the market value of a firm's equity is composed exclusively of its recursion value by employing an orthogonal polynomial fitting procedure that identifies the relative contribution that the linear and non-linear components of the relationship between equity value and its determining variables make towards overall equity value. The evidence from this procedure is that the non-linearities in equity valuation can be large and significant, particularly for firms where the recursion value of equity is comparatively small. Moreover, empirical work in this area is invariably based on market and/or accounting (book) variables that are scaled or deflated in order to facilitate comparisons between firms of different size. Given this, it is important that one appreciates how these deflation procedures might alter or even distort the underlying levels relationship between the market value of equity and its determining variables. Our analysis of this issue has shown that deflating data before regression procedures are applied can lead to a form of spurious correlation between the regression variables. This in turn can lead a researcher to the conclusion that there is a non-trivial relationship between the regression variables when in fact the data on which the regression analysis is based are completely unrelated. Moreover, if one assumes that the numerator and denominator of a deflated variable are normally distributed then the deflated variable itself may evolve in terms of a probability density function that possesses no convergent moments. This will mean that determining the significance of the regression coefficients associated with deflated variables on the assumption that the deflated variables are normally distributed can lead to seriously misleading inferences about the significance of the affected coefficients.

Selected references

Abramowitz, M. and Stegun, I. (eds) (1965) *Handbook of Mathematical Functions with Formulas, Graphs, and Mathematical Tables*, New York: Dover.

Akbar, S. and Stark, A. (2003) 'Discussion of scale and the scale effect in market-based accounting research', *Journal of Business Finance and Accounting*, 30: 57–72.

Ataullah, A., Rhys, H. and Tippett, M. (2009) 'Non-linear equity valuation', *Accounting and Business Research*, 39: 57–73.

Barth, M., Beaver, W. and Landsman, W. (1998) 'Relative valuation roles of equity, book value and net income as a function of financial health', *Journal of Accounting and Economics*, 25: 1–34.

Barth, M. and Clinch, G. (2009) 'Scale effects in capital markets-based accounting research', *Journal of Business Finance and Accounting*, 36: 253–88.

Easton, P. and Sommers, G. (2003) 'Scale and the scale effect in market-based accounting research', *Journal of Business Finance and Accounting*, 30: 25–56.

Freeman, H. (1963) *Introduction to Statistical Inference*, Reading, MA: Addison-Wesley.

Pearson, K. (1897) 'Mathematical contributions to the theory of evolution – on a form of spurious correlation which may arise when indices are used in the measurement of organs', *Proceedings of the Royal Society of London*, 60: 489–98.

Exercises

1. Consider a standardized random variable x that is symmetrical about its mean. Let x and y be functionally related through the formula $y = x^2$. Show that the coefficient of determination

$$R^2(x,y) = \frac{[\mathrm{Cov}(x,y)]^2}{\mathrm{Var}(x)\mathrm{Var}(y)}$$

between x and y (as in §10-8) is zero. What does this result tell you about the limitations of assessing the strength of the relationship between two variables in terms of the coefficient of determination?

2. It is asserted in §10-3 that the Fourier coefficient α_0 for the equity valuation function with respect to the Laguerre polynomial of order zero, $L_0(\eta) = 1$, is given by

$$\alpha_0 = \int_0^\infty e^{-\eta} P(\eta) L_0(\eta) d\eta = \theta \log\left(\frac{\theta}{1+\theta}\right) + 2$$

where

$$P(\eta) = \eta + \frac{1}{2} \int_{-1}^{1} \exp\left(-\frac{2\theta\eta}{1+z}\right) dz$$

is the equity valuation function. Evaluate the integral in the expression for α_0 and thereby confirm the above result.

3. It is asserted in §10-3 that the Fourier coefficient α_1 for the equity valuation function with respect to the Laguerre polynomial of order one, $L_1(\eta) = 1 - \eta$, is given by

$$\alpha_1 = \int_0^\infty e^{-\eta} P(\eta) L_1(\eta) d\eta = -1 - \frac{\theta}{1+\theta} - \theta \log\left(\frac{\theta}{1+\theta}\right)$$

where $P(\eta)$ is the equity valuation function defined in Exercise 2. Evaluate the integral in the expression for α_1 and thereby confirm the above result.

4. It is asserted in §10-3 that the Fourier coefficient α_m for the equity valuation function with respect to the Laguerre polynomial of order $m \geq 2$, $L_m(\eta)$, is given by

$$\alpha_m = \int_0^\infty e^{-\eta} P(\eta) L_m(\eta) d\eta = \frac{\theta(1+\theta)^m - (m+\theta)\theta^m}{m(m-1)(1+\theta)^m}$$

where $P(\eta)$ is the equity valuation function defined in Exercise 2,

$$L_m(\eta) = C_0^m - C_1^m \eta + C_2^m \frac{\eta^2}{2!} - C_3^m \frac{\eta^3}{3!} + \ldots + (-1)^m C_m^m \frac{\eta^m}{m!}$$

is the Laguerre polynomial of order m and

$$C_k^m = \frac{m!}{k!(m-k)!}$$

for $k = 1, 2, 3, \ldots, m$ is the binomial coefficient. Evaluate the integral expression for α_m and thereby confirm the above result.

5. In §9-6 of Chapter 9, it was assumed that the recursion value of equity $\eta(t)$ evolves in terms of the Ornstein–Uhlenbeck process

$$\frac{d\eta(t)}{dt} = r\eta(t) + \frac{dq(t)}{dt}$$

where r is the cost of equity and $dq(t)/dt$ is a white noise process with variance parameter ζ^2. In Exercise 1 of Chapter 9, it was shown that the solution of the Hamilton–Jacobi–Bellman equation associated with the Ornstein–Uhlenbeck process, and therefore the value of the firm's equity, will be

$$P(\eta) = \eta + \frac{P(0)}{2}\int_{-1}^{1} \exp\left[\frac{-2\theta\eta^2}{(1+z)^2}\right] dz$$

where $\theta = 2r/\zeta^2$ is a risk (or stability) parameter and $P(0)$ represents the adaptation value of the firm's equity should its recursion value η fall away to nothing. Show that the above equity valuation formula is scale-invariant under the dilation $\lambda = 1/\Theta$ (where Θ is an arbitrary real number) with a scaling dimension of $\Delta = 1$.

11 Equity valuation

Multivariate investment opportunity sets

§11-1. In §9-5 of Chapter 9, we developed an equity pricing formula based on the clean surplus identity, which, it will be recalled, is an equation that links the increment in the book value of a firm's equity to the accounting (i.e. book) profit that the firm earns over any given period of time. In particular, clean surplus accounting requires that all profits earned and all losses incurred by a firm are recorded in the firm's profit and loss account and that increments in the book value of the firm's equity are composed of the profit (or loss) appearing on the firm's profit and loss account less any provisions that have been made for the payment of dividends. Here we need to note, however, that there are occasions when accounting standards require firms to exclude certain profits and/or losses from the 'bottom' line earnings (i.e. profit or loss) figure reported in their financial statements (e.g. profits and losses on the disposal of fixed assets). This in turn will mean that the increment in the book value of the firm's equity will not be equal to the earnings figure appearing on the firm's profit and loss account for the period. Given this, our first brief in this chapter is to generalize the canonical equity pricing formula developed in Chapter 9 to remove its dependence on the clean surplus identity. Our analysis of this issue is based on two dirty surplus propositions. The first of these shows how the recursion value of equity is determined when the clean surplus identity does not hold, that is, when there is a form of dirty surplus accounting. The second proposition outlines how the system of stochastic differential equations that characterize the firm's investment opportunity set must be modified so as to encompass dirty surplus accounting. Our analysis of this second proposition is based on a multiplicity of determining variables. We do this because it is highly likely that in practice the market value of a firm's equity will hinge on a large number of determining variables and not just the two (abnormal earnings and the information variable) on which the canonical pricing formula developed in Chapter 9 is based. We then move on to assess the impact that the explicit incorporation of dividend payments into our modelling procedures can have on equity valuation. In common with results reported in the real options literature, our analysis shows that whilst the recursion value of equity does not hinge on the firm's dividend policy, the adaptation value of equity will in general be affected by the dividend policy invoked by the firm. Against this, our analysis also shows that, for parsimonious dividend payout assumptions (e.g. dividend payments that are proportional to the recursion value of equity), the 'structure' of the equity valuation formula is similar (although with some very important differences) to the canonical equity valuation formula developed in Chapter 9.

§11-2. We begin the analysis in this chapter by defining $b(t)$ as the book value of a firm's equity, $x(t)$ as the instantaneous accounting (or book) earnings (per unit time) attributable to equity, $D(t)$ as the instantaneous dividend (per unit time) paid to equity holders and $\varepsilon(t)$ as the instantaneous dirty surplus adjustment (per unit time), all at time t. It then follows that the increment in the book value of the firm's equity, $db(t) = b(t+dt) - b(t)$, over the instantaneous period from time t until time $t + dt$ will be described by the dirty surplus equation

$$db(t) = [x(t) + \varepsilon(t) - D(t)]dt$$

or, if stated on a per unit time basis,

$$\frac{db(t)}{dt} = x(t) + \varepsilon(t) - D(t)$$

Note that if we set the dirty surplus variable $\varepsilon(t)$ to be identically equal to zero then we will have the clean surplus identity as developed in §5-10 of Chapter 5. Now, it will be recalled here (as in §9-2) that the recursion value of equity $\eta(t)$ is the present value of the stream of future dividends the firm expects to pay computed under the assumption that the firm's existing investment opportunity set will remain in force indefinitely, or

$$\eta(t) = E_t\left[\int_t^\infty e^{-r(s-t)} D(s)ds\right]$$

where $E_t[\cdot]$ is the expectation operator taken at time t and r is the cost of capital (per unit time) applicable to equity. Moreover, we can use the dirty surplus equation in conjunction with the above expression for the recursion value of equity to link the expected present value of the firm's dividends to its bookkeeping and other information variables. To do this, we first note that the dirty surplus equation given earlier will mean that that the dividend payment at time s can be expressed as

$$D(s)ds = [x(s) + \varepsilon(s)]ds - db(s)$$

Substituting this result into the expression for the recursion value of equity $\eta(t)$ given above then gives

$$\eta(t) = E_t\left[\int_t^\infty e^{-r(s-t)}[x(s) + \varepsilon(s)]ds\right] - E_t\left[\int_t^\infty e^{-r(s-t)} db(s)\right]$$

Now, if we apply integration by parts to the final term on the right-hand side of this expression, it follows that

$$\int_t^\infty e^{-r(s-t)} db(s) = \left[e^{-r(s-t)} b(s)\right]_t^\infty + r\int_t^\infty e^{-r(s-t)} b(s)ds$$

We can then ensure that the recursion value of equity will remain finite for all t by imposing the following transversality requirement (as in §9-4):

$$\lim_{s\to\infty} e^{-r(s-t)} E_t[b(s)] = 0$$

This will mean that the final term in the above expression for the recursion value of equity can be evaluated as

$$E_t\left[\int_t^\infty e^{-r(s-t)}db(s)\right] = -b(t) + rE_t\left[\int_t^\infty e^{-r(s-t)}b(s)ds\right]$$

Moreover, substitution then shows that the recursion value of the firm's equity can be restated as

$$\eta(t) = E_t\left[\int_t^\infty e^{-r(s-t)}[x(s)+\varepsilon(s)]ds\right] + b(t) - rE_t\left[\int_t^\infty e^{-r(s-t)}b(s)ds\right]$$

or equivalently

$$\eta(t) = b(t) + E_t\left[\int_t^\infty e^{-r(s-t)}a(s)ds\right] + E_t\left[\int_t^\infty e^{-r(s-t)}\varepsilon(s)ds\right]$$

where $a(t) = x(t) - rb(t)$ is the abnormal earnings (per unit time) attributable to the firm's equity (as in §5-10). This shows that under dirty surplus accounting the expected present value of the future stream of dividends to be paid by the firm is equivalent to the book value of the firm's equity plus the expected present value of the stream of abnormal earnings and the expected present value of the stream of dirty surplus adjustments, where in both cases the expectation is taken at time t. Note how this result exhibits one crucial difference when compared with the 'equivalent' formulation based on the clean surplus identity as summarized in §5-10 and §9-5. This is that under the clean surplus identity there can, by definition, be no dirty surplus adjustments and so the recursion value of equity will be based on only the first two terms on the right-hand side of the above expression for the recursion value of equity. That is, when the clean surplus identity holds, the expected present value of the stream of dirty surplus adjustments, $E_t\left[\int_t^\infty e^{-i(s-t)}\varepsilon(s)ds\right]$, will be identically equal to zero. The dirty surplus integral given here has some important implications for the valuation of a firm's equity, and so we now develop them in further detail.

§11-3. We begin by supposing that the firm's investment opportunity set can be summarized in terms of the following vector system of stochastic differential equations:

$$\begin{pmatrix} \frac{da(t)}{dt} \\ \frac{dv(t)}{dt} \\ \frac{d\varepsilon(t)}{dt} \end{pmatrix} = \begin{pmatrix} c_{11} & c_{12} & c_{13} \\ c_{21} & c_{22} & c_{23} \\ c_{31} & c_{32} & c_{33} \end{pmatrix} \begin{pmatrix} a(t) \\ v(t) \\ \varepsilon(t) \end{pmatrix} + \eta^\delta(t) \begin{pmatrix} k_1 & 0 & 0 \\ 0 & k_2 & 0 \\ 0 & 0 & k_3 \end{pmatrix} \begin{pmatrix} \frac{dz_1(t)}{dt} \\ \frac{dz_2(t)}{dt} \\ \frac{dz_3(t)}{dt} \end{pmatrix}$$

or

$$\underset{\sim}{u}'(t) = Q\underset{\sim}{u}(t) + \eta^\delta(t)K\underset{\sim}{z}'(t)$$

Here $\underset{\sim}{u}(t)$ is the vector whose elements are the abnormal earnings $a(t)$ attributable to equity, the information variable $v(t)$ that captures all the information relevant to the value of the firm's equity but that has not, as yet, been incorporated into the firm's accounting records, and the dirty surplus variable $\varepsilon(t)$. $\underset{\sim}{u}'(t)$ is the vector whose elements are the derivatives of the variables comprising the firm's investment opportunity set. Q is the matrix whose elements are the structural coefficients associated with the firm's investment opportunity set and K is a matrix whose diagonal elements are a set of 'normalizing' constants (as in §9-2). All the off-diagonal terms of K are zero. The normalizing constants simplify the algebra associated with manipulating the firm's investment opportunity set and are computed according to the procedure laid down in §11-5 and §11-7 below. The elements of the vector $\underset{\sim}{z}'(t)$ are $dz_1(t)/dt$, which is a white noise process with variance parameter $\sigma_1^2, dz_2(t)/dt$, which is a white noise process with variance parameter σ_2^2, and $dz_3(t)/dt$, which is a white noise process with variance parameter σ_3^2. We assume, without loss of generality, that the three white noise processes are uncorrelated (as in §8-9 and §9-2). Finally, $0 \leq \delta \leq \frac{1}{2}$ is a real number that ensures that the market value of the firm's equity remains finite as the recursion value approaches a limiting value of zero. It also encapsulates the requirement that the variance associated with instantaneous changes in the variables comprising the firm's investment opportunity set become larger as the recursion value of equity grows in magnitude (as in §9-2).

There are several points about the investment opportunity set given here that require further amplification. First amongst these is that simple algebraic manipulation shows how the firm's abnormal earnings evolve in terms of the following process:

$$\frac{da(t)}{dt} = -c_{11}\left[\frac{-c_{12}\nu(t) - c_{13}\varepsilon(t)}{c_{11}} - a(t)\right]dt + k_1\eta^{\delta}(t)\frac{dz_1(t)}{dt}$$

Thus, the system of stochastic differential equations employed here implies that, apart from a stochastic component, the firm's current abnormal earnings $a(t)$ will gravitate towards a long-run mean of

$$\frac{-c_{12}\nu(t) - c_{13}\varepsilon(t)}{c_{11}}$$

The force with which it will do so is proportional to the difference between this long-run mean and the current instantaneous abnormal earnings $a(t)$, where the speed-of-adjustment coefficient is $c_{11} < 0$. The long-run mean of the abnormal earnings variable can be thought of as a weighted average of the current information variable $\nu(t)$ and the dirty surplus variable $\varepsilon(t)$. The weights applied to these variables to determine the long-run mean for $a(t)$ are $-c_{12}/c_{11}$ and $-c_{13}/c_{11}$, respectively. Furthermore, whilst one might normally expect the first of these weights, $-c_{12}/c_{11}$, to be positive, reflecting the fact that favourable information will usually imply larger future abnormal profits, there are conflicting forces determining the sign of the weight associated with the dirty surplus variable. Intuition suggests that positive dirty surplus adjustments would normally have favourable implications for future profitability, in which case $-c_{13}/c_{11}$ ought to be positive. However, this argument ignores a myriad other factors, such as the potential political and regulatory costs associated with a continuing history of 'excess' abnormal profits and the fact that, over time, excessive profits will normally dissipate under the influence of competitive pressures. These factors suggest that management will have incentives to use whatever flexibility is available to them in accounting standards to conceal the magnitude of current and future abnormal earnings. This points to the possibility of a negative value for $-c_{13}/c_{11}$. The sum result of these considerations is that it is probably reasonable to assume that c_{12} is positive, thereby implying that the weight associated with the information variable, $-c_{12}/c_{11}$, will also be positive. It is less clear, however, what sign the coefficient c_{13} will take, in which case it follows that the weight, $-c_{13}/c_{11}$, associated with the dirty surplus variable could be positive, negative or even zero.

The investment opportunity set defined earlier also implies that the information variable will evolve in accordance with the following differential equation:

$$\frac{d\nu(t)}{dt} = -c_{22}\left[\frac{-c_{21}a(t) - c_{23}\varepsilon(t)}{c_{22}} - \nu(t)\right]dt + k_2\eta^{\delta}(t)\frac{dz_2(t)}{dt}$$

This will mean that, apart from a stochastic component, the information variable gravitates towards a long-run mean of

$$\frac{-c_{21}a(t) - c_{23}\varepsilon(t)}{c_{22}}$$

with a speed-of-adjustment coefficient of $c_{22} < 0$. Here, it will be recalled that the information variable $\nu(t)$ captures all information that is relevant to the value of a firm's equity but that has not, as yet, been incorporated into the firm's accounting records (as in §9-1). It thus follows that $\nu(t)$ is prospective in nature and that, because of this, neither $a(t)$ nor $\varepsilon(t)$, both of which are generally retrospective in nature, can adequately reflect or capture movements in the long-run mean of the information variable $\nu(t)$. These arguments suggest that both c_{21} and c_{23} will be (close to) zero.

Finally, the investment opportunity set shows that the dirty surplus variable evolves in terms of the following differential equation:

$$\frac{d\varepsilon(t)}{dt} = -c_{33}\left[\frac{-c_{31}a(t) - c_{32}\nu(t)}{c_{33}} - \varepsilon(t)\right]dt + k_3\eta^{\delta}(t)\frac{dz_3(t)}{dt}$$

Hence, the dirty surplus variable will gravitate towards a long-run mean of

$$\frac{-c_{31}a(t) - c_{32}\nu(t)}{c_{33}}$$

with a speed-of-adjustment coefficient $c_{33} < 0$. Now, we have previously noted that potential political, regulatory and competitive factors will mean that managers have incentives to adopt accounting policies that reduce the firm's abnormal earnings. This suggests that the weight associated with the abnormal earnings variable, $-c_{31}/c_{33}$, will be positive, since managers can use the dirty surplus adjustment to reduce the firm's (headline) abnormal earnings. Furthermore, since favourable information $\nu(t)$ will normally have positive implications for future profitability (and therefore the manipulation of profits through the dirty surplus variable), it appears reasonable to assume that the weight associated with the information variable, $-c_{32}/c_{33}$, is also likely to be positive. This will mean that both the structural coefficients c_{31} and c_{32} are likely to be positive.

§11-4. We can make further progress towards determining the value of a firm's equity under the investment opportunity set defined in §11-3 by replicating the argument given in §9-4 to show that the expected present value of the stream of future abnormal earnings will be

$$E_t\left[\int_t^{\infty} e^{-r(s-t)}a(s)ds\right] = \frac{a(t)}{r} + \frac{1}{r}E_t\left[\int_t^{\infty} e^{-r(s-t)}\frac{da(s)}{ds}ds\right]$$

However, it will be recalled from the system of stochastic differential equations describing the firm's investment opportunity set (as in §11-3) that the abnormal earnings variable evolves in terms of the following differential equation:

$$\frac{da(s)}{ds} = c_{11}a(s) + c_{12}\nu(s) + c_{13}\varepsilon(s) + k_1\eta^{\delta}(s)\frac{dz_1(s)}{ds}$$

We can substitute this result into the expression for the present value of the future abnormal earnings stream and thereby show

$$E_t\left[\int_t^{\infty} e^{-r(s-t)}a(s)ds\right] =$$

$$\frac{a(t)}{r} + E_t\left[\frac{1}{r}\int_t^{\infty} e^{-r(s-t)}\left(c_{11}a(s) + c_{12}\nu(s) + c_{13}\varepsilon(s) + k_1\eta^{\delta}(s)\frac{dz_1(s)}{ds}\right)ds\right]$$

However, since $E_t[dz_1(s)/ds] = 0$ for all $s > t$, it necessarily follows that the above result can be restated as

$$E_t\left[\int_t^{\infty} e^{-r(s-t)}a(s)ds\right] =$$

$$\frac{a(r)}{r} + \frac{c_{11}}{r}E_t\left[\int_t^{\infty} e^{-r(s-t)}a(s)ds\right] + \frac{c_{12}}{r}E_t\left[\int_t^{\infty} e^{-r(s-t)}\nu(s)ds\right]$$

$$+ \frac{c_{13}}{r}E_t\left[\int_t^{\infty} e^{-r(s-t)}\varepsilon(s)ds\right]$$

We can then multiply through the above expression by r, in which case we have

$$a(t) = rE_t\left[\int_t^{\infty} e^{-r(s-t)}a(s)ds\right]$$

$$-\left\{c_{11}E_t\left[\int_t^{\infty} e^{-r(s-t)}a(s)ds\right] + c_{12}E_t\left[\int_t^{\infty} e^{-r(s-t)}\nu(s)ds\right] + c_{13}E_t\left[\int_t^{\infty} e^{-r(s-t)}\varepsilon(s)ds\right]\right\}$$

Similar calculations show that the information variable $\nu(t)$ will satisfy the following present-value condition:

$$\nu(t) = rE_t\left[\int_t^{\infty} e^{-r(s-t)}\nu(s)ds\right] - \left\{c_{21}E_t\left[\int_t^{\infty} e^{-r(s-t)}a(s)ds\right] + c_{22}E_t\left[\int_t^{\infty} e^{-r(s-t)}\nu(s)ds\right] + c_{23}E_t\left[\int_t^{\infty} e^{-r(s-t)}\varepsilon(s)ds\right]\right\}$$

Finally, the expected present value of the future stream of dirty surplus adjustments will satisfy the condition:

$$\varepsilon(t) = rE_t\left[\int_t^{\infty} e^{-r(s-t)}\varepsilon(s)ds\right] - \left\{c_{31}E_t\left[\int_t^{\infty} e^{-r(s-t)}a(s)ds\right] + c_{32}E_t\left[\int_t^{\infty} e^{-r(s-t)}\nu(s)ds\right] + c_{33}E_t\left[\int_t^{\infty} e^{-r(s-t)}\varepsilon(s)ds\right]\right\}$$

Now, we can state these latter three results in matrix form as follows:

$$\begin{pmatrix} a(t) \\ \nu(t) \\ \varepsilon(t) \end{pmatrix} = \left[r\begin{pmatrix} 1\,0\,0 \\ 0\,1\,0 \\ 0\,0\,1 \end{pmatrix} - \begin{pmatrix} c_{11}\ c_{12}\ c_{13} \\ c_{21}\ c_{22}\ c_{23} \\ c_{31}\ c_{32}\ c_{33} \end{pmatrix}\right]\begin{pmatrix} E_t\left[\int_t^{\infty} e^{-r(s-t)}a(s)ds\right] \\ E_t\left[\int_t^{\infty} e^{-r(s-t)}\nu(s)ds\right] \\ E_t\left[\int_t^{\infty} e^{-r(s-t)}\varepsilon(s)ds\right] \end{pmatrix}$$

or

$$\underset{\sim}{u}(t) = (rI - Q)\underset{\sim}{J}(t)$$

It follows from this that

$$\begin{pmatrix} E_t\left[\int_t^{\infty} e^{-r(s-t)}a(s)ds\right] \\ E_t\left[\int_t^{\infty} e^{-r(s-t)}\nu(s)ds\right] \\ E_t\left[\int_t^{\infty} e^{-r(s-t)}\varepsilon(s)ds\right] \end{pmatrix} = \underset{\sim}{J}(t) = (rI - Q)^{-1}\underset{\sim}{u}(t)$$

Now, we can pre-multiply the vector $\underset{\sim}{J}(t)$ by the vector $(\,1\ 0\ 1\,)$ and thereby show

$$(1\,0\,1)\begin{pmatrix} E_t\left[\int_t^{\infty} e^{-r(s-t)}a(s)ds\right] \\ E_t\left[\int_t^{\infty} e^{-r(s-t)}\nu(s)ds\right] \\ E_t\left[\int_t^{\infty} e^{-r(s-t)}\varepsilon(s)ds\right] \end{pmatrix} = E_t\left[\int_t^{\infty} e^{-r(s-t)}a(s)ds\right] + E_t\left[\int_t^{\infty} e^{-r(s-t)}\varepsilon(s)ds\right]$$

or equivalently

$$\begin{aligned}(1\ 0\ 1)\underset{\sim}{J}(t) &= (1\ 0\ 1)(rI - Q)^{-1}\underset{\sim}{u}(t)\\ &= E_t\left[\int_t^{\infty} e^{-r(s-t)}a(s)ds\right] + E_t\left[\int_t^{\infty} e^{-r(s-t)}\varepsilon(s)ds\right]\end{aligned}$$

This result then implies that the recursion value of the firm's equity can be stated as follows:

$$\begin{aligned}\eta(t) &= b(t) + E_t\left[\int_t^{\infty} e^{-r(s-t)}a(s)ds\right] + E_t\left[\int_t^{\infty} e^{-r(s-t)}\varepsilon(s)ds\right]\\ &= b(t) + (1\ 0\ 1)(rI - Q)^{-1}\underset{\sim}{u}(t)\end{aligned}$$

Although the analysis in this section is based on just three determining variables, it nonetheless lays down a general procedure for determining the recursion value of equity when there is a multiplicity of determining variables. The important argument in the above equation for $\eta(t)$ is the vector $(rI - Q)^{-1}\underset{\sim}{u}(t)$, whose elements are the expected present values of the variables comprising the firm's investment opportunity set. We can determine the recursion value of equity by simply specifying a vector comprised of zeroes and ones that identifies the determining variables comprising the recursion value of equity (as with the vector $(1\ 0\ 1)$ above) and then taking the inner product of this vector with $(rI - Q)^{-1}\underset{\sim}{u}(t)$. Adding the book value of equity to the outcome of this calculation will then determine the recursion value of the firm's equity. This calculation procedure will be the same irrespective of whether there are two, three or many more determining variables comprising the recursion value of equity.

§11-5. We can determine further properties of the stochastic process which describes the way the recursion value of equity evolves through time by differentiating through the expression for $\eta(t)$ given in §11-4 as follows:

$$\eta'(t) = \frac{d\eta(t)}{dt} = b'(t) + (1\ 0\ 1)(rI - Q)^{-1}\underset{\sim}{u}'(t)$$

where

$$b'(t) = \frac{db(t)}{dt} = x(t) + \varepsilon(t) - D(t) = a(t) + rb(t) + \varepsilon(t) - D(t)$$

encapsulates the dirty surplus identity developed in §11-2 above. Here, it will be recalled that:

$$(1\ 0\ 1)\underset{\sim}{u}(t) = (1\ 0\ 1)\begin{pmatrix} a(t) \\ v(t) \\ \varepsilon(t) \end{pmatrix} = a(t) + \varepsilon(t)$$

in which case the increment in the book value of equity can be described in terms of the following version of the dirty surplus identity:

$$b'(t) = rb(t) - D(t) + (1\ 0\ 1)\underset{\sim}{u}(t)$$

Moreover, this latter interpretation of the dirty surplus identity allows us to state the derivative for the recursion value of equity as follows:

$$\begin{aligned}\eta'(t) &= b'(t) + \begin{pmatrix}1 & 0 & 1\end{pmatrix}(rI - Q)^{-1}\underset{\sim}{u}'(t) \\ &= \left[rb(t) - D(t) + \begin{pmatrix}1 & 0 & 1\end{pmatrix}\underset{\sim}{u}(t)\right] + \begin{pmatrix}1 & 0 & 1\end{pmatrix}(rI - Q)^{-1}\underset{\sim}{u}'(t)\end{aligned}$$

From §11-4, however, we know that the firm's investment opportunity set is described by the following vector system of stochastic differential equations:

$$\underset{\sim}{u}'(t) = Q\underset{\sim}{u}(t) + \eta^{\delta}(t)K\underset{\sim}{z}'(t)$$

Hence, we can use this specification of the firm's investment opportunity set to show that the derivative for the recursion value of equity will be

$$\eta'(t) = \left[rb(t) - D(t) + \begin{pmatrix}1 & 0 & 1\end{pmatrix}\underset{\sim}{u}(t)\right] + \begin{pmatrix}1 & 0 & 1\end{pmatrix}(rI - Q)^{-1}[Q\underset{\sim}{u}(t) + \eta^{\delta}(t)K\underset{\sim}{z}'(t)]$$

or equivalently

$$\begin{aligned}\eta'(t) = rb(t) - D(t) &+ \begin{pmatrix}1 & 0 & 1\end{pmatrix}[I + (rI - Q)^{-1}Q]\underset{\sim}{u}(t) \\ &+ \eta^{\delta}(t)\begin{pmatrix}1 & 0 & 1\end{pmatrix}(rI - Q)^{-1}K\underset{\sim}{z}'(t)\end{aligned}$$

Now consider the term $rI - Q$ in the above equation and in particular the identity

$$(rI - Q) + Q = rI$$

We can premultiply the above equation by $(rI - Q)^{-1}$ and thereby show

$$\begin{aligned}(rI - Q)^{-1}(rI - Q) + (rI - Q)^{-1}Q &= (rI - Q)^{-1}[(rI - Q) + Q] \\ &= rI(rI - Q)^{-1} = r(rI - Q)^{-1}\end{aligned}$$

However, since $(rI - Q)^{-1}(rI - Q) = I$, the above result may be restated as

$$I + (rI - Q)^{-1}Q = r(rI - Q)^{-1}$$

Now, from the final part of §11-4, the recursion value of the firm's equity at time t can be expressed as $\eta(t) = b(t) + (1\ 0\ 1)(rI - Q)^{-1}\underset{\sim}{u}(t)$. This latter expression for the recursion value of equity when used in conjunction with the above result implies

$$rb(t) + \begin{pmatrix}1 & 0 & 1\end{pmatrix}[I + (rI - Q)^{-1}Q]\underset{\sim}{u}(t) = r\left[b(t) + \begin{pmatrix}1 & 0 & 1\end{pmatrix}(rI - Q)^{-1}\underset{\sim}{u}(t)\right] = r\eta(t)$$

We can then again use the fact that $\eta(t) = b(t) + (1\ 0\ 1)(rI - Q)^{-1}\underset{\sim}{u}(t)$ in conjunction with prior results in this section and thereby show that the derivative of the recursion value of equity will be

$$\begin{aligned}\eta'(t) = rb(t) - D(t) &+ \begin{pmatrix}1 & 0 & 1\end{pmatrix}[I + (rI - Q)^{-1}Q]\underset{\sim}{u}(t) \\ &+ \eta^{\delta}(t)\begin{pmatrix}1 & 0 & 1\end{pmatrix}(rI - Q)^{-1}K\underset{\sim}{z}'(t)\end{aligned}$$

Note, however, that this result can be restated as

$$\eta'(t) = r\eta(t) - D(t) + \eta^{\delta}(t)\begin{pmatrix}1 & 0 & 1\end{pmatrix}(rI - Q)^{-1}K\underset{\sim}{z}'(t)$$

We can further simplify the above expression for $\eta'(t)$ by recalling from §11-3 that K is a matrix whose diagonal elements are a set of 'normalizing' constants and whose off-diagonal elements are all zero. Numerical values for the normalizing constants are thus determined by the following identity:

$$\begin{pmatrix}1 & 0 & 1\end{pmatrix}(rI - Q)^{-1}K = \begin{pmatrix}1 & 1 & 1\end{pmatrix}$$

This will mean that the derivative of the recursion value of equity will evolve in terms of the following stochastic process:

$$\eta'(t) = r\eta(t) - D(t) + \eta^{\delta}(t)\begin{pmatrix}1 & 1 & 1\end{pmatrix}\underset{\sim}{z}'(t)$$

where, from §11-3 above,

$$\begin{pmatrix}1 & 1 & 1\end{pmatrix}\underset{\sim}{z}'(t) = \begin{pmatrix}1 & 1 & 1\end{pmatrix}\begin{pmatrix}\frac{dz_1(t)}{dt} \\ \frac{dz_2(t)}{dt} \\ \frac{dz_3(t)}{dt}\end{pmatrix} = \frac{dz_1(t)}{dt} + \frac{dz_2(t)}{dt} + \frac{dz_3(t)}{dt} = \frac{dq(t)}{dt} = q'(t)$$

is a white noise process with variance parameter $\zeta^2 = \sigma_1^2 + \sigma_2^2 + \sigma_3^2$. We can then restate the stochastic process describing the evolution of the derivative $\eta'(t)$ of the recursion value of equity in the following terms:

$$\eta'(t) = r\eta(t) - D(t) + \eta^{\delta}(t)q'(t)$$

or equivalently

$$\frac{d\eta(t)}{dt} = r\eta(t) - D(t) + \eta^{\delta}(t)\frac{dq(t)}{dt}$$

Moreover, if we multiply both sides of the above expression by dt then we will end up with

$$d\eta(t) = [r\eta(t) - D(t)]dt + \eta^{\delta}(t)dq(t)$$

This latter result shows that the increment $d\eta(t) = \eta(t + dt) - \eta(t)$ in the recursion value of equity over the instantaneous period from time t until time $t + dt$ will have a mean $E_t[d\eta(t)] = [r\eta(t) - D(t)]dt$, where, as previously, $E_t[\cdot]$ is the expectation operator taken at time t. Note that this also implies that the expected rate of growth in the recursion value,

$$\frac{E_t[d\eta(t)]}{\eta(t)} = \left[r - \frac{D(t)}{\eta(t)}\right]dt$$

hinges on the dividend policy $D(t)$ invoked by the firm. In particular, higher dividend payouts will mean that recursion value grows more slowly. We can also apply similar calculations to show that the variance of the increment in the recursion value of equity will be $\text{Var}_t[d\eta(t)] = \eta^{2\delta}(t)\varsigma^2 dt$. Note that when $\delta > 0$, the variance of increments in recursion value becomes larger as the recursion value itself grows in magnitude. This reflects the commonly held belief that variations in an economic variable (in this case the recursion value of equity) will become more pronounced as the affected variable grows in magnitude.

§11-6. The results obtained in §11-4 and §11-5 show that the recursion value of equity can be computed through the formula

$$\eta(t) = b(t) + \begin{pmatrix} 1 & 0 & 1 \end{pmatrix} (rI - Q)^{-1} \underset{\sim}{u}(t)$$

where $b(t)$ is the book value of the firm's equity at time t and, from §11-3, $\underset{\sim}{u}(t)$ is the vector whose elements are the abnormal earnings $a(t)$, the information variable $v(t)$ and the dirty surplus variable $\varepsilon(t)$. I is the identity matrix, whose diagonal elements are all unity and whose off-diagonal elements are zero, and r is the expected return on the firm's equity, that is, the cost of the firm's equity capital. Finally,

$$Q = \begin{pmatrix} c_{11} & c_{12} & c_{13} \\ c_{21} & c_{22} & c_{23} \\ c_{31} & c_{32} & c_{33} \end{pmatrix}$$

is the matrix whose elements are the structural coefficients associated with the firm's investment opportunity set. We can use this formulation for the recursion value of equity to illustrate the potential impact that the dirty surplus variable $\varepsilon(t)$ can have on the market value of a firm's equity. We assume that the structural coefficients c_{31} and c_{32} are both zero for expository convenience. This will mean that the dirty surplus variable evolves in terms of the following parsimonious process:

$$\frac{d\varepsilon(t)}{dt} = c_{33}\varepsilon(t) + k_3\eta^{\delta}(t)\frac{dz_3(t)}{dt}$$

This implies that the dirty surplus adjustment has an unconditional mean of zero, independent of the current magnitudes of the abnormal earnings and information variables. Whilst it is unlikely that such a simple model would apply in practice, it does provide a useful benchmark through which to compare models based on abnormal earnings and the information variable alone (as in the canonical equity valuation model developed in Chapter 9) with models that also incorporate a dirty surplus adjustment. Hence, if we follow §11-3 above in assuming that c_{13} and c_{23} are also zero then it follows from §11-4 that

$$\begin{pmatrix} 1 & 0 & 1 \end{pmatrix} (rI - Q)^{-1} \underset{\sim}{u}(t) = \begin{pmatrix} 1 & 0 & 1 \end{pmatrix} \begin{pmatrix} r - c_{11} & -c_{12} & 0 \\ -c_{21} & r - c_{22} & 0 \\ 0 & 0 & r - c_{33} \end{pmatrix}^{-1} \begin{pmatrix} a(t) \\ v(t) \\ \varepsilon(t) \end{pmatrix}$$

Here the reader will be able to confirm by direct calculation that

$$\begin{pmatrix} r-c_{11} & -c_{12} & 0 \\ -c_{21} & r-c_{22} & 0 \\ 0 & 0 & r-c_{33} \end{pmatrix}^{-1} = \begin{pmatrix} \dfrac{r-c_{22}}{\Delta} & \dfrac{c_{12}}{\Delta} & 0 \\ \dfrac{c_{21}}{\Delta} & \dfrac{r-c_{11}}{\Delta} & 0 \\ 0 & 0 & \dfrac{1}{r-c_{33}} \end{pmatrix}$$

where

$$\Delta = (r-c_{11})(r-c_{22}) - c_{12}c_{12}$$

Using this result, it follows that

$$\begin{pmatrix} 1 & 0 & 1 \end{pmatrix}(rI-Q)^{-1}\underset{\sim}{u}(t) = \frac{(r-c_{22})a(t)}{(r-c_{11})(r-c_{22})-c_{12}c_{12}} + \frac{c_{12}v(t)}{(r-c_{11})(r-c_{22})-c_{12}c_{21}} + \frac{\varepsilon(t)}{r-c_{33}}$$

Moreover, as previously noted (in §11-4 and §11-5), the recursion value of equity is given by $\eta(t) = b(t) + (\,1\ 0\ 1\,)(rI-Q)^{-1}\underset{\sim}{u}(t)$. Hence, it follows from this and the previous result that

$$\begin{aligned} \eta(t) &= b(t) + \begin{pmatrix} 1 & 0 & 1 \end{pmatrix}(rI-Q)^{-1}\underset{\sim}{u}(t) \\ &= b(t) + \frac{(r-c_{22})a(t)}{(r-c_{11})(r-c_{22})-c_{12}c_{12}} + \frac{c_{12}v(t)}{(r-c_{11})(r-c_{22})-c_{12}c_{21}} + \frac{\varepsilon(t)}{r-c_{33}} \end{aligned}$$

will be the recursion value of the firm's equity. Note how the coefficients associated with the abnormal earnings variable $a(t)$ and the information variable $v(t)$ in this formula are the same as those obtained for the canonical equity valuation model based on the clean surplus identity as given in §9-5. Thus, if this parsimonious interpretation of dirty surplus accounting applies in practice, it follows that the last term in the above formula, $\varepsilon(t)/(r-c_{33})$, will be the valuation bias in the recursion value of equity as a result of falsely assuming the validity of the clean surplus identity. At an empirical level, regression models that ignore the dirty surplus component of changes in the book value of equity will suffer from an omitted variables problem. This in turn will mean that parameter estimation based on models that ignore the dirty surplus adjustment will be inconsistent and inefficient. Moreover, since the canonical model of equity valuation developed in Chapter 9 shows that the overall market value of equity is parameterized in terms of its recursion value, it necessarily follows that any biases in recursion value will also be reflected as biases in the estimated market value of equity itself.

§11-7. In §11-3 above, we noted how the stochastic component of the firm's investment opportunity set is expressed in terms of a matrix K whose diagonal elements are a set of 'normalizing' constants. The off-diagonal elements of K are all zero. It will also be recalled from §11-5 that numerical values for these normalizing constants are determined from the identity

$$\begin{pmatrix}1 & 0 & 1\end{pmatrix}(rI-Q)^{-1}K=\begin{pmatrix}1 & 1 & 1\end{pmatrix}$$

We can post-multiply this expression by

$$K^{-1}=\begin{pmatrix}k_1^{-1} & 0 & 0\\ 0 & k_2^{-1} & 0\\ 0 & 0 & k_3^{-1}\end{pmatrix}$$

to give

$$\begin{aligned}\begin{pmatrix}1 & 0 & 1\end{pmatrix}(rI-Q)^{-1}KK^{-1} &= \begin{pmatrix}1 & 0 & 1\end{pmatrix}(rI-Q)^{-1}I\\ &= \begin{pmatrix}1 & 0 & 1\end{pmatrix}(rI-Q)^{-1}=\begin{pmatrix}1 & 1 & 1\end{pmatrix}K^{-1}\end{aligned}$$

Hence, if we continue with the interpretation of the structural matrix Q given in §11-6, it follows that the above equation will take the form

$$\begin{pmatrix}1 & 0 & 1\end{pmatrix}\begin{pmatrix}\dfrac{r-c_{22}}{\Delta} & \dfrac{c_{12}}{\Delta} & 0\\ \dfrac{c_{21}}{\Delta} & \dfrac{r-c_{11}}{\Delta} & 0\\ 0 & 0 & \dfrac{1}{r-c_{33}}\end{pmatrix}=\begin{pmatrix}1 & 1 & 1\end{pmatrix}\begin{pmatrix}k_1^{-1} & 0 & 0\\ 0 & k_2^{-1} & 0\\ 0 & 0 & k_3^{-1}\end{pmatrix}$$

where, as previously noted (in §11-6), $\Delta=(r-c_{11})(r-c_{22})-c_{12}c_{12}$. Moreover, evaluating the above expression shows

$$\begin{pmatrix}\dfrac{r-c_{22}}{(r-c_{11})(r-c_{22})-c_{12}c_{12}}\\ \dfrac{c_{12}}{(r-c_{11})(r-c_{22})-c_{12}c_{12}}\\ \dfrac{1}{r-c_{33}}\end{pmatrix}=\begin{pmatrix}k_1^{-1}\\ k_2^{-1}\\ k_3^{-1}\end{pmatrix}$$

in which case it follows that

$$k_1=\frac{(r-c_{11})(r-c_{22})-c_{12}c_{12}}{r-c_{22}},\quad k_2=\frac{(r-c_{11})(r-c_{22})-c_{12}c_{12}}{c_{12}}\quad\text{and}\quad k_3=r-c_{33}$$

Note that the expressions given here for k_1 and k_2 are the same as those summarized in §9-2. Here, it will be recalled that the analysis in Chapter 9 is based on the first two rows and the first two columns of the structural matrix

$$Q=\begin{pmatrix}c_{11} & c_{12} & 0\\ c_{21} & c_{22} & 0\\ 0 & 0 & c_{33}\end{pmatrix}$$

developed in §11-6 above, and so it is not surprising that the first two normalizing constants for this interpretation of the structural matrix are the same as those obtained for the structural matrix on which the canonical equity valuation model developed in Chapter 9 is based. It thus follows that the precise form of the vector system of stochastic differential equations that represents the investment opportunity set on which the analysis in §11-6 is based is given by

$$\begin{pmatrix} \frac{da(t)}{dt} \\ \frac{dv(t)}{dt} \\ \frac{d\varepsilon(t)}{dt} \end{pmatrix} = \underset{\sim}{u}'(t) = Q\underset{\sim}{u}(t) + \eta^{\delta}(t)K\underset{\sim}{z}'(t)$$

$$= \begin{pmatrix} c_{11} & c_{12} & 0 \\ c_{21} & c_{22} & 0 \\ 0 & 0 & c_{33} \end{pmatrix} \begin{pmatrix} a(t) \\ v(t) \\ \varepsilon(t) \end{pmatrix} + \eta^{\delta}(t) \begin{pmatrix} \frac{\Delta}{r - c_{22}} & 0 & 0 \\ 0 & \frac{\Delta}{c_{12}} & 0 \\ 0 & 0 & r - c_{33} \end{pmatrix} \begin{pmatrix} \frac{dz_1(t)}{dt} \\ \frac{dz_2(t)}{dt} \\ \frac{dz_3(t)}{dt} \end{pmatrix}$$

where, from §11-3, the evolution of the abnormal earnings variable $a(t)$, the information variable $v(t)$ and the dirty surplus adjustment $\varepsilon(t)$ are based on the uncorrelated white noise processes $dz_1(t)/dt$, $dz_2(t)/dt$ and $dz_3(t)/dt$, respectively. If, however, the off-diagonal components of the matrix K assume non-trivial values then $a(t)$, $v(t)$ and $\varepsilon(t)$ will all be correlated variables even though the white noise terms on which they are based are all uncorrelated.

§11-8. We have previously noted (in §9-7) that firms will normally have the option of changing or modifying their investment opportunity sets in order to use the resources available to them in alternative and potentially more profitable ways. We have also noted (in §9-1 and §9-7) that there are a variety of ways in which firms can exercise the option to change their investment opportunity sets, including liquidations, sell-offs, spin-offs, divestitures, CEO changes, mergers, takeovers, bankruptcies, restructurings and new capital investments. The potential to make changes like these gives rise to a second element of equity value that is known as the adaptation value of equity (as in §9-1). We can determine the contribution which adaptation value makes to the overall market value of equity by invoking the following 'no-arbitrage' condition:

$$P(\eta(t)) = D(t)dt + e^{-rdt}E_t[P(\eta(t+dt))]$$

Here $P(\eta(t))$ is the market value of the firm's equity, $\eta(t)$ is the recursion value of equity, $D(t)$ is the dividend payment (per unit time) made to equity holders at time t, r is the expected return (per unit time) on the firm's equity and, as previously, $E_t[\cdot]$ is the expectation operator taken at time t. This no-arbitrage condition is similar to that applied in §9-7, with the exception that it makes provision for the payment of dividends. Thus, the above arbitrage condition requires that the market value of equity 'today', $P(\eta(t))$, must be equal to the sum of the instantaneous dividend payment 'today', $D(t)dt$, and the expected discounted market value of equity 'tomorrow', $e^{-rdt}E_t[P(\eta(t+dt))]$. This in turn means that equity will be priced so that only 'normal' returns can be expected; that is, the expected return on the firm's equity is equal to the cost of capital for equity r. More important, however, is that we can follow procedures similar to those applied in §9-7 and thereby show that the market value of equity will satisfy the following version of the Hamilton–Jacobi–Bellman equation:

$$\frac{1}{2}\zeta^2\eta^{2\delta}\frac{d^2P}{d\eta^2}+(r\eta-D)\frac{dP}{d\eta}+[D-rP(\eta)]=0$$

where ζ^2 is the variance parameter associated with the white noise term $dq(t)/dt=q'(t)$ that captures the stochastic component of instantaneous changes in the recursion value of equity (as in §11-5).

Now, here it is important to note that direct substitution shows $P(\eta)=\eta$ to be a solution of the above differential equation, and this is so irrespective of the dividend policy invoked by the firm as captured by the function $D(t)$. This in turn means that the recursion value of equity η does not depend on the dividend policy implemented by the firm. Here, it will be recalled (as in §5-2) that the Miller and Modigliani dividend policy irrelevance theorem says that if, in a perfect capital market, a firm's existing investment opportunity set is applied indefinitely into the future then the future dividend policy that the firm implements will have no impact on the current market value of the firm's equity. In particular, the dividend payout rate determines merely how a given return to stockholders splits as between current dividends and current capital gains and does not affect either the size of the total return or the current market value of its equity stock. Hence, the fact that $P(\eta)=\eta$ is a solution of the Hamilton–Jacobi–Bellman equation irrespective of what particular form the dividend function $D(t)$ might take is merely a reflection of the Miller and Modigliani dividend policy irrelevance theorem. Given this, it is somewhat unfortunate that there is now persuasive empirical evidence suggesting that a firm's dividend policy can have a significant impact on the market value of its equity. Whilst a variety of explanations have been offered for this, a seldom-invoked reason arises out of the fact that when a firm makes a dividend payment, it increases the probability that it will have to exercise its adaptation options at some future point in time, thereby increasing the value of these options to the firm.

§11-9. We can illustrate the importance of the point being made here by invoking one of the few functional forms for the dividend function that leads to a tractable expression for the market value of equity. We thus assume that the firm makes dividend payments that are strictly proportional to the recursion value of its equity, namely,

$$D(t)=\alpha\eta(t)$$

where $0\leq\alpha<r$ is the constant of proportionality. Moreover, if we follow our previous analysis (as in §9-6) in assuming that the recursion value of equity evolves in terms of a continuous-time branching process then $\delta=\frac{1}{2}$ and, from §11-8, the market value of the firm's equity will satisfy the following version of the Hamilton–Jacobi–Bellman equation:

$$\frac{1}{2}\zeta^2\eta\frac{d^2P}{d\eta^2}+(r-\alpha)\eta\frac{dP}{d\eta}+[\alpha\eta-rP(\eta)]=0$$

Here, it will be recalled (as in §9-1) that the market value of a firm's equity is composed of two elements: first the recursion value that arises if the firm applies its existing investment opportunity set indefinitely into the future and second the adaptation value that arises from the option the firm possesses to modify or even abandon its existing investment opportunity set.

Given this, suppose that we seek a solution to the Hamilton–Jacobi–Bellman equation that takes the form

$$P(\eta) = \eta + X(\eta)$$

where $X(\eta)$ is a function that enables one to determine the adaptation value of the firm's equity and, as previously, η is the recursion value of its equity. Substituting the above expression into the Hamilton–Jacobi–Bellman equation then gives

$$\frac{1}{2}\zeta^2\eta\frac{d^2X}{d\eta^2} + (r-\alpha)\eta\left(1+\frac{dX}{d\eta}\right) + \{\alpha\eta - r[\eta + X(\eta)]\} = 0$$

We can cancel terms in this expression and thereby show that the adaptation value of equity can be determined from the following 'auxiliary' equation:

$$\frac{1}{2}\zeta^2\eta\frac{d^2X}{d\eta^2} + (r-\alpha)\eta\frac{dX}{d\eta} - rX(\eta) = 0$$

Unfortunately, no closed-form solutions are available for this auxiliary equation. Given this, we seek a solution of the auxiliary equation in the form of the following infinite power series expansion:

$$X(\eta) = \sum_{j=0}^{\infty} a_j\eta^{j+w}$$

where the a_j are coefficients and w is known as the 'exponent of singularity'. Moreover, we can differentiate through the power series expansion for $X(\eta)$ and thereby show

$$\frac{dX(\eta)}{d\eta} = \sum_{j=0}^{\infty} a_j(j+w)\eta^{j+w-1}$$

and

$$\frac{d^2X(\eta)}{d\eta^2} = \sum_{j=0}^{\infty} a_j(j+w)(j+w-1)\eta^{j+w-2}$$

Substituting the above power series expansions into the auxiliary equation then gives

$$\frac{1}{2}\zeta^2\sum_{j=0}^{\infty} a_j(j+w)(j+w-1)\eta^{j+w-1} + (r-\alpha)\sum_{j=0}^{\infty} a_j(j+w)\eta^{j+w} - r\sum_{j=0}^{\infty} a_j\eta^{j+w} = 0$$

Note, however, that in the final term in this expression we can replace j wherever it occurs by $j-1$, in which case we have

$$\sum_{j=0}^{\infty} a_j\eta^{j+w} = \sum_{j-1=0}^{\infty} a_{j-1}\eta^{j+w-1} = \sum_{j=1}^{\infty} a_{j-1}\eta^{j+w-1}$$

Similarly, for the penultimate term, we have

$$\sum_{j=0}^{\infty} a_j(j+w)\eta^{j+w} = \sum_{j-1=0}^{\infty} a_{j-1}(j+w-1)\eta^{j+w-1} = \sum_{j=1}^{\infty} a_{j-1}(j+w-1)\eta^{j+w-1}$$

These latter two expressions mean that we can restate the power series expression for the auxiliary equation in the following equivalent form:

$$\frac{1}{2}\zeta^2 \sum_{j=0}^{\infty}(j+w)(j+w-1)a_j\eta^{j+w-1} + (r-\alpha)\sum_{j=1}^{\infty}(j+w-1)a_{j-1}\eta^{j+w-1}$$
$$-r\sum_{j=1}^{\infty} a_{j-1}\eta^{j+w-1} = 0$$

Moreover, expanding out the term for $j=0$ in this expression leads to what is known as the 'indicial equation' for the auxiliary equation:

$$\frac{1}{2}\zeta^2 a_0 w(w-1)\eta^{w-1} = 0$$

This condition can only be satisfied if the exponents of singularity for the auxiliary equation are $w=0$ and $w=1$. Now, letting $w=1$ in the above power series expression for the auxiliary equation shows

$$\sum_{j=1}^{\infty}\left[\frac{1}{2}\zeta^2 j(j+1)a_j + (r-\alpha)ja_{j-1} - ra_{j-1}\right]\eta^j = 0$$

Note that this condition can only be satisfied if the coefficient associated with η^j is zero for $j = 1, 2, 3, \ldots, \infty$. This in turn will mean

$$\frac{1}{2}\zeta^2 j(j+1)a_j + (r-\alpha)ja_{j-1} - ra_{j-1} = 0$$

Solving this equation leads to the following recurrence relation for the coefficients of the power series expansion for $X(\eta)$:

$$a_j = \frac{2[r+(\alpha-r)j]}{j(j+1)\zeta^2}a_{j-1}$$

Now, suppose we substitute $j=1$ into this recurrence relation, in which case we have

$$a_1 = \frac{2[r+(\alpha-r)]}{2\zeta^2}a_0 = \frac{\alpha}{\zeta^2}a_0$$

Next, we can substitute $j=2$ into the recurrence relation to give

$$a_2 = \frac{2[r+(\alpha-r)2]}{2(2+1)\zeta^2}a_1 = \frac{2\alpha-r}{3\zeta^2}a_1 = \frac{\alpha(2\alpha-r)}{3\zeta^4}a_0$$

Likewise, letting $j = 3$ in the recurrence relation shows

$$a_3 = \frac{2[r+(\alpha-r)3]}{3(3+1)\zeta^2}a_2 = \frac{3\alpha-2r}{6\zeta^2}a_2 = \frac{\alpha(2\alpha-r)(3\alpha-2r)}{18\zeta^6}a_0$$

This procedure can be continued *ad infinitum*, in which case the reader will be able to confirm that

$$a_j = \frac{2^j\alpha(2\alpha-r)(3\alpha-2r)\cdots[j\alpha-(j-1)r]}{j!(j+1)!\zeta^{2j}}a_0$$

is the coefficient associated with η^{j+1} in the power series expansion for $X(\eta)$. It follows from this that

$$X(\eta) = \sum_{j=0}^{\infty} a_j\eta^{j+1} = a_0\left[\eta + \frac{\alpha}{\zeta^2}\eta^2 + \frac{\alpha(2\alpha-r)}{3\zeta^4}\eta^3 + \frac{\alpha(2\alpha-r)(3\alpha-2r)}{18\zeta^6}\eta^4 + \ldots\right]$$

will be a formal solution of the auxiliary equation. Here, however, it will be recalled (as in §9-10) that the adaptation value of equity always declines in magnitude as the recursion value of equity becomes larger. Unfortunately, the power series expansion given above for the auxiliary equation does not possess this property. We can demonstrate this by supposing the firm pays out a proportion $\alpha = \frac{1}{2}r$ of its recursion value as dividends, where it will be recalled from §11-2 that r is the cost of the firm's equity capital. It then follows from earlier analysis in this section that the coefficient associated with η^3 in the power series expansion for the auxiliary equation will be

$$a_2 = \frac{\alpha(2\alpha-r)}{3\zeta^4} = \frac{\frac{1}{2}r(2\times\frac{1}{2}r-r)}{3\zeta^4} = 0$$

Moreover, the recurrence relation developed earlier in this section shows that the coefficient associated with η^4 in the power series expansion for the auxiliary equation will be

$$a_3 = \frac{2[r+(\alpha-r)3]}{3(3+1)\zeta^2}a_2 = 0$$

Indeed, the recurrence relation shows that all coefficients beyond a_1 will be zero, and so the power series expansion for the auxiliary equation ends at the second term and takes the following form:

$$X(\eta) = a_0\left(\eta + \frac{\alpha}{\zeta^2}\eta^2\right) = a_0\left(\eta + \frac{r}{2\zeta^2}\eta^2\right)$$

Note for this solution that $X(\eta) \to \infty$ as $\eta \to \infty$. In other words, as the recursion value of equity grows in magnitude, $X(\eta)$ also becomes larger. This in turn means that $X(\eta)$ cannot represent the adaptation value of the firm's equity, since, as previously noted, the adaptation value of equity always falls in magnitude as the recursion value of equity becomes larger.

§11-10. We can address this problem of determining an appropriate functional form for the adaptation value of equity by seeking a second solution of the auxiliary equation that takes the form $Y(\eta) = u(\eta)X(\eta)$, where $u(\eta)$ is a twice-differentiable function of η. It then follows that

$$Y'(\eta) = u'(\eta)X(\eta) + u(\eta)X'(\eta)$$

and

$$Y''(\eta) = u''(\eta)X(\eta) + 2u'(\eta)X'(\eta) + u(\eta)X''(\eta)$$

When we substitute these latter two expressions into the auxiliary equation, we obtain

$$\begin{aligned}\frac{1}{2}\varsigma^2\eta\frac{d^2Y}{d\eta^2} + (r-\alpha)\eta\frac{dY}{d\eta} - rY(\eta) &= \frac{1}{2}\varsigma^2\eta[u''(\eta)X(\eta) + 2u'(\eta)X'(\eta)] \\ &\quad + (r-\alpha)\eta u'(\eta)X(\eta) \\ &\quad + u(\eta)\left[\frac{1}{2}\varsigma^2\eta X''(\eta) + (r-\alpha)\eta X'(\eta) - rX(\eta)\right] \\ &= 0\end{aligned}$$

Note that the final term on the right-hand side of the above expression is merely the auxiliary equation multiplied by $u(\eta)$ and, from §11-9, it will have to be equal to zero. We are then left with

$$\frac{1}{2}\varsigma^2\eta[u''(\eta)X(\eta) + 2u'(\eta)X'(\eta)] + (r-\alpha)\eta u'(\eta)X(\eta) = 0$$

We can separate this latter equation into terms involving the function $u(\eta)$ and terms involving the function $X(\eta)$ by dividing all terms in the equation by $\frac{1}{2}\varsigma^2\eta u'(\eta)X(\eta)$. Doing so, we have

$$\frac{u''(\eta)}{u'(\eta)} = -\left[\frac{2X'(\eta)}{X(\eta)} + \frac{2(r-\alpha)}{\varsigma^2}\right]$$

Now, if we integrate across both sides of this differential equation, we find

$$\log[u'(\eta)] = -2\log[X(\eta)] + \frac{2(\alpha - r)}{\varsigma^2}\eta + c_1$$

where c_1 is a constant of integration. However, it can be shown that c_1 is a redundant parameter in determining the adaptation value of equity (as with c_1 in §7-12) and, given this, we set it to zero. We can then apply the exponential operator to both sides of the above equation and thereby show

$$u'(\eta) = \frac{\exp\left[\dfrac{2(\alpha - r)\eta}{\varsigma^2}\right]}{X^2(\eta)}$$

Finally, if we integrate across both sides of this expression (again ignoring the redundant constant of integration), we find

$$u(\eta) = \int_{\eta}^{\infty} \frac{\exp\left[\frac{2(\alpha - r)y}{\zeta^2}\right]}{X^2(y)} dy$$

This in turn means that a second solution of the auxiliary equation will be

$$Y(\eta) = u(\eta)X(\eta) = X(\eta) \int_{\eta}^{\infty} \frac{\exp\left[\frac{2(\alpha - r)y}{\zeta^2}\right]}{X^2(y)} dy$$

Now, for this second solution of the auxiliary equation, it can be shown that

$$\lim_{\eta \to 0} Y(\eta) = \frac{1}{a_0}$$

where a_0 is the parameter associated with the power series expansion for $X(\eta)$ as summarized in §11-9 above. Likewise, it can also be shown that

$$\lim_{\eta \to \infty} Y(\eta) = 0$$

Hence, $Y(\eta)$ has the important property that it asymptotically declines towards zero as the recursion value of equity η grows in magnitude. This in turn will mean that when the firm is highly profitable (i.e. η is large) the adaptation value of equity $Y(\eta)$ will be relatively small and it is highly unlikely the firm will exercise the option it possesses to change its investment opportunity set in the foreseeable future. If, however, the firm is in a loss-making situation (i.e η is small), the adaptation value of equity $Y(\eta)$ will be relatively large and there is a much greater likelihood the firm will exercise its option to change its investment opportunity set. Moreover, from §11-9 above and from §9-8, we know that the market value of a firm's equity is the sum of its recursion value and its adaptation value:

$$P(\eta) = \eta + Y(\eta)$$

Substituting the expression for $Y(\eta)$ into the above expression for $P(\eta)$ shows that the market value of the firm's equity will be

$$P(\eta) = \eta + X(\eta) \int_{\eta}^{\infty} \frac{\exp\left[\frac{2(\alpha - r)y}{\zeta^2}\right]}{X^2(y)} dy$$

where $X(\eta)$ is the formal solution of the auxiliary equation determined in §11-9 above. Moreover, the fact that our earlier analysis shows that $Y(\eta)$ has a limiting value of $1/a_0$ as the recursion value of equity η approaches its lower limit of zero will mean

$$\lim_{\eta \to 0} P(\eta) = \lim_{\eta \to 0} \left\{ \eta + X(\eta) \int_{\eta}^{\infty} \frac{\exp\left[\frac{2(\alpha - r)y}{\zeta^2}\right]}{X^2(y)} dy \right\} = \frac{1}{a_0} = P(0)$$

where $P(0)$ represents the adaptation value of the firm's equity should its recursion value fall away to nothing. This in turn shows that $a_0 = 1/P(0)$ will be the parameter associated with the formal solution $X(\eta)$ of the auxiliary equation determined in §11-9 above.

Note also how the analysis in this section, and in particular the expression for $P(\eta)$ given above, confirms the conclusion reached in §9-13 that the market value of a firm's equity is potentially a highly non-linear function of its determining variables. This is of particular significance given the penchant amongst empirical researchers for applying purely linear methodologies to estimate the valuation relationships that exist in this area. It is not hard to show, however, that if, as the empirical evidence suggests, there is a non-linear relationship between equity prices and their determining variables then the purely linear methodologies that characterize empirical research in this area of the literature will constitute an unreliable basis for estimating the relevant valuation relationships.

§11-11. There is a second important issue that arises out of the non-linear pricing relationships considered in this chapter. This relates to the role that dividends play in the valuation of equity. We have previously observed (in §11-8) how the Miller and Modigliani dividend policy irrelevance theorem means that the dividend function $D(t)$ cannot enter into the (functional) expression for the recursion value of equity. However, the adaptation value of equity $Y(\eta)$ depends on the potential changes that a firm can make to its existing investment opportunity set, and the analysis of this chapter shows that the dividend function does enter into the (functional) expression for this component of equity value. In other words, whilst a firm's dividend policy will not influence the recursion value of equity, it can have a significant impact on the adaptation value of equity. In particular, dividend payments reduce the resources available to the firm and thereby adversely affect its capacity to 'ride out' unfavourable economic circumstances. We can demonstrate this by replicating the procedures alluded to in §9-10, in which case we have

$$\lim_{t\to\infty} \text{Prob}\,[\eta(t) = 0] = \exp\left[-\frac{2(r-\alpha)\eta(0)}{\varsigma^2}\right]$$

that is, in the steady state (i.e. as $t \to \infty$), the probability of the recursion value of equity falling away to nothing is $\exp[-2(r-\alpha)\eta(0)/\varsigma^2]$. Here, it will be recalled that $\eta(0)$ is the currently observed (i.e. time-zero) recursion value of the firm's equity. Note how this result shows that the probability of the recursion value eventually falling away to nothing increases exponentially as the firm increases its dividend pay-out rate η. This in turn means that the dividend policy implemented by the firm can have a significant impact on the probability that the firm will have to change its investment opportunity set, and therefore on the adaptation value of its equity.

We can illustrate the importance of this point by considering a firm with an adaptation value (should its recursion value fall away to nothing) of $P(0) = 1$ and whose dividend payout rate (as a proportion of its recursion value) is equal to one half the cost of its equity capital r. This means that the dividend payout rate will be $\alpha = \frac{1}{2}r$. From §11-9, this will also mean that the power series expansion for the auxiliary equation ends at the second term and thus takes the following form:

$$X(\eta) = a_0\left(\eta + \frac{r}{2\varsigma^2}\eta^2\right)$$

Using this result in conjunction with the value of the firm's equity as given in §11-10 then shows that the overall market value of the firm's equity will have to be

$$P(\eta) = \eta + \left(\eta + \frac{r}{2\varsigma^2}\eta^2\right) \int_\eta^\infty \frac{\exp\left(-\frac{r}{\varsigma^2}y\right)}{\left(y + \frac{r}{2\varsigma^2}y^2\right)^2} dy$$

Now recall from §9-10 that the risk (or stability) parameter relating to the evolution of the recursion value of equity is twice the expected rate of growth in the recursion value of equity divided by the variance parameter associated with the white noise term that captures the stochastic component of instantaneous increments in the recursion value of equity. Now, we know from §11-5 and §11-9 that in the present instance the expected rate of growth (per unit time) in the recursion value of equity is given by

$$\frac{1}{\eta(t)} \frac{E_t[d\eta(t)]}{dt} = r - \frac{D(t)}{\eta(t)} = r - \alpha = r - \frac{1}{2}r = \frac{1}{2}r$$

Likewise, the variance (per unit time) of the white noise term that captures the stochastic component of instantaneous increments in the recursion value of equity is given by

$$\frac{\mathrm{Var}_t[dq(t)]}{dt} = \varsigma^2$$

It thus follows that the risk parameter is given by

$$\frac{2(r-\alpha)}{\varsigma^2} = \frac{2(r - \frac{1}{2}r)}{\varsigma^2} = \frac{r}{\varsigma^2}$$

In Figures 11.1, 11.2 and 11.3 we plot $P(\eta)$ when the risk parameter r/ς^2 assumes values of $\frac{1}{2}$, 1 and $\frac{3}{2}$, respectively. Note that as the risk parameter becomes larger, the steady-state probability of the recursion value of equity falling away to nothing,

$$\exp\left[-\frac{2(r-\alpha)\eta(0)}{\varsigma^2}\right] = \exp\left(-\frac{r\eta}{\varsigma^2}\right)$$

declines in magnitude and the three figures show that the adaptation value of equity decays quickly away. Thus, when $r/\varsigma^2 = \frac{1}{2}$ and the recursion value of equity is $\eta = 1$, the steady-state probability of the recursion value of equity eventually falling away to nothing is $\exp(-r\eta/\varsigma^2) = e^{-0.5\times 1} = 0.6065$ and the adaptation value of equity will be $Y(\eta) = Y(1) = 0.2101$. When, however, $r/\varsigma^2 = 1$ and the recursion value of equity is $\eta = 1$, the steady-state probability of the recursion value of equity eventually falling away to nothing is $\exp(-r\eta/\varsigma^2) = e^{-1\times 1} = 0.3679$ and the adaptation value of equity falls to $Y(1) = 0.0987$. Finally, when $r/\varsigma^2 = \frac{3}{2}$ and the recursion value of equity is $\eta = 1$, the steady-state probability of the recursion value of equity eventually falling away to nothing is $\exp(-r\eta/\varsigma^2) = e^{-1.5\times 1} = 0.2231$ and the adaptation value of equity falls again to $Y(1) = 0.0563$. This continuous fall in the adaptation value of equity occurs because as the probability of the recursion value of equity eventually falling away to nothing, $\exp(-r\eta/\varsigma^2)$,

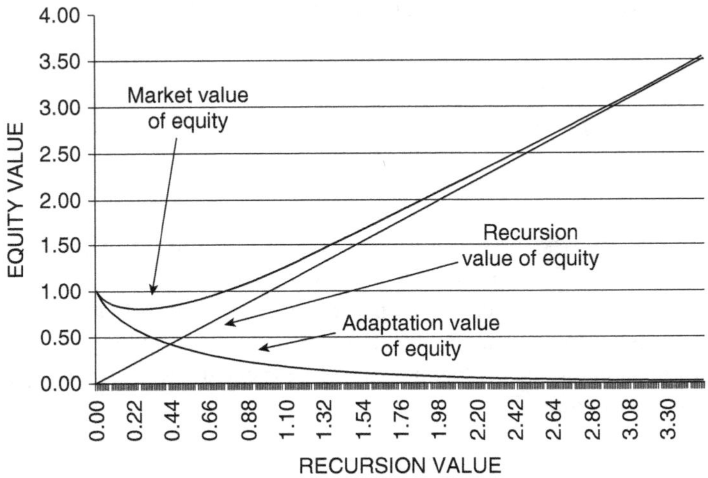

Figure 11.1 Graph of $P(\eta)$ against η when $P(0) = 1$ and the risk parameter $r/\zeta^2 = \frac{1}{2}$

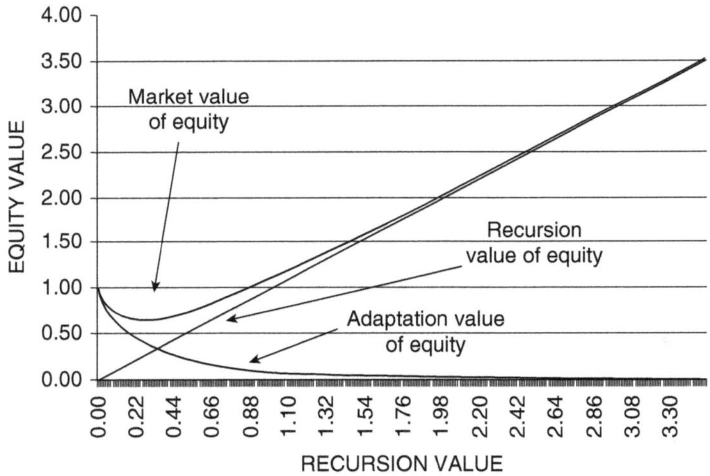

Figure 11.2 Graph of $P(\eta)$ against η when $P(0) = 1$ and the risk parameter $r/\zeta^2 = 1$

declines in magnitude, it becomes increasingly unlikely that the firm will have to exercise the adaptation options that are available to it. The value of these options will fall away because of this.

§11-12. We can determine further properties of the relationship between the adaptation value of equity for a dividend paying firm and the adaptation value for an equivalent non-dividend paying firm by making the substitution

$$y = \frac{2\eta}{1+z}$$

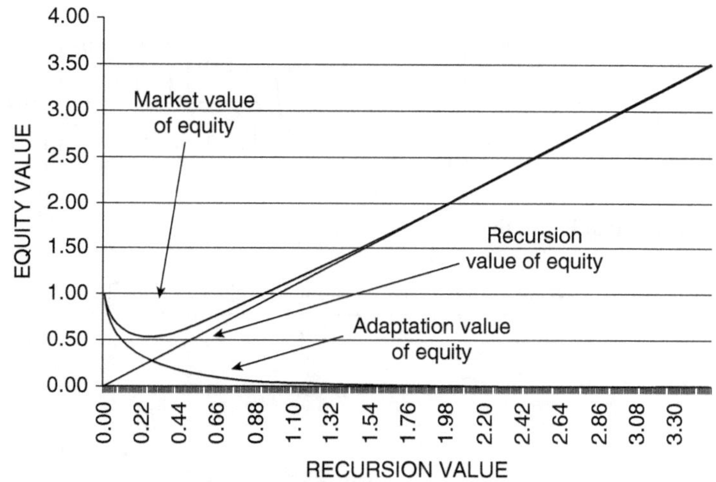

Figure 11.3 Graph of $P(\eta)$ against η when $P(0) = 1$ and the risk parameter $r/\zeta^2 = \frac{3}{2}$

in the expression for the adaptation value $Y(\eta)$ of a dividend paying firm as given in §11-10 above. It then follows that

$$\frac{dy}{dz} = -\frac{2\eta}{(1+z)^2}$$

or equivalently

$$dy = -\frac{2\eta dz}{(1+z)^2}$$

Note also that when $y = \eta$,

$$z = \frac{2\eta}{y} - 1 = \frac{2\eta}{\eta} - 1 = 1$$

Likewise, when $y = \infty$,

$$z = \frac{2\eta}{\infty} - 1 = -1$$

These calculations mean that the adaptation value of equity for a dividend-paying firm can be restated as

$$Y(\eta) = X(\eta) \int_{\eta}^{\infty} \frac{\exp\left[\dfrac{2(\alpha - r)y}{\zeta^2}\right]}{X^2(y)} dy = -2\eta X(\eta) \int_{1}^{-1} \frac{\exp\left[\dfrac{4(\alpha - r)\eta}{(1+z)\zeta^2}\right]}{\left[(1+z)X\left(\dfrac{2\eta}{1+z}\right)\right]^2} dz$$

Now, here we can use the fact that

$$Y(\eta) = -2\eta X(\eta)\int_{1}^{-1} \frac{\exp\left[\frac{4(\alpha-r)\eta}{(1+z)\zeta^2}\right]}{\left[(1+z)X\left(\frac{2\eta}{1+z}\right)\right]^2}dz = 2\eta X(\eta)\int_{-1}^{1} \frac{\exp\left[\frac{4(\alpha-r)\eta}{(1+z)\zeta^2}\right]}{\left[(1+z)X\left(\frac{2\eta}{1+z}\right)\right]^2}dz$$

Moreover, from §11-10, we also know that

$$2\eta X(\eta) = 2a_0\eta^2\left[1+\frac{\alpha}{\zeta^2}\eta+\frac{\alpha(2\alpha-r)}{3\zeta^4}\eta^2+\frac{\alpha(2\alpha-r)(3\alpha-2r)}{18\zeta^6}\eta^3+\ldots\right]$$

and

$$\left[(1+z)X\left(\frac{2\eta}{1+z}\right)\right]^2 = 4a_0^2\eta^2\left[1+\frac{\alpha}{\zeta^2}\frac{2\eta}{(1+z)}+\frac{\alpha(2\alpha-r)}{3\zeta^4}\left(\frac{2\eta}{1+z}\right)^2+\ldots\right]^2$$

Here it will also be recalled (as in §11-10) that $a_0 = 1/P(0)$ represents the adaptation value of the firm's equity should its recursion value η fall away to nothing. This in turn will mean

$$\frac{2\eta X(\eta)}{\left[(1+z)X\left(\frac{2\eta}{1+z}\right)\right]^2} = \frac{P(0)}{2}\frac{1+\frac{\alpha}{\zeta^2}\eta+\frac{\alpha(2\alpha-r)}{3\zeta^4}\eta^2+\frac{\alpha(2\alpha-r)(3\alpha-2r)}{18\zeta^6}\eta^3+\ldots}{\left[1+\frac{\alpha}{\zeta^2}\frac{2\eta}{1+z}+\frac{\alpha(2\alpha-r)}{3\zeta^4}\left(\frac{2\eta}{1+z}\right)^2+\ldots\right]^2}$$

Finally, since from §9-8 the risk (or stability) parameter relating to the evolution of the recursion value of equity for a non-dividend-paying firm is given by $\theta = 2r/\zeta^2$, it also follows that

$$\exp\left[-\frac{4r\eta}{(1+z)\zeta^2}\right] = \exp\left(-\frac{2\theta\eta}{1+z}\right)$$

Bringing these results together enables us to restate the adaptation value of equity for a dividend-paying firm in the following terms:

$$Y(\eta) = X(\eta)\int_{\eta}^{\infty}\frac{\exp\left[\frac{2(\alpha-r)y}{\zeta^2}\right]}{X^2(y)}dy$$

$$= \frac{P(0)}{2}\int_{-1}^{1}\exp\left(-\frac{2\theta\eta}{1+z}\right)\frac{\left[1+\frac{\alpha}{\zeta^2}\eta+\frac{\alpha(2\alpha-r)}{3\zeta^4}\eta^2+\ldots\right]\exp\left[\frac{4\alpha\eta}{\zeta^2(1+z)}\right]}{\left[1+\frac{\alpha}{\zeta^2}\frac{2\eta}{1+z}+\frac{\alpha(2\alpha-r)}{3\zeta^4}\left(\frac{2\eta}{1+z}\right)^2+\ldots\right]^2}dz$$

Now, here the reader will recall from §9-8 that

$$\frac{P(0)}{2}\int_{-1}^{1}\exp\left(-\frac{2\theta\eta}{1+z}\right)dz$$

is the adaptation value of equity for a non-dividend-paying firm. Hence, the above result shows that there is a complex non-linear relationship between the adaptation value of equity for a non-dividend-paying firm and the adaptation value of equity for an equivalent dividend-paying firm.

§11-13. Further progress towards determining the relationship between the adaptation value of equity for a dividend-paying firm as against the adaptation value for an equivalent non-dividend-paying firm can be obtained by considering the following component of the integral expression for $Y(\eta)$ in §11-12 above:

$$\frac{\exp\left[\frac{4\alpha\eta}{\zeta^2(1+z)}\right]}{\left[1+\frac{\alpha}{\zeta^2}\frac{2\eta}{1+z}+\frac{\alpha(2\alpha-r)}{3\zeta^4}\left(\frac{2\eta}{1+z}\right)^2+\ldots\right]^2}=\left\{\frac{\exp\left[\frac{2\alpha\eta}{\zeta^2(1+z)}\right]}{1+\frac{\alpha}{\zeta^2}\frac{2\eta}{1+z}+\frac{\alpha(2\alpha-r)}{3\zeta^4}\left(\frac{2\eta}{1+z}\right)^2+\ldots}\right\}^2$$

We can apply a Taylor series expansion to the numerator of the above expression and then recall (as in §11-12) that $y=2\eta/(1+z)$. The above expression then reduces to

$$\left[\frac{\exp\left(\frac{\alpha y}{\zeta^2}\right)}{1+\frac{\alpha y}{\zeta^2}+\frac{\alpha(2\alpha-r)y^2}{3\zeta^4}+\ldots}\right]^2=\left[\frac{1+\frac{\alpha y}{\zeta^2}+\frac{\alpha^2y^2}{2!\zeta^4}+\ldots}{1+\frac{\alpha y}{\zeta^2}+\frac{\alpha(2\alpha-r)y^2}{3\zeta^4}+\ldots}\right]^2$$

Note that the coefficient associated with y^j in the numerator of the above expression is given by

$$\frac{\alpha^j}{j!\zeta^{2j}}\ \text{for}\ j=1,2,3,\ \ldots,\infty$$

In contrast, we know from §11-9 above that the coefficient associated with y^j in the denominator of the above expression will be

$$\frac{2^j\alpha(2\alpha-r)(3\alpha-2r)\cdots[j\alpha-(j-1)r]}{j!(j+1)!\zeta^{2j}}$$

Thus, the ratio of the coefficient associated with y^j in the numerator of the above expression and the coefficient associated with y^j in the denominator of the same expression turns out to be

$$\frac{\frac{\alpha^j}{j!\zeta^{2j}}}{\frac{2^j\alpha(2\alpha-r)(3\alpha-2r)\cdots[j\alpha-(j-1)r]}{j!(j+1)!\zeta^{2j}}}=\frac{(j+1)!}{2^j\left(2-\frac{r}{\alpha}\right)\left(3-\frac{2r}{\alpha}\right)\cdots\left(j-\frac{(j-1)r}{\alpha}\right)}$$

Now, we can evaluate this expression by first noting that $(j+1)!/2^j \geq 1$ for $j = 1, 2, 3, \ldots, \infty$, with strict equality holding only when $j = 1$. Moreover, suppose also that there is an integral $m > 1$ for which $m\alpha - (m-1)r = 0$ (the general case for non-integral m is more difficult). It then follows that

$$\frac{r}{\alpha} = \frac{m}{m-1}$$

and

$$0 \leq j - \frac{(j-1)r}{\alpha} = j - \frac{(j-1)m}{m-1} \leq 1 \quad \text{for} \quad j = 1, 2, 3, \ldots, m$$

with strict equality holding only when $j = 1$ and $j = m$. Hence, these latter two results mean that

$$\frac{\dfrac{\alpha^j}{j!\zeta^{2j}}}{\dfrac{2^j\alpha(2\alpha-r)(3\alpha-2r)\cdots[j\alpha-(j-1)r]}{j!(j+1)!\zeta^{2j}}} \geq 1$$

with strict equality holding only when $j = 1$. Hence, this in turn will imply

$$\frac{\exp\left[\dfrac{4\alpha\eta}{\zeta^2(1+z)}\right]}{\left[1+\dfrac{\alpha}{\zeta^2}\dfrac{2\eta}{1+z}+\dfrac{\alpha(2\alpha-r)}{3\zeta^4}\left(\dfrac{2\eta}{1+z}\right)^2+\ldots\right]^2} > 1$$

Thus, if we multiply through the above expression by

$$\frac{P(0)}{2}\exp\left(-\frac{2\theta\eta}{1+z}\right)\left[1+\frac{\alpha}{\zeta^2}\eta+\frac{\alpha(2\alpha-r)}{3\zeta^4}\eta^2+\frac{\alpha(2\alpha-r)(3\alpha-2r)}{18\zeta^6}\eta^3+\ldots\right]$$

it follows that

$$\frac{\dfrac{P(0)}{2}\exp\left(-\dfrac{2\theta\eta}{1+z}\right)\left[1+\dfrac{\alpha}{\zeta^2}\eta+\dfrac{\alpha(2\alpha-r)}{3\zeta^4}\eta^2+\ldots\right]\exp\left[\dfrac{4\alpha\eta}{\zeta^2(1+z)}\right]}{\left[1+\dfrac{\alpha}{\zeta^2}\dfrac{2\eta}{1+z}+\dfrac{\alpha(2\alpha-r)}{3\zeta^4}\left(\dfrac{2\eta}{1+z}\right)^2+\ldots\right]^2} >$$
$$\frac{P(0)}{2}\exp\left(-\frac{2\theta\eta}{1+z}\right)\left[1+\frac{\alpha}{\zeta^2}\eta+\frac{\alpha(2\alpha-r)}{3\zeta^4}\eta^2+\frac{\alpha(2\alpha-r)(3\alpha-2r)}{18\zeta^6}\eta^3+\ldots\right]$$

Here, we can use the fact that $r/\alpha = m/(m-1)$ to restate the right-hand side of the above expression as follows:

$$\frac{P(0)}{2}\exp\left(-\frac{2\theta\eta}{1+z}\right)\left[1+\frac{\alpha}{\zeta^2}\eta+\frac{\alpha^2\left(2-\frac{m}{m-1}\right)}{3\zeta^4}\eta^2+\frac{\alpha^3\left(2-\frac{m}{m-1}\right)\left(3-\frac{2m}{m-1}\right)}{18\zeta^6}\eta^3+\ldots\right]$$

However, since we have noted earlier in this section that

$$j - \frac{(j-1)m}{m-1} \geq 0 \quad \text{for all} \quad j \leq m$$

it necessarily follows that

$$\frac{P(0)}{2}\exp\left(-\frac{2\theta\eta}{1+z}\right)\left[1+\frac{\alpha}{\zeta^2}\eta+\frac{\alpha^2\left(2-\frac{m}{m-1}\right)}{3\zeta^4}\eta^2+\ldots\right] > \frac{P(0)}{2}\exp\left(-\frac{2\theta\eta}{1+z}\right)$$

This in turn implies that

$$\frac{\frac{P(0)}{2}\exp\left(-\frac{2\theta\eta}{1+z}\right)\left[1+\frac{\alpha}{\zeta^2}\eta+\frac{\alpha(2\alpha-r)}{3\zeta^4}\eta^2+\ldots\right]\exp\left[\frac{4\alpha\eta}{\zeta^2(1+z)}\right]}{\left[1+\frac{\alpha}{\zeta^2}\frac{2\eta}{1+z}+\frac{\alpha(2\alpha-r)}{3\zeta^4}\left(\frac{2\eta}{1+z}\right)^2+\ldots\right]^2} > \frac{P(0)}{2}\exp\left(-\frac{2\theta\eta}{1+z}\right)$$

We can then integrate this expression with respect to z over the interval from -1 to 1, in which case it follows that

$$Y(\eta) = \frac{P(0)}{2}\int_{-1}^{1}\exp\left(-\frac{2\theta\eta}{1+z}\right)\frac{\left[1+\frac{\alpha}{\zeta^2}\eta+\frac{\alpha(2\alpha-r)}{3\zeta^4}\eta^2+\ldots\right]\exp\left[\frac{4\alpha\eta}{\zeta^2(1+z)}\right]}{\left[1+\frac{\alpha}{\zeta^2}\frac{2\eta}{1+z}+\frac{\alpha(2\alpha-r)^4}{3\zeta}\left(\frac{2\eta}{1+z}\right)^2+\ldots\right]^2}dz$$

$$> \frac{P(0)}{2}\int_{-1}^{1}\exp\left(-\frac{2\theta\eta}{1+z}\right)dz$$

From §11-12, however, this result may be stated in the following equivalent form:

$$Y(\eta) = X(\eta)\int_{\eta}^{\infty}\frac{\exp\left[\frac{2(\alpha-r)y}{\zeta^2}\right]}{X^2(y)}dy > \frac{P(0)}{2}\int_{-1}^{1}\exp\left(-\frac{2\theta\eta}{1+z}\right)dz$$

Now, we have previously noted (in §11-12) that

$$\frac{P(0)}{2}\int_{-1}^{1}\exp\left(-\frac{2\theta\eta}{1+z}\right)dz$$

is the adaptation value of equity for a non-dividend-paying firm. Hence, our analysis in this section has the important implication that the adaptation value of equity for a dividend-paying firm will always be larger than the adaptation value of equity for an equivalent non-dividend-paying firm. And this is as one would expect it to be, since, as noted in §11-11, dividend payments reduce the resources available to the firm and thereby increase the probability that the recursion value of the firm's equity will eventually fall away to zero. This in turn increases the likelihood that the firm will have to exercise its adaptation options, and so these options become more valuable as the firm increases the proportion α of its recursion value that it pays out as dividends.

§11-14. In this chapter, we have developed an equity valuation model that encompasses dirty surplus accounting and also where dividends are paid by the firm. We commenced our analysis with two dirty surplus propositions. The first of these shows how the recursion value of equity is determined when there is dirty surplus accounting, that is, when the clean surplus identity does not hold. The second shows that the recursion value of equity will be a weighted sum of the book value of equity, abnormal earnings, the information variable and the dirty surplus adjustment. Furthermore, this proposition also shows that ignoring the dirty surplus adjustment will, in general, induce biases in the functional expression for the recursion value of equity. Our analysis has also shown that whilst the Miller and Modigliani dividend policy irrelevance theorem applies to the recursion value of equity, it will not, in general, apply to the adaptation value of equity. Recursion value is computed under the assumption that the firm's investment opportunity set will not change, and since the dividend policy irrelevance theorem shows that in a perfect capital market without taxation, it is the cash flows associated with a given investment opportunity set and not dividends that determine equity value, it is clear that recursion value will have to be independent of the firm's dividend policy. However, the adaptation value of equity is determined by the potential changes that a firm can make to its existing investment opportunity set, and our analysis has shown that dividend payments can have a significant impact on this component of equity value. The analysis summarized in this chapter also confirms the conclusion reached in Chapter 9 that the market value of equity is potentially a highly non-linear function of its determining variables. Since most of the empirical work reported in this area of the literature is predicated on the assumption of a linear relationship between equity value and its determining variables, this raises the important issue of the potential biases that arise when the non-linearities induced by a firm's adaptation options are ignored by empirical researchers.

Selected references

Ashton, D., Cooke, T., Tippett, M. and Wang, P. (2004) 'Linear information dynamics, aggregation, dividends and "dirty surplus" accounting', *Accounting and Business Research*, 34: 277–99.

Isidro, H., O'Hanlon, J. and Young, S. (2004) 'Dirty surplus accounting flows: International evidence', *Accounting and Business Research*, 34: 383–411.

Isidro, H., O'Hanlon, J. and Young, S. (2004) 'Dirty surplus accounting flows and valuation errors', *Abacus*, 42: 302–44.

Jensen, G., Lundstrum, L. and Miller, R. (2010) 'What do dividend reductions signal?', *Journal of Corporate Finance*, 16: 736–47.

Landsman, W., Miller, B., Peasnell, K. and Yeh, S. (2011) 'Do investors understand *really* dirty surplus?', *Accounting Review*, 86: 237–58.

O'Hanlon, J. and Pope, P. (1999) 'The value-relevance of U.K. dirty surplus accounting flows', *British Accounting Review*, 31: 459–82.

Exercises

1. In §11-4, we determined the vector

$$\underset{\sim}{J}(t) = \begin{pmatrix} E_t\left[\int_t^\infty e^{-r(s-t)} a(s)ds\right] \\ E_t\left[\int_t^\infty e^{-r(s-t)} v(s)ds\right] \\ E_t\left[\int_t^\infty e^{-r(s-t)} \varepsilon(s)ds\right] \end{pmatrix}$$

whose elements are the present value of the stream of future abnormal earnings, the present value of the stream of information variables and the present value of the stream of dirty surplus adjustments. To do this, we had to solve the following equation:

$$\underset{\sim}{u}(t) = (rI - Q)\underset{\sim}{J}(t)$$

where

$$\underset{\sim}{u}(t) = \begin{pmatrix} a(t) \\ \nu(t) \\ \varepsilon(t) \end{pmatrix}$$

is the vector whose elements are the abnormal earnings, the information variable and the dirty surplus adjustment (all at time t), I is the identity matrix, Q is the matrix of structural coefficients and r is the expected return on the firm's equity. Cramer's Rule says that

$$E_t\left[\int_t^\infty e^{-r(s-t)}a(s)ds\right] = \frac{\det(rI - Q;\text{ with the first column replaced by }\underset{\sim}{u}(t))}{\det(rI - Q)}$$

where $\det(\cdot)$ is the determinant of the given matrix. Likewise,

$$E_t\left[\int_t^\infty e^{-r(s-t)}\nu(s)ds\right] = \frac{\det(rI - Q;\text{ with the second column replaced by }\underset{\sim}{u}(t))}{\det(rI - Q)}$$

and

$$E_t\left[\int_t^\infty e^{-r(s-t)}\varepsilon(s)ds\right] = \frac{\det(rI - Q;\text{ with the third column replaced by }\underset{\sim}{u}(t))}{\det(rI - Q)}$$

Use Cramer's Rule to determine the recursion value of equity when the matrix of structural coefficients is given by

$$Q = \begin{pmatrix} c_{11} & c_{12} & 0 \\ c_{21} & c_{22} & 0 \\ 0 & 0 & c_{33} \end{pmatrix}$$

and thereby confirm the results summarized in §11-6 above.

2. L'Hôpital's Rule states that if

$$\lim_{x\to\infty} f(x) = 0 \text{ and } \lim_{x\to\infty} g(x) = 0$$

and if

$$\lim_{x\to\infty}\frac{g'(x)}{f'(x)} \text{ exists}$$

then

$$\lim_{x\to\infty}\frac{g(x)}{f(x)}=\lim_{x\to\infty}\frac{g'(x)}{f'(x)}$$

Now consider the adaptation value of equity $Y(\eta)$ for the branching process as developed in §11-9 and §11-10:

$$Y(\eta)=X(\eta)\int_{\eta}^{\infty}\frac{\exp\left[\frac{2(\alpha-r)y}{\zeta^2}\right]}{X^2(y)}dy$$

where η is the recursion value of the firm's equity, ζ^2 is the variance parameter associated with instantaneous increments in the recursion value of equity, $0\leq\alpha<r$ is the proportional rate of dividend payments, r is the expected return on the firm's equity and

$$X(\eta)=a_0\left[\eta+\frac{\alpha}{\zeta^2}\eta^2+\frac{\alpha(2\alpha-r)}{3\zeta^4}\eta^3+\frac{\alpha(2\alpha-r)(3\alpha-2r)}{18\zeta^6}\eta^4+\ldots\right]$$

Use L'Hôpital's Rule to show

$$\lim_{\eta\to\infty}Y(\eta)=0$$

as given in §11-10.

3. A second interpretation of L'Hôpital's Rule states that if

$$\lim_{x\to 0}f(x)=0 \text{ and } \lim_{x\to 0}g(x)=0$$

and if

$$\lim_{x\to 0}\frac{g'(x)}{f'(x)}$$

exists, then

$$\lim_{x\to 0}\frac{g(x)}{f(x)}=\lim_{x\to 0}\frac{g'(x)}{f'(x)}$$

Use this interpretation of L'Hôpital's Rule to show

$$\lim_{\eta\to 0}Y(\eta)=\frac{1}{a_0}=P(0)$$

where $Y(\eta)$ is the adaptation value of the firm's equity defined in Exercise 3 above.

4. Suppose in §11-8 one lets $\delta = 0$ and that the firm makes dividend payments that are strictly proportional to the recursion value of its equity η. It then follows that the market value of the firm's equity $P(\eta)$ will satisfy the following interpretation of the Hamilton–Jacobi–Bellman equation:

$$\frac{1}{2}\zeta^2\frac{d^2P}{d\eta^2}+(r-\alpha)\eta\frac{dP}{d\eta}+[\alpha\eta - rP(\eta)]=0$$

where $\mathrm{Var}_t[dq(t)]/dt = \zeta^2$ is the variance (per unit time) of the white noise process that captures the stochastic component of instantaneous increments in the recursion value of equity, $0 \le \alpha < r$ is the proportional rate of dividend payments (as in §11-9) and r is the expected return on the firm's equity. Make the substitution

$$P(\eta) = \eta + X(\eta)$$

and thereby determine the auxiliary equation for the above interpretation of the Hamilton–Jacobi–Bellman equation. Determine the recurrence relation for the coefficients a_j of the following solution of the auxiliary equation:

$$X(\eta) = \sum_{j=0}^{\infty} a_j\eta^j$$

and thereby show that

$$X(\eta) = a_1\left[\eta + \frac{\alpha}{3\zeta^2}\eta^3 + \frac{\alpha(3\alpha-2r)}{30\zeta^4}\eta^5 + \frac{\alpha(3\alpha-2r)(5\alpha-4r)}{630\zeta^6}\eta^7 + \ldots\right]$$

is a formal solution of the auxiliary equation.

5. Use the formal solution for the auxiliary equation obtained in Exercise 4 and the procedures summarized in §11-10 to determine a second solution of the auxiliary equation. Show that this second solution captures the adaptation value of the firm's equity.

12 Equity valuation

Higher-order investment opportunity sets, momentum and acceleration

§12-1. In previous chapters, we have developed equity pricing formulae based on the assumption that that there are two complementary aspects to the valuation of a firm's equity. The first of these is determined by discounting the stream of expected future operating cash flows, or equivalently the dividends that the firm expects to pay, under the assumption that the firm will apply its existing investment opportunity set indefinitely into the future. This is usually referred to as the 'recursion value' of equity. The second component of equity value arises out of the fact that the firm will normally have the option to change or modify its investment opportunity set in order that it can use its resources in alternative and potentially more profitable ways. There are a variety of ways in which the firm can exercise this option to change its investment opportunity set, including liquidations, sell-offs, spin-offs, divestitures, CEO changes, mergers, takeovers, bankruptcies, restructurings and new capital investments. The potential to make changes like these gives rise to what is known as the 'adaptation value' of equity. Earlier chapters have assumed that if the recursion value falls away to nothing then the firm will be able to exchange its current investment opportunity set for a suite of assets and/or capital projects that have an inter-temporally *known and constant* adaptation value. However, it is highly likely that the adaptation value of equity will mirror recursion value in evolving stochastically through time. Unfortunately, the equity pricing formulae developed in previous chapters do not fully take account of the valuation implications arising from stochastic variations in the adaptation value of equity. Moreover, our analysis in earlier chapters also assumed that a firm's cash flows evolve through an investment opportunity set defined in terms of a first-order system of stochastic differential equations. However, there is mounting empirical evidence showing that the momentum and acceleration (i.e. the first and second derivatives) of the variables comprising the firm's investment opportunity set can also have a significant impact on the market value of a firm's equity. Unfortunately, when an investment opportunity set is defined in terms of a first-order system of stochastic differential equations, it cannot take account of these momentum and acceleration phenomena.

Our purpose in this chapter then is to build momentum, acceleration and stochastic variations in the adaptation value of equity into the equity valuation models developed in previous chapters. We begin our analysis of these issues in the next section by reiterating the fundamental proposition that underpins most of the equity valuation formulae developed in this book; namely, that the present value of the stream of future operating cash flows that a firm expects to earn is given by the sum of the book value of its equity and the present value of its stream of expected abnormal earnings. We then move into the main body of the chapter, where it is assumed that the variables comprising the firm's investment opportunity set evolve in terms of a second-order system of stochastic differential equations. We can use this assumption to show that the present value of the cash flows that a firm expects to earn can be stated in terms of both the levels and momentum (or first derivative) of the variables comprising the firm's investment opportunity set. This provides an analytical justification for the emerging empirical work that documents a significant association between earnings momentum and the market value of the firm's equity. Moreover, this result generalizes when the investment opportunity set is stated in terms of a higher-order system of stochastic differential equations. As a particular example, we show that if the investment opportunity set evolves in terms of a third-order system of stochastic differential equations then the present value of the cash flows that the firm expects to earn will be stated in terms of the levels, momentum (or first derivative) and acceleration (or second derivative) of the variables comprising the firm's investment opportunity set.

We then move on to demonstrate the significant impact that stochastic variations in adaptation value can have on the equity pricing formulae developed in previous chapters. Our analysis shows that the adaptation value of equity is a highly convex function of its determining variables, and this in turn implies that there will be a non-linear relationship between the market value of a firm's equity and the variables comprising its investment opportunity set. This again points to the biases that are likely to arise in empirical work that is based on the assumption that there is a purely linear relationship between the market value of a firm's equity and its determining variables. More important, however, is the fact that our analysis shows that the market value of a firm's equity grows in magnitude as the correlation between increments in the adaptation value of its equity and increments in the recursion value of its equity becomes more negative. This reflects the risk reduction benefits that arise from possessing a diversified portfolio of assets.

§12-2. In §9-1 of Chapter 9, we observed how the recursion value of a firm's equity $\eta(t)$ is defined as the present value of the firm's expected future cash flows (or equivalently the present value of the dividends that it expects to pay) given that it is indefinitely constrained to operate under its existing investment opportunity set. We also showed that the recursion value of equity can be determined from the following formula:

$$\eta(t) = b(t) + \int_t^\infty e^{-r(s-t)} E_t[a(s)]ds$$

where $b(t)$ is the book value of equity at time t, $a(t) = x(t) - rb(t)$ is the residual or abnormal earnings arising over the infinitesimal period from time t until to time $t + dt$ given that the firm is indefinitely constrained to operate under its existing investment opportunity set, $x(t)$ is the earnings reported on the firm's profit and loss account for the period from time t until time $t + dt, E_t[\cdot]$ is the expectation operator taken at time t and $r > 0$ is the cost of capital (on an annualized basis) applicable to equity. From §9-1 and §9-2, it will also be recalled that a firm's accounting procedures invariably capture information relevant to the valuation of equity with a lag – it can take many years for the full economic impact of a newly approved patent, a newly approved drug or the expansion (contraction) of a firm's order book to filter through to the firm's accounting records. Given this, we introduced an 'information' variable $\nu(t)$ as a component of the firm's investment opportunity set that summarizes all the information relevant to the valuation of equity that has not, as yet, found its way into the firm's accounting records. Moreover, our analysis in Chapter 9 assumed that the firm's investment opportunity set evolves in terms of a first-order system of stochastic differential equations. However, there is now compelling evidence that valuation models based on first-order processes of the kind employed in Chapter 9 generally underestimate equity values. Furthermore, investment opportunity sets based on the first-order processes employed in Chapter 9 cannot accommodate certain factors that one might expect to have a significant impact on the value of a firm's equity. Probably the most important of these is earnings momentum, which can only arise out of an investment opportunity set that is summarized in terms of a second- (or higher-) order system of stochastic differential equations.

§12-3. We can demonstrate this by supposing that the abnormal earnings $a(s)$ and the information variable $\nu(s)$ for a particular firm evolve in terms of an investment opportunity set that is characterized by the following reduced-form system of second-order stochastic differential equations:

$$\begin{pmatrix} \dfrac{d^2a(s)}{ds^2} \\ \dfrac{d^2\nu(s)}{ds^2} \end{pmatrix} = \begin{pmatrix} c_{11} & c_{12} \\ c_{21} & c_{22} \end{pmatrix} \begin{pmatrix} a(s) \\ \nu(s) \end{pmatrix} + \sqrt{\eta(s)} \begin{pmatrix} k_1 & 0 \\ 0 & k_2 \end{pmatrix} \begin{pmatrix} \dfrac{dz_1(s)}{ds} \\ \dfrac{dz_2(s)}{ds} \end{pmatrix}$$

or, in matrix notation,

$$\underset{\sim}{u}''(s) = Q\underset{\sim}{u}(s) + \sqrt{\eta(s)}K\underset{\sim}{z}'(s)$$

where $d^2a(s)/ds^2$ is the instantaneous acceleration in the abnormal earnings variable, $d^2\nu(s)/ds^2$ is the instantaneous acceleration in the information variable (both at time s) and Q is the matrix whose elements are the 'structural' coefficients of the model; namely, c_{11}, c_{12}, c_{21} and c_{22}. K is the matrix whose diagonal elements are the 'normalizing' constants

$$k_1 = \frac{(r^2 - c_{11})(r^2 - c_{22}) - c_{21}c_{12}}{r^2 - c_{22}} \quad \text{and} \quad k_2 = \frac{(r^2 - c_{11})(r^2 - c_{22}) - c_{21}c_{12}}{c_{12}}$$

respectively, and whose off-diagonal terms are all zero. Finally, $dz_1(s)/ds$ and $dz_2(s)/ds$ are uncorrelated white noise processes with variance parameters σ_1^2 and σ_2^2, respectively.

There are several points about the investment opportunity set given here that require emphasizing. We begin by noting how simple algebraic manipulation shows that the firm's abnormal earnings evolve in terms of the following process:

$$\frac{d^2a(s)}{ds^2} = -c_{11}\left[-\frac{c_{12}}{c_{11}}\nu(s) - a(s)\right] + k_1\sqrt{\eta(s)}\,\frac{dz_1(s)}{ds}$$

This means that, apart from a stochastic component, the firm's abnormal earnings accelerate towards a long-run mean of $(-c_{12}/c_{11})\nu(t)$. Moreover, the force with which the abnormal earnings will do so is proportional to the difference between this long-run mean and the current abnormal earnings, with the constant of proportionality, or speed-of-adjustment coefficient, being given by $-c_{11} > 0$. Larger values of the speed-of-adjustment coefficient imply that abnormal earnings will be more forcefully constrained to accelerate towards its long-run mean value. Note also that the stochastic component in the above equation hinges on the recursion value of equity $\eta(t)$. This assumption reflects the commonly held belief that the uncertainty associated with increments in an economic variable – in this instance abnormal earnings – become more pronounced as the affected variable grows in magnitude.

Similar considerations show that the differential equation for the information variable can be stated as

$$\frac{d^2 v(s)}{ds^2} = -c_{22}\left[-\frac{c_{21}}{c_{22}}a(s) - v(s)\right] + k_2\sqrt{\eta(s)}\,\frac{dz_2(s)}{ds}$$

This means that, apart from a stochastic component, the information variable $v(t)$ will accelerate towards a long-run mean of $(-c_{21}/c_{22})a(t)$. Again, the force with which it will do so is proportional to the difference between this long-run mean and the current value of the information variable – with the speed-of-adjustment coefficient being $-c_{22} > 0$. We have previously noted, however, that $v(t)$ captures all the value-relevant information that has not, as yet, found its way into the firm's bookkeeping records. It thus follows that $v(t)$ is prospective in nature and because of this it is unlikely that the abnormal earnings variable $a(t)$, which is generally retrospective in nature, can adequately reflect or capture movements in the information variable's long-run mean value. This in turn means that one would normally expect the structural coefficient c_{21} to be (close) to zero.

§12-4. We now recall that in §9-4 we applied integration by parts in order to show that the present value of the stream of future abnormal earnings will be

$$\int_t^\infty e^{-r(s-t)}a(s)ds = \left[-\frac{e^{-r(s-t)}}{r}a(s)\right]_t^\infty + \frac{1}{r}\int_t^\infty e^{-r(s-t)}\frac{da(s)}{ds}ds$$

Now suppose that we apply integration by parts to the final term on the right-hand side of this equation, in which case it follows that

$$\int_t^\infty e^{-r(s-t)}a(s)ds = \left[-\frac{e^{-r(s-t)}}{r}a(s)\right]_t^\infty + \left[-\frac{e^{-r(s-t)}}{r^2}\frac{da(s)}{ds}\right]_t^\infty + \frac{1}{r^2}\int_t^\infty e^{-r(s-t)}\frac{d^2a(s)}{ds^2}ds$$

However, we have previously noted (in §9-4) that the transversality requirement

$$\lim_{s\to\infty} e^{-r(s-t)}E_t[a(s)] = 0$$

where $E_t[\cdot]$ is the expectation operator (taken at time t), is a sufficient condition for the expected present value of the stream of future abnormal earnings to be convergent as the period over which it is computed becomes infinitely large. Similar considerations dictate that when the firm's investment opportunity set defines abnormal earnings in terms of a second-order system of stochastic differential equations, the following transversality requirement will ensure that the expected present value of the stream of future abnormal earnings will be convergent:

$$\lim_{s\to\infty} e^{-r(s-t)}E_t[a'(s)] = 0$$

where $a'(s) = da(s)/ds$ is the first derivative of the abnormal returns variable. We can then take expectations across the expression for the present value of the stream of future abnormal earnings in conjunction with the two transversality requirements given above and thereby show

$$E_t\left[\int_t^{\infty} e^{-r(s-t)} a(s)ds\right] = \frac{a(t)}{r} + \frac{a'(t)}{r^2} + \frac{1}{r^2}E_t\left[\int_t^{\infty} e^{-r(s-t)} a''(s)ds\right]$$

where $a''(s) = d^2a(s)/ds^2$ is the second derivative of the abnormal earnings variable. Now, recall from the system of stochastic differential equations describing the firm's investment opportunity set (as in §12-3) that the abnormal earnings variable will evolve in terms of the following differential equation:

$$\frac{d^2a(s)}{ds^2} = [c_{11}a(s) + c_{12}\nu(s)] + k_1\sqrt{\eta(s)}\frac{dz_1(s)}{ds}$$

Thus, we can substitute this result into the expression for the present value of the firm's expected abnormal earnings stream, in which case it follows that

$$E_t\left[\int_t^{\infty} e^{-r(s-t)} a(s)ds\right] =$$

$$\frac{a(t)}{r} + \frac{a'(t)}{r^2} + \frac{1}{r^2}E_t\left[\int_t^{\infty} e^{-r(s-t)}\left([c_{11}a(s) + c_{12}\nu(s)] + k_1\sqrt{\eta(s)}\,\frac{dz_1(s)}{ds}\right)ds\right]$$

However, since $E_t[dz_1(s)/ds] = 0$ for all $s > t$, it necessarily follows that the above result can be restated as

$$E_t\left[\int_t^{\infty} e^{-r(s-t)} a(s)ds\right] = \frac{a(t)}{r} + \frac{a'(t)}{r^2} + \frac{c_{11}}{r^2}E_t\left[\int_t^{\infty} e^{-r(s-t)} a(s)ds\right]$$

$$+ \frac{c_{12}}{r^2}E_t\left[\int_t^{\infty} e^{-r(s-t)} \nu(s)ds\right]$$

We can then collect terms in the above expression and thereby show

$$\left(1 - \frac{c_{11}}{r^2}\right)E_t\left[\int_t^{\infty} e^{-r(s-t)} a(s)ds\right] = \frac{a(t)}{r} + \frac{a'(t)}{r^2} + \frac{c_{12}}{r^2}E_t\left[\int_t^{\infty} e^{-r(s-t)} \nu(s)ds\right]$$

or equivalently

$$\int_t^{\infty} e^{-r(s-t)} E_t[a(s)]ds = \frac{ra(t)}{r^2 - c_{11}} + \frac{a'(t)}{r^2 - c_{11}} + \frac{c_{12}E_t\left[\int_t^{\infty} e^{-r(s-t)} \nu(s)ds\right]}{r^2 - c_{11}}$$

Now, it is clear from the above result that if we are to make progress towards determining the expected present value of the abnormal earnings stream then we will also have to evaluate the integral involving the present value of the stream of future information variables, namely,

$$\int_t^\infty e^{-r(s-t)}\nu(s)ds = \left[-\frac{e^{-r(s-t)}}{r}\nu(s)\right]_t^\infty + \left[-\frac{e^{-r(s-t)}}{r^2}\frac{d\nu(s)}{ds}\right]_t^\infty + \frac{1}{r^2}\int_t^\infty e^{-r(s-t)}\frac{d^2\nu(s)}{ds^2}ds$$

Here we can again apply the transversality requirements

$$\lim_{s\to\infty} e^{-r(s-t)}E_t[\nu(s)] = 0$$

and

$$\lim_{s\to\infty} e^{-r(s-t)}E_t[\nu'(s)] = 0$$

where $\nu'(s) = d\nu(s)/ds$ is the first derivative of the information variable, in order to ensure that the expected present value of the stream of future information variables will be convergent. We can then take expectations across the expression for the present value of the stream of future information variables in conjunction with the two transversality requirements given above and thereby show

$$E_t\left[\int_t^\infty e^{-r(s-t)}\nu(s)ds\right] = \frac{\nu(t)}{r} + \frac{\nu'(t)}{r^2} + \frac{1}{r^2}E_t\left[\int_t^\infty e^{-r(s-t)}\nu''(s)ds\right]$$

where $\nu''(s) = d^2\nu(s)/ds^2$ is the second derivative of the information variable. Now it will be recalled from the system of stochastic differential equations describing the firm's investment opportunity set (as in §12-3) that the information variable evolves in terms of the following differential equation:

$$\frac{d^2\nu(s)}{ds^2} = [c_{21}a(s) + c_{22}\nu(s)] + k_2\sqrt{\eta(s)}\frac{dz_2(s)}{ds}$$

We can substitute this result into the above expression for the expected present value of the stream of future information variables and then use the fact that $E_t[dz_2(s)/ds] = 0$ for all $s > t$, in which case it follows that

$$E_t\left[\int_t^\infty e^{-r(s-t)}\nu(s)ds\right] = \frac{\nu(t)}{r} + \frac{\nu'(t)}{r^2} + \frac{c_{21}}{r^2}E_t\left[\int_t^\infty e^{-r(s-t)}a(s)ds\right] + \frac{c_{22}}{r^2}E_t\left[\int_t^\infty e^{-r(s-t)}\nu(s)ds\right]$$

Collecting terms in the above equation shows

$$\left(1 - \frac{c_{22}}{r^2}\right)E_t\left[\int_t^\infty e^{-r(s-t)}\nu(s)ds\right] = \frac{\nu(t)}{r} + \frac{\nu'(t)}{r^2} + \frac{c_{21}}{r^2}E_t\left[\int_t^\infty e^{-r(s-t)}a(s)ds\right]$$

or equivalently

$$E_t\left[\int_t^\infty e^{-r(s-t)}v(s)ds\right]=\frac{rv(t)}{r^2-c_{22}}+\frac{v'(t)}{r^2-c_{22}}+\frac{c_{21}E_t\left[\int_t^\infty e^{-r(s-t)}a(s)ds\right]}{r^2-c_{22}}$$

Now, we have previously shown in this section that the present value of the expected stream of abnormal earnings will be

$$\int_t^\infty e^{-r(s-t)}E_t[a(s)]ds=\frac{ra(t)}{r^2-c_{11}}+\frac{a'(t)}{r^2-c_{11}}+\frac{c_{12}E_t\left[\int_t^\infty e^{-r(s-t)}v(s)ds\right]}{r^2-c_{11}}$$

Thus, we can use these latter two results to show that the present value of the stream of expected future abnormal earnings will be

$$\int_t^\infty e^{-r(s-t)}E_t[a(s)]ds=$$

$$\frac{ra(t)}{r^2-c_{11}}+\frac{a'(t)}{r^2-c_{11}}+\frac{c_{12}}{r^2-c_{11}}\left\{\frac{rv(t)}{r^2-c_{22}}+\frac{v'(t)}{r^2-c_{22}}+\frac{c_{21}}{r^2-c_{22}}E_t\left[\int_t^\infty e^{-r(s-t)}a(s)ds\right]\right\}$$

or equivalently

$$\int_t^\infty e^{-r(s-t)}E[a(s)]ds=\frac{r(r^2-c_{22})a(t)+(r^2-c_{22})a'(t)+rc_{12}v(t)+c_{12}v'(t)}{(r^2-c_{11})(r^2-c)_{22}-c_{12}c_{21}}$$

Note how this result shows that the present value of the stream of expected future abnormal earnings can be stated in terms of the firm's current earnings $a(t)$, the momentum in the firm's current earnings $a'(t)$, the current value of the information variable $v(t)$ and the momentum in the information variable $v'(t)$.

§12-5. It will be recalled from §12-2 that the recursion value of equity is determined by discounting the stream of future cash flows that the firm expects to earn, or equivalently the present value of the dividends it expects to pay over the life of the firm. In §12-2, we also reiterated that the expected present value of the stream of future cash flows that the firm expects to earn can be computed by reference to the following formula:

$$\eta(t)=b(t)+E_t\left[\int_t^\infty e^{-r(s-t)}a(s)ds\right]$$

where $b(t)$ is the book value of equity at time t, $a(t)$ is the instantaneous abnormal earnings, $E_t[\cdot]$ is the expectation operator taken at time t and $r>0$ is the cost of equity capital.

Now, if we substitute the expression for the stream of expected future abnormal earnings obtained in §12-4 into the above expression for $\eta(t)$, it follows that the recursion value of equity can be restated in terms of the following formula:

$$\eta(t) = b(t) + \frac{r(r^2 - c_{22})a(t) + (r^2 - c_{22})a'(t) + rc_{12}v(t) + c_{12}v'(t)}{(r^2 - c_{11})(r^2 - c_{22}) - c_{12}c_{21}}$$

This result has the important implication that the expected present value of the stream of future cash flows that the firm expects to earn hinges on both the levels and the momentum of the abnormal earnings and information variables, where the momentum in these variables is measured by their first derivatives; that is, $a'(t)$ and $v'(t)$, respectively. Hence, our analysis provides an analytical justification for the growing volume of empirical evidence that appears to show that the momentum of the variables comprising the firm's investment opportunity set can have a significant impact on the value of the firm's equity. Moreover, we can determine the time series properties of the recursion value of equity by differentiating through the above expression for $\eta(t)$. Doing so shows

$$\frac{d\eta(t)}{dt} = \frac{db(t)}{dt} + \frac{r(r^2 - c_{22})a'(t) + (r^2 - c_{22})a''(t) + rc_{12}v'(t) + c_{12}v''(t)}{(r^2 - c_{11})(r^2 - c_{22}) - c_{12}c_{21}}$$

Now, suppose that the 'clean surplus' requirement applies (as in §5-10 and §9-5), in which case increments in the book value of the firm's equity are composed of the profit (or loss) appearing on the firm's profit and loss account less any provisions that have been made for the payment of dividends. Thus, let $x(t)$ be the profit (on a per unit time basis) attributable to the firm's equity over the instantaneous period from time t until time $t + dt$. Likewise, let $D(t)$ be the dividend payment (again on a per unit time basis) made over the instantaneous period from time t until time $t + dt$. It then follows that the increment in the book value of equity over the period from time t until time $t + dt$ will be $db(t) = [x(t) - D(t)]dt$. Here, however, it will be recalled that the abnormal earnings attributable to equity over the instantaneous period from time t until time $t + dt$ will be $a(t) = x(t) - rb(t)$, where, as previously, r is the cost of capital for the firm's equity. This in turn will mean that the increment in the book value of equity over this period can be restated as

$$db(t) = [x(t) - D(t)]dt = [a(t) + rb(t) - D(t)]dt$$

or equivalently

$$\frac{db(t)}{dt} = a(t) + rb(t) - D(t)$$

if the increment in the book value of equity is stated on a per unit time basis. Now, we can take the expression given here for $db(t)/dt$ in conjunction with the expressions summarized in §12-3 for $d^2a(t)/dt^2 = a''(t)$ and $d^2v(t)/dt^2 = v''(t)$ and substitute them into the expression for $d\eta(t)/dt$ as given above. This will show that the increment in the recursion value of the firm's equity over the instantaneous period from time t until time $t+dt$ will be

$$\frac{d\eta(t)}{dt} = [a(t)+rb(t)-D(t)] + \frac{r(r^2-c_{22})a'(t)+rc_{12}\nu'(t)}{(r^2-c_{11})(r^2-c_{22})-c_{12}c_{21}}$$
$$+\frac{(r^2-c_{22})\left[c_{11}a(t)+c_{12}\nu(t)+k_1\sqrt{\eta(t)}\frac{dz_1(t)}{dt}\right]+c_{12}\left[c_{21}a(t)+c_{22}\nu(t)+k_2\sqrt{\eta(t)}\frac{dz_2(t)}{dt}\right]}{(r^2-c_{11})(r^2-c_{22})-c_{12}c_{21}}$$

But it will be recalled from §12-3 above that the firm's investment opportunity set incorporates two normalizing constants; namely,

$$k_1 = \frac{(r^2-c_{11})(r^2-c_{22})-c_{21}c_{12}}{r^2-c_{22}} \quad \text{and} \quad k_2 = \frac{(r^2-c_{11})(r^2-c_{22})-c_{21}c_{12}}{c_{12}}$$

This in turn will mean that the elements associated with the white noise terms in the above expression for $d\eta(t)/dt$ will simplify to:

$$\frac{(r^2-c_{22})k_1\sqrt{\eta(t)}\frac{dz_1(t)}{dt}}{(r^2-c_{11})(r^2-c_{22})-c_{12}c_{21}} = \sqrt{\eta(t)}\frac{dz_1(t)}{dt}$$

and

$$\frac{c_{12}k_2\sqrt{\eta(t)}\frac{dz_2(t)}{dt}}{(r^2-c_{11})(r^2-c_{22})-c_{12}c_{21}} = \sqrt{\eta(t)}\frac{dz_2(t)}{dt}$$

respectively. Moreover, if we use the fact that

$$a(t) = \frac{(r^2-c_{11})(r^2-c_{22})-c_{12}c_{21}}{(r^2-c_{11})(r^2-c_{22})-c_{12}c_{21}}a(t)$$

then the increment in the recursion value of equity can be restated as

$$\frac{d\eta(t)}{dt} = rb(t)-D(t)+\frac{[(r^2-c_{11})(r^2-c_{22})-c_{12}c_{21}]a(t)+r(r^2-c_{22})a'(t)+rc_{12}\nu'(t)}{(r^2-c_{11})(r^2-c_{22})-c_{12}c_{21}}$$
$$+\frac{(r^2-c_{22})[c_{11}a(t)+c_{12}\nu(t)]}{(r^2-c_{11})(r^2-c_{22})-c_{12}c_{21}}+\frac{c_{12}[c_{21}a(t)+c_{22}\nu(t)]}{(r^2-c_{11})(r^2-c_{22})-c_{12}c_{21}}$$
$$+\sqrt{\eta(t)}\left[\frac{dz_1(t)}{dt}+\frac{dz_2(t)}{dt}\right]$$

If we now collect terms in the above expression for $d\eta(t)/dt$ involving the abnormal earnings variable $a(t)$, we find

$$\frac{[(r^2-c_{22})(r^2-c_{11}+c_{11})-c_{12}c_{21}+c_{12}c_{21}]a(t)}{(r^2-c_{11})(r^2-c_{22})-c_{12}c_{21}} = \frac{r^2(r^2-c_{22})a(t)}{(r^2-c_{11})(r^2-c_{22})-c_{12}c_{21}}$$

Similarly, if we collect terms in the expression for $d\eta(t)/dt$ involving the information variable $\nu(t)$ we find

$$\frac{[(r^2-c_{22})c_{12}+c_{12}c_{22}]\nu(t)}{(r^2-c_{11})(r^2-c_{22})-c_{12}c_{21}}=\frac{r^2c_{12}\nu(t)}{(r^2-c_{11})(r^2-c_{22})-c_{12}c_{21}}$$

Bringing these results together shows that the increment in the recursion value of the firm's equity can be restated as

$$\frac{d\eta(t)}{dt}=r\left[b(t)+\frac{r(r^2-c_{22})a(t)+(r^2-c_{22})a'(t)+rc_{12}\nu(t)+c_{12}\nu'(t)}{(r^2-c_{11})(r^2-c_{22})-c_{12}c_{21}}\right]$$

$$-D(t)+\sqrt{\eta(t)}\left[\frac{dz_1(t)}{dt}+\frac{dz_2(t)}{dt}\right]$$

Hence, if we define

$$\frac{dq(t)}{dt}=\frac{dz_1(t)}{dt}+\frac{dz_2(t)}{dt}$$

as a white noise process with variance parameter $\zeta^2=\sigma_1^2+\sigma_2^2$ and use the fact that our calculations at the beginning of this section show that the recursion value is given by

$$\eta(t)=b(t)+\frac{r(r^2-c_{22})a(t)+(r^2-c_{22})a'(t)+rc_{12}\nu(t)+c_{12}\nu'(t)}{(r^2-c_{11})(r^2-c_{22})-c_{12}c_{21}}$$

then it follows that the increment in the recursion value of the firm's equity (per unit time) over the instantaneous period from time t until time $t+dt$ will be

$$\frac{d\eta(t)}{dt}=[r\eta(t)-D(t)]+\sqrt{\eta(t)}\frac{dq(t)}{dt}$$

It will be recalled from §9-6 and §11-5 that this is the differential equation of a continuous-time branching process. It shows that the rate of growth in the recursion value of equity hinges on the dividend policy $D(t)$ invoked by the firm as well as the stochastic perturbations arising from the white noise term $dq(t)/dt$. In particular, higher dividend payouts will mean that recursion value will on average grow more slowly. This in turn has the important implication that the expected present value of the future cash flows will evolve in terms of a first-order stochastic differential equation even though the variables on which it is based evolve in terms of an investment opportunity set that is defined in terms of a second-order system of stochastic differential equations. Indeed, as we shall see in §12-6 below, a general principle applies here; namely, that if the components of the firm's investment opportunity set evolve in terms of a vector system of differential equations of any given order then the present value of the cash flows that the firm expects to earn will nonetheless evolve in terms of a first-order stochastic differential equation.

§12-6. Our analysis so far has established the general principle that the momentum (i.e. the first derivatives) of the variables comprising a firm's investment opportunity set can have a significant impact on the present value of the future cash flows that the firm expects to earn. We now establish that this result generalizes in the sense that higher-order derivatives can also have a significant influence on the present value of the cash flows that the firm expects to receive. We can demonstrate this by supposing that the abnormal earnings and the information variable for a particular firm evolve in terms of an investment opportunity set that is characterized by the following reduced-form system of third-order stochastic differential equations:

$$\begin{pmatrix} \dfrac{d^3a(s)}{ds^3} \\ \dfrac{d^3\nu(s)}{ds^3} \end{pmatrix} = \begin{pmatrix} c_{11} & c_{12} \\ c_{21} & c_{22} \end{pmatrix} \begin{pmatrix} a(s) \\ \nu(s) \end{pmatrix} + \sqrt{\eta(s)} \begin{pmatrix} k_1 & 0 \\ 0 & k_2 \end{pmatrix} \begin{pmatrix} \dfrac{dz_1(s)}{ds} \\ \dfrac{dz_2(s)}{ds} \end{pmatrix}$$

or, in matrix notation,

$$\underset{\sim}{u}'''(s) = Q\underset{\sim}{u}(s) + \sqrt{\eta(s)}K\underset{\sim}{z}'(s)$$

where $d^3a(s)/ds^3 = a'''(s)$ is the instantaneous jerk in the abnormal earnings variable, $d^3\nu(s)/ds^3 = \nu'''(s)$ is the instantaneous jerk in the information variable (both at time s) and Q is the matrix whose elements are the 'structural' coefficients of the model; namely, c_{11}, c_{12}, c_{21} and c_{22}. K is the matrix whose diagonal elements are the 'normalizing' constants:

$$k_1 = \frac{(r^3 - c_{11})(r^3 - c_{22}) - c_{21}c_{12}}{r^3 - c_{22}} \quad \text{and} \quad k_2 = \frac{(r^3 - c_{11})(r^3 - c_{22}) - c_{21}c_{12}}{c_{12}}$$

respectively, and whose off-diagonal terms are all zero. Finally, $dz_1(s)/ds$ and $dz_2(s)/ds$ are uncorrelated white noise processes with variance parameters σ_1^2 and σ_2^2, respectively. Here it is important to note that the jerk in a variable is the rate of change in its acceleration. Investors may be interested in the jerk of a firm's abnormal earnings variable since this captures the rate of change in the way the abnormal earnings variable accelerates into the future. The greater the jerk, the greater the persistence in the acceleration of the abnormal earnings variable and, as we will demonstrate shortly, this leads to larger expected future cash flows and equity values. Moreover, simple algebraic manipulation of the firm's investment opportunity set shows that the jerk in a firm's abnormal earnings evolves in terms of the following process:

$$\frac{d^3a(s)}{ds^3} = -c_{11}\left[-\frac{c_{12}}{c_{11}}\nu(s) - a(s)\right] + k_1\sqrt{\eta(s)}\frac{dz_1(s)}{ds}$$

This means that, apart from a stochastic component, the firm's abnormal earnings will 'jerk' towards a long-run mean of $(-c_{12}/c_{11})\nu(t)$. Moreover, the force with which the firm's abnormal earnings will do so is proportional to the difference between this long-run mean and the current abnormal earnings and where the constant of proportionality, or speed-of-adjustment coefficient, is $-c_{11} > 0$. Larger values of the speed-of-adjustment coefficient imply that the abnormal earnings will be more forcefully constrained to jerk towards its long-run mean value.

Similar considerations show that the differential equation for the information variable can be stated as

$$\frac{d^3\nu(s)}{ds^3} = -c_{22}\left[-\frac{c_{21}}{c_{22}}a(s) - \nu(s)\right] + k_2\sqrt{\eta(s)}\frac{dz_2(s)}{ds}$$

This means that, apart from a stochastic component, the information variable $\nu(t)$ will jerk towards a long-run mean of $(-c_{21}/c_{22})a(t)$. Again, the force with which it will do so is proportional to the difference between this long-run mean and the current value of the information variable, with the speed-of-adjustment coefficient being $-c_{22} > 0$. We have previously noted (in §12-3), however, that $\nu(t)$ captures all value-relevant information that has not, as yet, found its way into the firm's accounting records. It thus follows that $\nu(t)$ is prospective in nature and that, because of this, it is unlikely that the abnormal earnings variable $a(t)$, which is generally retrospective in nature, can adequately reflect or capture movements in the information variable's long-run mean value. This in turn will mean that one would normally expect the structural coefficient c_{21} to be (close) to zero.

We can now again apply repeated integration by parts to the present value of the future stream of abnormal earnings and the present value of the future stream of information variables and thereby show that under the above investment opportunity set the present value of the cash flows the firm expects to earn will be

$$\eta(t) =$$

$$b(t) + \frac{r^2(r^3 - c_{22})a(t) + r(r^3 - c_{22})a'(t) + (r^3 - c_{22})a''(t) + r^2 c_{12}\nu(t) + rc_{12}\nu'(t) + c_{12}\nu''(t)}{(r^3 - c_{11})(r^3 - c_{22}) - c_{12}c_{21}}$$

Note how this result shows that the present value of the stream of future cash flows hinges on both the momentum ($a'(t)$ and $\nu'(t)$) and the acceleration ($a''(t)$ and $\nu''(t)$) of the variables comprising the firm's investment opportunity set. And here it is important to note that whilst there is an emerging empirical literature documenting a significant association between a firm's earnings momentum and/or acceleration and the market value of the firm's equity, the result given here provides an important analytical justification through which to theoretically underpin the empirical results reported in the literature of the area.

We can also differentiate through the above expression for $\eta(t)$ and thereby show that the instantaneous increments in the present value of the cash flows that the firm expects to earn will evolve in terms of a continuous-time branching process. This in turn means that the expected present value of the stream of future cash flows that the firm expects to earn will evolve as a first-order differential equation even though the variables on which it is based evolve in terms of a third-order system of stochastic differential equations. This is consistent with the general principle identified in §12-5 above; namely, that if the components of the firm's investment opportunity set evolve in terms of a vector system of differential equations of any given order then the present value of the cash flows that the firm expects to earn will nonetheless evolve in terms of the following process:

$$\frac{d\eta(t)}{dt} = [r\eta(t) - D(t)] + \sqrt{\eta(t)}\frac{dq(t)}{dt}$$

where r is the cost of equity capital, $D(t)$ is the instantaneous dividend payment at time t and $dq(t)/dt$ is a white noise process with variance parameter ζ^2 (as in §12-5).

There is one further and very important sense in which the results presented in this and the previous section generalize to investment opportunity sets characterized by higher-order systems of differential equations. We can illustrate this by supposing that the evolution of the variables comprising the firm's investment opportunity set are defined in terms of a fourth-order system of stochastic differential equations. It then follows that the present value of the cash flows that the firm expects to earn will hinge not only on the levels, momentum (first derivative) and acceleration (second derivative) of the abnormal earnings and information variables, but also on the jerk (or third derivative) of the abnormal earnings and information variables. Moreover, if the firm's investment opportunity set is characterized by even higher-order systems of stochastic differential equations then the present value of the cash flows that the firm expects to earn will turn on the snap (fourth derivative), crackle (fifth derivative) and pop (sixth derivative) of the abnormal earnings and information variables.

§12-7. In previous sections of this chapter, we have determined the recursion value of a firm's equity on the assumption that the firm is indefinitely constrained to operate within its existing investment opportunity set. We have previously noted (in §9-1), however, that there is a second component of equity value; namely, the adaptation value associated with a firm's ability to change its existing investment opportunity set. Earlier chapters assumed that if the recursion value of equity falls away to nothing then the firm will be able to exchange its current investment opportunity set for a suite of assets and/or capital projects that have an inter-temporally *known and constant* adaptation value. However, it is highly likely that the adaptation value of equity will mirror recursion value in evolving stochastically through time. We can address the obvious limitations this constant adaptation value assumption poses for the equity valuation models developed in previous chapters by supposing that adaptation value evolves in terms of the following 'technological uncertainty' process:

$$\frac{dB(t)}{dt} = \lambda B(t) + B(t)\sqrt{\eta(t)}\frac{dg(t)}{dt}$$

where $B(t)$ is the adaptation value of equity (conditional on the recursion value of the firm's equity falling away to nothing), $E_t[dB(t)/B(t)] = \lambda dt$ is the expected instantaneous rate of growth in the adaptation value of equity and $dg(t)/dt$ is a white noise process with variance parameter δ^2. Here, we would expect λ to be less than the cost of equity r, since the payment of dividends will reduce the adaptation value of equity in a similar (though not necessarily the same) way in which the payment of dividends reduces the recursion value of the firm's equity (as in §11-11 and §11-12). Moreover, the instantaneous covariance between proportionate variations in adaptation value and proportionate variations in the recursion value of equity will be

$$\frac{dB(t)}{B(t)}\frac{d\eta(t)}{\eta(t)} = \sqrt{\eta(t)}dg(t)\frac{1}{\sqrt{\eta(t)}}dq(t) = dg(t)dq(t) = \rho\delta\xi\, dt$$

where ρ is the correlation coefficient between the white noise process $dg(t)/dt$ that captures the uncertainty in adaptation value and the white noise process $dq(t)/dt$ that captures the uncertainty in recursion value (as in §12-5 above). Note also that the variance of instantaneous proportionate changes in adaptation value will be

$$Var_t\left[\frac{dB(t)}{B(t)}\right] = \delta^2\eta(t)dt$$

This in turn shows that if the recursion value of equity falls away to nothing ($\eta = 0$) then all uncertainty surrounding the adaptation value of equity is resolved (i.e. $\text{Var}_t[dB(t)/B(t)] = 0$). In these circumstances, the firm will replace its current investment opportunity set with the alternative opportunities reflected in the current adaptation value of equity $B(t)$.

Likewise, as the recursion value grows, there is increasing uncertainty about the rate of growth in the adaptation value of equity – reflecting the fact that it is increasingly unlikely the firm will change its investment opportunity set in the foreseeable future.

Now, the market value of the firm's equity $P(B(t), \eta(t))$ will have to satisfy the 'no-arbitrage' condition:

$$P(B(t), \eta(t)) = D(t)dt + e^{-rdt}E_t[P(B(t+dt), \eta(t+dt))]$$

where, as previously, r is the cost of equity capital, $D(t)$ is the instantaneous dividend payment (per unit time) made to equity holders at time t, and $E_t[\cdot]$ is the expectation operator taken at time t. This condition requires that the market value of equity 'today' must be equal to the dividend payment 'today' plus the expected discounted market value of equity 'tomorrow'. In other words, equity will be priced so that, on average, only 'normal' returns r are earned (as in §9-7 and §11-8). We can use the no-arbitrage condition given here in conjunction with the present value of the cash flows the firm expects to earn – as in §12-5 and §12-6 (depending on which investment opportunity set the firm has implemented) – and then follow procedures similar to those applied in §9-7 to show that the market value of equity will have to satisfy the Hamilton–Jacobi–Bellman equation:

$$\frac{1}{2}\zeta^2\eta\frac{\partial^2 P}{\partial\eta^2} + \rho\zeta\delta\eta B\frac{\partial^2 P}{\partial\eta\partial B} + \frac{1}{2}\delta^2 B^2\eta\frac{\partial^2 P}{\partial B^2} + \lambda B\frac{\partial P}{\partial B} + (r\eta - D)\frac{\partial P}{\partial\eta} + [D - rP(B, \eta)] = 0$$

Moreover, when the expected present value of the future cash flows from operating under the firm's existing investment opportunity set is 'small' ($\eta \to 0$), equity value will be composed mainly of the adaptation value associated with the firm's ability to change its investment opportunity set. This in turn implies that the Hamilton–Jacobi–Bellman equation will have to satisfy the boundary condition $P(B, 0) = B$. Furthermore, when the expected present value of the future cash flows that the firm expects to earn from operating under its existing investment opportunity set is 'large' ($\eta \to \infty$), the adaptation value associated with changing the investment opportunity set will be 'small'. This means the Hamilton–Jacobi–Bellman equation will also have to satisfy the boundary condition $\lim_{\eta\to\infty} P(B, \eta) = \eta$.

§12-8. Now, suppose we seek a solution to the Hamilton–Jacobi–Bellman equation in the form

$$P(B, \eta) = \eta + BY(\eta)$$

where $Y(\eta)$ is a function that captures the adaptation value of the firm's equity. Note how this expression divides the market value of the firm's equity into its two components; namely, its recursion value η and its adaptation value $BY(\eta)$. Substituting the above expression into the Hamilton–Jacobi–Bellman equation then gives

$$\frac{1}{2}\zeta^2\eta B\frac{d^2Y(\eta)}{d\eta^2} + \rho\zeta\delta\eta B\frac{dY(\eta)}{d\eta} + \lambda BY(\eta)$$
$$+ (r\eta - D)\left[1 + B\frac{dY(\eta)}{d\eta}\right] + [D - r\eta - rBY(\eta)] = 0$$

We can cancel and collect terms in this expression and thereby show that the adaptation value of equity will have to satisfy the following 'auxiliary' equation:

$$\frac{1}{2}\zeta^2\eta\frac{d^2Y(\eta)}{d\eta^2}+(r\eta+\rho\zeta\delta\eta-D)\frac{dY(\eta)}{d\eta}-(r-\lambda)Y(\eta)=0$$

Under this substitution, the first boundary condition for the auxiliary equation (as in §12-7 above) becomes $P(B,0)=BY(0)=B$, or $Y(0)=1$. Likewise, for the second boundary condition (again as in §12-7), we have $\lim_{\eta\to\infty}Y(\eta)=0$. The first of these boundary conditions, $Y(0)=1$, reflects the requirement that when the recursion value falls away to nothing, the market value of the firm's equity is composed entirely of adaptation value. The second boundary condition incorporates the requirement that when the recursion value is relatively 'large', the adaptation value will be relatively 'small'. Now let us assume (as in §11-9) that the firm pays dividends that are proportional to the recursion value of equity, namely, that $D(t)=\alpha\eta(t)$, where $0\le\alpha<r$ is the constant of proportionality. It then follows that the auxiliary equation may be stated as

$$\frac{1}{2}\zeta^2\eta\frac{d^2Y(\eta)}{d\eta^2}+(r+\rho\zeta\delta-\alpha)\eta\frac{dY(\eta)}{d\eta}-(r-\lambda)Y(\eta)=0$$

Unfortunately, no closed-form solutions are available for this auxiliary equation. However, we can follow procedures similar to those articulated in §11-9 and §11-10 and thereby show that the solution of the auxiliary equation can be stated in terms of the following integrated power series expansion:

$$Y(\eta)=X(\eta)\int_{\eta}^{\infty}\frac{e^{-\varphi y}}{X^2(y)}dy$$

where

$$X(\eta)=$$

$$\eta+\int_{j=1}^{\infty}\frac{2^j[(\alpha-\rho\zeta\delta)+\lambda][2(\alpha-\rho\zeta\delta)-(r-\lambda)]\cdots[j(\alpha-\rho\zeta\delta)-\{(j-1)r-\lambda\}]}{j!(j+1)!\zeta^{2j}}\eta^{j+1}$$

and

$$\varphi=\frac{2(r+\rho\zeta\delta-\alpha)}{\zeta^2}>0$$

is a risk (or stability) parameter (as in §9-10) that incorporates the correlation ρ between instantaneous changes in the adaptation value of equity and the recursion value of equity. In particular, it can be shown that the above solution satisfies the required boundary conditions; $Y(0)=1$ and $\lim_{\eta\to\infty}Y(\eta)=0$.

The above solution has several properties that need emphasizing. First, note that if we set $\lambda=\rho\zeta\delta=0$ then the solution is equivalent to that obtained in §11-9 and §11-10 for the equity value of a firm that has the option to exchange its current investment opportunity set for a suite of assets and/or capital projects that have an inter-temporally known and constant adaptation value. Given this, it is not surprising that graphs of the solution given here and those depicted in §11-10 are virtually identical. More important, however, is the fact that the term $e^{-\varphi y}$ that appears in the integral for $Y(\eta)$ grows in magnitude as the risk parameter φ becomes smaller. This in turn means that $Y(\eta)$ becomes larger as φ becomes smaller. Now, it is important to note here that the risk parameter φ falls in magnitude when the correlation ρ between increments in adaptation value and increments in recursion value becomes more and more negative. This shows that the adaptation value of equity will become larger as ρ becomes smaller. This, in turn, reflects the risk reduction benefits that arise for the firm from possessing a diversified portfolio of assets. Finally, using the substitution given at the beginning of §12-8 above, it follows that the market value equity will be

$$P(B,\eta) = \eta + BX(\eta)\int_{\eta}^{\infty} \frac{e^{-\varphi y}}{X^2(y)}dy$$

where, it will be recalled (as in §12-7), that B is the (stochastically varying) adaptation value of the firm's equity should the recursion value of equity fall away to nothing. Note how this valuation formula shows that under very general conditions (an adaptation value of equity that varies stochastically through time and an investment opportunity set that evolves in terms of higher-order systems of stochastic differential equations), the market value of a firm's equity $P(B,\eta)$ is a highly non-linear function of its determining variables. We would emphasize that this is of particular importance given the penchant amongst empirical researchers for applying purely linear methodologies to estimate the valuation relationships that exist in this area. It is not hard to show that if, as the empirical (and analytical) evidence indicates, there is a non-linear relationship between equity prices and their determining variables, then the purely linear methodologies that so dominate empirical work in this area of the literature will form an unreliable basis for estimating the relevant valuation relationships.

§12-9. Our principal purpose in this chapter has been to build the momentum and acceleration of variables comprising the firm's investment opportunity set and stochastic variations in the adaptation value of equity into the equity valuation models developed in previous chapters. There are several reasons for doing this. First, there is mounting empirical evidence showing that momentum and acceleration (i.e. the first and second derivatives, respectively, of the variables comprising the firm's investment opportunity set) can have a significant impact on the market value of a firm's equity. Unfortunately, when an investment opportunity set is defined in terms of the first-order systems of stochastic differential equations employed in previous chapters, it cannot take account of these momentum and acceleration phenomena. We have addressed this problem by demonstrating that if a firm's investment opportunity set evolves in terms of a second- (or higher-) order system of stochastic differential equations then the present value of the future cash flows that it expects to earn will be stated in terms of both the levels and the momentum (i.e. first derivative) of the variables comprising its investment opportunity set. This provides an analytical justification for the emerging empirical evidence that finds a significant association between earnings momentum and the market value of equity. Moreover, the results presented here generalize to higher-order systems of stochastic differential equations. It then follows that the acceleration (second derivative), jerk (third derivative), snap (fourth derivative), crackle (fifth derivative) and pop (sixth derivative) of the variables comprising its investment opportunity set can also have a significant impact on the present value of the cash flows that a firm expects to earn.

We have also demonstrated that if firms have the capacity to modify or change their investment opportunity sets then it is doubtful whether the expected present value rule can provide a complete description of the way equity prices are determined in practice. A firm's ability to modify or change its investment opportunity set is a valuable option that can make a significant contribution to the overall market value of its equity; and this will be in addition to the value emanating from the present value of the stream of future cash flows that the firm expects to make. Earlier chapters of this book assumed that if the recursion value of equity falls away to nothing then the firm will be able to exchange its current investment opportunity set for a suite of assets and/or capital projects that have an inter-temporally known and constant adaptation value. However, it is highly likely that the adaptation value of equity will mirror the recursion value in evolving stochastically through time. We have addressed the obvious limitations this constant adaptation value assumption poses for the equity valuation models developed in previous chapters by determining the auxiliary form of the Hamilton–Jacobi–Bellman equation when the adaptation value of equity evolves stochastically in time. The solution to this equation shows that the risk parameter associated with the recursion value of equity will fall as the correlation ρ between increments in adaptation value and increments in recursion value becomes more negative. This, in turn, will mean that the adaptation value of equity will become larger as ρ becomes smaller. This reflects the risk reduction benefits that arise for the firm from possessing a diversified portfolio of assets.

As in previous chapters, our analysis has also shown that the adaptation value of equity is a highly convex function of its determining variables and that there will be a non-linear relationship between the market value of a firm's equity and the variables comprising its investment opportunity set. This again points to the biases that are likely to arise in empirical work that is based on the assumption that there is a purely linear relationship between the market value of a firm's equity and its determining variables.

Selected references

Albrecht, W., Lookabill, L. and McKeown, J. (1977) 'The time-series properties of annual earnings', *Journal of Accounting Research*, 5: 226–44.

Brown, D. (1993) 'Earnings forecasting research: its implications for capital markets research', *International Journal of Forecasting*, 9: 295–320.

Chordia, T. and Shivakumar, L. (2006) 'Earnings and price momentum', *Journal of Financial Economics*, 80: 627–56.

Dichev, I. and Tang, V. (2009) 'Earnings volatility and earnings predictability', *Journal of Accounting and Economics*, 47: 160–81.

Hoel, P., Port, S. and Stone, C. (1987) *Introduction to Stochastic Processes*, Long Grove, IL: Waveland Press.

Lorek, K., Willinger, G. and Bathke, A. (2008) 'Statistically based quarterly earnings expectation models for nonseasonal firms', *Review of Quantitative Finance and Accounting*, 31: 105–19.

Myers, J., Myers, L. and Skinner, D. (2007) 'Earnings momentum and earnings management', *Journal of Accounting, Auditing, and Finance*, 22: 249–84.

Exercises

1. In §12-4, we have shown that under certain transversality conditions, the expected present value of the stream of future abnormal earnings will be

$$E_t\left[\int_t^\infty e^{-r(s-t)}a(s)ds\right] = \frac{a(t)}{r} + \frac{a'(t)}{r^2} + \frac{1}{r^2}E_t\left[\int_t^\infty e^{-r(s-t)}a''(s)ds\right]$$

where $a(s)$ is the abnormal earnings at time s and $a'(s) = da(s)/ds$ and $a''(s) = d^2a(s)/ds^2$ are its first and second derivatives, respectively. Use integration by parts and any further transversality conditions that may be required to show that the expected present value of the future stream of abnormal earnings can also be expressed as

$$E_t\left[\int_t^\infty e^{-r(s-t)}a(s)ds\right] = \frac{a(t)}{r} + \frac{a'(t)}{r^2} + \frac{a''(t)}{r^3} + \frac{1}{r^3}E_t\left[\int_t^\infty e^{-r(s-t)}a'''(s)ds\right]$$

where $a'''(s) = d^3a(s)/ds^3$ is the third derivative of the abnormal earnings variable. Use the assumption in §12-6 that the firm's investment opportunity set can be expressed in terms of a third-order system of stochastic differential equations to restate the expected present value of the stream of future abnormal earnings as follows:

$$E_t\left[\int_t^\infty e^{-r(s-t)}a(s)ds\right] = \frac{r^2a(t)}{r^3 - c_{11}} + \frac{ra'(t)}{r^3 - c_{11}} + \frac{a''(t)}{r^3 - c_{11}} + \frac{c_{12}}{r^3 - c_{11}}E_t\left[\int_t^\infty e^{-r(s-t)}v(s)ds\right]$$

Use similar procedures to show that the expected present value of the stream of future information variables can be represented as

$$E_t\left[\int_t^\infty e^{-r(s-t)}v(s)ds\right] = \frac{r^2v(t)}{r^3 - c_{22}} + \frac{rv'(t)}{r^3 - c_{22}} + \frac{v''(t)}{r^3 - c_{22}} + \frac{c_{21}}{r^3 - c_{22}}E_t\left[\int_t^\infty e^{-r(s-t)}a(s)ds\right]$$

Finally, simultaneously solve the above two equations and thereby show that the expected present value of the future stream of abnormal earnings can be represented as:

$$E_t\left[\int_t^\infty e^{-r(s-t)}a(s)ds\right] =$$

$$\frac{r^2(r^3 - c_{22})a(t) + r(r^3 - c_{22})a'(t) + (r^3 - c_{22})a''(t) + r^2c_{12}v(t) + rc_{12}v'(t) + c_{12}v''(t)}{(r^3 - c_{11})(r^3 - c_{22}) - c_{12}c_{21}}$$

2. In §12-8, we considered the auxiliary form of the Hamilton–Jacobi–Bellman equation; namely,

$$\frac{1}{2}\zeta^2\eta\frac{d^2Y(\eta)}{d\eta^2} + (r + \rho\zeta\delta - \alpha)\eta\frac{dY(\eta)}{d\eta} - (r - \lambda)Y(\eta) = 0$$

Let

$$\varphi = \frac{2(r+\rho\zeta\delta-\alpha)}{\zeta^2} > 0$$

be the appropriate form of the risk parameter and thereby show that

$$Y(\eta) = X(\eta)\int_{\eta}^{\infty} \frac{e^{-\varphi y}}{X^2(y)}dy$$

is a solution of the above differential equation. Show that $X(\eta)$ will take the form of a power series expansion and that, in particular,

$$X(\eta) = \sum_{j=0}^{\infty} a_j \eta^{j+1}$$

is a second solution of the auxiliary equation. Determine the coefficients a_j appearing in the expression for $X(\eta)$.

3. Use L'Hôpital's Rule (as in Exercises 2 and 3 of Chapter 11) and thereby show that

$$\lim_{\eta\to\infty} Y(\eta) = 0$$

and

$$\lim_{\eta\to 0} Y(\eta) = 1$$

where $Y(\eta)$ is as derived in Exercise 2. Explain how $Y(\eta)$ captures the adaptation value of equity.

4. In §12-8, it was shown that the market value of equity $P(B,\eta)$ is given by

$$P(B,\eta) = \eta + BY(\eta)$$

where η is the recursion value of equity, B is the adaptation value of equity conditional on the recursion value of equity falling away to nothing and $Y(\eta)$ is the solution of the auxiliary form of the Hamilton–Jacobi–Bellman equation as given in Exercise 2. Now suppose that $\rho = 0$ is the correlation between the white noise process $dg(t)/dt$ capturing the uncertainty in adaptation value and the white noise process $dq(t)/dt$ capturing the uncertainty in recursion value (as in §12-7; the case of a non-trivial correlation coefficient is more difficult). Apply the transformation

$$z = \frac{2\eta}{y} - 1$$

and thereby show that $Y(\eta)$ can be re-expressed as

$$Y(\eta) = 2\eta X(\eta)\int_{-1}^{1} \frac{\exp\left(-\frac{2\varphi\eta}{1+z}\right)}{\left[(1+z)X\left(\frac{2\eta}{1+z}\right)\right]^2}dz$$

where

$$\varphi = \frac{2(r-\alpha)}{\zeta^2} > 0$$

is the risk (or stability) parameter. Use this result to show that $P(B,\eta)$ is scale-invariant under the dilation $\lambda = 1/\Theta$ (where Θ is an arbitrary real number), with a scaling dimension of $\Delta = 1$ (as in §10-6 of Chapter 10).

5. The Wronskian determinant of the two solutions $X(\eta)$ and $Y(\eta)$ of the auxiliary equation defined in Exercise 2 is given by

$$\det\begin{pmatrix} X(\eta) & Y(\eta) \\ \dfrac{dX(\eta)}{d\eta} & \dfrac{dY(\eta)}{d\eta} \end{pmatrix} = X(\eta)\frac{dY(\eta)}{d\eta} - \frac{dX(\eta)}{d\eta}Y(\eta)$$

where det(·) is the determinant of the given matrix. Use the expression for the moment-generating function for a continuous-time branching process as given in §9-6 and thereby show that

$$\lim_{t\to\infty} E_0\left[X(\eta)\frac{dY(\eta)}{d\eta} - \frac{dX(\eta)}{d\eta}Y(\eta)\right] = \exp\left[-\frac{2(r-\alpha)\eta(0)}{\zeta^2}\right]$$

where $E_0[\cdot]$ is the expectation operator taken at time zero and $\eta(0)$ is the recursion value of equity at time zero. Use §9-10 and §11-11 to provide an appropriate interpretation of this result.

Index

Abnormal earnings (profit), 5, 130–1, 139, 208–15, 219, 229, 231, 235–6, 245, 254, 256–9, 264–5, 267, 282, 286–94, 296, 298
Abramowitz, M. 251
Acceleration, 4, 6, 179, 187, 203, 286–8, 296–8, 301–2
Accounting rate of return, 140, 142–3, 145, 148
Adaptation value of equity, 5, 208–9, 219, 221, 223, 225–8, 230–1, 234–6, 237, 239, 250, 254, 267–9, 271–9, 281–2, 286–7, 298–302; and dividends, 1–3, 5–6, 267–8, 274, 276–9, 281–2; and mean and variance of instantaneous changes, 298
Advanced corporation tax (see also dividends), 113–4
Akbar, S. 251
Albrecht, W. 302
Annual Percentage Rate (APR), 10, 18
Arbitrage portfolio, 56, 60, 64–5
Arbitrage Pricing Theory, see APT
Arnold, L. 176
APT, 64–5, 76; characteristic polynomial, 2, 53, 68–71, 73–4; eigenvalues (latent roots), 2; factors, 2; idiosyncratic return, 2; idiosyncratic variance, 43, 54, 76; strict factor model, 53, 76; variance-covariance matrix, 2
Ashton, D. 77, 231, 282
Ataullah, A. 251
Autoregressive process, 179, 203
Auxiliary equation, 269–274, 300, 302
Azevedo-Pereira, J. 7

Bai, J. 77
Bankruptcy costs, and firm value, 98–100
Barth, M. 251
Bathke, A. 302
Beaver, W. 251
Berger, P. 231
Bernstein, P. 131
Bernstein's error representation, 158, 171–2
Beta, 1–2, 40–9, 53–7, 59–64
Binomial distribution, 156; and mean and variance, 156
Bird in the hand argument, 112
Black, F. 131
Bond, 9–10, 25
Branching process, 218, 235, 268, 295, 297; and moment generating function, 218, 226; and mean and variance, 218; and probability of ultimate extinction, 226, 230, 275
Breeden, D. 50
Brisley, W. 76, 203
British Petroleum PLC, 145–7
Brown, D. 302
Brown, R. 25
Brown, Robert, 157
Brownian motion, 4, 155, 157; and difference equation form, 164; and normal distribution, 166–7; and pure and drift, 162–4; and stochastic differential equations, 166, 179
Burgstahler, D. 231

CAPM, 1–2, 40–3, 49, 53–5, 63, 76; debt to equity ratio, 88–9; two factor version, 48–9
Capital Asset Pricing Model, see CAPM
Capital gains, taxation and market value of firm, 96–7, 106, 112–3, 130
Capital market line, 35–40, 54, 58
Cash flow, see operating cash flow
Cauchy-Lorentz probability density, 249–50
Cavus, M. 7
Central Limit Theorem, 166, 170
Chamberlain, G. 77
Chapman, C. 152
Characteristic polynomial, (see also APT), 53, 68–71, 73–4, 76
Chordia, T. 302
Clean surplus, 4–5, 129, 214, 229, 254–6, 265, 282, 293
Clientele effect, 112–3
Clinch, G. 251
Coefficient of determination, see Correlation coefficient
Companies Act, 225
Connor, G. 77
Constant growth model, 100–2

Cooke, T. 231, 282
Correlation coefficient (or correlation matrix), 30, 53, 57, 66–70, 73–6, 234, 248–9, 251, 287, 298, 300–2
Cost of debt, 83–4, 100; weighted average cost of capital, 91–5, 103
Cost of equity, 84, 87–8, 90, 93–5, 100–2, 106, 110, 112, 116, 119, 121, 142, 146–7, 148–9, 151, 208, 217, 219, 220, 225, 228–9, 235–6, 264, 267, 287, 292, 297, 298–9; and weighted average cost of capital, 92–4, and constant (Gordon) growth model, 100–102
Covariance (of returns), 30–1, 41–5, 47, 54–6, 58, 60, 65–6, 245, 247, 298
Cox, D. 176, 231
Cox, J. 176
Crackle, 6, 298, 302
Current ratio, 62

Davidson, I. 77
Debt to equity ratio (see also return on shares, see also leverage), 2; bankruptcy costs, 80–1, 98–100; cost of equity, 84–9; market imperfections, 6, 98–100; market value of the firm, 80–1; optimal capital structure, 2, 80–1; weighted average cost of capital, 6, 91–5
Deflated variables (see also scaling) 234, 243–51
Denis, D. 131
Depreciation, 138, 142
Descartes' rule of signs, 149, 151
Determinant (of matrix), 68
Dichev, I. 231, 302
Dimson, E. 25
Dirty surplus, 5–6, 254–8, 260–2, 264–5, 267, 282
Discount rate (see also equity value), 1, 89–91, 95–6, 107–8, 110, 137–8; and capital gains taxes, 96–7; and Laplace transform, 124–5
Dividends, and 'classical' (double) system of taxation, 113–14; and constant (Gordon) growth model, 100–102; and functional forms and equity value, 3, 100–2, 114–22, 131; and the imputation system of taxation, 113–14
Dividend policy irrelevance theorem (see also return on shares, see also dividends), 2–3, 106–13, 268, 274–82; and adaptation value, 6; and operating cash flows 2–3, 108–10, 120–2, 128–131; and taxation, 112–4, 130–1
Dixit, A. 177
Dodd, D. 131

Easton, P. 251
Edwards, J. 152
Effective rate of interest, see Interest
Eigenvalue (see also APT), 68, 70–6, 182–3, 189–90, 203
Eigenvector (see also APT), 70–1, 73–5, 183, 188–9, 202
Einstein, A. 155–6, 163, 168
Equity risk premium, 42–3
Equity value (see also dividends, see also dividend policy irrelevance theorem, see also operating cash flows), and accounting earnings, 229–30; and clean surplus, 129; and constant (Gordon) growth model, 100–2; and discount rate, 1, 107–8, 137; and Fourier-Laguerre polynomial approximation, 237–43; and fundamental value, 1, 106; and intrinsic, long-term worth, 1, 106; and investment opportunity set, 208–9; and leverage, 80–7; and operating cash flows and Gauss-Laguerre quadrature, 3, 125–8, 131; and price-earnings multiples, 1
Error function, 124
Error vector, 56–7, 61–4
Expected return on portfolios and shares (see also cost of equity), 28–9, 42–46, 49, 54, 65, 67, 137; and normal distribution, 29–30
Exponent of singularity, 269

Factor loading, 75
Factor models (see also APT), 53–54; and asset prices, 2
Fair value, 225
Fama, E. 19, 25, 50, 77
Feller, W. 176
Ferris, S. 131
Firm size, 55, 57, 59, 61, 64, 76
Fisher, F. 152
Fisher, I. 131
Fixed asset, 225, 254
Flat rate of interest, 12
Fokker-Planck equation, 4, 155, 171–2, 176
Fourier(-Laguerre) coefficients, 237–8, 240
Freeman, H. 251
French, K. 19, 25, 50, 77
Friedman, A. 203
FRS 10: Goodwill and Intangible Assets, 225
FRS 11: Impairment of Fixed Assets and Goodwill, 225
FRS 15: Tangible Fixed Assets, 225
Funds flow equation: dividends and equity value, 107–8

Gauss-Laguerre quadrature, 3, 125–8, 131
Generalized method of moments (GMM), 173
Global minimum variance portfolio, 33–5, 54, 58
Goodwill, 225
Gordon growth model, 102
Graham, B. 131
Guo, Q. 77

Hamilton-Jacobi-Bellman equation, 107–9, 221–3, 268–9, 299–300, 302
Harcourt, G. 152
Hoel, P. 177, 204, 302
Hopwood, A. 152
Howell, S. 7

Ibbotson and Associates, 25
Identity matrix, 68, 75, 264
Idiosyncratic return or variance, see APT
Indicial equation, 270
Inefficient portfolio, 53–4, 56–7, 59–64, 76
Infinite power series expansion, see power series expansion
Information variable, 5–6, 208–9, 211, 213–4, 216, 219, 229–31, 235–6, 245, 254, 256–8, 260, 264–5, 267, 282, 287–9, 291–3, 295–8
Ingersoll, J. 176
Intangible asset, 225
Interest: continuous compounding, 17–19; effective rate, 10, 16, 18; flat rate, 12–16; linear interpolation, 13, 25; Newton-Raphson technique (algorithm), 14–16, 25; nominal rate, 10, 16–18
Investment opportunity set, 3–6, 106, 110–12, 114, 128, 130, 155, 179–82, 186–8, 199, 203, 208–10, 212–3, 215, 219, 221, 225, 227, 228–31, 234–6, 254–9, 261–2, 264–5, 267–9, 273–4, 282, 286–91, 293–9, 301–2; and stochastic differential equations, 166, 179–99, 201–3, 235, 254, 256–9, 260–5, 286–91, 293–302
Investment rate, 9–11
Isidro, H. 282
Iteration procedure, 14–16, 141–4, 147–51; and approximation error, 141–2
Itô, K. 4, 155, 174–6
Itô's lemma, 175–6, 243

Jensen, G. 282
Jerk, 6, 201, 296–8, 302

Karlin, S. 176
Kay, J. 152
Kernel, 56

Laguerre (orthogonal) polynomial, 126–8, 234, 237–42, 250
Landsman, W. 251, 282
Laplace, Pierre-Simon, 155
Laplace model of accumulated errors, 4, 155–7, 174–6; and Bernstein's representation of the measurement error, 158, 171–2; and mean, variance and covariance, 156–9; and mean, variance and covariance of weighted average measurement error, 159–62, 166–7, 169–70
Laplace transform, 123–5
Latent roots (see Eigenvalue)
Leverage, and the market value of the firm, 80–7
Linear interpolation: method of, 13, 25
Lintner, J. 113, 131
Liquidity, 62–64
Logarithmic return, see Return on shares: continuous compounding
Lookabill, L. 302
Lorek, K. 302
Lundstrum, L. 282

McGowan, J. 152
McHugh, A. 152
McKeown, J. 302
Majluf, N. 103
Market portfolio, 35–47, 49; expected return on, 38–42, 44–6, 48–9, 54; variance of, 38–43
Market price of risk, 35, 37
Market to book ratio, 55, 57, 59, 61, 64, 76
Markowitz, H. 50
Markowitz efficient frontier, 35
Markowitz locus, 32–4, 36–40, 44–6, 53–5, 58
Marsh, P. 25
Mayer, C. 152
Maximum likelihood, 173
Method of moments, see generalized method of moments (GMM)
Miller, B. 282
Miller, H. 176, 231
Miller, M. 81, 85, 103, 106, 108, 112, 131, 268, 274, 282
Miller, R. 282
Minimum variance zero beta portfolio, 43, 45–9
Modigliani, F. 81, 85, 103, 106, 108, 112, 131, 268, 274, 282
Moment generating function; and branching process 218, 225–6
Momentum, 4, 6, 179, 187, 203, 286–8, 292–3, 295, 297–8, 301
Mortgage repayment schedule, 11–13, 16
Myers, J. 302
Myers, L. 302
Myers, S. 103

Newton, D. 7
Newton-Raphson technique (algorithm), 14–16, 25; and method of linear interpolation, 16
Ng, S. 77
No-arbitrage condition, 2, 53, 56, 60, 64–5, 68, 76, 83, 219–21, 235, 267, 299
Nominal rate of interest, see Interest
Normal distribution, 29–30, 167, 170, 173, 217, 223, 249, 250–1
Normalizing constants, 210, 215, 257, 263, 265–7, 288, 294, 296
Null vector, 56

Ofek, E. 231
O'Hanlon, J. 282
Ohlson, J. 231
Øksendal, B. 177
Omitted variables problem, 265
Onatski, A. 77
Operating cash flows, 1–3, 5–6, 12, 23–4, 89, 97, 106, 108–14, 116–31, 137–9, 142, 149–52, 208–9, 214, 223, 234–5, 282, 286–7, 292–3, 295–8, 299, 301–2; and Laplace transform, 123–5
Ornstein and Uhlenbeck process, see Uhlenbeck and Ornstein process
Orthogonal polynomial, see Laguerre polynomial
Orthogonal portfolio, 53–60; and market portfolio, 53
Osobov, I. 131

Par value, 9
Patel, K. 7
Paxson, D. 7
Pearson, K. 251
Peasnell, K. 152, 282
Perfect capital market, 2, 81, 98, 103, 130–1, 268, 282
Pindyck, R. 177
Pop, 6, 298, 302
Pope, P. 282
Port, S. 177, 204, 302
Power series expansion, 269–71, 278–81, 300–1
Principal, 9, 11–14, 16

Recurrence relation, 270–1
Recursion value of equity, 5–6, 208–11, 214–21, 223, 225–31, 234–7, 239–44, 250, 254–7, 261–5, 267–9, 271, 273–5, 278, 281–2, 286–8, 292–3, 295, 299–302; and dividends, 209, 214, 235, 254–6, 263, 267–8, 271, 274, 276–9, 281, 286–7, 292–3, 295, 297–300.
Redemption payment, 9
Residual earnings, see abnormal earnings
Return on shares (see also expected return on portfolios and shares), arithmetic mean, 20–21, 23, 25; continuous compounding, 18–23, 25; debt to equity ratio, 2, 80–7; dividends, 18–19, 21–2; discrete compounding, 18–20, 22–3, 25; and accounting profit, 3, 137–40, 151–2; geometric mean, 20, 23, 25; infrequent (thin) trading, 3, 23–4; rights issue, 21–2; small firm effect, 19
Return on superannuation fund, 23–4
Rhys, H. 251
Riesz representation theorem, 237
Risk free (asset), 35–8, 40–3, 45, 48–9, 54, 58
Risk parameter, see stability measure

Roll, R. 76
Rothschild, M. 77
Ross, S. selected references: 50, 76, 176
Row echelon form, 71, 73
Rubinstein, M. 7, 50

Scaling, 234, 243–51
Scrap (liquidation) value; 137, 140, 142, 147
Seed value, 15, 144–6, 148–9
Sen, N. 131
SFAS 157: Fair Value Measurements, 225
Share value, see equity value
Sharpe, W. 50
Shields, M. 152
Shivakumar, L. 302
Signalling hypothesis, 113, 131
Size, see Firm size
Small firm effect, 19
Snap, 6, 298, 302
Sommers, G. 251
Song, X. 77
Speed of adjustment coefficient, 168–9, 175, 210–11, 288–9, 296–7
Spurious correlation, 5, 234, 245–9, 251
Square root law, 156–7, 163, 168
Stability measure (parameter), 221, 223, 225, 227–8, 235, 239, 243, 275, 278, 300, 302
Standard deviation of return on portfolios and shares, see Variance of return on portfolios and shares
Stark, A. 7, 251
Staunton, M. 25
Steady state probability density, 171–3, 274–6
Steele, A. 152
Stegun, I. 251
Stochastic differential equation, 4–6, 155, 166, 168–71, 175–6, 179–81, 187, 189–90, 199, 201, 203, 208–10, 212–3, 218, 243, 254, 256–7, 259, 262, 267, 286–8, 289–91, 295–8, 301–2; and parameter estimation, 170–1, 173, 179, 199–201, 203, 236, 265
Stone, C. 177, 204, 302
Strict factor model, see APT
Structural matrix (coefficients), 181, 183, 189–90, 210, 219, 229, 235–6, 257–8, 264, 266, 288–9, 296–7
Student's '*t*' probability density, 249
Superannuation fund returns, 23–4
Supply side, 3–4, 155, 176, 179, 235
Swary, I. 231
Systems of stochastic differential equations, see stochastic differential equations
Systematic (market) risk, 43

Tang, V. 302
Taylor, H. 176
Tippett, M. 77, 231, 251, 282

Trace (of a matrix), 68–70
Transversality condition, 109, 129, 211–2, 255, 289–91
Two factor CAPM, see CAPM

Uhlenbeck and Ornstein process, 4, 155, 167–76, 216–7, 231; and discrete time interpretation, 167–71; and Itô's lemma, 175–6; and mean and variance, 159–62, 169–70, 173, 216–7
Unsystematic risk, 43
Updating procedure, see Iteration procedure

Variance-Covariance matrix, 2, 43–5, 47–8, 54–60
Variance of return on portfolios and shares, 19, 25, 29–35, 38–50, 53–60, 65–9, 75–6
Van Zijl, T. 50
Villamil, A. 103

Wang, P. 282
Weighted average cost of capital, 2, 91–5, 103; and bankruptcy costs, 98–100
Wiener's theorem, 159–62, 166–7, 169–70, 176, 187, 199, 217; and normal distribution, 166–7, 169–70
Williams, J. 1, 7, 106, 131
Willinger, G. 302
Wymer, R. 203

Yee, K. 231
Yeh, S. 282
Young, S. 282
Yui, H. 131

Zero beta portfolio, see Minimum variance zero beta portfolio
Zhang, G. 231
Zima, P. 25

For Product Safety Concerns and Information please contact our EU
representative GPSR@taylorandfrancis.com
Taylor & Francis Verlag GmbH, Kaufingerstraße 24, 80331 München, Germany

www.ingramcontent.com/pod-product-compliance
Lightning Source LLC
LaVergne TN
LVHW080807011026
849160LV00015B/1561

* 9 7 8 0 4 1 5 6 9 6 0 3 6 *